C000235001

Impoliteness in Interaction

Pragmatics & Beyond New Series (P&BNS)

Pragmatics & Beyond New Series is a continuation of Pragmatics & Beyond and its Companion Series. The New Series offers a selection of high quality work covering the full richness of Pragmatics as an interdisciplinary field, within language sciences.

Editor

Andreas H. Jucker
University of Zurich, English Department
Plattenstrasse 47, CH-8032 Zurich, Switzerland
e-mail: ahjucker@es.uzh.ch

Associate Editors

Jacob L. Mey
University of Southern Denmark

Herman Parret
Belgian National Science Foundation, Universities of Louvain and Antwerp

Jef Verschueren
Belgian National Science Foundation, University of Antwerp

Editorial Board

Shoshana Blum-Kulka
Hebrew University of Jerusalem

Jean Caron
Université de Poitiers

Robyn Carston
University College London

Bruce Fraser
Boston University

Thorstein Fretheim
University of Trondheim

John C. Heritage
University of California at Los Angeles

Susan C. Herring
Indiana University

Masako K. Hiraga
St.Paul's (Rikkyo) University

David Holdcroft
University of Leeds

Sachiko Ide
Japan Women's University

Catherine Kerbrat-Orecchioni
University of Lyon 2

Claudia de Lemos
University of Campinas, Brazil

Marina Sbisà
University of Trieste

Emanuel A. Schegloff
University of California at Los Angeles

Deborah Schiffrin
Georgetown University

Paul Osamu Takahara
Kobe City University of Foreign Studies

Sandra A. Thompson
University of California at Santa Barbara

Teun A. van Dijk
Pompeu Fabra, Barcelona

Richard J. Watts
University of Berne

Volume 167

Impoliteness in Interaction
by Derek Bousfield

Impoliteness in Interaction

Derek Bousfield
University of Central Lancashire, UK

John Benjamins Publishing Company
Amsterdam / Philadelphia

TM The paper used in this publication meets the minimum requirements of American National Standard for Information Sciences – Permanence of Paper for Printed Library Materials, ANSI z39.48-1984.

Library of Congress Cataloging-in-Publication Data

Bousfield, Derek.
Impoliteness in interaction / Derek Bousfield.
p. cm. (Pragmatics & Beyond New Series, ISSN 0922-842X ; v. 167)
Includes bibliographical references and index.
1. Interpersonal communication. 2. Politeness (Linguistics) 3. Discourse analysis. I. Title.
P94.7.B68 2008
401'.41--dc22 2007031921
ISBN 978 90 272 5411 5 (Hb ; alk. paper)
ISBN 978 90 272 5439 9 (Pb ; alk. paper)
ISBN 978 90 272 9147 9 (Eb)

© 2008 – John Benjamins B.V.
Paperback 2010
No part of this book may be reproduced in any form, by print, photoprint, microfilm, or any other means, without written permission from the publisher.

John Benjamins Publishing Co. · P.O. Box 36224 · 1020 ME Amsterdam · The Netherlands
John Benjamins North America · P.O. Box 27519 · Philadelphia PA 19118-0519 · USA

Table of contents

CHAPTER 5

Acknowledgements

In Chapter 7: material drawn from Derek Bousfield (2007a) "Beginnings, middles and ends: a biopsy of the dynamics of impolite exchanges', Journal of Pragmatics 39 (12): 2185–2216, by permission of the publishers, Elsevier. In Chapter 8: material drawn from Derek Bousfield (2007b) 'Impoliteness, preference organization and conducivity', Multilingua 26 (1/2): 1–33, by permission of the publishers, Mouton de Gruyter.

Preface

In the truest style of thanking individuals for their help, patience and assistance it is absolutely guaranteed that I will forget to thank someone I really should here. The book before you grew out of my PhD thesis – a project funded by the Economic and Social Research Council. I acknowledge their support here.

Many friends and colleagues have commented on early draft sections of this book and on the ideas that are now contained within it. In most cases, exhaustively. Amongst those I have to thank are Dawn Archer, Jonathan Culpeper, Lesley Jeffries, Dan McIntyre, Rocio Montoro, Miriam Locher, and Richard J. Watts. I am grateful to the series editor, Andreas Jucker, for his helpful comments on the ms, and to Patricia Laplae and Isja Conen of John Benjamins for facilitating a thoroughly quick and efficient publishing process.

This book is dedicated to my beautiful, happy, fun-filled daughters, Tegan and Darci. This is despite the fact that this book contains the kind of language and behaviour that, as a parent, I never, ever, want to witness coming from them.

Finally, Dawn. My gorgeous, patient, supportive, understanding wife Dawn. Her love and support have seen me through. Thankyou Dawn. I love you.

CHAPTER 1

Impoliteness in interaction

> [C]onflictive illocutions tend, thankfully, to be rather marginal to human linguistic behaviour in normal circumstances. (Leech 1983: 105)

> If you can't clean up your act, fuck you and the donkey you rode in on. (Moore 2002: 226)

1.1 Introduction

Despite Leech's (1983) view, above, we must recognise that there are discourses in which conflictive illocutions (just one set of which is impoliteness) are not marginal human phenomena. Indeed, Culpeper, Bousfield and Wichmann (2003) point out that there are discourses in which conflictive illocutions are rather more central than may be the case in discourses which can be considered to be operating within 'normal circumstances'. Culpeper et al. note that:

> Conflictive talk has been found to play a role – and often a central one – in, for example, army training discourse (Culpeper 1996), courtroom discourse (Lakoff 1989; Penman 1990), family discourse (Vuchinich 1990), adolescent discourse (Labov 1972; Goodwin and Goodwin 1990), doctor-patient discourse (Mehan 1990), therapeutic discourse (Labov and Fanshel 1977), 'Everyday conversation' (Beebe 1995) and fictional texts (Culpeper 1998; Liu 1986; Tannen 1990). (Culpeper et al. 2003: 1545–1546)

As non-marginal human linguistic phenomena within certain types of discourse the concepts of conflictive illocutions (in general) and of impoliteness (in particular) within interaction are therefore worthy of study, critical consideration, and research. However since 1973, for Pragmaticians and, perhaps to a lesser extent, Sociolinguists, research on social interaction has tended to concentrate on collaborative or supportive illocutions, that is, on the linguistic expression and communication of politeness – impoliteness has been largely ignored. Eelen (2001) has noted this. It is what he calls the 'conceptual bias' in approaches to politeness. Both Bousfield (2006a) and Locher and Bousfield (2008), in arguing for the need for research into impoliteness cite the incredible imbalance between these two essentially linked fields of enquiry:

> As long ago as 1999 Fraser noted that since the publication of Lakoff's seminal paper in 1973, well over 1,000 books and articles had been published on the phenomena of politeness. (Bousfield 2006a: 9)

> In the face of [the] continual rise in interest for politeness phenomena our understanding of impoliteness, by contrast, has merely crawled forward [...] The paucity of research into impoliteness is telling, especially when we consider that several researchers (e.g. Craig, Tracey and Spisak 1986; Culpeper, Bousfield and Wichmann 2003; Tracy 1990) have argued that any adequate account of the dynamics of interpersonal communication (e.g. a model of Politeness) should consider hostile as well as cooperative communication.
> (Locher and Bousfield 2008: 2)

It is on this basis that this book aims to take the dual steps towards (i) increasing our understanding of impoliteness in interaction and (ii) redressing the balance, however slightly, with regards to studies concerned with politeness.

1.2 The scope of the present book

The object of the present book is the investigation and analysis of the use of impoliteness in a small number of different discourses. It is an attempt to understand how participants manage impoliteness both offensively and defensively in extended instances of spoken discourse and how they manipulate and exploit conversational expectations to the same end. It is also a step towards an understanding of how impolite discourses are triggered in the first place. More specifically, it seeks to understand and account for the triggering, onset, sequencing and, ultimately, the resolution of exchanges which can be characterised by the impoliteness which takes place. The book seeks to explore such interactions within the contexts in which they occur.

1.3 Motivation for the book: Why is the phenomena of impoliteness worth investigating?

The present book aims at filling the gap, or rather, at taking steps to address the conceptual bias (see Eelen 1999, 2001), which exists in current approaches to politeness with regards to impoliteness. It aims to show that consideration of politeness theories can only be complete when impoliteness is considered. Similarly, this book seeks to consider impolite face threatening acts in the context in which they are produced as it is felt (see Penman 1990) that too many theories (cf. Brown and Levinson 1987; Lachenicht 1980; and Leech 1983) consider (im)politeness within the context of a single turn at talk. Such approaches whilst valuable and necessary milestones on the research road to discovery are simply that – research milestones. They neither adequately describe nor predict how (im)politeness may be used by speakers in extended, real-life interactions. It is felt that investigating the phenomena of impoliteness can have significant contributions both to existing academic research and to 'the wider world.'

1.3.1 As a contribution to existing research

Thomas tells us that although much has been written on Politeness, comparatively little is based on empirical research (Thomas 1995: 149). Similarly, Culpeper (1996) argues for, and posits a theoretical approach to non-harmonious communication through impoliteness which Culpeper considers is parallel but opposite in orientation to Brown and Levinson's (1987) politeness theory. Again, while attractive, this model is theoretical and with the exception of the work completed for Culpeper et al. (2003) it has not been empirically tested to any great degree. Furthermore, as Fraser points out (1990: 235), Brown and Levinson's study, while well articulated, seems to be the one most systematically challenged. For example, one major criticism of Brown and Levinson's model is that given by Penman (1990: 16), in that the '...methods of analysis [by Brown and Levinson] were not developed for the systematic, sequential interpretation of ongoing discourse. All of the examples given by Brown and Levinson are single utterances drawn out of the context of ongoing discourse'. As Culpeper's approach is a parallel-but-opposite model of Brown and Levinson's, it runs the risk of falling foul of at least some of the same criticisms, this one included. The present book then aims to work towards a model which (1) is based upon firm empirical evidence and (2) concerns 'in-context' discourse. Furthermore, in working towards such a model I am illuminating discourses that have thus far received little, if any, attention. In this way it is hoped that this book has a significant contribution to make to existing research on both politeness and impoliteness.

1.3.2 As a contribution to "the wider world"

Brown and Levinson claim (1987: 1) that their politeness theory, 'must surely be the model' for diplomatic protocol, and that politeness 'presupposes that potential for aggression as it seeks to disarm it'. This isn't entirely true. Brown and Levinson suggest that Politeness *proactively* disarms aggression – before it surfaces, and they say that it '...makes possible communication between *potentially* aggressive parties' (1987: 1, as cited by Culpeper 1996: 356. My emphasis.). In effect, their model cannot adequately account for aggression *after* it has surfaced which necessitates *reactive* disarmament. This is where this book is relevant. Not only will the present text make a contribution to 'diplomatic protocol', but it will also come to the aid of those who are the targets of verbal aggression. For when one is placed in a confrontational, non-harmonious situation, a powerful tool in neutralising aggression can be had by having the knowledge of (1) the types of impoliteness that may be used, and (2) the effective linguistic 'management' and 'defence' options that are available within the discourse and the situational context in which one is operating.[1]

With the data that I use in this book there are a number of critical areas from this theme which will benefit from the present research:

- Given the changing nature of government, with the removal of some of government's functions, coupled with new government systems of delivering services, primarily through privatisation, the very nature of the traditional 'public servant – private citizen' relationship is changing rapidly. Such changes in governance raise difficult questions concerning "power", "rights" and "ethics".
- Public perceptions of the powers of these privately funded public servants, as well as the ethics of the exercising of power by, or deference to, such 'privatised' public servants is still largely unknown in society.
- Even with an attempt at the concretisation and formalisation of citizens' rights in a fluid and changing world, people are having to discover, or rather create for themselves some concept of just what their rights are. Such a changing, non-solidified situation could easily contribute to a culture in which people are quick to complain. Given this premise, confrontational, and non-harmonious communication is bound to ensue.

For these reasons, studying how and under what conditions impoliteness is generated is an important and worthy object of study. Such a study will also lead towards indicating how interactants deal with such impoliteness; it will, in effect, show how impoliteness may potentially be countered, controlled and managed.

1. It should be noted that although I consider impolite usage and impolite management/defensive options as 'strategies' throughout this book, they are, nevertheless, *artificially* identified as discrete entities purely for the purpose of analysis and ease of discussion.

1.4 Aims of the book

The aim of the present work is to investigate the use of impolite utterances and how they are received and dealt with in the interactive spoken discourses studied. This is attempted in stages by recourse to the following research questions.

1.4.1 The research questions

To begin any study of impoliteness one needs to know: *What is impoliteness?* This is the main research question for which I construct a working definition in Chapter 4. Following on from this, and considering the broad research question: *How is impoliteness used in conflictive exchanges?* I found a continuing process of refinement to have been necessary. In short, the nature of the data, the process of analysis and the findings, have all continually informed, been informed by, and re-informed the project as to the exact nature of the questions asked. The research questions (below), have been shaped by both (i) the literature and by earlier studies dealing with, and surrounding (im)politeness; and by, (ii) the data sets that were available for study. These all contributed to the creation of a set of research questions which, when addressed, have allowed me to posit a descriptive, data-driven model concerning impoliteness in interaction.

Briefly, the data for the present text were taken from terrestrial British ITV, Channel 4 and BBC television 'fly on the wall' documentaries about military and civilian police training, vehicle parking disputes, metropolitan and motorway policing and a restaurant kitchen. The reason these documentary serials were chosen is that they all seemed to be contexts in which impolite utterances may occur. On this basis, that there are contexts in which impoliteness may occur, I envisage a research project which asks the overarching question:

> What is the nature and role of impoliteness in interactional communication?

This is based on the observation that otherwise promising models of impoliteness, like those posited in Culpeper (1996) and Lachenicht (1980) were (i) largely untested empirically, (ii) still experimental in their outlook, and/or (iii) applied only to highly specific types of discourse. This led to the conclusion that existing models may not be able to account for how impoliteness was, actually, being deployed. This led to the sub-question:

> How is impoliteness actually realised in interactive communication?

Observation of what actually happens, (as presented in Chapter 5), led to the further question:

> How can impoliteness 'strategies' be combined in utterances?

Following from this, a general belief or overall hypothesis was that just as it is possible, linguistically, to offend one's interlocutor, through impoliteness for example, it is equally possible to defend, linguistically, oneself against such offensive, impolite attacks, which led to the research questions:

> How can impoliteness be countered?
> Are the countering strategies offensive or defensive?
> What defence strategies are available to interactants within a given situational context?

Furthermore, I hypothesised that some strategies of issuing and countering impoliteness are more effective than others depending upon the impolite offensive and counter strategies being used, the context of the discourse, and the overall rights, powers and obligations of the participants in the particular speech event in question. These considerations lead to the question:

> What are the communicative options available to interactants when faced with impoliteness?

I noted that attempts to counter, or even accept impolite face attacks could in certain discourses and certain contexts lead to further impolite attacks and a general escalation of verbal conflict in discourse. This lead to the questions:

> What triggers impolite face attack?
> How does the discourse build up and pan out, dynamically, throughout the discourse?

These questions, in turn, lead to the question:

> What are the dynamic phenomena typifying discourses which contain active impoliteness?

Finally, in light of this mix of originally hypothesised and data driven questions, the question now, is, what is the best way of organising the book for the investigation of these research questions and the presentation of the findings?

1.5 Concerning the data

Within this research project I necessarily take a 'mixed' or eclectic approach to answering the Research Questions that were raised above. I adopt and adapt existing established critical and descriptive frameworks from a number of different areas of linguistic research. This, alone, reflects both the wide application and (at least, potentially) the extensive implications which research on im/politeness enjoys.

In conjunction with the eclectic blend of approaches adopted within this study, I develop a new framework based upon the analysis of a number of extracts taken from 'impolite-rich' data sets. This framework is constructed, explored and discussed throughout Chapters 5, 6, 7 and 8. I discuss in depth some main approaches to politeness (cf. Brown and Levinson (1987, Leech 1983) and impoliteness (cf. Culpeper 1996, Lachenicht 1980) which are applied in support of my initial findings (as presented in Chapter 5).

1.5.1 The types of data used

The type of data used in this study are in the form of 101 example extracts mostly taken from video-taped television serial documentaries – the so-called 'fly-on-the-wall' documentaries prevalent on British terrestrial television channels during the late 1990s and early 2000s. There are, of course, a number of methodological advantages and a number of methodological disadvantages regarding the use of such data. Suffice it to say at this stage that the major advantage of using data of this nature is that the extracts are readily available. Issues of access are, therefore, significantly diminished. The selection process however is a methodological issue of no small import. I collected the television data by recording the programmes and then chose extracts which appeared to contain conflictive, impolite illocutions. The chosen extracts represent the discourse types of driver-clamper encounters; military training discourse; police-public encounters; employer-to-employee discourse and person to person encounters. These discourses can be subdivided into different Activity Types (cf. Levinson [1979] 1992. See also Chapter 7, below), which I discuss below (see Section 1.5.3 below).

One major issue, however, is that for all their attractiveness even fly-on-the-wall documentaries might not be what social scientists would strictly call 'naturally occurring data'. At the very least, such data suffers from the Observer's Paradox given that a full film crew happens to be present, and recording, during the unfolding of the otherwise 'everyday' discourses, activities and utterances which I am seeking to analyse. Clearly, the presence of such a unit *has* to affect the actions of the participants.

1.5.2 The transcription conventions

The transcription conventions used in this study are represented in Table 1, below. These conventions are based on several sources (Ochs 1979; Gumperz 1992; Eggins and Slade 1997). The system of transcription used throughout this study is the stave method. I have chosen this method over more standard, CA style 'turn' based transcriptions, as the stave system allows for easier viewing of which interactant said what, when, in relation to the other interactants in the exchange. Similarly, such phenomena as interruptions, or two interactants speaking at the same time are easily represented in stave transcription without the need to utilise additional keystroke symbols such as '/' used in CA transcription or '[' and ']' which are used by turn-based transcriptions for overlapping speech.

Table 1. Transcription conventions

Transcription conventions	
#	Stave number (where # is a numerical unit: 1,2,3, etc…).
S#	Speaker identification within extract ('S1' = 'speaker 1', 'S2' = speaker 2, and so on).
<indistinct>	The speaker's contribution is indistinct.
< text >	Transcriber unsure of speaker's contribution
<bleeped>	The speaker's contribution is indistinct and unrecoverable due to 'censorship' of profanities by the programme's editor.
.	Audible pause of up to ½ second.
..	Audible pause of between ½ and 1 second. (Further points '.' indicate further time segments of up to ½ second each).
=	Latching contribution: One speaker begins their contribution immediately another speaker ends their contribution.
CAPS	Loud. Extreme emphatic stress (e.g. SHOUTING).
<spits/slaps>	Nonverbal expression.
[*other*]	Other activity important to the understanding of the speaker's contribution. e.g. [*dials mobile telephone*].
Edit/End	Edit point signifying a non-contiguous part of the extract, or End point signifying no further exchanges were recorded or available.

1.5.3 The data sets

The data is taken from a number of television 'docusoaps', or 'fly-on-the-wall' documentary serials. Extracts have been taken from the following series on the basis that they appeared to contain at least some confrontational discourse:[2] In every case, each type of encounter is represented in **bold** with the Activity Types (cf. Levinson 1992) I consider, represented in *italics*.

- **Driver-clamper encounters**: The BBC's *The Clampers* and ITV's *Parking Wars.*
  - *On-street, informal complaint/argument*: Between driver and clamper/clamping official.
  - *Off-Street, informal complaint/argument*: Between driver and council/privatised vehicle storage staff.
  - *Formal Appeal*: Between driver and court appointed adjudicator.
- **Person-to-person encounters**: The BBC's *The Clampers, Soldiers to be* and ITV's *Parking Wars*:
  - *Argument*: Between peers (e.g. recruit-to-recruit, driver-to-driver).
- **Military discourse**: The BBC's *Soldiers to be* and *Redcaps.*
  - *Informal 'dressing down'*: Non-commissioned officer (NCO) -to-recruit.
  - *Formal 'dressing down'*: NCO or Officer to recruit under formal circumstances.
- **Police-public encounters**: The BBC's: *Motorway Life* and *Raw Blues.*
  - *Stop and enquiry:* Between officer and member of public.
  - *Arrest:* Between officer and member of public.
- **Employer-employee discourse**: Channel 4's *Boiling Point.*
  - *Dressing down:* Owner to employee.
  - *Critical evaluation:* Owner to employee

The Clampers and *Parking Wars* are television programme documentaries which are primarily concerned with the day to day activities of the London Councils' privatised traffic wardens, including the 'clampers', those traffic wardens whose task it is to apply clamps to illegally parked cars and to tow them away. They also follow, both, the activities of private citizens in confrontation with one another over such things as driving ability, driving style and parking places, and the activities of legal officials who adjudicate in disputes over the penalties that have been applied by the traffic wardens.[3]

---

2. Note: there is no claim to equality of treatment in these data sets for each specific discoursal activity type. The simple fact of the matter is, despite my best efforts, there is simply not an adequate amount of each type of discoursal activity type available, at the time of the study, to be able to acquire a large, equally weighted sample. Future research will be easier due to the expansion of public interest in television 'reality' shows since the commencement of this study.

3. The full list of 'officials' includes traffic wardens acting as ticketers, clampers and those who tow away illegally parked vehicles; direct employees of the council, namely, public servants who

As one might imagine these activities have the potential to result in confrontational interactions. The 'face' (cf. Goffman 1967; Brown and Levinson 1987. See also Chapter 3, this book) of drivers is directly threatened by such occurrences as the receipt of a parking indictment (a ticket), the clamping of their vehicle, or even the forced removal of the vehicle (it being towed away) to a council authority-appointed facility. It not only threatens the 'negative' face (cf. Brown and Levinson 1987) of the driver, by impeding their movements, it also threatens their 'positive' face, given that it is an official disapproval of their choice of parking position. The fact that the officials have the legal authority to perform such actions is not, always, considered an adequately mitigating factor for such a Face Threatening Act. This, in part, is fostered by the apparent belief on the part of some drivers that the parking rules are almost draconian in both their scope and in the way in which they are enforced. Evidence of this can be seen in the dialogues given by a number of disgruntled motorists direct to the camera, as well as to the clamping officials, both directly and indirectly. Associating the clampers with *Adolf Hitler* (examples [18], Section 5.1.9; and again in [42], Section 6.1.2) specifically and with *Nazism* in general (example [19], Section 5.1.9); or by shouting to camera that 'They [the parking officials] need strangling' (see, Bousfield 1999), who are within earshot, are some of the more indirect ways in which this view is expressed. Direct views have been expressed by reference to the clampers as being 'Muggers in uniform' (Anonymous cyclist and local home owner, The Clampers) and complaints that there has been no compassion on the part of the adjudicating official (Unsuccessful individual during an appeal hearing, *The Clampers*, example [23], Section 5.3, staves 14–15) or that there is nowhere to park legally, in London, on a weekday after 9 a.m. (Clamped individual, *The Clampers*).[4] While such claims may be exaggerations, it is clear that they indicate a lack of belief in, respect for, and/or acceptance of the power, the obligations, the right and the authority of the clampers as being mitigating factors. Without the acceptance of these elements as mitigating factors then, being indicted via a ticket, a clamp, or by the removal of one's vehicle, can be seen as a triggering, antecedent, offending event (see Jay 1992, 2000. See also Chapter 4, Section 4.5.4) under which impolite discourse can commence and ensue. This said, *The Clampers* and *Parking Wars* are less rich in impoliteness than the military training discourses, and, as such, they represent good data sets for testing and probing the limits of impoliteness.

work at the council's vehicle storage pound (where towed vehicles are stored); court appointed bailiffs who operate to collect unpaid parking fines or offenders' vehicles; and adjudicators, who hear from drivers appealing against fines levied on parking tickets, clamps, or towed vehicles.

4. Indeed, another individual reported and admitted, to camera, to having violent thoughts towards the clampers, despite describing himself as being normally 'a placid person'.

Soldiers to be and *Redcaps* are serial television programmes dealing with military training discourse. It is a common factor of many military organisations that confrontational and impolite linguistic behaviour is produced during the training process for two main reasons: (1) The extreme inequality of power which is rigidly enforced, and (2) The particular training philosophy, which, Culpeper theorises, aims to depersonalise recruits in order to break them down physically and psychologically in order that they may be remolded as model soldiers (Culpeper 1996, and personal communication). It is for these reasons that these two programme series have been chosen. Note that *Soldiers to be* is concerned with recruits to basic military training, whereas *Redcaps* is concerned with the advanced military training of soldiers wishing to become Royal Military Policemen.[5] Some *Soldiers to be* extracts concern not only NCOs conversing with recruits impolitely, but also concerns recruits conversing with other recruits (i.e. interactants of an equal power), impolitely. It is interesting to note that there is no direct official recognition, either via the military, or the academic authorities, that such impolite linguistic behaviour takes place during military training. This is not to suggest that there is an overt conspiracy of denial. A survey of papers and works concerned with the training of recruits shows that the relevant literature almost predominantly ignores the use of linguistically impolite behaviour during training. Where it is dealt with, then it is considered indirectly, as being assumed to be 'given knowledge' on much the same level as one would assume that infantry recruits are going to be (i) taught to use small arms, (ii) fed and clothed, and so on. i.e. it is considered a fact of military life, one which does not need stating. Indeed, the view of impoliteness is that it is considered to be vital for the education of recruits. For example, Fitzpatrick, who is not unrepresentative, notes that, '[the recruits] are going to have to adjust themselves to the new environment. They are going to be in camp under a rather strict supervisory [environment], *perhaps not always sympathetic* [...]' (1945: 207–8, my emphasis).

Given what we can see in the Army Training data used in this study (see appendices), and what I will argue in the following chapters (see Chapters 5, 6, 7 and 8), with the environment being, *not always sympathetic*, (in that the face wants of the recruits are not always being directly considered during training), then we can see that such a comment is, itself, somewhat indirect and understated.

Goldhamer (1974: 107, cited in Marshall-Hasdell 1994) considers the use of drill to be, educationally, highly beneficial to the recruits, '[Drill] develops discipline, alertness, the habit of fulfilling commands, and a sense of collectivism that makes it possible to unify efforts of all the men in a general mission.' Further,

5. Note that the title 'Redcaps' refers to the Royal Military Police's distinctive red peaked cap.

Goldhamer (1974: 107) considers drill training to contribute to the 'physical and psychological hardening' of the recruits. Given that (as we can see by recourse to the appendices), linguistic impoliteness is a central part of drill training when infractions, or errors, are detected, then its role in contributing both to the ability of recruits to act in unison and to their physical and psychological hardening appears to validate Culpeper's theory (1996, and personal communication), as to the use of impoliteness in military training.

Additionally, despite the paucity of direct work on impoliteness between trainers and recruits in military training discourse, work does exist on the phenomena of 'Hazing'. Hazing is a Canadian-American English term for the demanding and often humiliating physical and linguistic 'initiation' of new inductees into a military unit or other social group by older and/or existing members. This, apparently, is seen as a group-bonding phenomenon by Winslow (1999) who notes that, hazing, while not officially sanctioned, is tolerated, at least to an extent.

Motorway Life and *Raw Blues* are data sets which concern the training and everyday activities of trained police officers. Policework has the potential to be an unrewarding and unenviable occupation given the wide and varied range of activities which the police are expected to both perform and deal with. *Motorway Life* deals specifically with police officers assigned to motorway patrol duties whilst *Raw Blues* deals with, first, the training of new officers, and second the on-duty activities of those officers in London's Metropolitan Police Force. Again, as one might imagine, from the range of activities and events which pervade police officers' work, there is a potential for conflictive, impolite discourse to occur. The comparisons to be made between military and civil police training; police-to-public and clamper-to-public interactions and motorway duties to metropolitan duties make *Motorway Life* and *Raw Blues* good data sets for a study such as this one.

Finally Channel 4's *Boiling Point* is a programme that concerns the activities of British chef Gordon Ramsay in the day to day running of his London restaurant *Ramsay's*. *Ramsay's* has a reputation for excellence, indicated by the accolade of having initially two, and then winning three Michelin stars (three stars being the maximum). Gordon Ramsay himself has a certain 'no nonesense' reputation when dealing with his staff during the running of the restaurant, especially at busy, high stress times.[6] Extracts from this programme have been included therefore, to investigate the role that impoliteness plays in employer to employee relationships.

6. The series detailed life in *Ramsay's* kitchens when the restaurant first tried, and failed, to win its third Michelin star. It was after the screening of this series that Gordon Ramsay won his third Michelin star.

1.5.4 Considerations about the data sets

There are a number of caveats concerning the use of such data that need to be borne in mind. We must acknowledge that one of the likely goals of any television series, especially of this nature, is to entertain the viewing public. Culpeper (1998, 2005) makes a convincing argument for the link between impoliteness and entertainment. It is likely, therefore, that the BBC and the independent television production companies, whose programmes are being discussed here, have biased their own selection of scenes for inclusion in the screened series towards the more confrontational and impolite ones. As a consequence, any inferences about the norms of interaction between individuals in the specific contexts denoted must be made with some caution. More specifically, while some instances of interaction between, say, parking officials and private car owners were clearly confrontationally charged to the point of impoliteness and aggressiveness (both linguistic and physical), one cannot claim that *all*, or even the majority of interactions are *always* confrontationally charged to such a level just because it may very well *seem* that way by observation of the complete set of scenes included in the data sets here studied. We may note that while this clearly effects any qualitative approach, it would, more particularly, render a quantitative approach virtually nonsensical given the nature of the data sets available.

1.5.5 The observer's paradox

The existence of an operating and all too obvious camera crew, which is recording the unfolding interactions, leads, unequivocally, to the problem of the Observer's Paradox. It is quite conceivable that the presence of the camera crew may, in some cases, have led to more restrained conversational behaviour or may have led to more extreme conversational behaviour. Indeed, in the data transcribed and analysed, there are indications that both of these phenomena occurred. What this means, again, is that we cannot, make generalisations concerning the norms of interaction between individuals in such discoursal contexts. There is an additional issue regarding the Observer's Paradox which has directly informed the methodology of the current research project. Given the Observer's Paradox, not every individual filmed was happy to be identified in the programme, and, of course, other individuals, who did agree to be identified, clearly restrained their 'normal' or 'natural' conversational behaviour in the contexts of the extracts. This made the issue of finding relevant extracts that one could ethically and legally use, somewhat problematic. There is one major issue here: Despite the richness of some examples, I made the decision, based on ethical and moral grounds not to use any extract where an individual had not agreed to be identified and, thus, in the programmes, had had their face 'blurred'. What this means is that the video-taped data here has, of course, been through a number of layers of editing, selection, and analysis before even reaching the stage of being transcribed. This we need to bear in mind.

1.5.6 The advantages of using this type of data

There are clear benefits to using this type of data over some other types that have been utilised in other, similar, research projects. For example, in their study of Interpersonal Linguistic Conflict, Brenneis and Lein (1977) and Lein and Brenneis (1978) came up with what they considered was a straightforward method of studying conflict discourse. It was a method which Bavelas et al. (1985) claims could serve as a prototype for a wide variety of initial investigations into this area.

What Brenneis and Lein (1977) and Lein and Brenneis (1978) did was to arrange for a conflict to occur by asking children to role-play an argument. The benefits of this type of method are that 'conflictive discourse' is (a) readily available, and (b) on a topic that we can specify at a moment's notice. After all, they asked the children to role-play arguments about, for example, 'whose ball it is' or 'who is the strongest'. Brenneis and Lein (1977) and Lein and Brenneis (1978) point out that the children seem to have become quite absorbed in their roles and to have generated spontaneous and lengthy disputes (which were tape-recorded and transcribed). However, there is a number of issues above and beyond that of the Observer's Paradox which need to be borne in mind concerning this method of generating and collecting such data. To begin, there are at least two levels of artificiality here which preclude us from viewing such data as 'naturally occurring'. Firstly, the children were *asked* to argue. That is, their arguments were not, naturally, but rather, artificially induced. Secondly, the children were asked *to role-play* the arguments. That is, the arguments were a non-serious undertaking, but were being artificially created and acted out. Despite Brenneis and Lein's (1977) claims that the children became absorbed and spontaneous, possibly allowing some of them to slip out of role-play type acting and into 'real' argument, these interactions were still artificially stimulated purely by the process of the children being *asked* to argue. As such we need to bear the caveat, about the role of roleplay in inducing impolite containing discourses, in mind.

Another study of conflict, which has an interesting method of data 'collection', is that of Camras (1977). Like Brenneis and Lein, Camras also studied conflict between children and indeed there are some interesting similarities between the two projects. However, while Brenneis and Lein (1977) *asked* children to *role-play* arguments, Camras (1977), sidestepping the issue of artificiality that is attached to 'acting,' attempted to *create* genuine, spontaneous conflict between interactants. He did this by presenting a pair of children with a desirable object (a caged gerbil) that only one of the pair was able to play with at any given time. The ensuing interaction was filmed, which provided a permanent record of both the visual and auditory information produced. Again, Observer's Paradox aside, the benefits here, (as in the use of the televised extracts), are that not only can the verbal data be viewed, transcribed and analysed, but the visual aspects, the non-verbal paralanguage, such as gestures, facial expressions, and even physical contact between interactants can also potentially be viewed and interpreted through analysis. However, a significant and inescapable issue here is the way in which Camras (1977) collects or rather, generates data. As with Brenneis and Lein (1977), in creating arguments between children, we must acknowledge that their arguments were not *naturally*, but rather *artificially* induced. Additionally a much more serious issue with Camras's method of data 'collection' is one that transgresses ethical considerations. Camras, after all created, that is, purposefully and deliberately caused two children to argue. It is not as if he gave the children a gerbil with which to play and then recorded any *truly* spontaneous argument that occurred, (which, still, would have been of dubious worth and morality). For in presenting the desirable object and stating that only one child at a time could play with it, he engineered a situation whereby conflict *would*, on the balance of probabilities, occur. Even if he did so for the sole purpose of research, this, in my view, is ethically questionable and of dubious validity.

The role of roleplay in impolite discourses is represented clearly in one extract from the Raw Blues data set.[7] Here the difference between the Brenneis and Lein and Lein and Brenneis studies and the present research project is that the interactants were not asked to argue, rather they were asked to roleplay the situation – in just this one roleplay, by two particular police officer recruits, the situation became impolite and physically aggressive between the police officers and the 'suspect'. Taken from **Raw Blues.**

[1] ***Context***: *A police roleplaying exercise. Two police officers are asked to stop, speak to, and eventually search a local member of the black community who is acting the part of a suspected drug dealer. S1 is one of the police officers, S2 is the volunteer civilian playing the 'suspected drug dealer'.*

7. Note also, that ALL training data could be considered to involve role play: military recruits are 'asked' to practice armed attacks, field survival and other tasks commensurate with real battlefield conditions. The point here is that it is not the role play, itself, which is the central focus, aim or trigger for impoliteness but activities performed whilst 'roleplaying'. This is unlike Brennies and Lein's (1977) and Lein and Brenneis' (1978) studies where roleplaying the argument was the aim.

***Edit**: The trainer explains that he is looking for how PC Hutton handles the stop, how considerate the PC is to the individual's needs, expectations of the police, how/what information he gives to the individual by way of explanation and so on. During this, it is apparent that PC Hutton, S1, has expressed an intention to search S2 as a result of the radioed allegations that have resulted in this situation in the first place.*

[…]

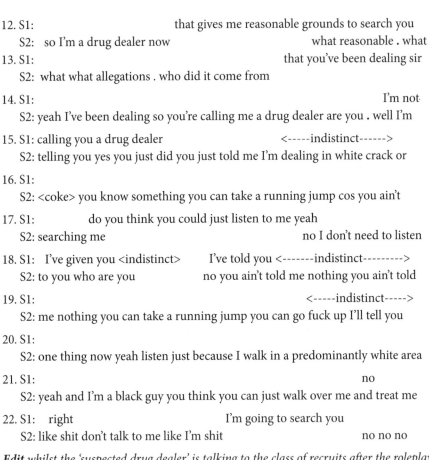

12. S1: that gives me reasonable grounds to search you
    S2: so I'm a drug dealer now what reasonable . what
13. S1: that you've been dealing sir
    S2: what what allegations . who did it come from

14. S1: I'm not
    S2: yeah I've been dealing so you're calling me a drug dealer are you . well I'm

15. S1: calling you a drug dealer <-----indistinct------>
    S2: telling you yes you just did you just told me I'm dealing in white crack or

16. S1:
    S2: <coke> you know something you can take a running jump cos you ain't

17. S1: do you think you could just listen to me yeah
    S2: searching me no I don't need to listen

18. S1: I've given you <indistinct> I've told you <-------indistinct--------->
    S2: to you who are you no you ain't told me nothing you ain't told

19. S1: <-----indistinct----->
    S2: me nothing you can take a running jump you can go fuck up I'll tell you

20. S1:
    S2: one thing now yeah listen just because I walk in a predominantly white area

21. S1: no
    S2: yeah and I'm a black guy you think you can just walk over me and treat me

22. S1: right I'm going to search you
    S2: like shit don't talk to me like I'm shit no no no

***Edit** whilst the 'suspected drug dealer' is talking to the class of recruits after the roleplay sessions. Return to the roleplay session.*

23. S1: <------ indistinct ------>
    S2: what grounds have you given me

Edit whilst the 'suspected drug dealer' is talking to the class of recruits after the role-play sessions. Returns to the roleplay session.

24. S1: [here S1 takes
    S2: you know something I think you're a stranger to the truth

25. S1: hold of S2's arm as the first move in searching him]
    S2: no don't touch me

26. S1:
    S2: [twists away]don't put your hands on me *

[* a scuffle between S1 and S2 ensues in which S1, the police officer, eventually puts S2 in a restraining head lock. The roleplay session is stopped at this point].

End.

Here we can see the roleplaying exercise, which became impolitely charged, ended in the somewhat face threatening situation of the police officers restraining the individual playing the 'suspect'.

The difference between Camras' data, and the situation in example [1] above, is that there was no certainty that impoliteness would occur in the latter situation. In fact, PCs Hutton and Haggar were the only ones of their class NOT to successfully search the 'suspect' without overt, gratuitous impoliteness and physical conflict arising from how they handled the situation. In short, Brenneis and Lein (1977) and Camras (1977) sought to *generate* their conflictive data whereas I have sought to *observe* it in my data sets.

The data for Culpeper's (1996) exposition of impoliteness came from a 'fly-on-the-wall' television documentary entitled 'Soldier Girls'. This was a programme following the basic military training of females being inducted into the U.S. military. Clearly, data of this nature has most of the benefits and all of the issues that the data for my research have, as discussed above. The data is (relatively) 'naturally occurring', readily available and is permanent in that, with it being available on videocassette, can be returned to, and re-assessed, at a later date. Clearly, it also suffers from the Observer's Paradox as stipulated above. However, because Culpeper bases the 'real-life' data of his approach to impoliteness (1996) only on 'Soldier Girls', the theory does tend to suffer from limitations of wider applicability and, thus, external validity. The specific reason I have attempted to include data from a number of discourses (military, public to private, police-to-public, employer to employee) is to increase the applicability and, thus, the external validity of the research findings. In that respect, the research that I am undertaking here could be seen to be a next, logical step in understanding impoliteness.

1.6 Outline of the book

This book is organised into eight chapters. Following this introductory chapter, Chapter 2 is concerned with the Gricean (1975) approach to implicature. As this study is interested in impoliteness it is, therefore also interested in the models and theories that underpin such phenomena. Grice has been much maligned in recent years, mostly unfairly given the misunderstandings that Grice's Cooperative Principle has had to endure. This chapter seeks to give a particular reading of the Gricean approach to implicature which is in keeping, not only with impoliteness, but also politeness and general meaning communication beyond that which is actually said.

Chapter 3: Brown and Levinson's approach to face has, in some ways, quite rightly, been much criticised and corrected over recent years. However, some of Brown and Levinson's underlying assumptions regarding the universality of face are, once reconsidered, relatively sound, others, however, are not. This chapter explores the conceptualisations of their, and others' approaches to the phenomenon, before suggesting an approach for use within the present study.

Chapter 4: Of the many approaches to politeness that exist, most ignore impoliteness as inconsequential or as 'parasitic' upon politeness (Culpeper 1996). This chapter seeks to interrogate and challenge the major existing approaches to politeness and impoliteness before suggesting an outline structure/approach for a model of impoliteness. This outline structure is elaborated upon and otherwise 'fleshed out' in the subsequent chapters.

Chapter 5: I explore and critique the approach to impoliteness based on face-directed strategies. I develop the outline structure of the model of impoliteness I'm suggesting here in this book along theoretical, 'out-of-context' lines to provide a prototypical 'blueprint' of impoliteness production before moving onto the next chapter.

Chapter 6: I explore the dynamic nature of impoliteness at the utterance level, investigating the multi-layered nature of the phenomena whereby many effects are produced by single utterances.

Chapter 7: Here I fully discuss the phenomenon within the context of continuous and developing discourses with the complex interplay of impolite moves and countermoves made by interlocutors within impolite containing exchanges which sheds greater light on the richness of (countering) impoliteness within exchanges. The discussion in this chapter moves from impoliteness being considered largely 'out-of-context' to a more context-sensitive understanding that comes to fruition in the following chapter. Furthermore, I explore 'next-turn' counter/defensive moves to the impolite utterances explored in Chapters 5 and 6 to give an idea as to the resources which are open to interactants in the maintenance of their own face.

Chapter 8: Here I explore the conversational resources that are open and available to interactants in symmetrical and assymetrical exchanges. I discuss the manipulation and exploitation of interactants' expectations as to the structure and format of 'prototypical' conversation. I explore the activity types in which interactants are engaged and using/facing impoliteness and how sophisticated language users change the very 'rules of conversation' whilst overwhelming the schematically expected norms.

Chapter 9: Here I summarise the argument made throughout the book, drawing together the threads woven throughout. Further, I conclude with a discussion of the implications of this book to the field of politeness and impoliteness studies, thereby suggesting areas of future research.

CHAPTER 2

Implicature

(Mis)Understanding Grice

The concept of implicature is a fundamental and far-reaching one for studies concerned with politeness and impoliteness – the present one included. With the exception of such direct, baldly expressed phrases as, 'take a seat' and 'quiet!' (both of which can be polite or impolite depending on the context) what interactants communicate, either politely or impolitely, is often very different from the core, unvarnished, propositional content of their message(s). Academically, different views of politeness and impoliteness have, by and large, adopted either a Gricean (1975, 1978, 1981, 1989) maxim-based approach or a Sperber and Wilson (1995) relevance-theory approach. Both, however, have their issues and I will explain the reasons, here, why I choose to follow a Gricean approach in this model. This seems especially prudent in light of the fact that there are at least two major and decidedly different interpretations of the Cooperative Principle, partly because Grice's own writings and conceptualisations of the CP are (a) less than watertight, which I explore below, and (b) were continually developed right up until his death in 1988.

2.1 Grice's cooperative principle

Fundamental to many 'traditional' approaches to politeness (Brown and Levinson 1987; Leech 1983, 2007; Fraser 1975; Fraser and Nolan 1981) is Grice's (1975) principle of cooperation. This, however, has not precluded different researchers from interpreting Grice in their own way, to suit their own ends. One primary aim of this section, beyond that of merely describing Grice's approach (1975) is to put on record my position and my understanding of the Cooperative Principle. I must stress that the following discussion is not, nor is it intended to be an exhaustive critique of Grice's Cooperative Principle, it is merely a conceptualisation of the Cooperative Principle and its subsequent maxims (see below) in relation to the generation and communication of im/politeness.

Grice's (1975) Cooperative Principle (hereafter shortened to CP) assumes a tacit understanding between interlocutors to co-operate in an interactive event in a meaningful way. The CP is formulated in Grice's own words as:

> [...] a rough general principle which participants will be expected (ceteris paribus) to observe, namely: Make your conversational contribution such as is required at the stage at which it occurs, by the accepted purpose or direction of the talk exchange in which you are engaged. (Grice 1975: 45)

What this 'rough general principle' means is that in conversation individuals work on the assumption that there are general expectations to interaction which will be observed by all members unless there are indications to the contrary. Under this 'rough general principle', Grice suggests four conversational categories or 'maxims' as they have come to be known which we generally expect our interlocutors to follow.

- **Maxim of Quantity:**
  1. Make your contribution as informative as is required (for the current purpose of the exchange)
  2. Do not make your contribution more informative than is required
- **Maxim of Quality:** Try to make your contribution one that is true
  1. Do not say what you believe to be false
  2. Do not say that for which you lack adequate evidence
- **Maxim of Relation:** Be relevant
- **Maxim of Manner:** Be perspicuous: –
  1. Avoid obscurity of expression
  2. Avoid ambiguity
  3. Be brief (avoid unnecessary prolixity)
  4. Be orderly (Grice 1975: 45–46)

Grice (1975) highlights two interesting issues concerning the category of manner. First, Grice emphasises that, unlike what seems to be the norm within the other maxims, utterances that are the concern of the maxim of Manner relate not to what is said, but to how what is to be said is said. Clearly, therefore, non-verbal, prosodic and paralinguistic information may well be included under the category of manner. Consider the following: If I was to wish someone, 'have a good day' then I could be seen to be (a) being conventionally polite (within an appropriate context) and, (b) operating within the maxim of manner (given our appropriate context). However, note the following example taken from one of the examples in my data sets:

[2] **The Clampers, Extract 8.**
Context: *Two 'Clampers' proceed to clamp an illegally parked car. Just as they have finished, the car's driver, a workman who was doing a job for a local homeowner, returns to his car to find it clamped, and the clampers still there. After an impolitely charged exchange, the Clampers return to their van to leave whilst S4 phones the clamping fines office to pay his release fee. As he is dialling the numbers he finds something to say to the retreating clampers: S1 – 'Ray' the clamping supervisor; S4 – Returning workman and owner of the clamped van.*

14. S1: I will do
S4: <sarcastically> *have a good day*

I should note here how S4's sarcastic tone breaks ('flouts' – see below) the maxim of manner to implicate the opposite, impolite belief from the one he utters to S1 (for a fuller discussion of sarcasm, see Section 5.2, below). Second, Grice points out that the list of sub-maxims for Manner may be incomplete and may well include others (Grice 1975: 46).

Grice was well aware that interlocutors rarely abided by these maxims in conversational or communicative exchanges. Grice understood that users of language often transgressed the expectation that we would follow these maxims and did so for particular, interactional reasons. Transgression, or 'non-observance', of these conversational maxims can take a number of forms. These include:

1. *Violating a maxim*: The unostentatious or covert non-observance of a maxim. The speaker in violating a maxim, '...will be liable to mislead.' (Grice 1975: 49)
2. *Opting out of a maxim*, which effectively makes plain, allows to be understood or indicates clearly that the interactant is unwilling to co-operate in the way the maxim(s) require. (Grice 1975: 49)
3. *A Clash of maxims*: An interactant may be unable, for example, to fulfil the first maxim of Quantity (Be as informative as is required) without breaking the second maxim of Quality (Have adequate evidence for what you say). (Grice 1975: 49)
4. *Flouting a maxim*: The intentional and blatant non-observance of a maxim at the level of what is said. This blatancy is overt, that is, it is designed to be noticed by the speaker's interlocutor(s) and is therefore designed to generate a conversational implicature, (Grice 1975: 49; 1981: 85). A flout is of course one possible mechanism by which unpleasant or impolite beliefs may be conveyed either politely or impolitely

5. *Suspending a maxim*: The non-observance of any maxim because there is no (or perceived to be no) expectation on the part of any interlocutor that they must all be fulfilled, (Thomas 1986: 44)
6. *Infringing a maxim*, (Grice 1981: 185 as cited in Thomas 1986: 38[1]): The unmotivated or unintentional non-observance of a maxim. Essentially, Thomas argues (1986: 38) transgressions of this nature are generated through a speaker's imperfect linguistic performance rather than a desire to generate conversational implicatures, to be uncooperative or to mislead. One such way in which someone may be said to have infringed a maxim could be where an utterance meaning X is said, which could be constructed as meaning Y by the hearer. However, the speaker is unaware, or, at least, apparently unaware that the utterance could be interpreted and, thus, taken as meaning Y by the hearer. Of course, not every misinterpretation need involve an infringement. The point here is that an infringement is one possible mechanism, however inadvertent, by which such speech acts may be performed.

2.1.1 Interpreting Grice

How we interpret and conceptualise Grice's CP is an issue of some import. A number of critics of Grice's theory of conversational implicature (1975) have expressed differing standpoints on how Grice's CP should indeed be interpreted, understood and deployed. One major reason for this is Grice's writing style which while readily accessible is arguably rather 'loose' in nature. This looseness has potentially arisen as a result of the fact that Grice's early work on the subject was prepared and presented as a series of lectures and his thinking on the topic was still developing right up until 1988. It is this issue, of looseness, that has allowed researchers and critics of Grice to view what he argued in such a way as to suit their own ends and purposes: whether that be, either, the exploitation and application of his approach or the criticism of it in support of their own ideas. Additionally, we should note a point made by Thomas:

> [...] few of those who in recent years have drawn so heavily on Grice's theories appear to have noticed the many ambiguities which exist in his work, or if they

1. There is an interesting issue with this reference. Examination of Grice (1981: 185) shows no trace of Grice actually discussing the infringement of a maxim. Indeed, even by 1989, Grice was still not considering the concept in the way that Thomas does. That said, the concept of infringement is still, in this researcher's view, a viable method of non-observance of a maxim. It remains a mystery to me why Thomas (1986) did not claim for herself the concept of 'infringement' as just such an additional way of not observing the maxims of Grice's CP. Thomas (1986) is in effect selling herself short here.

> have noticed, have taken the trouble to define the way in which they themselves have interpreted the concept of 'conversational cooperation' or are using the term 'cooperative'. (Thomas 1986: 26)

Thomas is effectively summing up one of the major issues here in that the very term 'conversational cooperation' is itself ambiguous and misleading in some rather important respects. Indeed, in one reading of Grice's (1975) work, impoliteness would be considered to be some of the most 'uncooperative' behaviour. In another, impoliteness is actually considered to be 'cooperative' behaviour. As such, for the purposes of this book, I will discuss the different major interpretations of Grice, and then clearly define my own position in relation to these competing views.

2.1.1.1 *Grice: Should we observe the maxims at the level of what is said?*

Thomas (1986: 26) identifies one particular and rather extreme conceptualisation of Grice (1975) which she views as '[...] a complete misrepresentation of what Grice was concerned to do.' This view would seem to insist that the maxims of Quantity, Quality, Relation and Manner must at all times be observed at the level of what is said. In the words of one of the main proponents of this view:

> The conversational postulates [maxims] make us believe that the speaker knows the truth and is saying what he knows in a clear, simple and relevant manner. (Apostel 1979: 294, as cited in Thomas 1986: 26)

However, given that Grice has unequivocally stated (Grice 1981: 185) that the ostentatious non-observance of a maxim at the level of what is said (i.e. a flout) in no way contravenes the CP, we can safely disregard this interpretation of Grice's CP and the subsequent maxims. Indeed, a flout of a maxim is the very mechanism that is required in order to generate a conversational implicature.

2.1.1.2 *Grice: As social cooperation or linguistic cooperation?*

One possible reading of the CP is that it is a system of social cooperation or 'social goal sharing' (Thomas 1986: 29). In the words of one proponent:

> [T]he Gricean maxims attempt to describe cooperative communication in which the participants strive after the same goal and are equally interested in achieving this goal. (Kiefer 1979: 60)

Clearly then, by the social goal sharing definition, Grice's view of cooperation means that an interlocutor would share with their intended addressee some common goal or purpose which is significantly beyond that of merely efficient message communication.

A significant number of linguistic researchers, both explicitly and implicitly, appear to have taken and interpreted Grice's CP as operating as just such a system of social 'goal sharing' cooperation. Thomas identifies Apostel (1980), Bollobas (1981), Corliss (1981), Kasher (1976, 1977), Kiefer (1979), Pratt (1977, 1981) and Sampson (1982) as being amongst them. They are joined by Fraser (1990), Fish (1999) and Watts (2003). Note that though actively believing that Grice is propounding the CP as a model of 'social goal sharing', most of the above do take pains to disassociate themselves from the viability of such a system for linguistic research. However, this said, such researchers as Watts do appear to take this interpretation to be the one intended by Grice. Watts (2003: 20), in making a number of points towards opening, both, his discussion of the nature of politeness, and a critique of his own earlier work on politic verbal behaviour (1992) suggests the following:

> My original definition assumes:
> 1. that all social interaction is geared towards cooperation, an assumption which the literature on conflictual discourse and impoliteness has shown to be false.
> [...]
> Point 1 can only be dispensed with only if we are prepared to abandon the Gricean assumption of cooperation. (Watts 2003: 20)

This suggests a 'social-goal sharing' reading of Grice and Grice's use of the term 'cooperation'. We should note also the points supporting this reading of Grice which Watts (2003:203) makes when critiquing earlier models of politeness:

> [...] it comes as no surprise that Grice's Cooperative Principle was the cornerstone of models [which originated from work in the 1970s and 1980s] that explain polite utterances as one way of achieving mutual cooperation or contributing towards the establishment and maintenance of mutual face. At the same time these models also recognise that such utterances appear to violate one or more of the Gricean maxims. So there's an inherent contradiction in their work; polite language is a form of cooperative behaviour but does not seem to abide by Grice's Cooperative Principle. (Watts 2003: 203)

And herein lies the root of the problem. Clearly, a view like Watts's above which equates the cooperative behaviour implied by politeness with the cooperative behaviour enshrined in Grice (1975, 1989) assumes either (i) that polite behaviour is in no way socially cooperative which would be somewhat disengenious to say the least, or more likely, (ii) that Grice's theory of cooperation is a theory of social cooperation.[2] This, as we will see, simply cannot be the case.

---

2. Either way, the fact remains that Watts (2003: 203) is confusing two separate definitions of 'cooperation' here.

It would certainly seem that a social goal sharing view of the CP starts to become highly problematic when we consider cases of discourse in which conflicting goals, non-cooperation and impoliteness occur (cf. Watts's comments above). However, Grice's own writings clearly indicate that social cooperation or social goal sharing is not the intended purview of the CP. Immediately following his own definition of the CP; the maxims of Quantity, Quality, Relation and Manner, Grice says that, "There are, of course, all sorts of other maxims (aesthetic, *social* or moral in character)" (Grice 1975: 47. My emphasis). Now, it could be argued that had Grice intended his CP to be a model of social cooperation (and his maxims, therefore, as being socially directed maxims), then he would not have indicated 'social' maxims as being an 'other' type of maxim to the ones he himself had just stipulated for the CP; its categories and subordinate maxims. What really confirms Grice's position is the fact that he explicitly indicates that while he once considered the CP as a possible system of 'social goal sharing', he soon abandoned this view. This is because there are issues between social cooperation, and the types of cooperation in which the CP must sometimes operate, which simply do not coincide. In Grice's own words:

> For a time, I was attracted by the idea that observance of the CP and the maxims, in a talk exchange, could be thought of as a quasi-contractual matter, with parallels outside the realm of discourse. If you pass by when I am struggling with my stranded car, I no doubt have some degree of expectation that you will offer help, but once you join me under the hood, my expectations become stronger and take more specific forms; [...] and talk exchanges seemed to me to exhibit, characteristically, certain features that jointly distinguish cooperative transactions:
>
> 1. The participants have some common immediate aim.
> 2. The contributions of the participants should be dovetailed, mutually dependent.
> 3. There is some sort of understanding (which may be explicit but which is often tacit) that [...] the transaction should continue in appropriate style unless both parties are agreeable that it should terminate.
>
> But while some such quasi-contractual basis as this may apply to some cases, there are too many types of exchange, like quarrelling [...] that it fails to fit comfortably. (Grice 1975: 48)

Indeed, Grice's view was to develop substantially over the years. In his retrospective epilogue he reconceptualises the above. In an elaboration of point [1], he says:

> 1. The participants have some common immediate aim, like getting a car mended; their ultimate aims may, of course, be independent and even in conflict – each may want to get the car mended in order to drive off, leaving the other stranded.

> In characteristic talk exchanges there is a common aim even if, as in over-the-wall chat, it is a second-order one, namely that each party should, for the time being, identify himself with the transitory conversational interests of the other. (Grice 1989: 29)

We could therefore argue that one implication of viewing the CP as a principle of social goal sharing would be that conversation should immediately cease, or at the very least become highly problematical when 'quarrelling' or other conflictive or impolite discourse begins to occur which is precisely what Watts (2003) was alluding to. Clearly conversation does not always cease in these types of discourse – such as those discussed in this book. What this means is that conflictive, impolite, non-socially cooperative talk can and does still occur. The channel of communication in impolite, conflictive exchanges remains open as both participants want to, or are forced to by an imbalance in power relations and permitted actions within a certain context, maintain the channel as open. Essentially, for im/politeness to occur it has to be communicated. After all, Grice in his retrospective epilogue opines that:

> While the conversational maxims have, on the whole been quite well received, the same cannot, I think, be said about my invocation of a supreme principle of conversational cooperation. One source of trouble has been that it has been felt even in the talk-exchanges of civilized people browbeating disputation and conversational sharp practice are far too common to be offenses [sic] against the fundamental dictates of conversational practice. Another source of discomfort has perhaps been the thought that, whether its tone is agreeable or disagreeable, much of our talk-exchange is too haphazard to be directed toward any end cooperative or otherwise. Chitchat goes nowhere, unless making the time pass is a journey. (Grice 1989: 368–9)[3]

How then does the CP account for such 'conversational sharp practice' and 'browbeating disputation' which can be seen as, and constitute, competitive, impolite, 'socially uncooperative' behaviour? A pseudo-solution to this problem relies upon the social goal-sharing proponents arguing for a structure that accounts for the existence of communication in these areas of disagreement, conflict and 'non-cooperation'. Fish (1999) proposes an 'Uncooperative Principle' which simply put, mirrors the existing CP and reverses the conversational categories and their subsequent maxims. This, one feels, is rather unnecessary as there is a clearer, simpler, and in my view more attractive interpretation of Grice's cooperative principle which, other problems with Grice aside, accounts for all types

3. My thanks go to Professor Ken Turner for directing me to this specific reference in light of the point I am attempting to make.

of communication. It is viewing Grice's CP as a principle of linguistic cooperation (see Thomas 1986). Indeed, the point needs to be made that one needs to be cooperative, in a linguistic sense, in order to communicate a lack of cooperation in a social sense: i.e., when one is, for example, arguing with, or being impolite to, an interlocutor. After all, if one wants to be impolite, such impoliteness has to be communicated.

The view of Grice's CP as a principle of linguistic cooperation assumes that the only goal of a given communication is the transmission of information. Thomas (1986) terms this view as 'linguistic goal sharing' as opposed to 'social goal sharing'. Thomas argues (1986: 28) that Grice only intended the CP to apply to the conventions of interaction and presupposes no shared aims between interactants other than that of correctly establishing the speaker's illocutionary intent and getting the hearer(s) to understand the proposition which is being expressed or implied. Indeed, this would seem to fit with what we have just seen of Grice's (1975, 1989) own writings. Thomas (1986: 29) goes on to point out that, in this view, the CP does not presuppose that the proposition expressed, entailed or implied is necessarily polite, relevant to any of the hearer's real (extra-linguistic) social goals or even truthful. Indeed, it bears re-iterating here that Grice himself notes that speakers' aims '[...] may even be in conflict' (Grice 1989: 29). In effect, Thomas (1986) is arguing, correctly in my view, that the CP operates purely to allow your interlocutor to understand what you are saying or implying. This is regardless of whether the content of your message happens to be what the social goal sharers would consider 'cooperative' or 'uncooperative'; regardless of whether it be harmonious communication or conflictive; and, more importantly for this book, regardless of whether it be polite or impolite. Indeed, we must accept Leech and Thomas's observation of the CP in that it '[...] makes no claims about the good intentions of the speakers' (Leech and Thomas 1990: 181).

To summarise Thomas's (1986) view, the social goal sharing view of the CP states: Say to your interlocutor what they want to hear, whereas the linguistic goal sharing view of the CP states: Use language in such a way that your interlocutor can understand what you are stating, presupposing[4] or implying. I believe it is upon this view – that Grice's CP is a model of linguistic cooperation – that the approach to politeness of Brown and Levinson (1987) is founded. Furthermore it is clear to me that this understanding of the CP is, for obvious reasons, absolutely necessary for a full(er) understanding and conceptualisation of im/politeness and its use.

4. For presupposition and conversational implicature see Grice (1989: 269–282).

2.1.2 Issues with the CP

There are of course a great many other issues concerning Grice's principle of co-operation and it seems that with each passing year there are researchers suggesting refinements to, correctives for, elaborations of, or replacements of the model. Hawley (2002), Spencer-Oatey and Jiang (2003) and Mooney (2004) are just some of the most recent. However, to explore all of the issues, criticisms, and suggestions for 'improvement' here is beyond the scope and scale of this book. As such I confine the discussion in the pages following to a consideration of only those features which are of direct relevance to the study of impoliteness in use.

Indeed, one primary concern in this regard is that Grice's definition (1975, 1989) of the CP is not watertight. The description of how the CP's categories and subsequent maxims operate is, in fact, rather loose. For example, the CP maxim of Quantity stipulates that one is expected to: 'Make your contribution as informative as is required (for the current purpose of the exchange)' and 'Do not make your contribution more informative than is required'. Yet while one given utterance may well be considered by one conversational participant to have been performed in accordance with the CP category of Quantity, it may well be considered by another to be less than informative given the context at hand or some other factor influencing the communicative event. Of course, the same can be said for every one of the categories of the CP as well as their subsequent maxims. How do we know that our hearer will consider an utterance to be maximally efficient with regards to Relation, Quality or Manner either? Indeed, one does not have to think too long or hard to recover at least one instance from personal experience whereby either an utterance of one's own was 'taken the wrong way', or an utterance from another was interpreted in a certain way which, it later turned out, was not the speaker's intended meaning. In short the instructions to, amongst others, 'be relevant', 'be perspicuous', 'avoid unnecessary prolixity' or 'make your contribution one that is true' are all relative terms. They are relative to the situation, the context and perhaps most importantly they are relative to the individual persons engaged in a communicative event. As such, we must accept that the categorical requirements of either acting in accordance with, or of not observing Grice's (1975) CP, its categories and their subsequent maxims are decisions that are both subjectively and contextually based. They are decisions made by the speaker, hearer and even analyst, which are relative to themselves and how they interpret the situational context at any given point in space and time.[5] In short, the issue here is to do with intention. Indeed, Strawson (1990: 154) points out that the CP

5. As such, it would seem that Grice was rather unwise in wording the (sub-)maxims as imperatives.

suffers from problems with regards to speakers' intentionality which are core to Grice's account of meaning. While I could elaborate upon this point here I do deal with intention later in this book (see Section 4.5.3 below) and the discussion made in this later section, in relation to im/politeness, also applies to the Grice's account of meaning.

We should bear in mind that such decisions are dependent upon the salient factors of the context at hand, such as the power relations, social distance and affect between the interactants, those same interactants' shared background knowledge, and their socio-discoursal roles, rights and obligations within the given context, to name but a few. Indeed, on this score, Mooney (2004) successfully re-casts Grice's CP and the subsequent categories and their maxims as applicable within specific, given activity types (Levinson 1992). In one clear and concise move Mooney helps Grice to sidestep the issues surrounding the CP with regards to its 'loose' nature in that, according to Mooney, interactants now consider quality, quantity, manner and relation within a specific, contextualised, type of activity. She thus quietens many of Grice's critics. The full importance of this position will become clear later when I discuss and justify the need for a framework that can account for impoliteness which, while linked, is essentially separate and distinct from existing frameworks which primarily deal with politeness (cf. Eelen 2001).

2.2 Sperber and Wilson's relevance theory

Developed as a reaction to Grice's approach, Sperber and Wilson place the concept of implicature on a more explicitly cognitive footing. Their approach subsumes all of the CP's categories (Quality, Quantity, Manner and Relation) under one, overarching, super-maxim – that of Relevance. Arguing that relation is always an issue in terms of implicature recognition, Sperber and Wilson provide a theoretically attractive approach to the phenomenon, so much so that a number of researchers, many who have worked within the "postmodern" approach to politeness, have adopted the theory at the expense of Grice. Escandell-Vidall (1996), Jary (1998), Jucker (1988), Locher (2004), Terkourafi (1999), Watts (2003) are amongst those who explicitly reject Grice's (1975, 1989) CP and turn to relevance theory. However, the reason I do not explore such approaches, nor adopt the theory itself, here, is that, as Turner (2000, see also Xie (2003: 813)) points out, relevance theory has a deep-rooted and irreparable weakness in its "conceptual incoherence." Thus far, in my view, all efforts at explaining politeness phenomena with relevance theory have failed for this very reason (cf. Fraser 1999). There are other analytical issues as well. The main ones being the fact that relevance theory as used here for these approaches to politeness, is a theory, not about the communication of such politeness, but rather, of the interpretation and perception of it. In short the theory over-privileges the recipient/receiver (hearer) at the expense of the originator (speaker) of any given 'im/polite' utterance. Watts suggests that:

> [a] theory of (im)polite behaviour needs to take the perspectives of the speakers and the hearers adequately into consideration, firstly, because speakers are also hearers, and vice-versa, and secondly, because social interaction is negotiated. (Watts 2003: 23)

As such, we must note that relevance theory does not take the perspectives of both the speakers and the hearers into account in the way required, as negotiation of 'what-was-meant' does not enter a relevance theory account of meaning in general, or a relevance theory account of im/politeness in particular. Additionally, Watts (2003: 212) notes that relevance theory rarely, if ever, concerns itself with stretches of natural verbal interaction. As any theory of politeness, as Watts himself argues, must be able to account for how im/polite discourse builds up and pans out as, '[i]t is impossible to evaluate (im)polite behaviour out of the context of real, ongoing verbal interaction.' (Watts 2003: 23) then relevance theory fundamentally fails in this respect. This said, I certainly view it as a priority for researchers within pragmatics to attempt to clarify relevance theory and rid it of its 'conceptual incoherence'. Once done it needs to be applied, systematically, to stretches of ongoing, real-life interaction from a multitude of different discourse types. However, such an undertaking is at least one project in its own right – well beyond the scope and scale of the present study. As such, and for the other reasons stated above, I still view Grice's CP as the best way of understanding and accounting for implicature being what was meant beyond what was said.

CHAPTER 3

Face within a model of im/politeness

Central to many of the classic and postmodern approaches to politeness and impoliteness is the concept of 'face'. Based primarily on Goffman's ([1955] 1967) approach to the concept, just how face should be conceptualised is a matter of both deep concern and fierce debate within and across approaches to human interaction. In the chapter following this one I will explore the most clearly expressed and articulated perspectives on politeness and impoliteness and, based on observations, arguments and conclusions made there, I will construct, layer upon layer, the multi-faceted nature of impoliteness in interaction. Given the complex model of impoliteness which I intend to construct and communicate throughout this book, it is critical, at this stage, to attend to the concept of face. I should, however, note that I cannot here hope to definitively answer all concerns or satisfy all critics of research on face. I confine the argument in this chapter to the discussion of the most salient issues (as I see them) concerning the concept of face as it applies to the study of impoliteness.

3.1 An early conceptualisation of face as related to models of im/politeness

Goffman (1967) defines face as being:

> [...] the positive social value a person effectively claims for himself by the line others assume he has taken during a particular contact. Face is an image of self delineated in terms of approved social attributes – albeit an image that others may share, as when a person makes a good showing for his profession or religion by making a good showing for himself. (Goffman 1967: 5)

Crucially for the present book, the concept of 'face' is at the core of Brown and Levinson's (1987) approach to politeness and Culpeper's (1996, 2005) approach to impoliteness. Whilst I make a fuller discussion and extensive critique of these models in the following chapter, it is necessary and sufficed to say here that in Brown and Levinson's own interpretation and understanding of the concept, 'face' is perhaps best understood as an individual's feeling of self-worth or self image (Thomas 1995: 169). Brown and Levinson (1987), taking a Durkheimian line (1915) of *approach* and *withdraw* (see also Terkourafi 2008: 50–51), subdivide 'face' into 'Positive Face' and 'Negative Face', which can be summarised as follows, (Brown and Levinson 1987: 62):

- *Negative face*: the want of every 'competent adult member' that his/her actions be unimpeded by others.
- *Positive face*: the want of every member that his/her wants be desirable to at least some others.

According to Brown and Levinson (1987: 62) members of a given society treat 'face' not as norms or values which members of that society subscribe to, but as basic *wants* which every member of a society, on some level, knows every other member desires, and which in general are in the interests of every member to (at least) partially satisfy. They also argue that face can be, and routinely is, ignored in cases of urgent co-operation, in the interests of efficiency and in cases of social breakdown (effrontery) (1987: 62). Indeed, as Thomas points out face is, '[...] damaged, maintained or enhanced through interaction with others' (Thomas 1995: 169) which echoes Brown and Levinson's own view on this (1987: 61).

3.2 Issues with early conceptualisations of face

As Watts (2003) has noted, de Kadt (1998) is but one of a long line of researchers who have criticised Brown and Levinson's concept of (negative) face (see also Gu 1990; Lee-Wong 1999; Locher 2004; Mao 1994; Matsumoto 1988). In short, the upshot of these many criticisms is that Brown and Levinson seem to assume an interlocutor's face is both universally applicable across all cultures worldwide, and internally generated and highly individualistic, despite Brown and Levinson advocating the concept as 'a public self image' (Brown and Levinson 1987: 62) which, as Locher (2004: 53) rightly points out suggests both an external and an internal view to face. However, Locher (2004: 55) does go on to argue that the distinction between external and internal aspects gets confused and increasingly lost during Brown and Levinson's extensive and otherwise illuminating analysis.

What the critics of Brown and Levinson's essentially (but not wholly) 'internally generated' view of face are not fully recognising is O'Driscoll's (1996) argument that there are two layers, or a *dualism*, to face. O'Driscoll has noted the confusion in Brown and Levinson that Locher (2004) mentions. He explains it thus:

> Goffman (1967: 5) refers to the origin of face in "the line others assume [a person] has taken". It is "an image". Thus it is bestowed from the outside and post-factum (note the perfective aspect here). B[rown] & L[evinson], on the other hand,

> stress that face consists of "wants" (1987: 62). Thus it is bestowed from the inside, and pre-facto. B[rown] & L[evinson], however, confuse the issue somewhat by also referring to face as "something that...can be lost, maintained or enhanced" (1987: 61), thus also using the term in Goffman's sense. (O'Driscoll 1996: 6)

As Locher (2004) notes, many researchers who criticise Brown and Levinson's stance do so because they ignore the dual internal-and-external aspects of face either in their own conceptualisations or in Brown and Levinson's approach to positive and negative face wants.

3.3 The dualism perspective

For O'Driscoll (1996) positive and negative face are not primary concepts that are wanted, in and of themselves, by interactants, rather they are synthesised compounds derived from wider, underlying basic positive and negative 'wants':

> [...] there are *positive wants* – the need to come together, make contact and identify with others; to have ties; to belong; to merge.
>
> At the other end there are *negative wants* – the need to go off alone, avoid contact and be individuated; to be independent; to separate.
>
> Since there are obviously degrees of proximity, politeness addressed to face dualism is scalar. It can be either very *positively or negatively polite* or only slightly so. (O'Driscoll 1996: 4, emphasis in third paragraph is mine)

Unfortunately for O'Driscoll here his wording is ambiguous. One reading could be that whilst the strength of any given utterance can vary from slightly-to-very polite or, conversely for us here, from slightly-to-very impolite, the face-direction of the utterance seems to be to *either* positive face/wants *or* negative face/wants. Not both. But this leads us into confusion. The reading of face suggested by O'Driscoll as dichotomous is, ultimately, a problem. However, it is a problem which would stem, at least partially, from the fact that face, in Brown and Levinson's terms, is indeed implicitly viewed as constituting aspects which are dichotomous polar opposites (see the discussion in Brown and Levinson 1987: 17–18). This is exemplified (and, occasionally, further misunderstood) in the nomenclatures: 'Positive' and 'Negative' face and, indeed, the 'Internal' and 'External' aspects to face (as mentioned above; more on this later). 'Positive-Negative'; 'Internal-External' are semantic opposites that most schematically hold in their heads. The aspects of face that Brown and Levinson, and O'Driscoll refer to are, thus, open to be somewhat erroneously, viewed as polar, dichotomous opposites as I will show in the next chapter and, indeed, throughout this book. However, Brown and Levinson's approach to face is so deeply ingrained in the most central approaches to politeness and impoliteness that, whilst I am attempting both, (i) a re-conceptualisation of their original view of face along both internally expected and externally realised lines, and (ii) a systematic challenge to the idea of a positive/negative face *dichotomy*, it is still necessary and even advisable to refer to these latter aspects of face (from time to time) throughout the book in order, firstly, to give further evidence as to why the *dichotomy* should be abandoned; secondly, to support the logical advancement of other researchers' arguments who have been restricted in fully developing their theories as a result of the limitations that the *dichotomy-view* of face has inadvertently placed on them and their approaches and; thirdly, as I view evolutionary (rather than revolutionary) approaches to the development of politeness and impoliteness to be the ones most likely to gain 'academic currency' and, thus, are more likely to receive the all-important rigour of testing by other researchers who apply the models to other types of discourses. What is interesting about O'Driscoll's argument is that he ultimately clarifies and develops his view of face, not as dichotomous – as his above comments could suggest – but as scalar:

> The concept of dualism when applied to the word 'face' prompts a Janus-like picture, with face looking both ways. However, it should be clear … that the corresponding dual nature of politeness is not a binary choice but rather a matter of degree. Politeness dualism operates on a spectrum. The total effect of an utterance may be either very positively or very negatively polite or it may only be slightly so. (O'Driscoll 1996: 28)

Of course the main problem here is the ambiguity of the phrase "…very positively *or* very negatively polite …". This said, I'm in agreement with his position as clarified above. Just to be absolutely clear here, it is not the desires of (at least 'western') individuals to the *approval* of others and the *freedom from imposition* from others that I am contesting here. I consider that these notions of face are merely two already identified and identifiable aspects to notions of face. What I'm contesting is the rather strong resistance of Brown and Levinson (1987: 17–18) to the idea (identified as long ago as 1984 by Harris) that positive and negative face oriented utterances can co-occur within a single utterance (see, for example, Chapter 5, Section 5.5.4 and Chapter 8, Section 8.4.3: the full discussion of 'Challenge' as a linguistic impoliteness strategy which simultaneously attacks the target's *freedom of action* and *desire for approval*).

3.4 The 'universality' of positive and negative face

As noted in the previous section, many researchers working with Pacific Rim cultures (Japanese, Chinese, Indo-China) have hotly contested the role and strength of the concept of negative face outside of a so-called 'western' setting. For example Matsumoto suggests that:

> What is of paramount concern to a Japanese is not his/her own territory, but the position in relation to the others in the group and his/her acceptance by those others. Loss of face is associated with the perception by others that one has not comprehended and acknowledged the structure and hierarchy of the group…A Japanese generally must understand where s/he stands in relation to other members of the group or society, and must acknowledge his/her dependence on others.
> (Matsumoto 1988: 405)

There are two points to be made here. First, there seems to be a sense of confusion as to what negative face actually is here. With loss of face associated with the perception by others that one has not comprehended and acknowledged the structure and hierarchy of the group, then this seems to suggest, or imply, notions of (dis)approval which is more the purview of positive and not negative face. This 'confusion' of face is not limited to researchers working with Japanese culture:

> The Chinese negative face is not threatened by the speaker's impeding the hearer's freedom to act, but it is threatened when self cannot live up to what s/he has claimed or when what the self has done is likely to incur *ill fame* or *reputation*.
> (Gu 1990: 241–242. Emphasis added)

Ill fame or *reputation* are aspects of (dis)approval. With positive face being the want to be approved of by others in one's society then, in my view, *Ill fame* or *reputation* must be considered aspects of positive face, and not aspects of negative face as Gu seems to claim. This 'confusion' may actually be a result of the fact that there appears to be no sharply defined line between positive and negative face, as I argue below and throughout the book.

Second, this is not to say that non 'western' cultures and, therefore, some more culturally motivated notions of face (e.g. Spencer-Oatey's work 1992-to-2007) do not have the aspects of the desire to be free from restriction (freedom of action) or the desire to be the subject of others' approval encapsulated within them. Following O'Driscoll, I view these as two fundamental and even universal aspects of face amongst a hitherto unidentified number of aspects. The type, quantity, strength and salience of different aspects of face will vary from culture – to – culture, discourse – to – discourse and, of course, context – to – context. Indeed, part of the problem with researchers such as Gu 1990; Lee-Wong 1999; Mao 1994; Matsumoto 1988 criticising the inapplicability to non-western cultures of the aspect of face of being free from imposition (Brown and Levinson's negative face) is the assumption, unchallenged by most, that the two aspects of face identified by Brown and Levinson are supposed to be of equal weight, importance and value in every culture. This, clearly, isn't the case. It is evidenced, amongst many other things, by the fact that British culture is often viewed, perhaps simplistically, as a negative-face culture, and the US, just as simplistically, a positive-face culture. This very observation which has been made by many researchers over the years must inevitably lead us to considering these two identified aspects of face as being of different strengths and, thus of differing importance in different cultures. This isn't to say that the desire to be approved of, in some direct or peripheral way is non-existent in UK culture, nor that the desire to be free from imposition is simply non-existent in US culture (far from it, in some sections), rather that (traditionally at least) the desire for freedom from imposition and the desire for approval are more important, respectively, in these two cultures (with all other things being equal). One suspects the same could be true for the other cultures that have been held up as antithetical counterexamples to Brown and Levinson's position in the past. Therefore, what I'm contesting is the largely implicit view that Brown and Levinson meant their two aspects of face to be viewed always as mutually exclusive and of equal weight universally, across all cultures, discourses and contexts. As I will argue further in the next chapter the dichotomy view must fail, at least partly given the evidence I present in this book that 'positive' and 'negative' face is, apparently, always an issue (to a greater or lesser degree) in most impoliteness strategies within the interactional exchanges as they build up and proceed.

3.5 A return to Goffman?

De Kadt's (1998) suggestion is that we seriously reconsider Goffman's (1967) notion of face over Brown and Levinson's, in particular Goffman's idea that face is 'public property' in that it is something which is only realised in social interaction and is dependent upon others. It is not something that the individual builds *purely* for him or herself. Face is, in de Kadt's terms, mutually constructed (de Kadt 1998: 176) and, thus, in Goffman's (1967:10) and Held's (1995: 64–65) undertsanding 'on loan' from society:

> [...] while his social face can be his most personal possession and the center of his security and pleasure, it is only on loan to him from society; it will be withdrawn unless he conducts himself in a way that is worthy of it.
>
> (Goffman 1967: 10)

In short, this heralds Thomas's (1995: 169) and Brown and Levinson's (1987: 61) own view that face is maintained, enhanced or damaged in interaction with others. Terkourafi (2008) takes the view of re-considering Goffman's position on face over Brown and Levinson's even further with her extremely 'stripped down' notion of face. She utterly rejects Brown and Levinson's view of an internally generated aspect to face. Face in Terkourafi's view is constituted or threatened purely in interaction, that is, face is *only* constituted externally.

> Individuals alone do not 'have' face and cannot 'gain' or 'lose' face. Rather [face] is grounded in the interactional dyad. Without an Other to whom they may be directed, face concerns cannot arise. The moment an Other enter's the Self's perceptual field creating the possibility of to approach or to withdraw, that is the moment when face concerns prototypically arise. To adapt a well known expression, face is 'in the eye of the beholder.' (Terkourafi 2008: 52)

Furthermore, for Terkourafi, face is not, as she argues that Brown and Levinson (1987: 97 & 305) and Lakoff (1989: 103) seem to assume:

> [...] an optional add-on, (almost) a luxury attended to time permitting but otherwise easily and quickly dispensed with in the interests of urgency, clarity, and generally efficient information exchange, or when the speaker is powerful enough to "not care". (Terkourafi 2008: 46)

For Terkourafi, face is either enhanced (what she calls 'constituted') or damaged, and this always takes place in interaction. There is no middle ground. Essentially, for Terkourafi, there is 'no faceless communication' (Scollon and Scollon 1995: 38; see also Locher 2004: 55). As we can see, we're moving away from the classic (Brown and Levinson) view of face as a pre-existing static monolith to be threatened, damaged, repaired or enhanced and which is internally generated and projected by the individual into the interactional space between participants, to a more fluid consideration of face, one in which the concept is both dynamic and mobile, and is created, strengthened or weakened in (often extended) interaction. After all, Terkourafi points out that face is constituted over multiple turns and this is what Goffman meant when he said that "[a] person's face clearly is something that is not lodged in or on his body, but rather something that is diffusely located in the flow of events in the encounter [...]" (Goffman 1967: 7).

I agree with Terkourafi's insistence that there is, and can be, no communication without face being an issue, which has implications for Brown and Levinson's model of politeness, as we will see in the following chapter. However, I cannot agree that the individual interactant does not bring *something* concerning their own face to the interaction. After all, surely we approach interactions with *expectations* as to how we would like our face(s) to be constituted. Such expectations of how face should be constituted are, necessarily, internal. They are brought by an individual to the interaction based on her/his own feeling of self-worth and her/his understanding of the context of previous, similar encounters (with whom one is meeting, the situation the interactants are in, and so on). Such expectations are held right up to the point at which the interaction starts and, indeed, must survive in some (albeit modified) form throughout the exchange. As Goffman notes:

> If the encounter sustains an image of him that he has long taken for granted, he probably will have few feelings about the matter. If events establish a face for him that is better than he might have expected, he is likely to 'feel good'; if his ordinary expectations are not fulfilled, one expects that he will 'feel bad' or 'feel hurt'. (Goffman 1967: 6)

Essentially, when the *reality* of the socially and interactionally constituted face differs markedly from the individual's (internal and cognitive) expectation of how their face should be constituted – especially where face is constituted at a somewhat 'lower' level that expected – then things can really get interesting: tensions can ensue requiring, perhaps, remedial face/politeness work, an individual's re-assesment of their standing in society in relation to their feeling of self-worth including a defence of their expectations in an attempt to bring actual face in line with the expected, or an attack on a threatener's face or other, similar 'repositioning'. In short, face expectations not matching face reality may well result, amongst other things, in the communication, manipulation or management of impoliteness or aggression, linguistic or otherwise.

The view I suggest here is not new. Goffman, and de Kadt are but two researchers who have expressed ideas on face being *mutually* constructed. Such an approach seems to fit my argument of what happens with expectations of how face will be constituted and the reality of face constitution. Indeed Goffman's and de Kadt's ideas here fit perfectly with army training, kitchen, and police training data (amongst others). I should note in all these extracts the preponderence of public 'dressing downs' (a formal or informal activity type in which one or more individuals receive a reprimand) of interactants who have, or are perceived as having committed an infraction. Despite the institutionally long 'accepted' centrality of what I here term impoliteness in, say, army training discourse, (cf. Fitzpatrick 1945, Marshall-Hasdell 1994) the face threat/damage suffered by recruits at the hands of training NCOs, is still keenly felt (as evidenced by recruits' reports to camera and their reactions to the impoliteness which range from limited 'defensive moves' (see Chapter 7, Section 7.2.1.3) to a degree of psychological collapse (i.e crying). The fact that the public (informal) dressing downs are issued in front of the recruits' localised 'society' or 'community of practice' (their squadmates) may potentially add to the face damage, despite the 'centrality' of impolite utterances in this institutional type of discourse, as the recruits' face is constructed, mutually supported, and loaned to them by (amongst others) each of their individual squad mates as well as the corporal or sergeant who is training them. As Terkourafi (2008: 52–53) explains:

> […] the intentionality (or directedness) of Face toward an Other means that Self will have several faces concurrently, as many as there are Others involved in a situation. Putting this somewhat schematically, if I am interacting with an interlocutor in front of an audience, I make (and am aware of making) a bid for face not only in the eyes of my interlocutor, but also in the eyes of each of the members of that audience taken seperately and as a group. And the same applies to each of them.

Goffman also makes an interesting point:

> In any case, while his social face can be his most personal possession and the center of his security and pleasure, it is only on loan to him from society; it will be withdrawn unless he conducts himself in a way that is worthy of it. Approved attributes and their relation to face make of every man his own jailer; this is a fundamental social constraint even though each man may like his cell.
>
> (Goffman 1967: 10)

In short, stoically standing one's ground in the face of an impolite verbal ear bashing seems to be the *raison d'etre* of impolite verbal action in army training (and other group) discourses. In army training it is part of what can be termed 'Common Enemy Syndrome.' How you deal with the frequent and regular attacks on your individual face, within the context of group-constructed face promotes (or ameliorates) that group sense of face – in short, can your squadmates rely on you when you're under pressure? Can your superiors rely on you to get things right and not to fold when under pressure? Face, in multi-interactant exchanges of this nature is necessarily multi-faceted – following Terkourafi, there is not just one 'blanket' aspect of face per individual, rather face is constituted between dyads of interactants and multiplied throughout the interactants to produce many discrete but potentially linked (by social group bonds) aspects of face. With two interactants (a dyad) there are two salient types of face being constituted and shaped as the interaction proceeds. With three interactants there are six salient types of face being constituted and shaped as the interaction proceeds (3 interactants multiplied by 2 types of face constituted for each individual). Just to re-iterate, just because it is sometimes group face being attacked, in insitutionally impolite settings (and, thus, may be 'expected' to an extent), does not mean to say it is not keenly felt by recruits – as evidenced by their reactions in at least some of the extracts.

I am therefore also contesting moves towards purely 'external' notions of face. Rather, I prefer to view face as internally expected and externally realised in interaction requiring, in actuality, some fine tuning or outright re-modification/manipulation. Indeed, in a similar vein, Lee-Wong (1999) following Gu (1990) and Mao (1994) considers face maintenance to be '… an act of balancing – the perception of self in relation to other' (Lee-Wong 1999: 24). Matsumoto (1988: 415) argues that face is intimately bound up with showing recognition of one's relative position in the communicative context and with the maintenance of the social ranking order. Whilst, in these researchers' cases they were dealing with Chinese (Gu, Lee-Wong, Mao) and Japanese (Matsumoto) respectively, their comments on what are essentially group oriented, socially hierarchical cultures also apply to some Western cultural settings and contexts, especially those of some discourses here discussed. Army training, as we will see (and as both Culpeper 1996 and Marshall-Hasdell 1994 have at least tacitly argued) is concerned with essentially stripping away the individualism of the recruit and recasting that individual into the role of soldier – i.e. as an integral member of a larger socially and mutually dependent group/network.

In summary, I view the concept of face as follows:

- Face is individually (internally, cognitively, historically) expected by the Self but is interactionally (externally, mutually, continuously) constituted between Self and Other.
- With regards to the 'continuous' aspect of face: Following the initial constitution, face is enhanced or threatened/damaged in interactional dyads (2 participants) throughout the exchange potentially spanning many turns of interaction until the communication ends. Self's understanding of how Self's face was constituted and developed during this interaction then passes into the self's episodic memory and become part of self's internal expectations of face for future interactions with the immediately recent or a different Other.
- 'Positive' and 'Negative' face, that is the desire for approval, and the desire to be free from imposition are applicable to most, if not all cultures but are of differing strengths and saliency dependent upon context.
- 'Positive' and 'Negative' face are but two identified aspects of face. There are others which are applicable to different cultures and contexts and these, too, will be of differing strengths and saliency.
- 'Group face' is created by the sum of faces constituted through interactional dyads and is often dependent upon previous, socially cooperative interactions with like-minded, and like-faced people.
- Constitution of the face of one member of a group can have an impact on the face constitution and face expectation of other members of a group.

It is on this basis that I view face within a model of impoliteness.

CHAPTER 4

Perspectives on politeness and impoliteness

In this chapter I explore and discuss both the literature and the background concerning the concept of impoliteness. In this way I construct a working definition of the term 'impoliteness' for use throughout this book and identify more clearly some terms relating to impoliteness and associated phenomena that may be ambiguous in nature.

Whilst it is undoubtedly true that impoliteness does not constitute an unproblematic opposite to politeness (Mills 2003, 2005), Culpeper (1996: 355) argues that impoliteness is very much the parasite of politeness. By this he means that models and approaches developed to account for and explain impoliteness have evolved out of existing approaches which were originally developed for politeness. On this basis it seems that before discussing the current theoretical approaches to impoliteness the most logical place to begin is with a critical review of current theoretical and conceptual standpoints underpinning politeness, its predicted manifestations in interaction, and how such models have attempted to account for the notion of impoliteness.

However, this is perhaps much easier said than done. Fraser (1990: 219), points out that there is little common understanding of the concept of politeness, "... and how to account for it is certainly problematic." Further, Watts (2003: 9) notes, "(im)politeness is a term that is struggled over at present, has been struggled over in the past and will, in all probability, continue to be struggled over in the future." This problem, of accounting for or defining politeness is, perhaps, hardly surprising given the "nearly geometric" (Xie 2003: 811) or "mammoth-like" (Chen 2001: 87) increase in the number of texts dealing with, critiquing, correcting or commenting upon politeness models since Lakoff's seminal work (1973). It is perhaps no small wonder then that Eelen (2001) and Watts (2003) have identified at least 10 different conceptualisations operating from within linguistic paradigms purporting to account for politeness phenomena in interaction (Arndt and Janney 1985; Blum-Kulka 1992; Brown and Levinson 1978, 1987; Lakoff 1973, 1989, 2006; Leech 1983, 2003, 2005, 2007; Fraser 1990; Fraser and Nolen 1981; Gu 1990; Ide 1989; Janney and Arndt 1992; Locher 2004; Watts 1989, 1991, 1992, 2003). Despite such a seemingly wide choice of models, Watts makes a pertinent remark:

> The fact remains that only Leech and Brown and Levinson have elaborated their positions in sufficient detail to allow them to be tested through application to real-language data. (Watts 2003: 63)

Throughout this book I take a view of impoliteness which has evolved out of the predominantly 'face-management' approach to politeness. Following and agreeing with Culpeper (1996, 2005) I only minimally deal with Leech's (1983) maxim (or later (2007) 'constraint') based view, seeing it as a useful complement to face-management approaches rather than a stand-alone model in its own right. As such I will discuss in this chapter only those approaches which directly relate to the exploration and validation of the model of impoliteness suggested in this book. These are:

1. The Social Norm or 'lay person's' view of politeness
2. The Conversational Maxim / Constraint based view posited by Lakoff (1973) and developed by Leech (1983, 2007)
3. The Face Management view developed by Brown and Levinson (1987) and critiqued by many others.

I shall present and discuss each of these in turn, but I should note that Brown and Levinson's (1987) face management view is, arguably, the most academically popular of all the approaches to politeness and, to date, has been the approach that has inspired the most extensively articulated models (Culpeper 1996, 1998, 2005; Culpeper et al. 2003).

4.1 Social norm politeness

> A dinner guest once suggested to the French Marshal Ferdinand Foch that there was nothing but wind in French politeness. Foch retorted, "Neither is there anything but wind in a pneumatic tyre, yet it eases wonderfully the jolts along life's highway." (As cited in Fraser 1990: 219)

Stipulating so-called 'correct' personal conduct in society, in effect 'good manners', the 'Social Norm' view is effectively the lay-person's conceptual understanding of the phenomena of politeness. Or to put it another way, this view, according to Fraser (1990: 220), "reflects the historical understanding of politeness generally embraced by the public within the English-speaking world." He further argues that this approach,

> [...] assumes that each society has a particular set of social norms consisting of more or less explicit rules that prescribe certain behaviour, state of affairs, or way of thinking in a context. (Fraser 1990: 220)

Both Fraser (1990) and Kasher (1986) cite Locke's *Ladies book of Etiquette and Manual of Politeness* (1872) as a typical text exemplifying the social norm approach. Examples that Fraser (1990) cites from Locke's (1872: 5 and 7) text include:

> [...] avoid topics which may be supposed to have any direct reference to events or circumstances which may be painful.
>
> [in the event a lady unintentionally raises a troublesome subject, she is instructed thus] do not stop abruptly, when you perceive that it causes pain, and above all, do not make the matter worse by apologising; turn to another subject as soon as possible, and pay no attention to the agitation your unfortunate remark may have excited.
>
> Never question the veracity of any statement made in general conversation.
>
> (Locke 1872, as cited in Fraser 1990: 220)

The social norm approach has been criticised by some (Thomas 1986: 150), as an inadequate platform upon which to investigate linguistic politeness phenomena. Indeed, Fraser concludes, 'I think it is safe to say that the social-norm view has few adherents among current researchers' (Fraser 1990: 221). However, things have changed since 1990 which seem to indicate that a divorce from the social norm approach for linguistic conceptualisations of im/politeness may not only be a mistaken move, but, theoretically, an impossible one.

First, we must recognise that most, if not all of the approaches to politeness rely in at least some way upon social norms. After all, the very concept of politeness is a socially oriented one. For example, Brown and Levinson's model (1987), despite being a linguistic theory of face management (see 4.3 below) does consider, on one level, those activities that require the deployment of mitigating politeness to include: 'the raising of dangerously emotional or divisive topics' (Brown and Levinson 1987: 67). By way of comparison, this is somewhat similar to Locke's 'avoid topics which may be supposed to have any direct reference to events or circumstances which may be painful', which is, as we saw above, 'social norm' politeness. Similarly, Brown and Levinson (1987: 66) also argue that expressions of criticism, disapproval, contempt or ridicule are linguistically threatening and, for the sake of politeness, need to be mitigated.[1] Again, such expressions may

1. See also Leech's (1983) Agreement maxim, or (2007) constraint no. # 7: Agreement; and Spencer-Oatey's (1992) face 'needs': 'Need for consideration, need to be valued, need for rela-

be implicated within the third example from Locke given above, namely: 'Never question the veracity of any statement made in general conversation'.

There are, undoubtedly, many more comparable examples to be made. This said, it is not to say that the concept of 'linguistic politeness' is weakened by the reliance of its elements upon socially grounded lay users' expectations of politeness. Far from it, for without such social expectations it could be argued that any theory or model of politeness becomes untenable or even entirely unnecessary. Language, we must not forget, is here to serve our society, not the other way around. As Xie (2003) notes:

> [...] we human beings do not and cannot possibly live in isolation; rather we are in essence "at once biological, psychological and cultural/social beings" (Pyysiainen 2001:167) and need to interact constantly with other people, and politeness is one of the things we should bear in mind to ensure smooth and successful interaction. (Xie 2003:811)

Without social expectations then it is difficult to see how one interlocutor could offend another linguistically, (either intentionally or otherwise). As such, 'politeness' – the set of devices which can be used for avoiding or otherwise mitigating linguistic offence in interaction – would be entirely unnecessary. Because of the previously overlooked and unfashionable view that 'social norms' once had within politeness theories, researchers struggled with an incomplete grasp of the phenomena of politeness (and associated parallel phenomena such as impoliteness). It was only when researchers following a 'postmodern' approach to politeness made a distinction between 1st order, lay, or socially (and societally) understood approaches to the phenomenon, and 2nd order, theoretical, or linguistically grounded approaches, that the dangers inherent in ignoring social and even historical norms became explicitly apparent: by ignoring social expectations of politeness and how such expectations have developed historically within a society, then you are no longer looking *at politeness*. Indeed, Ehlich (1992) points out that the historicity of politeness may well be a useful starting point after all for future developments in politeness research – a cry enthusiastically and convincingly taken up by Watts (2003:32–46). Further, both Eelen (2001:252) and Watts (2003:8–9) are but two amongst a whole school of researchers, working with this postmodern approach to human linguistic interaction who insist that a theory of politeness should, amongst other things, be based upon and concern itself with how lay members understand and evaluate the social norms governing interaction which, obviously, includes im/politeness. As such, the view I take here, whilst

tional identity'. Pitched as requirements for politeness, all are, nevertheless, socially motivated needs or constraints.

ostensibly a so-called, 2nd order ('classic' or theoretical) approach to linguistically communicated impoliteness, nevertheless is cognisant of the need to take into account so-called 1st order ('postmodern' or lay users') notions and understandings of the term. This is the approach I take and develop throughout this book.

4.2 Conversational maxim politeness

Lakoff (1973) was amongst the first linguistic theorists to posit the need for a model of politeness. Her work first influenced and then was expanded upon and superseded by the work of later researchers. For this reason I will not dwell on her model here.[2] Rather, I will discuss in brief the work of the main inheritor of the legacy of the 'conversational maxim' approach to politeness: Leech (1983, 2007).

4.2.1 Interpersonal rhetoric

Leech (1983, 2007) theorises a model of Interpersonal Rhetoric (IR) in which the Cooperative Principle of Grice (CP) stands as one of two primary stanchions that support the bridge of communication; the other stanchion, equal in importance to the Gricean CP is the Politeness Principle (PP). Leech sees the PP as 'rescuing' the CP in that where the CP explains *how* people create implicatures in communication by deviating from or transgressing a tacitly expected 'norm', the PP can explain *why* people deviate from communicating completely in accordance with that norm (Grice's CP). In this way, argues Leech, the CP and PP are complementary and necessary. As I hope to show, this is, potentially, a rather narrow and, unfortunately for such an attractive model, a somewhat limiting view.

4.2.1.1 *The politeness principle*

Leech's Politeness Principle (hereafter PP) states that with all other things being equal one should, 'Minimise the expression of impolite beliefs, Maximise the expression of polite beliefs' (Leech 1983: 81). Summarising further, Leech subdivides the PP into six maxims (which he later renames and expands as 'constraints' (2007)), as shown in Table 2, below.

According to Leech, the PP's (1983) maxims are further divided into sub-maxims. Here the first sub-maxim (identified as the (a) sub-maxims above) is what Leech calls 'Positive Politeness'. The second sub-maxim (identified as square-bracketed (b) sub-maxims above) is what Leech calls 'Negative Politeness'

2. Lakoff (2006) has returned to her model – what fruits this will bring are yet to be seen.

(as opposed to Brown and Levinson's (1987) rather different use for these terms). The maxims and sub-maxims are not equally important: Leech argues that the 'Positive Politeness' sub maxim in each case is more important than the 'Negative Politeness' sub maxim within interaction. Taking the Tact maxim, for example, minimising the cost to other is, generally, held to be more important that maximising the benefit to the other. Furthermore, these PP maxims tend to be paired according to pragmatic scales (Leech 1983: 123). The Tact and Generosity maxims are paired together as they deal with a bipolar 'cost-benefit' scale; the maxims of Approbation and Modesty are paired together as they also deal with a bipolar scale: the 'praise-dispraise' scale. The remaining two maxims are paired as they deal with discrete but linked unipolar scales, the scales of agreement and sympathy respectively.

Table 2. Leech's (1983) Politeness maxims and sub-maxims (Leech 1983: 32)

	Maxim/ Constraint	Positive Politeness	Negative Politeness
I.	**Tact**	(a) Minimise cost to other	[(b) Maximise benefit to other]
II.	**Generosity**	(a) Minimise benefit to self	[(b) Maximise cost to self]
III.	**Approbation**	(a) Minimise dispraise of other	[(b) Maximise praise of other]
IV.	**Modesty**	(a) Minimise praise of self	[(b) Maximise dispraise of self]
V.	**Agreement**	(a) Minimise disagreement between self and other	[(b) Maximise agreement between self and other]
VI.	**Sympathy**	(a) Minimise antipathy between self and other	[(b) Maximise sympathy between self and other].

On the basis of these pairs, Leech also considers that (I) Tact influences what we say more powerfully and more significantly than does (II) Generosity. Likewise (III) Approbation is considered more important than (IV) Modesty. We should also note that interactants may adhere to more than one Politeness maxim within a given utterance (at the same time). It is often the case that one maxim is the primary maxim with other maxims operating in support by being invoked by implication. Further, Leech argues that politeness needs to be communicated and suggests that if politeness is not communicated then we should assume that a polite attitude is absent.

Whilst an attractive approach there are however a number of issues with Leech's PP both in how it deals with politeness and, more importantly for us here, in how it would or could deal with impoliteness. Spencer-Oatey and Jiang (2003 drawing upon Spencer-Oatey 2000) take issue with the fact that the politeness maxims all have what they term, 'universal valences':

> [...] in other words one pole of a given maxim is seen as more desirable than the other. For example with regards to *modesty-pride*, Leech implies 'the more modest the better'. (Spencer-Oatey and Jiang 2003: 1635)

However, different discourses and different contexts (such as those discussed in this book) may alter the valences as to which aspect of each maxim is considered the more desirable. For example, in sales discourse it may well be more appropriate or desirable to take, or emphasise, a Leech-style negative politeness approach to the Tact maxim, being 'maximise benefit to other', over the positive politeness approach, 'minimise the cost to other' even though both are still, clearly, salient issues.

Furthermore, and perhaps more seriously, in seeing the PP as an equal and necessary half of Interpersonal Rhetoric (IR), in that it stands alongside, complements, and 'rescues' the CP, Leech (1983) could be seen to adopt the view of Grice (1975) as a 'Social Goal Sharing' model, (see Section 2.1.1.2 above) *when* the CP stands alongside the PP as the component parts of Interpersonal Rhetoric. Note that for Interpersonal Rhetoric to succeed, Leech (1983) proposes an 'agreement maxim' which is pitched as 'Minimise disagreement between self and other [maximise agreement between self and other]'. This, I would argue is evidence of social goal sharing and not linguistic goal sharing. Indeed, Leech himself appears to validate the social goal sharing view of the CP (when considered *within* the IR) when he says:

> Here we should consider the general social function of these two principles. The CP enables one participant in a conversation to communicate on the assumption that the other participant is being *cooperative*. In this the CP has the function of regulating what we say so that it contributes to some assumed illocutionary or discoursal goal(s). It could be argued, however, that the PP has a higher regulative role than this: to maintain social equilibrium and the friendly relations which enable us to assume that our interlocutors are being *cooperative* in the first place. To put matters at their most basic: unless you are polite to your neighbour, the channel of communication between you will break down, and you will no longer be able to borrow his mower. (Leech 1983: 82. My emphasis)

Bearing in mind that Leech argues that the PP stands alongside, complements, and rescues the CP, we should note that the second use of the word 'cooperative' (line 7) is arguably being used in the 'social goal sharing' sense as opposed to the first use of the word 'cooperative' (in line 3) which could appear to be used in a 'linguistic goal sharing' sense. But note also that (i) Leech considers the general *social* function of the CP and the PP (in lines 1–2) and (ii) that the 'social goal sharing' sense is assumed to have a '...*higher* regulative role...' (in line 5) than the 'linguistic goal sharing' sense. Effectively, when Leech argues that the CP and the

PP operate together (as components of IR), thereby allowing us to assume that we and our interlocutors are being cooperative by maintaining social equilibrium, and of working towards some assumed illocutionary or discoursal goal, he implicitly assumes that this goal is a common, and therefore, *social goal* – hence his example of borrowing the lawn mower. To put it another way, in arguing that Interpersonal Rhetoric (IR) consists of the PP and the CP standing side-by-side (which the IR clearly does when we consider *only* politeness but not impoliteness), Leech appears to assume that the CP's role is one which operates (when we consider it *within* Interpersonal Rhetoric) as a *social goal sharing principle* (see Chapter 2, Section 2.1.1.2). He has, in fact, given a new facet to the CP when it is considered within Interpersonal Rhetoric. It needs to be noted that this is satisfactory only while dealing within the bounds of Interpersonal Rhetoric, which is oriented towards politeness (politeness being essentially a social theory). However, the point here is that Leech makes little attempt to explain how the CP, or the wider IR in which he places it, may attempt to deal with impoliteness or other conflictive, aggressive communication. Even if they would not, in at least one sense (of shared goals), be termed 'social' communication both of which can and perhaps should be seen to be aspects of an 'Interpersonal Rhetoric'. After all, as Billig argues, '[…] it is impossible to have habitual politeness without the possibility of rudeness.' (Billig 2001: 39). However, if we were to ask: "Would Leech's assumption of how the IR operates work for conflictive situations?" I would have to argue that, in this form, it probably would not. This is precisely what Jucker (1988: 376) means when he says Leech's approach can only be applied to certain (i.e. socially cooperative: polite) types of interaction and not others (i.e. socially uncooperative: impolite). We must remember that Grice pointed out that although the form of cooperation (which Leech is describing by using the lawn mower example), which is quasi-contractual, may apply in some cases, 'there are too many types of exchange, like quarrelling […] that it fails to fit comfortably' (Grice 1975: 48). As I have alluded above we must not forget that for either politeness or impoliteness to be communicated we *do* have to assume CP cooperation (in a linguistic sense). Indeed, Brown and Levinson (1987) see the CP as operating as an underpin to politeness not alongside it as Leech maintains. Brown and Levinson (1987: 5) point out that we can find cooperation, as they put it, "at a deeper level" (see also Locher 2004: 65) in virtually all uncooperative behaviour (except, for example, where someone 'withdraws' from the interaction – see Chapter 7, Section 7.3.5). Locher, following Brown and Levinson (1987: 5) does not agree that politeness can be conceptualised in the same way that cooperation is, namely in terms of principles and maxims. To do so would mean that, '[…] politeness would have to be found at a deeper level in impolite behaviour as well if it were to have principle status' (Locher 2004: 65) or to put it another way, even when people are being impolite we would have to assume that on some deeper level they are still trying to be polite. In short, Brown and Levinson, and Locher are viewing the CP first and foremost as a principle of linguistic co-operation. So, as with the argument given above for the 'social goal sharing' view of the CP, with Leech's (1983: 82) assumption of 'maintaining social equilibrium', just *how could* Leech's approach cope with conflictive, impolite interaction? Or indeed with interaction involving any form of non-cooperation in a 'social goal sharing' sense?

As argued in Bousfield (1999, 2004) and, latterly, in Leech (2007), in much the same way as the adherence to or the non-observance of Grice's (1975) CP maxims can help individuals interpret a particular participant's goals and motivations so too there *may well* be a wealth of motivational and goal-oriented knowledge to be gleaned from observation of how interactants adhere to, or transgress, Leech's PP. Just as Grice's CP maxims can be broken in various ways (see Section 2.1, above) we may be able to say that Leech's PP maxims, or constraints, can be violated (covertly broken), flouted (overtly broken), infringed, suspended, or opted out of. In short, we could say that some intentional linguistic impoliteness occurs at the level where one (or more) of Leech's PP maxims is flouted, that is ostentatiously, to generate an im/polite implicature. Accidental offences, such as *Faux pas* and *gaffes* (see Section 4.4.3, below), would, clearly, occur at the 'infringement' level. Emergency or other urgent situations would entail the 'suspension' of the PP (cf. *bald, on record*, Brown and Levinson (1987)), and opting out of the PP would encompass those situations where people choose to *stay silent* when politeness might otherwise have been expected (see Culpeper 1996), or where even stated politeness may be considered to be offensive to the recipient (cf. *don't do the FTA*, Brown and Levinson (1987)).

The problem with this view is that, whilst attractive, it nevertheless still presupposes that politeness is a 'norm' for all speakers across all discourses, and that impoliteness is, in some way, *always* deviant linguistic behaviour *to be avoided* (see Leech (1983: 105); see also Mills (2005)). Leech (2005: 18) argues, "My position, incidentally, is that a theory of politeness is inevitably also a theory of impoliteness, since impoliteness is a non-observance or violation of the constraints of politeness." Such a view fits Mills's (2005) argument that impoliteness is a break from the hypothesized norms of a community of practice. However, even this positioning of Leech's approach does not fully answer Jucker's (1988) concerns, as noted above. In short, this view, in privileging politeness and seeing impoliteness as always socially aberrant, ignores the fact that impoliteness, whilst not 'normal' in a lay sense, is nevertheless ubiquitous across and within virtually all modes of human communication and can be quite-prevalent-to-centrally-important in many discourses (Bousfield 2007a, b; Culpeper et al. 2003). As such Leech's model appears to be one of predominantly social cooperation and not of socially influenced (sociopragmatic) linguistic im/politeness.

Additionally there are questions as to the model's methodological stability and rigidity. As Jucker (1988: 377) has noted, the number of maxims are arbitrary – this criticism still applies to the 2005 version. Thomas, (1995) also notes that the number is unrestricted and that there is no clear and motivated limit to the number that may be available. This, Thomas claims (1995), makes the model untenable at best and unfalsifiable at worst. It is interesting that Brown and Levinson (1987) also level this charge at Leech, especially given that Leech (1999, personal written communication) notes that "[…] the same could be said for Brown and Levinson's 30+ (super) strategies."

Furthermore, perhaps oversimplistically, Leech's theory has been classified as belonging to the indirectness approach (Held 1992: 139). On this basis, Locher criticises Leech's (1983: 108) equation of indirectness with politeness as

> […] an overgeneralization, due to his connecting politeness to a violation of the CP [a] direct utterance can be the appropriate polite form in a specific context, while indirectness could even be impolite. (Locher 2004: 65)

Such claims are, unfortunately, not uncommon. In defence of Leech here, it should be noted that it is Locher, along with Held (1992), who is guilty of overgeneralisation rather than Leech. Whilst it is true that Leech does, largely, link politeness to a *flout* (not, note, a *violation*) of the CP, he does, in a lesser quoted section of his book explicitly note that indirectness can sometimes be more impolite:

> […] in this case obliquity works in the opposite direction: because 'You have something to declare' is an impolite belief, the more indirect kinds of question [e.g. 'Haven't you something to declare?'] are progressively more impolite, more threatening, than the ordinary *yes-no* question. (Leech 1983: 171)

This is, in point of fact, also an issue for the main 'face management' view (Brown and Levinson 1987) as we will see in Section 4.3, below. I will make another discussion in elaboration of this issue in relation to impoliteness there.

Another more serious issue regarding Leech's model is the insistence on there being 'Absolute' and 'Relative' varieties of politeness. The terms, perhaps unhappy ones, have led some researchers to (mis)understand what it is that Leech (1983) was trying to say here. This has led to something of a clarification by Leech in a later recasting of the model (2005). Essentially, Leech suggests that his model is one which, in general, deals with absolute politeness – but he acknowledges the existence of relative politeness. Both of which he defines:

> [A]bsolute politeness [is] a scale, or rather a set of scales [...] having a negative and a positive pole. Some illocutions (*eg* orders) are inherently impolite, and others (*eg* offers) are inherently polite. Negative politeness therefore consists in minimizing the impoliteness of impolite illocutions, and positive politeness consists in maximizing the politeness of polite illocutions [...]. I shall be dealing with strategies for producing and interpreting polite illocutions, and placing them on a scale of absolute politeness.
>
> At the same time, I am aware that people typically use 'polite' in a relative sense: that is, relative to some norm of behaviour which, for a particular setting, they regard as typical. The norm may be that of a particular culture or language community. For example, I have been seriously told that 'Poles/Russians/etc. are never polite', and it is commonly said that 'the Chinese and the Japanese are very polite in comparison with Europeans', and so on. These stereotypic comments are often based on partial evidence, and one of the tasks of what I earlier called 'socio-pragmatics' is to examine the extent to which language communities do differ in their application of the PP. (Leech 1983: 83)

I think it necessary to acknowledge that Leech, perhaps a little unfairly, attracted some severe criticism for this stance which, amongst other things, seems to suggest im/politeness resides in lexico-syntactic structures irrespective of the context in which they occur. Fraser was amongst the first to lead a counter-charge to the idea that some illocutions are inherently polite or inherently impolite.

> Sentences are not *ipso facto* polite, nor are languages more or less polite. It is only speakers who are polite, and then only if their utterances reflect an adherence to the obligations they carry in that particular conversation. (Fraser 1990: 233)

His position was, and is, indicative of that of too many other researchers to list here. The main problem (and consequent solution) is actually very simple. The terms 'absolute' and 'relative' politeness are clearly unhappy ones and, indeed, Leech (2005) has discarded these terms in favour of 'Semantic politeness' (replacing 'Absolute politeness') and 'Pragmatic politeness' (replacing 'Relative politeness'). As a brief aside, it is probably fair to say that the majority of work into politeness since the early 1990s has been within pragmatic politeness. Indeed, the postmodernist approaches to politeness, typified and led by the work of Locher (2004), Watts (1992, 2003) and Locher and Watts (2005, 2008), are entirely within what Leech would call pragmatic politeness. Is Leech's precarious position on this issue at least so easily rescued by a simple change in terminology? The answer is, perhaps surprisingly, yes.

What Leech was attempting to communicate was that *semantically* some illocutions / phrases are conventionally considered to be polite or impolite. In other terms, he was attempting to note that some utterances are *conventionalised* in lay usage to an extent that they *appear to be* inherently polite or impolite. To put it another way, Culpeper (2005: 41) has noted that whilst no individual words or phrases are inherently polite or impolite out of context, many phrases, such as "Hello, how are you?" and "You fucking cunt!", are *conventionally* considered, across many different discourses, as being polite and impolite respectively (see also Jay 1992: 2). Terkourafi (2008) in working towards a unified theory of politeness, impoliteness and rudeness takes this a step further when she argues that:

> [...] some linguistic expressions (conventionalised ones) do facework more frequently (and therefore, more economically) than others.
>
> (Terkourafi 2008: 48)

Terkourafi elaborates upon this when she discusses correlations between linguistic expressions and the situations in which they are used:

> The use, in a particular situation, of an expression which is regularly used to achieve a certain perlocutionary effect in that situation – in other words, which is conventionalised relative to that context –[3] will, then, increase one's chances of achieving that perlocutionary effect *to the extent that* one's experience and one's interlocutor's experience are similar enough to have led to the development of similar linguistic dispositions, or overlapping *habitus*. In this way, conventionalised expressions emerge as one's safest bet *so long as* interlocutors' experiences are similar, and the expression is used in a context relative to which it is conventionalised. [...] Lacking an indication to the contrary [...] simply uttering the expression in that context will achieve the perlocutionary effect conventionally associated with it *ipso facto*.
>
> (Terkourafi 2008: 66. Emphasis in the original)

Essentially then we can say that 'semantic politeness' is enacted *pragmalinguistically*, that is – some lexico-syntactic forms are conventionally held to be im/polite across multiple, regularly occurring, well known (to the interactants) discourses and discourse-contexts and, as such, their enactment produces the pragmatic effect(s) that the participants conventionally believe or understand it to hold. Thus, 'pragmatic politeness' is enacted *sociopragmatically*, that is – some im/politeness is non-conventional and, thus, neologistic and is, more or less, purely pragmatic in its use, expression and interpretation. As such, the communication of im/politeness is entirely down to the users' understanding and grasp of the context in which the lexico-syntactic (linguistic) forms are issued, by reference to

3. As Terkourafi (2008) notes: Conventionalisation on this view includes intonation. Corpus studies of intonation are still very recent, but at first sight they confirm that a stereotyped intonational pattern is part and parcel of conventionalisation (cf. Wichmann 2004; Terkourafi 2006).

Grice's CP. In this way we are acknowledging Leech's (2005) view that it is preposterous to talk just about a semantic (absolute) variety or just about a pragmatic (relative) variety of politeness. We are retaining both an academic, and a lay users' balance between the semantic and pragmatic varieties. Such a balance is important for all approaches to im/politeness as, by-and-large, lay users *do* consider politeness and impoliteness to reside in certain linguistic structures (that is, within semantic or *pragmalinguistic* im/politeness); similarly lay users do, at least tacitly, produce, communicate and understand non-conventional politeness and impoliteness (pragmatic or *sociopragmatic* im/politeness). That lay users of language communicate im/politeness both pragmalinguistically and sociopragmatically is the view I take here for the model laid out in this book.

In conclusion, perhaps it should be noted that in all fairness to Leech (1983), the IR was never intended to be a model which would account for impoliteness or other conflictive illocutions. However, herein lies another issue. How can we have a model which purports to 'rescue' Grice's CP by giving you a reason why people do not abide by the CP maxims (in order to be polite) which then virtually fails to consider any other reason why people do not abide by the maxims (ie, in order to be 'impolite')? In short, and following Billig's (2001) view to its logical conclusion, we can't consider politeness without impoliteness (cf. Eelen 2001). A model of politeness must, at the very least, be able to be extended to consider, unproblematically, impoliteness on a more equal footing than has thus far been the case. If not, we run the risk of ignoring or being unable to adequately account for those discourses in which conflictive and impolite illocutions are more prevalent. Leech's (1983, 2005) model does not operate in this way. All this said, and following Culpeper (1996), Leech's still-developing model, which, importantly for the argument I make in the next section (4.3), for all its issues is a largely function-based model which can be used to complement the essentially form-based approach of Brown and Levinson (1987).

4.3 Politeness: The face management view

The face management view typified by Brown and Levinson (1987) is, perhaps, the most extensive exposition and thus the best known, most investigated, commented upon, and critiqued of all the approaches to Politeness discussed within this book. Indeed, while, in discussing this theory, I will be largely limiting myself to its core concepts, it is as Pérez de Ayala (2001: 144) has noted, impossible to disregard the many authors who have attempted to refine the face management view of politeness. Such is the preponderance of different authors' correctives, refinements, alterations and interpretations of politeness in Brown and Levinson's terms, that it must be noted the essentially truthful position mentioned by Brown and Gilman (1989: 164) when they say '[…] investigators who want to work with the Brown/ Levinson theory of politeness must pick a version.' What follows is mine.

As discussed more fully in the previous chapter (3), at the core of Brown and Levinson's theory of Politeness is the concept of 'face' as proposed by Goffman. Goffman defines face as being:

> […] the positive social value a person effectively claims for himself by the line others assume he has taken during a particular contact. Face is an image of self delineated in terms of approved social attributes – albeit an image that others may share, as when a person makes a good showing for his profession or religion by making a good showing for himself. (Goffman 1967: 5)

Brown and Levinson (1987), subdivide 'face' into 'Positive Face' and 'Negative Face', (Brown and Levinson 1987: 62):

- **Negative face:** the want of every 'competent adult member' that his/her actions be unimpeded by others.
- **Positive face:** the want of every member that his/her wants be desirable to at least some others.

According to Brown and Levinson (1987: 62) members of a given society treat face, not as norms or values which members of that society subscribe to (as with the 'Social Norm' view above), but as basic wants which every member of a society knows every other member desires, and which in general are in the interests of every member to (at least) partially satisfy. They also admit that face can be, and routinely is, ignored in cases of urgent co-operation, in the interests of efficiency and in cases of social breakdown (effrontery) (1987: 62). Furthermore, as Thomas points out face is, '[...] damaged, maintained or enhanced through interaction with others' (Thomas 1995: 169).

Within their approach, Brown and Levinson, like Leech, suggest that certain illocutionary acts inherently threaten either aspect of the face of another person (1987: 60). In their terminology, such acts are called 'Face Threatening Acts', or FTAs. They propose five 'superstrategies' for mitigating FTAs. It must be noted at this point that Brown and Levinson's approach is clearly a theory interested in the creation and maintenance of social harmony and social cooperation. As an aside I should note here that in Brown and Levinson there is nothing *explicit* on confrontational or disharmonious communication, which is ultimately indicated through, I argue, impoliteness.

The superstrategies that Brown and Levinson claim can be deployed for politeness work are:

1. **Bald on record politeness** – The FTA is performed "[...] in the most direct, clear, unambiguous and concise way possible" (Brown and Levinson 1987: 69). In short, the utterance is maximally efficient with regards to Grice's conversational maxims.

2. **Positive politeness** – The FTA is performed utilising strategies oriented towards redressing the positive face threat to the hearer. The linguistic output strategies include (Brown and Levinson 1987: 103–129):

   Claim common ground
   - Notice, attend to H (his interests, wants, needs, goods)
   - Exaggerate (interest, approval, sympathy with H)
   - Intensify interest to H
   - Use in-group identity markers: in-group language or dialect, jargon, slang, contraction or ellipses
   - Seek agreement: safe topics, repetition
   - Avoid disagreement: token agreement, pseudo-agreement, white lies, hedging opinions
   - Presuppose/raise/assert common ground: gossip, small talk, point of view operations, presupposition manipulations
   - Joke

   Convey that S and H are co-operators
   - Assert or presuppose S's knowledge of and concern for H's wants
   - Offer, promise
   - Be optimistic
   - Include both S and H in the activity
   - Give (or ask for) reasons
   - Assume or assert reciprocity

   Fulfil H's want for some X
   - Give gifts to H (goods, sympathy, understanding, cooperation)

3. **Negative politeness** – The FTA is performed utilising strategies oriented towards redressing the negative face threat to the hearer. The linguistic output strategies include (Brown and Levinson 1987: 129–211):

   Be indirect
   - Be conventionally indirect

   Don't presume/assume
   - Question, hedge: hedge on illocutionary force, prosodic/kinesic hedges

Don't coerce H
- Be pessimistic
- Minimize the imposition, R*x*
- Give deference

Communicate S's want to not impinge on H
- Apologize: admit the impingement, indicate reluctance, give overwhelming reasons, beg forgiveness
- Impersonalize S and H: use performatives, imperatives, impersonal verbs, passive and circumstantial voices, replace the pronouns 'I' and 'you' by indefinites, pluralize the 'I' and 'you' pronouns, use point-of-view distancing
- State the FTA as a general rule
- Nominalize

Redress other wants of H's
- Go on record as incurring a debt, or as not indebting H

4. **Off-record** – the FTA is performed 'Off Record', typically through the deployment of an indirect illocutionary act which has more than one interpretation and, thus, allows for plausible deniability on the part of the utterer if the intended recipient takes offence at the face threat inherent in the utterance. The linguistic output strategies include (Brown and Levinson 1987: 211–227):

Invite conversational implicatures:
- Give hints
- Give association rules
- Presuppose
- Understate
- Overstate
- Use tautologies
- Use contradictions
- Be ironic
- Use metaphors
- Use rhetorical questions

Be vague or ambiguous: Violate the manner maxim:
- Be ambiguous
- Be vague
- Over-generalize
- Displace H
- Be incomplete, use ellipsis

5. **Don't perform the FTA** – The FTA, judged to be too threatening to the intended recipient, is, therefore, in the interests of social harmony, not performed.

The ranking of superstrategies can be represented diagrammatically, as in Figure 1, below.

Greater detail surrounding the types of illocutionary acts which Brown and Levinson consider to be FTAs, as well as a more detailed look at the redressive strategies that can be used within each of the superstrategies can be found in Brown and Levinson (1987). It is not necessary to go into them in great detail here other than to point out that the choices on this five-point model are not ranked equally. Brown and Levinson point out that addressers will choose an appropriate superstrategy (and subsequent strategy) based on their evaluation of the risk to the addressee's face. That is, the lower the face threat 'inherent' in the FTA utterance being issued, the lower the number of the superstrategy chosen. i.e. if there is little face threat to you, I am likely to choose the '1. Bald, on record' superstrategy. If there is huge face threat for you, I am likely to opt for '4. Off Record', or even, '5. Don't do the FTA' (essentially, 'stay silent', or 'change the topic of conversation', for example.)

In performing '2. Positive Politeness', the speaker does not necessarily orient the strategy to the imposition that the FTA represents. Rather the main strategy is 'social groundwork', to, as Brown and Levinson (1987: 103) put it, 'Claim common ground', 'Convey S and H are cooperators' or 'Fulfil H's need/want for X'. The speaker typically attends to the hearer's face wants 'e.g. by treating him as a

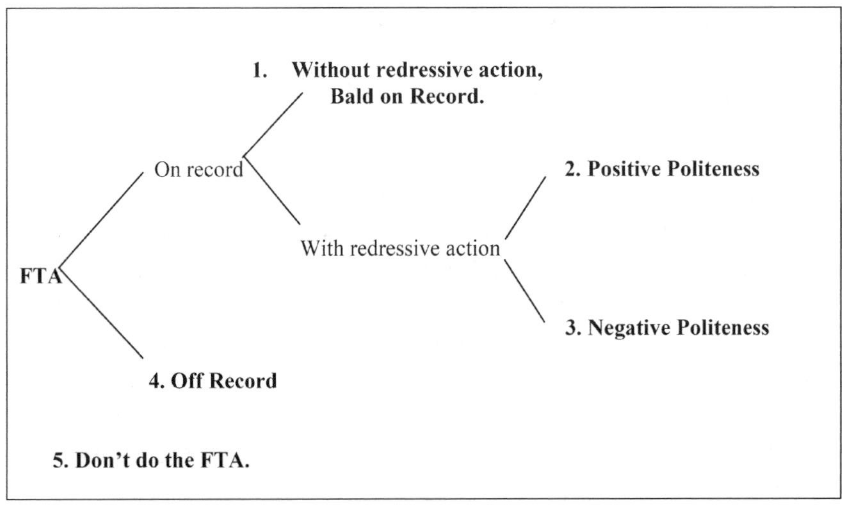

Figure 1. Possible strategies for doing FTAs (Brown and Levinson 1987: 60)

member of an in-group, a friend, a person whose wants and personality traits are known and liked' (Brown and Levinson 1987: 70).

With '3. Negative Politeness' we see a specific focus on directly mitigating the imposition that the FTA represents thus 'softening' it. This is usually achieved through such devices as apologising for the transgression, phrasing the utterance as a question, hedging, using negatives and other such 'softening', devices. As Culpeper (1994: 165) metaphorically puts it, 'positive facework attempts to provide the pill with a sugar coating; negative facework attempts to soften the blow.'

'4. Off record' strategies, including metaphor, understatement, tautologies, hints, and other means of indirect communication, theoretically allow the speaker to attribute more than one intention to the utterance. In this way, the speaker can 'plausibly deny' having performed the FTA, if challenged by an addressee or other receiver.

With the possible exception of 'Don't perform the FTA', the 'Bald on record' superstrategy, on the surface, seems to be the simplest one. However, when we consider both the effects of how people have conceptualised and explained the '1. Bald on Record' superstrategy in the past, and how some people view 'impoliteness' within Brown and Levinson (1987), we see that this superstrategy is, in fact, quite complex and requires some serious consideration.

4.3.1 Issues with Brown & Levinson: The 'bald, on record' superstrategy

Brown and Levinson (1987) do not explicate, in any great depth, the *bald, on record* superstrategy. While they do take up and explain in detail their 4 superstrategies for doing (mitigating) FTAs politely, for the *bald, on record* strategy, however, they in their own words, '[...] simply outline the uses to which *bald, on record* utterances are put, since all the outputs are the same: follow Grice's Maxims' (Brown and Levinson 1987: 94).

This lack of explication leads to a number of serious issues which ultimately undermine the entire viability of their approach, and of approaches to impoliteness built upon it (Culpeper 1996, 2005; Culpeper et al. 2003; Lachenicht 1980). To begin, it can be argued that simply stating what bald on record is in a particular context is a rather complex issue. In describing the bald on record strategy, Thomas (1995: 170) notes that, 'There are times when external factors constrain an individual to speak very directly (and in full conformity with the Gricean maxims)'. She points out that in emergencies or in highly task oriented situations, a speaker is likely to focus on the *propositional* content of a message and pay little attention to the *interpersonal* aspect of what is said.

Both Short (1996) and Thomas (1995) suggest that linguistic impoliteness can be accommodated within Brown and Levinson's (1987) 'bald, on record' super-strategy (see also, Liu 1986). Thomas states:

> Far from employing a bald-on-record strategy because the speaker estimates that the degree of face threat is small [...] in each of the examples which follow, the speaker takes no redressive action because he has deliberately chosen to be maximally offensive:
> [...]
> *Mr Tam Dalyell, M.P., in the British House of Commons (referring to the then Prime Minister, Margaret Thatcher):*
>
> 'I say that she is a bounder, a liar, a deceiver and a crook.'
>
> *Australian Judge in the court case brought by the British government to try to prevent the publication of the memoirs of Peter Wright, an ex-member of MI5. The Judge is referring to the evidence given by the then British Cabinet Secretary, sir Robert Armstrong:*
>
> 'His evidence is palpably false and utter humbug.' (Thomas 1995: 171)

Remember that Brown and Levinson's definition of *bald on record* utterances are those which are issued 'in the most direct, clear, unambiguous and concise way as possible [...] following the specifications of Grice's Maxims of Co-operation' (1987: 69). In addition, Brown and Levinson (1987: 69) suggest that *bald on record* politeness is used in specific circumstances:

> (a) S and H both tacitly agree that the relevance of face demands may be suspended in the interests of urgency or efficiency; (b) where danger to H's face is *very* small, as in offers, requests, suggestions that are clearly in H's interest and do not require great sacrifices of S (e.g., 'Come in' or 'Do sit down'); and (c) where S is vastly superior in power to H, or can enlist audience support to destroy H's face without losing his own. (Brown and Levinson 1987: 69. Original emphasis)

Bearing this in mind, we should now consider an example, given in Thomas (1995: 170), of what she considers to be a bald on record utterance used in an emergency situation:

> [*The speaker knows that a bomb has been planted in the stand at his racecourse. He thinks his young nephew is hiding in the stands*]
>
> [...] Toby, get off the stands. The stands are not safe. Toby, for Christ's sake do what I say. This is not a game. Come on you little bugger [...] for once in your life be told.

As noted in Culpeper et al. (2003), first, the example does not adhere to Grice's (1975) maxims, and thus a key part of Brown and Levinson's (1987: 69 & 94) definition of bald on record. A maximally efficient bald on record version might be simply: 'Toby, get off the stands'. This would fit Thomas' suggestion that in emergencies, 'the speaker is likely to focus on the propositional content of the message, and pay little attention to the interpersonal aspect of what is said' (1995: 170). Thomas' original version is inefficient through the use of linguistic devices that attack face. In the final sentence the utterance, *you little bugger* is an abusive term of address, and *for once in your life* implicates, via the maxim of quality, the impolite belief that Toby is generally disobedient. Clearly, the focus is not purely on the propositional content, but also has an important interpersonal aspect. What seems to be happening here is that the speaker employs a short-term goal of causing face damage, in order to achieve the long-term benefit of saving his nephew's life.

Additionally we should note that there are 'maximally offensive' examples given in Thomas (1995) that fall outside the specific contexts for bald on record mentioned by Brown and Levinson (1987: 69). Thomas' example, given above, of Tam Dalyell's reference to Margaret Thatcher (the then Prime Minister) in the British House of Commons: 'I say that she is a bounder, a liar, a deceiver, a crook', clearly does not fit Brown and Levinson's (1987: 69 & 94) contexts. There is also the issue of whether such offensive phenomena as this can be labelled as bald, on record *politeness* when politeness is defined by Brown and Levinson (1987: 1, my emphasis):

> [...] politeness, like formal diplomatic protocol (for which it must surely be the model), presupposes that potential for aggression *as it seeks to disarm it*, and makes possible communication between potentially aggressive parties.

In short the superstrategy 'bald, on record' does not and indeed cannot adequately describe the variety of phenomena, including impoliteness phenomena, that has been placed within it.

The development of all these issues stems from one apparently inescapable truth: The *bald, on record* superstrategy cannot and does not exist outside of the theorist's vacuum. There is, essentially, a 'form-function' mismatch. By way of elaboration around the main point being made here I wish to revisit the example of *bald, on record impoliteness* which was presented by Culpeper, Bousfield and Wichmann (2003).

> The following interaction, which we cite to illustrate 'bald on record impoliteness', involves S1, a clamper who is preparing to ticket a car in a road next to a primary school, and parents of children who often park in order to drop their children unto the school. Prior to this interaction, a number of parents have been ticketed and one has had her vehicle removed. The conversation between S1, and

> S2, S3 (both are parents) and S4 (The school's headmistress) has been confrontational up to this point.
>
> S1: we'll start with you madam <to S4> I work for TFM parking okay
> S2: has made no attempt to respond
> S3: excuse me excuse me you are
> S4:
>
> S1: I did the first time I met you okay where's you car?
> S2:
> S3: a parking attendant alright act like one okay *shut up and act like a parking attendant*
> S4:
>
> Bald on record impoliteness occurs when S3 says *shut up and act like a parking attendant*. Here we see two imperative commands that are deployed baldly with the purpose of aggravating the face of the parking attendant. It might also be noted that S3 is in a position of relative powerlessness, and so this does not match one of the contexts in which Brown and Levinson (1987: 69) attribute to bald on record *politeness.* (Culpeper et al. 2003: 1556, original emphasis)

What is of most interest here is that Culpeper et al. (2003), when discussing *negative face impoliteness*, refer back to the above example and say:

> Note also that *shut up*, which we commented on under the heading bald on record impoliteness, *is also an aggressive means of impeding speech.*
> (Culpeper, Bousfield and Wichmann 2003: 1559, my emphasis)

We must accept that if we are 'impeding speech' then that is, in Brown and Levinson's (1987) terms, *a negative face threat* as we are imposing on the target's freedom of action. We must therefore understand that every single *bald, on record* utterance attacks or threatens some (or both, if we retain the Brown and Levinson notion) aspect(s) of face in *functional* terms.[4] As such, even if we were

4. This is not to say that Brown and Levinson (1987) would consider the *Bald, on record* strategy to be devoid of face issues. Rather, the point I'm making is that *Bald, on record* is a *form* based superstrategy, whereas 'Positive Im/Politeness' and 'Negative Im/Politeness', being oriented towards Positive and Negative face respectively, are essentially *function* based superstrategies. When we also consider that the *Off-Record* superstrategy can include off-record utterances which are orientated to positive and / or negative face, then we can see that Brown and Levinson have intermixed and linked *form* and *function* in their 5-point model. Indeed, this is perhaps unsurprising when we consider that *Bald, on record-in-form* utterances also have a function (as do, arguably, all communicative utterances). Indeed, because *Bald, on record-in-form* utterances have in Brown and Levinson's terms a positive/negative face – oriented *function* it seems odd that such utterances would not be captured under the positive or negative im/politeness superstrategies. It therefore seems to make sense to simply do away with the *Bald, on Record* superstrategy, as part of wider reforms to the model, as it does not operate in the same way or on the same level as the positive, negative and off-record superstrategies do when we seperate *form* from *function.*

to retain the positive/negative face distinction from Brown and Levinson, then *bald, on record im/politeness* does not and cannot exist when we take into account (a) context, and, more importantly here, (b) the fact that there is no communication without face (see Locher 2004; Scollon and Scollon 2001; Terkourafi 2008, for an elaboration of this point). After all, even in the example above, Culpeper et al. (2003: 1556) note, "Here we see two imperative commands that are deployed baldly *with the purpose of aggravating the face of the parking attendant.*" As Brown and Levinson (1987) insist on two aspects of face, we must accept that (at least) one of them is aggravated / damaged here. Therefore, *bald, on record impoliteness* or *politeness* cannot and does not exist outside of the theorist's vacuum – it is superfluous as it simply describes the formal/structural aspects of utterances, and does not adequately account for the face-functional aspects of those utterances. As such, it really has no place in a model of impoliteness that attempts to capture real-world interactions and which rejects notions of outright absolute, or 'context-independent' im/politeness.

4.3.1.1 *On-record and off-record: Positive politeness and negative politeness*

In addition to the issue regarding the viability of the 'bald, on record' superstrategy is the applicability and even the viability of the positive-negative dichotomy.

To begin with, the 'positive politeness' and 'negative politeness' superstrategies are pitched, only, as on-record varieties. However, it stands to reason, given the argument that there can be no communication without face being an issue (Locher 2004; Scollon and Scollon 1995), that off-record utterances are therefore as equally face-directed as their on-record counterparts. In short, there should be as many options for performing im/politeness via off-record means as via on-record means. This, (along with the removal of the 'bald, on record superstrategy') would *seem* to suggest that Brown and Levinson's model, as depicted in Figure 1, above, would need to be recast as follows in Figure 2.

This revised model would account for the previously considered *bald, on record*, set of utterances within the 'On-record' superstrategy given, as I have argued above, that even so-called *bald, on record* utterances do impinge upon, or attack, some aspect of the recipient's face. Indeed, there is some sympathy for this from Brown and Levinson (1987: 18) who do say that 'we may have been in error to set up the three superstrategies, positive politeness, negative politeness, and off-record, as ranked unidimensionally to achieve mutual exclusivity.'

As I will argue below (see Sections 4.5.1 and 4.6.1.3), during the discussion of those models developed to account for impoliteness, even the level of re-modelling suggested in Figure 2, here, does not go far enough to accurately account for im/politeness in interaction.

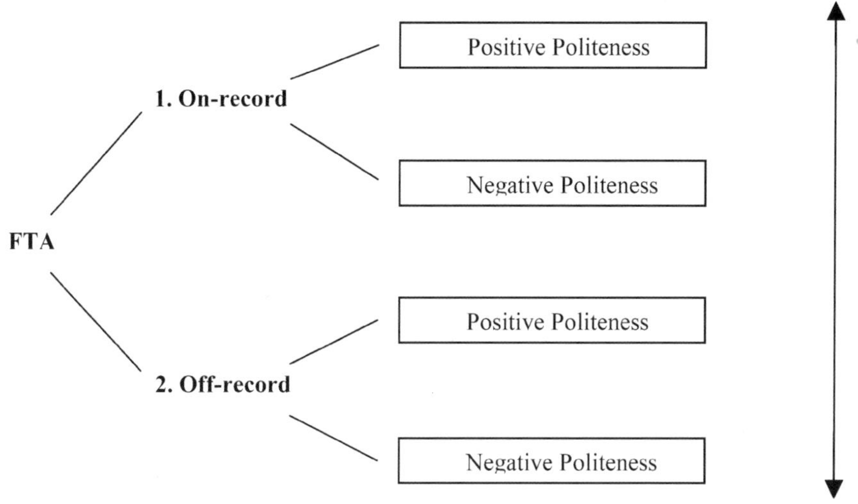

Figure 2. Revised politeness hierarchy

4.3.2 Issues with Brown and Levinson: Werkhofer's (1992) criticisms and the implications for a model of impoliteness

Werkhofer (1992), in what Watts (2003: 110) describes as one of the severest criticisms, initially notes a number of other issues with Brown and Levinson's overall view of politeness – issues which need to be considered or at least recognised for any research on impoliteness to take place. Werkhofer (1992: 155) notes that Brown and Levinson's 'model person' (1987) is an attempt to systematically reconstruct the rationality that underlies polite talk,

> ie that the model is not an attempt to reconstruct what might be going on in a person's mind but rather a means to the end of solving a 'problem' in linguistic pragmatics and not in the psychology or sociology of language ([Werkhofer] 1992: 155). (Watts 2003: 110)

I must point out that the very idea of a 'model person' (in Brown and Levinson's (1987) terms) poses serious problems for any account of impoliteness which is based on Brown and Levinson's politeness model (though see Bousfield 2010: 105–106). I note, with interest, that Culpeper (1996) and Culpeper et al. (2003) in their expositions of impoliteness, studiously choose to avoid this issue, as, indeed, I do, here. I accept that future research into impoliteness based on the face-management view must take this into consideration and attempt to account for it. Thus acknowledged, I do not intend to undertake such research in this book.

Watts (2003: 111 and 113) notes that Werkhofer (1992) also argues that politeness is an act, set of acts, or a stretch of behaviour; and that a polite interaction could stretch over a number of turns at talk. Brown and Levinson (1987) however, seem locked in enshrining single acts of politeness within single utterances. Here, Werkhofer (1992) implicitly raises the point that Brown and Levinson (1987) (and, we must accept by implication Culpeper (1996)) do not consider the effects of (im)politeness across a discoursal exchange as it builds up and pans out. This we remedy to an extent in Culpeper et al. (2003) and indeed, building upon Bousfield (2007a) this I elaborate upon in more depth in this book (see Chapters 5, 6 and 7).

Watts (2003: 112) explains that Werkhofer (1992) comments on the lack of discussion in Brown and Levinson approach's for what happens if the face-threatening event has actually occurred. In short Brown and Levinson (1987) and Culpeper (1996) fail to account for interactant responses to face threatening/damaging impoliteness. Again this we attend to, to an extent, in Culpeper et al. (2003) and again, building upon Bousfield (2007a) I elaborate upon this very concept in later chapters.

Watts (2003: 112) notes Werkhofer's (1992) argument that the rational procedure to commit a FTA and the appropriate politeness strategy in the utterance is sequential, where the speaker must go 'step by step' from selecting whether to utter the FTA or Opt Out; (in choosing the FTA) to choose on record or off record; (in choosing on record) to choose positive or negative politeness. There is no way, Werkhofer argues in which a later step might feed back into earlier ones and this indicates that the whole process is unconstrained by social factors. Now, although I must point out that whilst Brown and Levinson do resist the mixing of strategies and the mixing of types of face-oriented utterance, it is merely *their conceptualisation* of how interactants act that is at fault, not necessarily their whole model on this score. As I will show in Chapters 7 and 8, speakers in issuing or dealing with impoliteness can and do 'feed back' their utterances to earlier 'steps' in the selection process as part of highly dynamic and elaborately constructed set of complex interactional moves. If interactants can do this when dealing with and in impoliteness (as I will show that they do here, see Chapters 5 through 8), then, surely, interactants can do this when dealing in and with politeness too.

Finally as Werkhofer (1992) notes, Brown and Levinson (1987) make no mention of the role of bystanders in the social interaction. In relation to this Watts (2003: 11) asks if we are really just concerned with the speaker and the hearer. Indeed, I broaden the concern of research into impoliteness to include the bystanders/audience (intended or not) later in this book (see Section 7.1.2.1) as their roles have a significant bearing on the issuing of utterances which communicate impoliteness.

On a final note in this section, despite the savaging that Brown and Levinson have received in recent years, I genuinely believe that a work of such insight, magnitude and complexity still has a considerable amount to tell us. Erroneous in parts it may be – Brown and Levinson have admitted as such – however, I do feel that, following trial and revision leading to the inevitably required correctives, amendments and clarifications we are, and have been, essentially looking at the *sort* of model that can, and will, develop into a predictive theory of im/politeness. In this light, the present book is to be seen, merely, as a means to this eventual end – a model arising out of a set of essential correctives, amendments and clarifications to the classic approach. The quest for a 'holy grail' theory goes on.

4.4 Impoliteness and types of face threat

In the next section I will define how I use and understand the term 'impoliteness' within this book. Before that, however, in order to differentiate impoliteness from other varieties of linguistic offence, I consider the types of action that may lead to face damage. Goffman (1967: 14) suggests that there are three types of action which constitute a threat to face:

4.4.1 Intentional threats to face

"[T]he offending person may appear to have acted maliciously and spitefully, with the intention of causing open insult." (Goffman 1967: 14). For example, the following interchange contains an offence which, clearly, aims at aggravating the face of the intended recipient. Here, S1 is a traffic warden; S2 owns the car which has received a parking penalty, taken from **The Clampers, Extract 5** (pertinent sections *italicised*):

[3]

[…]

15. S1: I'm afraid
    S2: you have no authority to put a ticket on a disabled err car

16. S1: I have sir= I'd what do you mean I did do
    S2: =why didn't you do it before then

17. S1: it before
    S2: I've parked here every day because I have a prescription

18. S1: yes sir I never
    S2: from the chemist you don't put any tickets on my car

19. S1: really I'm not
    S2: and then and then you just come in and out of the blue and put

20. S1: I'm not always down here sir
    S2: one on *ohh fuck off*

[…]

It is my understanding that utterances within this category of threat to face constitute impoliteness, i.e. where there is a clear intention to be maximally offensive.

4.4.2 Incidental threats to face

"There are incidental offences; these arise as an unplanned but sometimes anticipated by-product of action – action the offender performs in spite of its offensive consequences, though not out of spite." (Goffman 1967: 14). In the following example, S1 is a tribunal officer for London's Southwark council. He hears and decides upon appeals concerning all types of parking offences. S2 and S3 are a husband and wife (respectively) who are appealing against a ticket which they have received. This extract is taken from the final stages of their appeal hearing, taken from **The Clampers, Extract 2:**

[4]

1. S1:well look I must draw this to a close . *I've listened to you very carefully*
   S2:
   S3:

2. S1: *and I'm . do understand entirely what your point is* but *I can't allow*
   S2:
   S3:

3. S1: *your appeal I'm afraid=* erm erm *I can't say that the*
   S2: =Oh why not I I
   S3:

4. S1: *ticket has been incorrectly issued because it's been correctly*
   S2:
   S3:

5. S1: *issued not incorrectly issued* I
   S2: we're not we're not arguing that
   S3: but it hasn't been
6. S1: well[5] in my opinion it has
   S2: what happens if a
   S3: correctly issued but
7. S1:
   S2: sign changes overnight
   S3:

[…]

This act of denying an appeal (of 'disagreeing' with one's interlocutor) is not impoliteness in that the *intention* is not to cause face damage to the vehicle's owners, but simply to explain that their appeal has been unsuccessful and that the initial indictment for illegal parking stands. However, face damage *is* likely to be an anticipated by-product of the action of denying an appeal (indeed of 'disagreeing' generally). The action would appear to have been done *in spite* of the offensive consequences but not *out of spite* for the vehicle's owners. This kind of by-product offence is captured within existing politeness frameworks. Note that S1, understanding the potential offensive consequences of denying an appeal feels the need to show empathy with the vehicle's owners (*I'm . do understand entirely what your point is*), to express regret (*I'm afraid*), and to express his inability (rather than as his own decision) to allow the appeal (*I can't allow your appeal* and *I can't say that the ticket has been incorrectly issued because it's been correctly issued*). In other words, he predominantly uses 'positive politeness' (Brown and Levinson 1987) (see Culpeper et al. (2003)).

4.4.3 Accidental threats to face

Here, in Goffman's terms, the offending person, "may appear to have acted innocently; his offence seems to be unintended and unwitting […] In our society one calls such threats to face *faux pas, gaffes,* boners or bricks." (Goffman 1967: 14). An 'unwitting' offence might consist of something like the following example, reconstructed, from a conversation taking place between a high ranking male member of the Lancaster university senate (S1) and a female member of staff (S2):

5. This has not been included as an example of 'incidental offence' as the politeness status of this utterance, and, in particular, the operation of 'well', as a hedge, is not at all clear in light of this extract's prosodic and paralinguistic factors.

[5]

1. S1: <Sincerely> *Oh, when is it due?*
   S2: <Pause> I'm not pregnant.

Here S1 has unwittingly drawn attention to the fact that S2 looks overweight. Such an action could be construed as 'face threatening', certainly within a Western cultural setting.

Whilst Goffman's categorisation is helpful, it does not capture the 'fuzzy' instances one finds in real data. For example, the following exchange occurs at the very end of a dispute which has taken place between S1, a parking official, and S2, the owner of a clamped van. S2 has been disputing S1's right to clamp, and the ethics of clamping. Neither participant has been willing to concede to the other and eventually S2 'closes' the exchange, taken from **The Clampers, Extract 1.**

[6]

[…]

33. S1: that's right I clamped your car sir and I won't dispute that fact that I
    S2:
34. S1: clamped your car well that's fine by me if
    S2: *well end of conversation*
35. S1: you don't want to talk we don't have to talk
    S2:

End.

The problem which concerns us here is that we cannot be sure whether S2's utterance was performed maliciously, with "the intention of causing open insult" (Goffman 1967: 14) towards S1 (by snubbing him, cf. Culpeper 1996), or whether S2 simply grew tired of the discussion, and its apparent lack of progress and thus decided to end the conversation *in spite* of the offensive consequences of doing so though not *out of spite* for S1.

I have considered the intent to threaten face, the incidental generation of face threat and the accidental damage to face that a specific action can cause. However, this three-way distinction rests, at least primarily, upon the speaker's intention (see Section 4.5.3 'Intention' below).

4.5 Impoliteness

As argued in Culpeper et al. (2003), we know that conflictive, verbally aggressive, 'non-socially-cooperative' and impolite communication can and does take place. We also know that approaches to politeness are conceptually biased (Eelen 1999, 2001) and generally assume impoliteness to be 'marginal' (cf. Leech 1983:105), and/or that it can be dealt with within the existing structures (Liu 1986; Short 1996; Thomas 1995). As we have already seen, the 'Bald, on Record' strategy cannot adequately account for impoliteness and as such it may be necessary to construct a framework that does account for it – but is one really needed?

Craig et al. (1986), Eelen (1999, 2001), Fraser (1990, 1999), Kasper (1990) and Tracy (1990), amongst others, argue that to provide an adequate account of the dynamics of interpersonal communication models of politeness should also consider hostile as well as cooperative communication, and that such hostile behaviour should be considered complementary to politeness (Kasper 1990). Culpeper et al. (2003), following Eelen (1999, 2001), note that while all the leading politeness theories at least mention the notion of impoliteness, the problem is that in practice they all focus solidly on politeness, with the result that their comments on impoliteness are descriptively inadequate and often conceptually biased (i.e. it is assumed that the concepts used to explain politeness can straightforwardly be applied to impoliteness – see Eelen, 1999, Chapter 1 and Eelen, 2001, Chapter 3, for an elaboration of this point). In short, current approaches to politeness have been unable to fully account for the confrontational interaction in impolite discourses. Clearly, then, some sort of framework *is* needed to account for such linguistic behaviour.

4.5.1 A framework for impoliteness?

Moving now from the general background, to the more specific aspects concerning this book, within this section I attempt to lay some of the groundwork for the construction of a framework which can account for impoliteness which is further explored and developed in Chapters 5 through 8.

4.5.2 Defining impoliteness

Before I examine or undertake to produce a descriptive framework which accounts for impoliteness there is another issue. How should we define impoliteness? I take impoliteness to be the broad opposite of politeness, in that, rather than seeking to mitigate face-threatening acts (FTAs), impoliteness constitutes the communication of intentionally gratuitous and conflictive verbal face-threatening acts (FTAs) which are purposefully delivered:

i. Unmitigated, in contexts where mitigation is required, and/or,
ii. With deliberate *aggression*, that is, with the face threat exacerbated, 'boosted', or maximised in some way to heighten the face damage inflicted.

Furthermore, for impoliteness to be considered successful impoliteness, the intention of the speaker (or 'author') to 'offend' (threaten/damage face) must be understood by those in a receiver role.

With the above definition then, quite obviously, impoliteness does not exist where one, but not both of the participants (in two-party interaction) intends / perceives face-threat. Whilst this might appear to be problematic, it is easily explained, thus:

i. If the Speaker (or someone in a producer role) intends face-damage and the Hearer (or someone in a receiver role) *perceives* the Speaker's (Producer's) intention to damage face (cf. Goffman 1967: 14), then *impoliteness is successfully conveyed*. We should note that such impoliteness may later be defended against by the hearer or a third party using a counter-strategy (see Chapter 7, below).
ii. If the Speaker/Producer intends face-damage but the Hearer/Receiver fails to *perceive* the speaker's intent/any face-damage, then *the attempt at impoliteness fails*.[6]
iii. If the Speaker/Producer does not intend face-damage but the Hearer/Receiver *constructs* the Speaker's/Producer's utterance as being intentionally face-damaging then this could be *Accidental face-damage* (as opposed to *Intentional or*

6. Though it should be noted that two of the possible defensive counter strategies identified by Culpeper, Bousfield and Wichmann (2003: 1566–1567) and discussed by Bousfield (2007a), of 'dismiss, make light of face damage, joke' and 'ignore the face attack' mean that it is virtually impossible for the analyst to identify whether (i) the impoliteness was successfully conveyed, but defended against; or (ii) the attempt at impoliteness failed. Such is the nature of impoliteness in interaction. Further, within this category is the possibility of the speaker intending face-damage, the hearer understanding that face-damage was intended but the face-damaging effects on the hearer are negligible. For example, my nephew calling me a 'pooh-pooh head!' or daughter saying 'naughty daddy!' when, in the name of safety, I stop them from engaging in life-and-limb risking acts of fun and horseplay that they really want to try. I'm not at all offended by such comments in these situations but I understand they are intended to (a) harm and, (b) exert power over me. Hence these thankfully rare occurrences in my family discourse are instances of "failed impoliteness".

Incidental face-damage; see Goffman 1967: 14), which could be caused by one or more of the following: *Rudeness* (e.g. inadequate levels of politeness); *Insensitivity* (on the part of the Speaker/Producer); *Hypersensitivity* (on the part of the Hearer/Receiver); *a clash of expectations*; *a cultural misunderstanding*; *misidentification (by the speaker or the hearer) of the Community of Practice or Activity Type in which they are engaged*; some combination of these, or some other hitherto unidentified means of inadvertently causing offence or of perceiving offence when none was intended.

iv. If the Speaker/Producer does not intend face-damage but the Hearer/Receiver constructs the Speaker's/Producer's utterance as being unintentionally face-damaging then this could be one of the following: *Incidental* or *Accidental face-damage* (as opposed to *Intentional face-damage*; see Goffman 1967: 14), which could be caused by one, or more of the following: *Rudeness* (e.g. inadequate levels of politeness); *Insensitivity* (on the part of the Speaker/Producer); *Hypersensitivity* (on the part of the Hearer/Receiver); *a clash of expectations*; *a cultural misunderstanding*; *misidentification (by the speaker) of the Community of Practice or Activity Type in which they are engaged*; some combination of these, or some other hitherto unidentified means of inadvertently causing offence or of perceiving offence when none was intended.

Note that, following Culpeper et al. (2003), I am primarily concerned with what other researchers have referred to as 'strategic' (Bandura 1973; Lakoff 1989) or 'instrumental' (Beebe 1995) impoliteness (see Section 4.5.4, below for an elaboration on 'instrumentality'). This is to say that it is impoliteness which fulfills a specific, goal oriented function. It fulfils, in Beebe's words, 'a function that the speaker intended, and was not [simply] failed politeness' (Beebe 1995: 166). 'Failed politeness' defined as too little or too much politeness work in a particular context.

I focus mainly on 'genuine' or 'sincere' impoliteness, as opposed to 'ritual' or 'mock' impoliteness (see Labov 1972; and Leech 1983: 144, respectively for an elaboration of these types of offence. See also Chapter 5, Section 5.2, *Mock impoliteness*, below). However, such a definition as that given above raises two further issues (1) how do we attribute 'intention' on the part of an interlocutor? And, (2) what, precisely, do we mean by the term aggression?

4.5.3 Intention

A central concept to any approach to a linguistic issue within pragmatics (this one included) is that of intention, or more specifically, *attributing* intention. As Culpeper et al. (2003) note,

> Interlocutors do not wear their intentions on their sleeves and one interlocutor does not have access to the internal states of other interlocutors. However, speakers' intentions are fundamental to speech act theory. As a consequence, the fact that Brown and Levinson's (1987) politeness theory is built on speech act theory means that it also has speakers' intentions at its heart. However, even within conversation analysis and other more sociologically oriented approaches to interaction, there is an admission that participants in conversation do attribute intentions and purposes of some kind to talk. Grimshaw (1990: 281), reviewing a collection of sociolinguistic investigations into 'conflict talk', makes the following points:
>
> '[The] attribution of purposiveness to participant behaviours, will be sharply criticized by those students of talk (e.g. conversation analysts) who argue that this implies the ability to "get into people's heads" and requires unwarranted inferences and claims. The researchers whose work is reported here do not contest the position that what is in people's heads is accessible neither to analysts nor to interlocutors (nor even, ultimately, fully accessible to those whose behaviour is under investigation). I believe most of them will also argue, however, that the availability of ethnographic context *and* of an optimally complete behaviour record permits analysts to make such inferences and attributions which are "for-the-most-practical-purposes" (paraphrasing Garfinkel) no less plausible than those of actual participants. This claim is subject to qualification but the disambiguation process is that which we ourselves employ in interaction – where, it must be conceded, we sometimes err.' (Culpeper et al. 2003: 1552)

For Culpeper et al. (2003) then there is no claim that one can retrieve the actual intentions of speakers, but rather, that 'plausible' intentions can be reconstructed, given adequate evidence. Indeed, Mooney (2004: 900) suggests intention is *reconstructed* rather than *retrieved* by drawing upon such features pertaining to a communicative event as '[…] past encounters, knowledge of social roles and so on.' (Mooney 2004: 901). Other applicable features must invariably include: the discoursal roles of the particpants, the context, the co-text, the activity type one is engaged in, previous events, affect between the interactants and, of course, the power, rights and obligations of the interactants, to name but a few. Some or all of these features (along with others, where relevant) may well provide evidence adequate enough for an addressee to reconstruct the plausible intention(s) of a given speaker at a particular point within a linguistic exchange.

4.5.4 Aggression

> Aggression: act of beginning a quarrel or war; unprovoked attack;
> (Psych.) hostile or destructive tendency or behaviour.
>
> (Oxford Concise Dictionary, 7th Edition)

I concentrate upon 'aggression' as part of a definition of impoliteness as it is the one, lowest and most common denominator to such phenomena as 'conflict' or 'confrontation' which underlie impoliteness. That said, it must be noted that the one interesting aspect of 'aggression' is that definitions of the concept are dependent upon the particular field of study in which one is operating. Kemp (2001:51–52), interested in cross-cultural studies, provides an interesting, enigmatic and yet thoroughly pragmatic answer to the question of how we should define the term 'aggression'. Kemp notes that:

> The UN set up an International Law Commission to establish such a definition [of aggression], but it could find little consensus and, in the end came to the remarkable conclusion that aggression 'should not be defined'. To quote one of the commissioners the 'notion of aggression is a notion *per se*, a primary notion, which by its very essence, is not susceptible of definition'. (Rifaat 1979:225)
>
> In the end the UN's 1974 definition represented less a definition than a recognition that aggression could only be determined when and where it occurred depending on the social and practical circumstances.
>
> This failure to establish a consensus is reflected in people's attempts to define aggression, which have proved equally problematic (Derriennic 1972; Goode 1978; Skolnich 1968; Tedeschi, Smith and Brown 1974; Van der Dennan 1980).
> (Kemp 2001:51–52)

While the UN was primarily attempting to define State Aggression post World War II, Kemp notes that:

> There may be lessons in the UN's failings that can be drawn upon in scientific attempts to understand aggression. (Kemp 2001:51–52)

This latter comment is particularly important for the argument made throughout this book. It is clear that a watertight definition, universally applicable, may not only be impossible to produce, but, rather, given the very context specific nature of the concept of aggression, dispreferable. Despite the problems inherent in identifying a cross-disciplinary definition acceptable to all, what we should aim for here is a useful *working* definition – one that sufficiently defines the salient aspects of the concept of aggression, but does not seek to constrain the concept with supposed 'necessary' aspects for an all-encompassing view. In short, the definition should remain open, and should hold for the arguments made here, but not be so defined by its use within this book. To this end, a brief exploration of the differing ways in which a number of discrete but related theoretical fields define the term would seem to be prudent.

Hydén, an academic concerned with theories of Social Work, considers two varieties of aggression: verbal aggression and physical violence. Verbal aggression, she argues, can be symptomatic of problematic interpersonal relationships (1995: 55). According to Hydén (1995: 55–56), '[t]he concept of "verbal aggression" here refers to a verbal act which has the *intent* (or *perceived intent*) to symbolically hurt or to threaten to hurt another'. Physical violence '[...] refers to an act that has the *intent* (or *perceived intent*) of causing physical harm to another'. (Hydén 1995: 56. My emphasis.). The concept of 'violence' which Hydén considers here is, '[...] *a tactic of reaching a certain goal*.' (1995: 56. My emphasis.). This subscribes to a widespread, yet fundamentally split notion of the essence of violence. The concept of violence as a tactic of reaching a certain goal concerns whether it is better conceptualised as a tactic of coercive control, used to attain or maintain power (Yllö 1993) or as a conflict tactic (Straus and Gelles 1990).

However, the concept of violence being used to maintain or attain power, or as a conflict tactic, could, indeed, should be extended to the concept of verbal aggression. It would be counterintuitive to consider that verbal aggression occurred solely for its own sake. Surely, it is deployed as a conflict tactic and/or, as a device for attaining or maintaining power in a specific situation or context. It is, in short, *instrumental*.

Björkqvist, Österman and Kaukiainen (2000) working within the field of developmental psychology consider aggression to be, possibly, the result of having social intelligence but lacking empathy with an individual, or, as they put it in the title of their paper: SOCIAL INTELLIGENCE – EMPATHY = AGGRESSION? They note that '[...] aggression is not only physical by its nature, but it may take a wide variety of forms.' (2000: 191–192). They outline three varieties of aggression: physical, direct verbal and indirect aggression. Interestingly, they consider the three varieties to be not only three separate strategies but also constituting three developmental phases, partly overlapping, partly following each other during human development from childhood through to adolescence and beyond (2000: 192). They suggest that 'Small children who have not yet developed verbal and social skills to any considerable degree, will have to resort to physical aggression.' (2000: 192). Björkqvist et al. do not mention it but this would seem to be suggestive of an element of frustration which provokes the perceived need, in the child, for aggressive action. This should be borne in mind.

Björkqvist et al. (2000: 192) further note that, 'When verbal and social skills develop, these facilitate expression of aggression without having to resort to physical force.' This, of course, does not mean the element of frustration, inherent in the concept of physical aggression, necessarily need be absent; indeed, it would appear to remain. Finally Björkqvist et al. note that:

> When social intelligence develops sufficiently [to allow the individual the use of all three types of aggression], the individual is fully capable of indirect aggressive behaviour: (s)he is able to induce psychological, sometimes even physical, harm to a target person by mere social manipulation, without putting him/herself at direct risk of retaliation. (Björkqvist et al. 2000: 192)

Of the three types of aggression here, studies of impoliteness would be most interested in Björkqvist et al.'s concepts of, primarily, direct verbal and indirect aggression. However, it needs to be noted that the concept and realisation of indirect aggression would be an area for future research on impoliteness.[7]

Berkowitz (1993), also working within the field of psychology, defines aggression as behaviour intended to injure someone physically or psychologically. He distinguishes physical from psychological aggression. Following Berkowitz, medical researchers Hillbrand and Spitz (1999: 360) use a broad definition of psychological aggression to include what Spielberger et al. (1985) referred to as the AHA! syndrome (anger, hostility, aggression). Anger is considered to be an emotional state associated with the development of hostile attitudes and aggressive behaviour; hostility is a broad concept involving angry feelings and negative, destructive attitudes that often motivate aggressive behaviour; aggression is the overt manifestation of the intent to harm someone in some way.

However, social learning theorist Bandura, (1973), points out that there are problems with defining concepts, such as anger and hostility which would also apply to defining the concepts of aggression and impoliteness. He notes that attempts to define *any* concept, '[...] essentially represent an invitation for a stroll through a semantic jungle.' (1973: 2). Despite the apparent futility, he notes that such a journey, is, nevertheless worthwhile by being, '[...] instructive because it reveals important issues about the phenomena selected for analysis.' (Bandura 1973: 2). He goes on to argue against the position of some researchers who cognitively separate aggression into instrumental and hostile varieties:

> Instrumental aggression, which is aimed at securing extraneous rewards other than the victim's suffering, is distinguished from hostile aggression, the sole aim of which is presumably to inflict injury on others. Since hurtful and destructive actions were largely attributed to aggressive drive forces, so-called instrumental aggression received only passing notice. The differentiation generally conveys the

7. Especially in light of a high profile example of indirect aggression, c. 2000–2001 when the then British government minister, Mo Mowlam was, allegedly, 'briefed against' both by, and to, senior members of the British government. The indirect aggression, via specific individuals' social manipulation caused a considerable amount of face damage and, indeed, professional harm to Mo Mowlam who later resigned in the face of the campaign. Indirect aggression, in effect, ruined her career.

> impression that aggressive behavior (sic) performed for rewarding outcomes represents a form of pseudoaggression relegated to the subsidiary status of a means to other ends. According to this valuation, the holocaust in Hiroshima, which was ordered to force a quick end to the war, would represent a mere instrumental act. So would any act of war, for that matter.
>
> In point of fact, so-called hostile aggression is equally instrumental except that the actions are used to produce injurious outcomes rather than to gain status, power, resources, or some other types of results. Whatever its merits, the distinction reflects differences in desired outcomes, not in instrumentality. It would therefore be more accurate to differentiate aggressive actions in terms of their functional value rather than in terms of whether or not they are instrumental. Most aggressive acts serve ends other than solely to produce injury.
>
> (Bandura 1973: 3)

Hurst Tatsuki (2000), exploring the use of aggression in complaints, notes that,

> Frustration can be attributed to the environment, an object, a person or the subject himself (sic). The subject can respond to that frustration by lashing out, turning it inward, or denying its existence. (Hurst Tatsuki 2000: 1005)

Hurst Tatsuki further notes that complaints, which are one of the possible responses to frustration are considered, along with apologies and denials, to be a form of aggression. She says,

> Contrary to the popular connotation of hostility, aggression can be defined as '... some form of coping behavior that may then be either constructive or destructive in effect' (Rosenzweig 1978a: 2). This means that aggression can be seen as an assertive response to a problem or frustration. (Hurst Tatsuki 2000: 1005)

We can note the similarity of Hurst Tatsuki's position (vis-à-vis the notion of hostility with aggression), with Bandura's position. What is significant is the concept of aggression being a possible response to a frustrating incident, object, individual, or other phenomena. Jay (1992), discussing a five-stage model of anger, has already begun to explore the concept of an assertive response with, and to, the notion of an 'Offending Event.'

Jay (1992), working in the area of 'Neuro-Psycho-Social' theories of speech, discusses the causes and forms of cursing including the phenomena that can trigger such language. Jay (1992: 9) defines cursing as wishing harm on a person, and uses the term comprehensively to include swearing, obscenity, profanity, blasphemy, name calling, insulting, verbal aggression, taboo speech, ethnic-racial slurs, vulgarity, slang and scatology. He argues (1992, 2000) that it is an "Offending Event" which can trigger such language. Offending Events are constituted of major elements that vary from situation to situation. In short, Offending Events are both person and context dependent:

> The major elements of the offending event involve the person or event that evokes the anger and the social-physical location of the event. These factors amount to the who, what, where, and when of anger. What provokes anger can vary from person to person and from time to time. (Jay 1992: 98)

What Jay (1992) seeks are the correlative features of the event and the offender which provoke anger and verbal aggression as a response. The elements of the Offending Event are, '... the *most* important in determining how anger is expressed verbally.' (Jay 1992: 98. Original emphasis.). Jay (1992: 98) notes that the particular weighting of the individual elements, in any given situation, is not totally known.[8] He further notes that the weightings, in all probability, vary from speaker to speaker and from situation to situation. In line with current psychological and sociological studies of language, he notes the most salient elements of an Offending Event as being:

> ***The Offender***: The offender or wrongdoer has certain qualities, real or imagined, accurate and inaccurate. The important point is that these offender factors will be used to select the appropriate semantic dimensions when retaliating with a taboo word.
>
> *Age*: child, teenager, adult, elder are the most salient features. Very young and very old offenders provoke less anger than teenagers and adults.
>
> *Sex*: one of the most powerful dimensions of human communication is the gender of the speaker or listener, especially with respect to swearing and insulting behaviors (sic – passim). The word *bitch* is targeted at females and the phrase *son of a bitch* at males, for example.
>
> *Status*: perceived social or economic status such as rich/poor, amount of education, employer/employee, occupation, or religious authority affect the way one uses anger. High status, rich, employers, or religious figures are less likely to be the targets of spoken anger or direct anger speech acts relative to others. The presence of a police uniform, military uniform, or other types of dress may signal the inhibition of direct expression.

---

8. The weightings of such factors, if known, could help us to discern more precisely what it is that *triggers* the onset of impolite containing exchanges in the first place. Furthermore, such weightings would, clearly, be of greater benefit to a study of impoliteness than, and a complement to, the values of P, D and R from Brown and Levinson's (1987) Wx = D(S,H) + P(H,S) + Rx, which they assume apply to interactants using politeness.

Ethnic Group: racial/minority or assumed ethnic origin is a feature that is used to select an expression when the speaker is angered by the (ethnic) offender.

Physical Appearance: any noticeable deviation from "normal." Body size, abnormal facial features, weight, deformities, and body movement or locomotion cover the majority of these angry insults noting physical differences. In this case, the offended would use the abnormality as a subject of the insult, such as calling an obese person a "pig"...

Social-Physical Setting: relaxed/business, private/public, homogenous/mixed grouping, relatives/strangers. In each of the first of these pairings there are less constraints on communication. One is likely to hear anger expressed under these conditions where its expression is not highly sanctioned. Strangers, new acquaintances, or those who the speaker cannot change through anger will be less likely to be the targets of it relative to those offenders with a close relationship with the offended.

Non-human Wrongdoer: chased by a dog, hit by bird droppings, seeing poor weather conditions. These events occur where a person did not cause the anger; instead the anger came from some event or action that was more accidental or non-intentional in nature. This dimension is included in the event scenario because many of the anger expression that use taboo words are of this non-human category. In these instances the person is angry and emits an expletive, the force and offensiveness of which are related to the degree of insult or injury experienced. The intent is not to communicate anger but to express frustration.

Self as Wrongdoer: in this case the offending person or behavior is one's self. The purpose of self directed anger is to perform a self-corrective procedure. For example, you shut the car door on your new raincoat and say to yourself, "Next time pull the jacket in before you shut the door, dumb ass!" The expression performs a teaching function and at the same time allows you to let off a little steam. The use of a full sentence is probably less likely than the use of one word expletives such as, *dammit*, *shit*, or *you dumb ass* in a case of self-frustration.

***The Event*:** Here the focus is on the nature of the action or lack of action on the part of the wrongdoer that offended the person. The event could be some type of behavior that was expected but not provided, some type of language or communication, or the manner in which the event occurred. The temporal and physical qualities of the event are weighed, in conjunction with the spontaneity or intentionality of the cause of the event. The major dimensions are listed here.

Behavior: unexpected, deviant, ill-mannered, aggressive, crude or vulgar. Examples of these would be crowding in a line, cheating in a game, or sneezing on someone. The behavior may be evaluated by its morality or legality, which are used especially in the cases of undesirable sexual or social behavior.

> *Language*: speech or comment that incites the source. Besides physical action, what another person says or the manner in which the language is spoken may provoke another. These linguistic or verbal behaviors (sic) are the basis of slander, libel, verbal abuse, and "fighting words" laws in the culture. The verbal behavior may provoke immediate anger or delayed retribution through legal or officially sanctioned channels.
>
> *Intentionality*: whether the event was caused, or occurred by accident. That is, intentionality influences the perception of a wrongful act. The more intentional the act appears to the speaker, the greater the justification for an angry response. If the event was purely accidental, less anger is expressed.
>
> *Damage*: The event can be measured in terms of its duration, degree of physical pain, cost in dollars, waste of time or energy. The more damage done by the event and the more likely that the damage cannot be repaired, the more anger is associated with the event. In other words, big damage means big anger.
>
> (Jay 1992: 98–100)

When we look at such elements as *non-human wrongdoer* and *self as wrongdoer*, then we have to note that this model is not a model that *solely* concerns itself with the concept of communication. After all, communication, via verbal language, can be held to be questionable when applied to animals such as the family's pet dog, or the proverbial pigeon flying overhead.[9] Similarly, 'communication' can be said to be in question when one is ranting at the rainclouds, or cursing oneself for trapping a coat in the car door. In all these cases there is no autonomous human interlocutor with which to engage. It should be noted that despite the fact that I have pointed out Jay's (1992) sole concern is not about the concept of communication, this is not meant as a criticism or comment on a presumed deficiency of the model. That this is not a first concern is hardly surprising. Jay is concerned with the *expression* of cursing and curse words, as defined above, and not necessarily with the communication of such words. That said, when we take this into account, we can see how such a model could be a useful 'way in' when applied to a theory of the communication of angry, aggressive, and impolite terminology.

In summary, we can now see how, in response to an offending event, feelings of frustration could be triggered in an interlocutor (see Section 7.2.1). In turn, this could lead to the expression of some form of instrumental verbal aggression, for example, impoliteness. Such a speech act could, itself, be seen as a triggering, offending event and could, in turn, lead to feelings of frustration or anger in another interlocutor which could, in turn, lead to the expression of a new impoliteness. This very concept will be discussed and explored in depth in Chapter 7.

---

9. But note they can still be the cause, or the 'Offending Event', which triggers the utterance.

Thus far we have moved from the general background which situates and defines Grice (1975) and critiques the ability of approaches to politeness to accommodate impoliteness, to a more specific, and precise, foreground which justifies a need for a model dealing with, and defines, impoliteness. In the remaining sections of this chapter I compare and critique existing models of impoliteness, ultimately choosing one which is best suited for use and adaptation within this study.

4.6 Models of impoliteness and aggravation

There have been in my view three innovative approaches to explain impolite or aggravating linguistic behaviour. Two approaches, Lachenicht (1980) and Culpeper (1996) are so finely detailed, and at first sight, of startling similarity, that I intend to compare and contrast them and their relative strengths and weaknesses later in the following section. In this section however, I should note, in brief, the model of Austin (1990). As Culpeper et al. (2003) have noted Lachenicht (1980), Austin (1990) and Culpeper (1996) do appear to have a lot in common. They all derive a framework from Brown and Levinson (1987) and both Austin (1990) and Culpeper (1996) talk about 'face attack'. However, there is a fundamental difference. Culpeper et al. (2003) point out that Austin (1990) is a hearer-based account of how utterances can be interpreted as offensive. They note that she shows (1990: 285) how apparent compliments like *You have been a capable and decorative chairman* could, even if it may have been intended as a straightforward compliment, have offensive implications for the hearer in a particular context. The main point made by Culpeper et al. (2003), which is worth reporting here is that while Austin's (1990) paper is a useful reminder that Brown and Levinson (1987) underestimate both the role of the hearer and of the context, Austin, like Sperber and Wilson (1986) (see Section 2.2. Relevance, above) steadfastly overlooks the role of the speaker. Her paper is not about the *communication* of impoliteness, but rather the interpretation and perception of it. Her examples include cases that may simply have involved the miscommunication of politeness (e.g. too little or too much politeness work in a particular context). In other words, her examples may simply involve 'unintentional' or 'incidental' face threat (Section 4.4.2), and 'accidental' face threat (Section 4.4.3). Culpeper et al. (2003) further note that a particular weakness of Austin's (1990) paper is that her interpretations of offence are untested. It is both a priority and a challenge for future research to test the perlocutionary and interactional offensive effects of linguistic impoliteness.

4.6.1 Culpeper (1996) and Lachenicht (1980)

Despite the appeals by researchers of later years to provide adequate frameworks for the description of impolite, rude or aggravating behaviour, Lachenicht (1980), in what has been described as a 'rarely cited but nevertheless meritorious paper' (Turner 1996: 7), had already posited just such a model in 'Aggravating language: a study of abusive and insulting language'. Culpeper (1996), unaware of Lachenicht's study, covers similar territory in his paper 'Towards an anatomy of impoliteness'.

Both Lachenicht (1980) and Culpeper (1996) take Brown and Levinson's model of politeness as the underlying point of departure for their own work. Lachenicht (1980: 607) considers the use of 'aggravating language' as a rational attempt to 'hurt' or damage the addressee. 'Hurt', Lachenicht says (1980: 607) is achieved by (a) conveying that the addressee is not liked and does not belong and by (b) interfering with the addressee's freedom of action. Culpeper (1996: 349–350) takes a similar view when he suggests that 'impoliteness' is defined as the use of utterances or actions that attack one's interlocutor and cause disharmony and/or social disruption (rather than promoting or maintaining social harmony, which is the purpose of politeness of course). Culpeper (1996: 349–350) views impoliteness as attacking the addressee's face wants (positive or negative). We can see the similarity between the two approaches when we consider, again, how Lachenicht (1980: 607) considers 'hurt' to be achieved: by (a) conveying that the addressee is not liked and does not belong (positive aggravation) and by (b) interfering with the addressee's freedom of action (negative aggravation).

The apparent similarity of the two models' approach to such verbally aggressive behaviour begins to diverge when we consider the respective 'architectures' the models assume. Lachenicht (1980) considers four 'aggravation' superstrategies and suggests aggravation can be explained by, and adjoined to, Brown and Levinson's (1987) framework as follows (Lachenicht 1980: 619).

The aggravation strategies that can be selected are, in order of degree of threat, as follows:

(i) Off record: ambiguous insults, insinuations, hints, and irony. This strategy is of much the same kind as the politeness strategy, and is designed to enable the insulter to meet an aggrieved challenge from the injured person with an assertion of innocence.
(ii) Bald on Record: directly produced FTAs and impositions ('Shut that door', 'Do your work', 'Don't talk', etc.) of the same kind as in the politeness strategy.
(iii) Positive aggravation: an aggravation strategy that is designed to show the addressee that he is not approved of, is not esteemed, does not belong, and will not receive cooperation.

(iv) Negative aggravation: An aggravation strategy that is designed to impose on the addressee, to interfere with his freedom of action, and to attack his social position and the basis of his social action. (Lachenicht 1980: 619)

Note that the first two strategies are not in fact part of a new impoliteness framework, but are taken from Brown and Levinson's (1987) politeness framework. Positive aggravation and negative aggravation appear to be distinguished in terms of their orientation to positive and negative face wants (cf. Brown and Levinson 1987).

Similarly, as one can see, Lachenicht (1980) neglects to consider silence or 'opting out' (Grice 1975) as a potential strategy to aggravate or 'hurt' one's interlocutor. Thomas quite rightly points out (1995: 175) that silence, where there is an expectation that something should be said, could be a ' [...] massive FTA.' Furthermore, Lachenicht (1980: 619) considers that off record strategies will, typically, be used against powerful addressees, positive aggravation against friends and intimates and negative aggravation against those more socially distant. He is, in effect, attempting to unproblematically apply politeness variables to aggravation strategies. Unfortunately, as I will show, this is not as simple as he foresees, and the lack of any testing on this score is a weakness for Lachenicht (1980).

Culpeper (1996) explores the possibility of a parallel structure to Brown and Levinson (1987). Impoliteness superstrategies for Culpeper are 'opposite' in terms of orientation to face (i.e. instead of maintaining or enhancing face, they are designed to attack face), but not necessarily opposite in other pragmatic ways (e.g. from a Gricean point of view, the opposite of on record is off-record). The five superstrategies from Culpeper (1996) are summarised, and compared to Lachenicht's position here:

1. ***Bald on record impoliteness.*** This is distinct from how both Brown and Levinson (1987), and Lachenicht (1980), envisage 'Bald on Record'. Lachenicht (1980) suggests that utterances in Brown and Levinson's ([1978] 1987) bald on record superstrategy can be *either* polite *or* aggravating. However, Culpeper (1996: 356) suggests that bald on record *im*politeness is somewhat distinct from Brown and Levinson's ([1978], 1987) own bald on record strategy. Culpeper suggests it is deployed for *polite* purposes in fairly specific circumstances: for example, where there is little face at stake, where there is an emergency situation, and where there is *no* intention of damaging the face of the hearer. In contrast, utterances within Culpeper's (1996) bald on record *im*politeness superstrategy are typically deployed where there *is* much face at stake, and where there *is* an intention on the part of the speaker to attack the face of the hearer. (For further discussion regarding the 'Bald, on record' superstrategy, see Section 4.6 below).

2. ***Positive impoliteness.*** Culpeper (1996) suggests that this superstrategy exists for the use of strategies designed to damage the addressee's positive face wants. When we compare this to Lachenicht's (1980) view of Positive Aggravation, being, namely that which wilfully and intentionally conveys to the addressee that he or she is not liked, will not be co-operated with and/or does not belong, then we can see the similarity across the two approaches. The strategies each researcher suggests are compared in Table 3, below.

Table 3. Lachenicht's (1980) and Culpeper's (1996) positive face damaging strategies

Lachenicht (1980)	Culpeper (1996)
Positive Aggravation Positive aggravation attempts to convey to the addressee that the speaker does not want what he wants. Strategies consist of:	**Positive Impoliteness** The use of strategies designed to damage the addressee's positive face wants. The linguistic output strategies include:
1.1 Deny Common Ground.	**1.1** Ignore, snub, fail to attend to H's interests, wants, needs, goods, etc.
1.1.1 Convey that *h* is not liked	
1.1.1.1 Express dislike for *h* and *h*'s things	**1.2** Exclude the other from activity.
1.1.1.2 Use non-valid imperatives	**1.3** Disassociate from the other. Deny common ground, or association.
1.1.1.3 Offend *h*'s sensibilities and beliefs	
1.1.1.4 Wish *h* ill	**1.4** Be disinterested, unconcerned, unsympathetic.
1.1.1.5 Use Sarcasm	
1.1.2 Deny in group membership and opinions	**1.5** Use inappropriate identity markers.
	1.6 Use obscure or secretive language.
1.1.2.1 Use negative politeness	**1.7** Seek disagreement. - sensitive topics or just disagree outright (act as 'Devil's advocate').
1.1.2.2 Deny in group status	
1.1.2.3 Disclaim common opinions	**1.8** Avoid agreement. - avoid agreeing with H's position (whether S actually does or not).
1.2 Convey that *s* and *h* are not co-operators	**1.9** Make the other feel uncomfortable.
1.2.1 Show that not taking *h*'s wants into account	**1.10** Use taboo language - swear, be abusive, express strong views opposed to H's.
1.2.1.1 Ignore *h* and interrupt *h*'s speech	**1.11** Call H names – use derogatory nominations.
1.2.1.2 Show disinterest in h's projects	
1.2.1.3 Don't give or ask	**1.12** Etc…
1.2.2 Deny reflexivity	
1.2.2.1 Don't give or ask	
1.2.2.2 Use negative politeness	
1.2.3 Deny h's wants	
1.2.3.1 Refuse	

3. ***Negative impoliteness.*** The use of strategies designed to damage the addressee's negative face wants. When we compare this to Lachenicht's (1980) view of Negative Aggravation, being, namely, that which wilfully and intentionally impedes or interferes with the addressee's own freedom of action, again we can see the similarity of the two models. Again, the strategies each researcher suggests are compared in Table 4, below.

Table 4. Lachenicht's (1980) and Culpeper's (1996) negative face damaging strategies

Lachenicht (1980)		Culpeper (1996)	
2.0	**Negative Aggravation**	**2.0**	**Negative Impoliteness**
Negative aggravation attempts to impinge upon *h*:		The use of strategies designed to damage the addressee's negative face wants. The linguistic output strategies include:	
2.1	Communicate ability and want to coerce *h*	**2.1**	Frighten – instil a belief that action detrimental to other will occur.
2.1.1	Stress and increase *s*'s power	**2.2**	Condescend, scorn or ridicule – emphasise own power, use diminutives to other (or other's position), be contemptuous, belittle, do not take H seriously
2.1.1.1	Be indirect		
2.1.1.2	Use speech of powerful persons		
2.1.1.3	Refer to *s*'s status/power		
2.1.1.4	Question	**2.3**	Invade the other's space – literally (positioning closer than relationship permits) or metaphorically (ask for intimate information given the relationship)..
2.1.1.5	Insist on *h* being humble		
2.1.2	Minimise *h*'s power		
2.1.2.1	Tease and bait		
2.1.2.2	Use inappropriate positive politeness	**2.4**	Explicitly associate H with negative aspect – personalise, use pronouns, 'I' and 'you'.
2.1.2.3	Indebt *h*		
2.1.2.4	Deflate	**2.5**	Put H's indebtedness on record.
2.2	Coerce and Impinge on *h*	**2.6**	Hinder – physically (block passage), conversationally (deny turn, interrupt).
2.2.1	Challenge		
2.2.1.1	Challenge indirectly	**2.7**	Etc…
2.2.1.2	Challenge explicitly		
2.2.1.3	Refer to rights and obligations		
2.2.1.4	Disagree/contradict		
2.2.2	Increase imposition		
2.2.2.1	Increase imposition weight		
2.2.3	Use force		
2.2.3.1	Use threats and violence		

4. ***Sarcasm or mock politeness.*** For Culpeper (1996), sarcasm or mock politeness is a superstrategy in its own right. Here the face threatening acts are performed with the use of politeness strategies that are obviously insincere, and thus remain surface realisations. Sarcasm (mock politeness for social disharmony) is clearly the opposite of banter (mock impoliteness for social harmony).[10] For Lachenicht (1980), however, sarcasm is an aggravation sub-strategy (see '1.1.1.5 Use Sarcasm' in Table 3 above) falling within the remit of the positive aggravation strategy of 'Deny common ground, convey that *h* is not liked'. Similarly, using inappropriate positive politeness (one form of 'mock politeness') is, for Lachenicht (1980), an aggravation sub-strategy falling within the remit of the negative aggravation strategy of 'Communicate Ability and Want to Coerce the Addressee, Minimise Addressee's Power' (see 2.1.2.2, in Table 4 above). In effect then, while Culpeper (1996) gathers such phenomena into one impolite superstrategy, Lachenicht (1980) distributes such phenomena around his framework in an attempt to account for them.

5. ***Withhold politeness.*** Keep silent when politeness work is expected, necessary or 'mandatory' and hence damage the hearer's face. As noted already, Lachenicht (1980) fails to consider the offensive or aggravating effects that withholding politeness may have.

4.6.1.1 *Considerations concerning Culpeper (1996) and Lachenicht (1980)*

It must be noted that the fact that these frameworks are inspired by Brown and Levinson's (1987) model means that weaknesses associated with their model tend to be inherited. Specifically, this means that little is said about matters to do with sequencing in discourse (see Chapters 6, 7 and 8) or even prosodic aspects (see Culpeper 2005 and the Conclusion, Chapter 9, this text). Furthermore, as Culpeper (1996: 358) points out, Brown and Levinson (1987) is primarily geared to handling matters relating to linguistic form, and impolite implicatures, while ostensibly handled in their Off-record superstrategy can nevertheless slip through their framework, as they themselves admit (see Brown and Levinson 1987: 11). Culpeper (1996) suggests Leech's (1983) model of politeness, which is primarily concerned with linguistic content, may be used to complement that of Brown and Levinson (1987).

10. Culpeper's (1996) understanding of sarcasm is, clearly, close to Leech's conception of irony (1983: 82–142).

Impoliteness and the 'weightiness' issue. In performing FTAs politely, Brown and Levinson (1987: 15 and 76–78) suggest a formula for assessing the seriousness or weightiness of such a speech act. Where Wx is the numerical value of the FTA 'x', D(S,H) is the value that measures the social distance between the speaker and the hearer; P(H,S) is a measure of the power that the hearer has over the speaker and Rx is a value that measures the degree to which the FTA 'x' is rated as an imposition in a given culture, they suggest the formula: Wx = D(S,H) + P(H,S) + Rx. Brown and Levinson (1987) argue that the higher the weightiness of a particular FTA to be performed suggests the type of strategy to be used. In order of ranking, where the weightiness runs from lowest to highest risk: Bald on Record politeness, Positive Politeness, Negative Politeness, Off-Record, Withhold the FTA.

The issue here is that both Culpeper (1996) in positing a parallel impolite structure to Brown and Levinson's (1987) model; and Lachenicht (1980) in positing his additional 'aggravation' arm to Brown and Levinson's (1987) architecture, adopt Brown and Levinson's formula for assessing the weightiness of an FTA. Culpeper (1996: 357) explicitly adopts Wx = D(S,H) + P(H,S) + Rx, saying that it 'still applies for impoliteness'. However, he does caution that he adopts the formula in lieu of additional, future research, which, he argues, may further indicate, 'how impoliteness strategies relate to the degree of face attack of an act and how they promote the overall impoliteness of an utterance.' (Culpeper 1996: 357). Lachenicht (1980: 619) also adopts the weightiness formula, implicating this when he says, '[A] speaker will assess the risk he can take in aggravating his (sic!) hearer, and [will] select an 'aggravation' strategy that will produce an FTA of the required weight.' Couple this with the way in which Lachenicht (1980: 619) suggests the superstrategies are arranged in ascending order of degree of face threat (Off Record – Bald on Record – Positive then Negative aggravation), and the adoption of Wx = D(S,H) + P(H,S) + Rx is clear. However, Turner (1999), to name but one researcher, roundly criticises Brown and Levinson's (1987) formula, Wx = D(S,H) + P(H,S) + Rx, for assessing the weightiness of FTAs on two main points. First, the 'Power', 'Distance' and 'Ranking' categories are not nearly enough to begin to explain the overwhelming complexity of human relations. Even such fundamentally basic factors as 'Affect' (how 'Speaker' and 'Hearer' like each other; see Slugoski 1985), and the 'situation' in which FTAs are issued, are ignored. Second, the scalar values of the categories D, P and R are not stipulated in any *definite* way, thus the formula – which purports to be precise – is, in fact, woefully imprecise with regards the categorisation of the weight of an FTA and of the complexity of human relations regarding the 'value' of such categories. In other words, how individual persons *qualitatively* view such factors as P, D and even R belies the imposition of a *quantitative* scale from 0 to *n*, where *n* is some small number. It is clearly time to re-assess the values pertaining to the creation, mitigation or enhancement of

FTAs. Indeed, many researchers have suggested revisions and corrections to the formula for assessing FTAs. For example, Turner (1999), like other researchers calling for revision, makes a suggestion for the inclusion of 'Affect'. However, it seems apparent that many more features are needed. The features from Jay (1992, 2000 – see Section 4.5.4, above), would be ideal as initial concepts to consider given that they can be adapted to account for the situational context in which im/politeness is produced, not to mention the triggering event which precedes it.

4.6.1.2 *Considering Lachenicht (1980)*

As noted elsewhere (Culpeper et al. 2003), the chief merits of Lachenicht's (1980) work undoubtedly lie in the fact that it provides both an extensive review of linguistic strategies that may be used to aggravate face and, unlike Culpeper (1996), it considers that strategies for aggravating face can be mixed (see Chapter 6, this text). Note that Brown and Levinson (1987: 17–20) resist the idea that politeness strategies can be mixed (for example, positive politeness markers occurring in negative politeness strategies such as indirect requests), despite claims by other researchers (e.g. Craig et al. 1986: 452–3) to the contrary. The mixing of impolite strategies is, therefore, a primary research area for this book (see Chapter 5 and, especially, Chapter 6).

There are, however, a number of issues concerning the consistency, speculative nature, and validity of Lachenicht's (1980) model. For example, Lachenicht claims (1980: 631) that '[p]ositive aggravation informs the hearer that he is not liked, will not be cooperated with, and does not belong. Essentially it attacks his need for freedom of action, for status, and for power'. But, as indicated by other references and claims in other parts of Lachenicht (1980) and throughout Brown and Levinson (1987: passim) attacks on 'freedom of action' concern 'negative' and not 'positive' face. Brown and Levinson (1987: 61) point out that positive face is the desire that an individual's wants and needs are respected by others, whereas negative face is the desire for 'freedom of action'. If positive and negative aggravation are supposed to relate to positive and negative face, as defined by Brown and Levinson (1987), they fundamentally fail to do so. However, given the discussion I made in Chapter 3, above, this is largely a moot point. Another significant issue is that Lachenicht's (1980) model is based upon and describes anecdotal, constructed examples, and written material from a number of dictionaries of insults. No 'real life' conversational data, either written or verbal, are utilised. Turner (1996: 7) writes, 'It might be stressed that the paper is an essay not in analysis but in constructivism and so the specific details are subject to trial and revision by the data that are collected.' Indeed, lack of any such trials or revisions of Lachenicht (1980) relegates numerous claims made therein to purely hypothetical ones. Examples include:

> It is very interesting that non-valid imperatives may be changed into less severe insults by adding a number of politeness forms, or by making the imperatives into indirect requests:
>
> (a) You can drop dead!
> (b) Get lost, please.
> (c) You can go jump in the lake!
> (d) Oh, do please hang yourself.
>
> These expressions are noticeably less insulting than the direct imperatives. (Lachenicht 1980: 639)

This claim, clearly, is an empirical issue – one which requires testing in order to ascertain its veracity. Furthermore, such additions of politeness work to utterances that are clearly impolite-in-content may be interpreted as insincere. As such, they probably fit in better with Culpeper's (1996) overall approach within the superstrategy 'mock politeness' (Culpeper 1996: 352) and by the utilisation of a complementary model that deals with function over form. The one that Culpeper (1996) and Culpeper et al. (2003) suggest is Leech's (1983) Politeness Principle (see Section 4.2 above). Lachenicht also argues that 'Probably swearing is past its prime today, for the decline of religious belief has made it less useful. Today, it is manly 'God-damns' and 'bloodys' that are popular' (1980: 641). This, again, is an empirical issue, as is Lachenicht's (1980: 652) claim that men frequently employ the sub-strategy 'Ignore *h*'s remarks and interrupt *h*'s speech' against women.

4.6.1.3 *Considering Culpeper (1996, 2005)*

Culpeper's (1996) model, on the other hand, has the benefit of being tested, to a degree, with real life data, across various discourses, (see Bousfield 1999, 2004; Cashman 2006; Culpeper 1996, 2005 and Culpeper et al. 2003). Culpeper (1996) includes an analysis of the conflictive and impolite illocutions in U.S. army training discourse. Culpeper, et al. (2003). Use a slightly modified version of Culpeper (1996) to provide an analysis of the impolite and conflictive illocutions in extracts concerning vehicle parking disputes. Lauer (1996) deploys Culpeper (1996) in the analysis of impoliteness in letters of complaint and Cashman (2006) shows how Culpeper's (2005) model accounts for the impolite interactions within bilingual Spanish/English children's interaction. The conclusions made in these studies is that Culpeper (1996) and the developments of this model, with some few modifications at root level, (including some additional strategies) give adequate analysing power across both verbal and written data from real life situations. As such, it is the most promising candidate for use, application and testing in this book.

However, there are a number of issues, beyond those already discussed, which surround Culpeper (1996, 2005) that need to be considered. Culpeper (1996), in line with Brown and Levinson's (1987) original proposal, indicates that the linguistic output strategies listed above in Table 3 and 4 are only *some* of those that can be deployed within each superstrategy for 'positive' or 'negative' face damage. That is, the lists presented in Culpeper (1996) are explicitly *open-ended* lists. This makes the model somewhat robust, in that it can adapt to changes in linguistic usage over time. However, the fact is that it also lays the model open to the criticism that its very 'open endedness' may be something of a weakness as there is really no clear, distinct or motivated way of restricting the number of strategies within the model. This means that the very dynamic nature of the model is also a weakness, for if we are able to simply invent a new strategy for every new regularity in language then the model could soon become impervious to counterexamples, (or, as Thomas (1995: 167) claims for Leech's (1983) PP, this dynamism, '... makes the theory at best inelegant, at worst virtually unfalsifiable'). This, it needs to be noted, is another problem inherited from Brown and Levinson (1987). However, despite the impressive work of Cashman (2006), in my view, research into impoliteness should not unduly concern itself with the discovery of additional linguistic output strategies but should now be concentrated upon how the discourse 'builds up', how context affects the generation of impoliteness and how the *dynamism* of impolite illocutions is dealt with. Again, this is research I undertake and discuss in Chapters 5, 6, 7 and 8.

In its 2005 incarnation, the model proposed and developed by Culpeper suggests a shift in the focus of intentional, impolite face-attack away from a Brown and Levinson style 5-point model of offensive superstrategies (Bald, on Record; Positive Impoliteness; Negative Impoliteness; Sarcasm; Withhold Politeness). Culpeper (2005: 40) begins to argue for the adoption of a more contextually and culturally sensitive model of face. The one he suggests should be adopted is Spencer-Oatey's (2002) approach.[11] However, as Cashman (2006) has argued, despite his promising move here, Culpeper (2005: 41–42) does still refer to the original Brown and Levinson 5-point model and does not fully integrate Spencer-Oatey's approach within his own. However, by *relating* Spencer-Oatey's approach to the existing, classic model that he and his later co-authors have expounded Culpeper is able to produce an evolutionary development of this approach to impoliteness.

11. Spencer-Oatey's approach (2002: 540–542) identifies tow distinct but associated phenomena: FACE and SOCIALITY RIGHTS. FACE, she considers as being made up of QUALITY FACE – the desire to be viewed positively, and SOCIAL IDENTITY FACE – the desire to be respected and accepted in our social roles. SOCIALITY RIGHTS she considers as being made up of EQUITY RIGHTS – the desire to be treated fairly and not unduly imposed upon by others, and ASSOCIATION RIGHTS – a belief that we are entitled to associate with and have positive relationships with others.

In doing so his approach remains sympathetic and complementary to the work done previously on this model. However, simply relating Brown and Levinson's Postitive/Negative approach to face Spencer-Oatey's (2002) approach to rapport management (including 'Face' and 'Sociality Rights'); by, in short, linking the two together, simply doesn't solve the issue of the, more often than not multi-face-directedness of the linguistic impoliteness strategies. Indeed, when we consider that Spencer-Oatey (2007: 16) argues that face is a multi-faceted phenomenon, then it is obvious that the linguistic impoliteness strategies identified by Culpeper (1996), Culpeper et al. (2003) and Cashman (2006) don't purely indict one type of face, or one type of sociality right, over another. I would therefore suggest though that the evolutionary steps that Culpeper (2005: 41–42) makes have not *yet* gone far enough to solve such issues facing the model.[12]

The 5-point model identifies a number of separate ways ('superstrategies') in which impoliteness can be generated and conveyed. I should stress here that what follows is a paraphrased explanation of the model in its most recent (2005) incarnation:

(1) **Bald on record impoliteness**
According to the developments of the model (Culpeper 1996, 2005), *bald, on record impoliteness* is seen as typically being deployed where there *is* much face at stake, and where there *is* an intention on the part of the speaker to attack the face of the hearer and/or where the speaker does not have the power to (safely) utter an impolite utterance. That is, the utterance is deployed in a direct, clear and unambiguous manner (fully in accordance with Grice's ([1975]1989) maxims), "...where face is not irrelevant, or minimized" (Culpeper 2005: 41).

(2) **Positive impoliteness** (Attacking your want to be approved of, which Culpeper (2005: 40) explicitly links with Spencer-Oatey's (2002) QUALITY FACE and elements of SOCIALITY FACE).
Positive Impoliteness, according to the latest instantiation of the model (Culpeper 2005: 41) involves "the use of strategies deployed to damage the recipient's positive face wants." Examples of such strategies from Culpeper 1996 include 'ignore, snub the other', 'exclude the other from the activity', 'disassociate from the other', 'be disinterested, unconcerned, unsympathetic', 'use inappropriate identity markers', 'use obscure or secretive language', 'seek disagreement', 'make the other feel uncomfortable (e.g. do not avoid silence, joke, or use small talk)', 'use taboo words', 'call the other names', etc.

12. As, indeed, I am sure Culpeper would agree.

(3) **Negative impoliteness** (Attacking your freedom of action, which Culpeper (2005: 40) explicitly links with Spencer-Oatey's (2002) Equity Rights. Further, he (2005: 41) suggests that this negative face also overlaps with Association Rights, to some extent.)
Negative Impoliteness, according to the latest instantiation of the model (Culpeper 2005: 41) involves "the use of strategies deployed to damage the recipient's negative face wants." Examples of such strategies from Culpeper 1996 include 'frighten', 'condescend, scorn, or ridicule', 'invade the other's space', 'explicitly associate the other with a negative aspect', 'put the other's indebtedness on record', etc.

(4) **Off-record impoliteness**
This superstrategy was introduced by Culpeper (2005: 43–44) as a replacement to the 'meta-strategic' nature of sarcasm (which had previously been considered on the same level as the other superstrategies; cf. Culpeper 1996). 'Off-record impoliteness' is one where the offence is conveyed indirectly by way of an implicature and could be cancelled (e.g., denied, or an account, post-modification or other type of elaboration offered, etc.) but where, according to Culpeper (2005: 44). "...one attributable intention clearly outweighs any others".

(5) **Withhold politeness** (Keep silent or fail to act where politeness work is expected)
Culpeper (1996: 357) notes that impoliteness may be realised through, "[...] the absence of politeness work where it would be expected." Culpeper (2005: 42) gives the example that "failing to thank someone for a present may be taken as deliberate impoliteness." Culpeper further notes that Brown and Levinson would appear to agree with the face-threatening aspects and implications surrounding the withholding of politeness when they claim:

> [...] politeness has to be communicated, and the absence of communicated politeness may, *ceteris paribus*, be taken as the absence of a polite attitude.
> (Brown and Levinson 1987: 5, as cited in Culpeper 1996: 357)

Obviously, as might be supposed from what I have argued above (Section 4.3.1) there is also an issue with the viability of the 'bald, on record' superstrategy where it occurs in impoliteness models, just as there is where it occurs in the original politeness model. There is also the issue of equally balanced on- and off-record superstrategies containing positive/negative strategies for performing and communicating impoliteness (see Figure 2, above). However, this leads us to the next, perhaps more fundamental issue in that a strict positive/negative dichotomy does not, in actual fact, exist. In light of the discussion made above and the following example, the distinction may simply be unsustainable. Take, for example, the following (adapted from Bousfield 2006: 11–12).

A student knocks on my door and enters my office outside of my office hours, hastily saying (before I can utter a word of welcome or protest) "Derek, I'm really sorry to bother you but I need a little help and advice and I don't know who else could help." Here, cast in Brown and Levinson's (1987) terms, the student is making the attempt to mitigate their impingement on my freedom of action (my *negative face want* to be unimpeded in my work outside of office hours) by the expression of an apology (…I'm really sorry…), linked to the acknowledgement that my negative face *is* being impinged upon, (…to bother you…), the expression of the student having limited choice (…I need…) which is linked with a minimiser for what may, actually, take up significant effort on my part in terms of time and resources (…a little…). However, (in the context of relatively informal British Universities), beyond the use of my first name (Derek…) as an indicator of supposed social proximity between tutors and students (an attempt at establishing solidarity and hence, the use of 'Derek' is arguably an invocation of *my positive face*) what is not considered under Brown and Levinson's (1987) ostensibly form-based approach is that by virtue of coming to me and asking for my help, via expressions linked to the hyperbolic (…I don't know who else could help) the student is enhancing my *positive face* by assuming that I, as sole *Oracle* and *Fount of Wisdom*, may have the (best placed) knowledge/ability/wherewithal within the department to help them in their dilemma. This is hardly an isolated example of supposedly 'dichotomous' face aspects (see Chapter 3) being present in other-face-directed expressions. Most utterances will, even only secondarily, implicate both aspects of face on, or at, some level. Indeed, given that (a) face is always an issue in interaction, and (b) the systematic way in which 'positive' and 'negative' face strategies have already been found to regularly *combine* in interaction (see Culpeper, Bousfield and Wichmann 2003: 1560–1562; Harris 2001) then it would appear that the positive/negative face distinction becomes simply superfluous (see also Haugh 2006: 18–19 for a discussion on this score). As such, the model of superstrategies that Culpeper (1996, 2005) and Culpeper, et al. (2003) have proposed and modified for the expression and communication of impoliteness could be restructured along simpler lines with two overarching 'tactics',[13] thus:

13. I choose the term 'tactic' to clearly differentiate what I propose here from the concept of '(super)strategy'. However, I do recognise that both are unhappy terms. In military discourse, 'strategies' are grand plans which, necessarily, require the successful completion of 'tactics' within them to succeed. In short, the terms 'strategy' as adopted by Brown and Levinson are misnamed – they should have been 'tactics' and the 'tactics' I name here, should be indentified as 'strategies' – but historical nomenclatures have a way of sticking.

1. **On record impoliteness**
   The use of strategies designed to *explicitly* (a) attack the face of an interactant, (b) construct the face of an interactant in a non-harmonious or outright conflictive way, (c) deny the expected face wants, needs, or rights of the interactant, or some combination thereof. The attack is made in an unambiguous way given the context in which it occurs.
2. **Off record impoliteness**
   The use of strategies where the threat or damage to an interactant's face is conveyed indirectly by way of an implicature (cf. Grice [1975] 1989) and can be cancelled (e.g., denied, or an account / post-modification / elaboration offered, etc.) but where "…one attributable intention clearly outweighs any others" (Culpeper 2005: 44), given the context in which it occurs.

   Sarcasm and the *Withholding of Politeness where it is expected* would also come under this heading, as follows:

   (a) Sarcasm
   Sarcasm constitutes the use of individual or combined strategies which, on the surface, appear to be appropriate but which are meant to be taken as meaning the opposite in terms of face-management. The utterance that appears, on the surface, to positively constitute, maintain, or enhance the face of the intended recipient(s) actually threatens, attacks and/or damages the face of the recipient(s) (see Culpeper 2005) given the context in which it occurs.[14]

   (b) Withhold politeness
   More specifically, withhold politeness where politeness would appear to be expected or mandatory. Withholding politeness is within the Off-Record category as "[…] politeness has to be communicated […] the absence of communicated politeness may, *ceteris paribus*, be taken as the absence of a polite attitude." Brown and Levinson (1987: 5).

It is on this basis that I analyse, present and discuss the examples throughout the remainder of this book including, where appropriate, further justification for the adoption of this simplified model. At this point it suffices to say that, in defence of the reduction of bald, on record superstrategy and the reconceptualisation and clarification of 'positive' face directed and 'negative' face directed utterances

14. Note: I take Sarcasm (cf. Culpeper 1996, 2005) to be the opposite in functional terms to Banter (cf. Leech 1983) despite the apparently identical nature of the forms that each 'tactic' takes. Therefore, Banter, being the functional opposite to Sarcasm, is Sarcasm's polite 'mirror-tactic' (for want of a better phrase). As ever, every tactic and strategy in interaction is context-dependent for its effectiveness and understandability.

within the 'On-Record' tactic, as Brown and Levinson themselves admit that 'we may have been in error to set up the three superstrategies, positive politeness, negative politeness, and off-record, as ranked unidimensionally to achieve mutual exclusivity.' (1987: 18).

They go on to note that, what's 'on-record' for one, may be 'off-record' for another (1987: 19–20). What this means is that even the conflation of the five point model into the two tactic approach for managing FTAs, as presented here, does not *de jure* guarantee mutual exclusivity. Rather they are *de facto* mutually exclusive as with each FTA,[15] on- and off-record utterances are *contextually dictated* as being in complementary distribution but this is not to say that multiple FTAs within a stretch of ongoing discourse will not be a collection of mixed on and off-record im/polite utterances, as we will see in subsequent chapters.

I should note also that the individual strategies postulated by Culpeper (1996), Culpeper, Bousfield and Wichmann (2003), Cashman (2006) (amongst others), which can combine in multitudinous ways for the purposes of enhancing or boosting the face damage inflicted, are all deployable with(in) any of the above tactics chosen. Furthermore this model is, I believe, robust, in that it is applicable alongside traditional (e.g. Goffman 1967), culture-specific (e.g. Brown and Levinson 1987), or more contextually and culturally sensitive (e.g. Spencer-Oatey 2002, 2005) models of face. The point to be made here is that this modified model of impoliteness is an adaptable adjunct to existing and foreseeable models of face.[16] It is on the basis of this simplified model that I analyse and comment on the examples in Chapter 5, below.

4.7 Conclusion

In this chapter I have explored and discussed both the literature and the background underpinning the concept of impoliteness, thereby working to construct definitions of critical terms for use and understanding throughout the remainder of this book. I have defined how I understand and use Grice's CP; I have explored

15. Of course, saying what an individual FTA is, is another question entirely. Even a single word utterance may be performing multiple FTAs simultaneously, even as on- or off-record ones.

16. What is meant here is that should an otherwise attractive model of what is considered here as being face (such as Spencer-Oatey's 2002 approach to 'rapport-management') ultimately prove unable to resist attempts at falsification, then the model of impoliteness proposed here should be able to adopt a successor model of face. In short, models of face are to be considered 'upgrade bolt-ons' as appropriate to this approach to impoliteness.

contemporary models of politeness to seek the best fit with impoliteness; I have considered the types of threat to face that interlocutors may make, relating them to a working definition of impoliteness which is, itself, rooted in cross-disciplinary understandings of the concept of aggression and I have compared and extensively discussed two theories which purport to deal with linguistic impoliteness or aggravation before coming to my own understanding of how best to conceptualise the most appropriate model, currently.

In the following chapters I continue to test the model with real life data from the corpus constructed, in Chapter 5; move on to discuss the dynamics of impolite utterances (Chapter 6), and impolite exchanges across discourses (Chapter 7); I discuss the impolite effects of exploiting and manipulating participant expectations in discoursal exhanges (Chapter 8) and, following a summary of what I have observed, I suggest areas for future consideration and study in impoliteness in the concluding chapter (9).

CHAPTER 5

The realisation of impoliteness

In the previous chapter I discussed the issues surrounding the viability of the 'bald, on record' superstrategy and those surrounding the 'positive' and 'negative' face-oriented varieties of im/politeness. Chief amongst the models purporting to account for impoliteness which are affected by the removal of the 'bald, on record' superstrategy and the conflation of the positive and negative face-oriented superstrategies are Lachenicht (1980) and Culpeper (1996). Discussion has already been made (Chapter 4) regarding the suitability, in other ways, of these two models. Lachenicht's model, whilst both attractive and innovatively pioneering, now seems hopelessly dated and it has not enjoyed the critical reception enjoyed by Culpeper's (1996, 2005; et al. 2003) approach.

Despite the limitations of Culpeper's (1996, 2005) model, as I outlined in the previous chapter, the 'linguistic impoliteness output strategies' that he suggested as positive-face and negative-face oriented are still applicable within the reconceptualised 'on-/off-record impoliteness' model I have proposed. Impoliteness can be communicated through the use of particular, identifiable strategies, within an appropriate situational context and activity type.

In the present chapter I explain and discuss how impolite utterances are realised by interlocutors in the data sets here studied. More specifically, in this, the first chapter in which I discuss examples of communicated, intentional face-threat/damage (impoliteness) in real-life interaction, I begin to attend to the initial research questions, presented in Chapter 1, namely: *What is the nature and role of impoliteness in interactional communication?* By beginning with a sub-question to the above, namely: *How is impoliteness actually realised in interactive communication?* we will be able to move in the following chapters to investigate the questions, *What triggers impolite face attack? What are the communicative options available to interactants when faced with impoliteness? How can impoliteness be countered?* and *Are the countering strategies offensive or defensive?*, and if defensive, *What defence strategies are available to interactants within a given situational context?*

What we need to be bear in mind, however, are the following issues:

a. Some of the categories/strategies of impoliteness, appear to have quite hard, discrete edges, whilst others have relatively fuzzy edges.

b. Some of the categories seem to be very different from others in nature – for example, sarcasm, which I have identifed as a sub-tactic of 'off-record impoliteness' appears to operate as a second-order device.
c. The fact remains that, as will be apparent from the discussion of the examples given in this chapter, individual impoliteness strategies (cf. Culpeper 1996), rarely occur on their own. Rather, in any given extract, they tend to co-occur, with others, as combined strategies in various ways and in various forms for various effects.

Indeed, combined-strategy impolite utterances occur in most examples in the data sets studied and, whilst I will make reference to the phenemenon here in this chapter, I will discuss the issue at some length in Chapters 6 and 7.

In order to begin this process it is best to consider the impolite utterances within the data sets through an existing model of impoliteness. There is, however, an issue to bear in mind regarding the few significant models and approaches to 'impoliteness' that exist (cf. Austin 1990; Beebe 1995; Culpeper 1996; Culpeper et al. 2003; Harris 2001; Kienpointner 1997; Lachenicht 1980; Rudanko 2006). While at least some of the papers purporting to deal with the phenomena that I have here termed impoliteness (see Chapter 4) can indeed be used, unproblematically, to predict *some* aspects of the types of impoliteness that occur in the data sets here studied, none could fully account for how impoliteness is actually expressed in all the situations of the extracts taken from this corpus. This is an indication of the limitations of these models – limitations which the majority of the papers are, in fact, tacitly self aware.[1]

Thus noted, it is, nevertheless, wise to use an existing model for some very good reasons. The model I have chosen is one based on Culpeper's (1996) exposition supported by Leech's (1983) maxim-based approach to Politeness.[2] The reasons for this are twofold: A narrow view, or rather, a potential criticism of creating a new model, is that, the new model, being based upon the impoliteness that occurs in the data sets here studied, only, *truly*, describes the impoliteness of this corpus. One would have to be wary of generalising beyond such discourses, or even, beyond such examples. Therefore (and for the second reason), using an existing model, which is founded upon other examples in another data set, allows

1. Indeed, Culpeper (1996), in working '*Towards* an Anatomy of Impoliteness', and Kienpointner (1997), in looking at '*Varieties* of Rudeness', tacitly acknowledge that they are not exhaustive.

2. Indeed, Culpeper himself combines his own strategies with the maxim-based approach of Leech (1983) to more adequately describe the phenomena he identifies in the 'Soldier Girls' data (cf. Culpeper 1996).

us to avoid such a criticism. In this chapter I shall be suggesting essential correctives to Culpeper's (1996) exposition and in future chapters (5, 6 and 7) I shall be suggesting conceptual extensions to Culpeper's (1996) model, in order that impoliteness can be more adequately explained and accounted for in the extended discourse(s) of the corpus constructed.

5.1 Realisations of impoliteness

Given the extensive redevelopment of the existing, Culpeper-led, classically-inspired model made in Chapter 4, it might be easy to assume that nothing of that approach survives. Nothing could be further from the truth. As I suggested in Chapter 4, the strategies for communicating politeness suggested by Culpeper (1996), Culpeper et al. (2003) and, latterly, Cashman (2006) are all still realisable using the amended 'on/off-record' model outlined in the previous chapter. The following discussion made throughout the remainder of this chapter explores the communication of impoliteness via the previously proposed strategies. However, before we begin, we need to note here that the different strategies suggested by Culpeper (1996) seem to be of an unequal status. Thus noted, I will pick up this point in Section 5.2, below.

Instances of impoliteness are many and varied throughout all of the data sets included in this study. To present every example would require lengthening just this one section to an unacceptable size, which would also detract from the aim of this chapter as well as from the book as a whole. Instead I present a few examples of each type of impolite utterance strategy to be found within each of the data sets studied.

5.1.1 Snub

The first is originally one of a large set of utterances which Culpeper (1996) viewed as attacking the intended recipient's want to be approved of. However, 'snubbing' an interlocutor not only shows disapproval, but also impedes the interactant from conversing with the snubber. This is but one instance in which the positive-negative dichotomy is problematic, though, of course, face is still being threatened here. In the following example we see apparent instances of a conversational participant attempting to 'snub' their interlocutor. Taken from **The Clampers, Extract 1**.

[7] ***Context:*** *Ray and Miguel, clamping supervisor and assistant respectively, have arrived to remove the clamp from a van. The van's owner is waiting for them. After engag-*

ing Ray in an impolite round of haranguing, challenging, complaints and accusations, the van's owner finally tries to close the conversation as Ray is still trying to speak. S1 is Ray, the clamping supervisor, S2, the van's owner, S3 – Miguel – does not speak throughout this portion of the extract.

[…]

22. S1: well I fully appreciate what you're saying but what
    S2: legalised extortion does it

23. S1: I'm saying to you I can take your notes I can take your notes on
    S2: I'm sure you do I'm sure you hear it ten times a day

24. S1: board but there's nothing I personally can do I simply work do my
    S2: just do your job

25. S1: job for the council I do my job for the coun if you want me to
    S2: *I don't care what you do*

26. S1: explain then if you want to be like that then I can walk away I don't
    S2:

27. S1: have to talk to you if I don't want to if you're going to be rude to me
    S2:

28. S1: yeah I that's fine then sir I
    S2: *I don't really want to talk to you* you're not going to do anything

29. S1:
    S2: about it are you

[…]

Here, the two utterances of *I don't care what you do* (stave 25) and *I don't really want to talk to you* (stave 28) seem to be moves, by S2, to *snub* S1. They show a clear unwillingness on the part of S2 to attend to S1's apparent need to exonerate himself as indeed S1 attempts to do through abrogating blame for the clamping.[3] In failing to attend to what S1 is saying in this way, in effect, being dismissive of S1's stated needs, S2's utterances effectively amount to an aggravated, and thus, impolite, attack against S1's face.

3. Abrogation, as a linguistic defensive counter strategy, will be discussed in full in Chapter 7. At this point it needs to be noted that the act of clamping can be viewed as a Face Threatening 'trigger' responsible for causing S2 to embark on an impolite filled exchange with S1.

5.1.2 Disassociate from the other – for example, deny association or common ground with the other; avoid sitting together (Culpeper 1996: 357)

In this example, we can see an example of disassociation as an impolite strategy, taken from **Parking Wars, Extract 74.**

[8] ***Context***: *This exchange takes place in a Welsh town where residents and students live side by side. A dispute has arisen between one resident, S1, and one student, S2, over one parking space. They are in the street discussing incidents which have occurred on previous occasions.*

1. S1: why is it that you get out of the car with this attitude [raises his hands
S2: [sighs and
2. S1: triumphantly] no no you've been seen doing it yes with
S2: shakes head] have I really
3. S1: this attitude and your language is foul so it's foul
S2: phew right let me just turn that
4. S1: oh right
S2: one around on you *you were the one who has been shouting*
5. S1: Ah aye aye
S2: *and swearing at me I haven't been <indistinct> you know that I've*
6. S1: yes yes
S2: *got everybody on my side and all your neighbours went out <and say*
7. S1:
S2: *the same thing> and all your local <people> that have lived here*
8. S1: yes yes yes
S2: *for a long time*

[…]

Here S2 opts for a form of social/group disassociation as part of a general criticism of S1's past language and behaviour with the claim that *you know that I've got everybody on my side* which would implicate, via the maxims of Quality and Relation (Grice 1975), that of the group of people captured in 'everybody' (presumably, the local neighbours of both participants), none support S1 or his position. This would mean, therefore, that they are not associated with either it or him on this issue. Such a phenomenon could be seen as a socially extended version of the impolite strategy of *Disassociate from the other – for example, deny association or common ground with the other; avoid sitting together* presented in Culpeper

(1996: 357). In the context of the above example, the on-record *disassociate* strategy may also be seen to be operating as a specific sub-strategy of the *criticism* impolite strategy (see Section 5.3.1, below), which appears to be communicated in an off-record manner by implicitly associating the interlocutor with a 'negative image'. The combined, multi-function aspects of individual utterances being, simultaneously, more than one impoliteness strategy is more fully explored in Chapter 6 (Section 6.2.1), where I discuss complex impoliteness.

Other instances of the *disassociate* impoliteness strategy may well include disassociating the other from a *formally* organised group of which others may consider themselves to be a part, as in the following example taken from the military training data set, **Soldiers To Be, Extract 28**.

[9] ***Context:*** *Recruit rifleman Parry has, for the second time, been fighting with his fellow recruits while under the influence of alcohol. This second time he beat a recruit so badly that the other recruit was sent for medical treatment. The attack was relatively unprovoked and is primarily due to Parry's inability to conduct himself in an appropriate manner while under the influence of alcohol. As the second offence of this nature, Parry's punishment cannot be dealt with by either his platoon commander or his company commander. He is to be referred to the OC – Officer Commanding – the training regiment. In the meantime (S1) the CSM – Company Sergeant Major – a very senior and experienced N.C.O. has called Parry (S2) into his office. The reasons for this are unclear. It may be because the CSM is angry with Parry and wishes this to be known by him, or it may be in order for the CSM to be able to make a recommendation to the Commanding Officer when Parry's case comes up based on how he reacts to the line of questioning.*

[…]

10. S1: *I'm hoping the OC recommends you to be discharged from the army*
    S2:

11. S1: *. I don't want you . because you are a pathetic individual* do you
    S2:

12. S1: understand
    S2:

[…]

Here we see S1 disassociate himself on a personal level from S2 by saying *I don't want you* (and indirectly disassociating S2 from the army in general when he says *I'm hoping the OC recommends you to be discharged from the army*). Of course, discharge need not, necessarily be a matter of impolite disassociation. The clause, *because you are a pathetic individual* is crucial to our understanding here as, through the additional use of the insulting *pathetic individual* (captured in Culpeper's (1996)

Call h names – use derogatory nominations), S1, in the role of sergeant major, is disassociating recruit Parry from himself, and by implication, from the army.

5.1.3 Be uninterested, unconcerned, unsympathetic (adapted from Culpeper 1996: 357)

The following is notable as an impolite strategy for the unsympathetic tack taken by one of the interactants. Example taken from **Soldiers To Be, Extract 32.**

[10] ***Context***: *Recruit Wilson, S2, is finding the training hard. She is short and finds it hard to keep up with the rest of the platoon on march. Furthermore, once back at camp she falls asleep in class for which she is disciplined. She decides to PVR – that is, she decides to take Premature Voluntary Release – from the army. She calls on the platoon sergeant, S1, who takes a rather interesting tack in order to encourage her to stay.*

1. S1: it's now twenty past eight you have your P V R letter in to me by
   S2:
2. S1: quarter to nine and three reasons why you wish to P V R
   S2: <indistinct>
3. S1: right.now let's see..let's go back to.week one....this is what week one
   S2:
4. S1: says 'recruit Wilson is a quiet member of the section and platoon . is
   S2:
5. S1: immature' what would you say about that ... would that acc *hey don't*
   S2: [starts crying at accusation of immaturity]
6. S1: *stand there bubbling because it makes no difference to me you can*
   S2:
7. S1: *bubble all you want* stand there look at me and answer my question
   S2:
8. S1: does that accurately reflect you.I think it does.you are immature right
   S2:

[...]

Here S1 shows himself to be unsympathetic to S2's crying with the phrase (staves 5–7) *hey don't stand there bubbling because it makes no difference to me you can bubble all you want*. Such an utterance can be captured within the impolite linguistic strategy of *Be disinterested* (sic! cf. 'uninterested'*), unconcerned, unsympathetic* (Culpeper 1996: 357). It is worth noting here that S2 only started crying when faced with the accusation that she is immature. By crying, it could well be that she self-proves the accusation which has made her so upset and, thus, self-damages (or confirms the damage).

5.1.4 Use inappropriate identity markers Culpeper (1996: 357)

In the next example we can see instances of impoliteness that are inappropriate identity markers, one of which is also sarcastic. This extract is taken from **Soldiers To Be, Extract 28.** (See Section 5.1.2, example [9], above, for context)

[11]

1. S1: right come in .... *right my young fellow* explain your fucking actions
   S2:
2. S1: to me because I am not a happy ted.[4]
   S2:

[...]

6. S1: you know something *my young feller* I . it's a good job you was not in
   S2:
7. S1: the army ten years ago when I was at a rank where I could actually
   S2:
8. S1: beat the living daylights out of you
   S2:

[...]

12. S1: me Parry   you have got a drink problem *my friend* do you
    S2:   yes sir
13. S1: understand that
    S2:   yes sir

[...]

In no less than three instances does S1 appear to use insincere and inappropriate identity markers. The use of the first two – *my young fellow* (stave 1) and *my young feller* (stave 6) – appear to be overtly patronizing and insincere. The third instance of an inappropriate identity marker is perhaps the clearer example with the use of the phrase *my friend* (stave 12). Clearly, the relationship pertaining between these two; the CSM and the sometimes-violent-when-drunk recruit; is not so close as to permit either to consider themselves friends of the other and so the

4. *happy ted[dy bear]; not a.* This is a colloquial term indicating one is upset; not happy with the actions of another, or of an event which has taken/due to take place.

use is somewhat sarcastically inappropriate. Such usage could be captured within Culpeper's (1996: 357) *Use inappropriate identity markers – for example, use title and surname when a close relationship pertains, or a nickname when a distant relationship pertains*. Note, as mentioned, this example clearly shows that there is a significant degree of overlap with the *Sarcasm* strategy (cf. Culpeper 1996, 2005). Indeed, sarcasm appears to be one of the most likely strategies to combine with other tactics and strategies.

Other instances of this type are hard to find within my data sets. Within military discourse, anecdotal evidence outside of the data sets would consider the use of *Mister* to be a polite way of addressing an officer of a lower rank than oneself, but is potentially impolite when used by a non-commissioned officer, or by a private soldier to an officer, as the following example shows:

[12] ***Context:*** *In Tom Clancy's novel, 'Red Storm Rising', set in the mid 1980s, the government of the USSR, faced with a crippling fuel shortage, decide on the radical course of action of invading the Middle East to secure oil. In order to do so, without undue interference from western nations, the Soviets make moves to disband NATO politically. The KGB engineer the placing of a bomb, apparently by a West German agent, in the Kremlin. The bomb kills a number of politicians, staff and visiting 'Young Oktoberists' – children of Communist party members. Enraged and apparently 'justified', the USSR declares war on West Germany and invades – the ploy to separate the NATO nations, and sow confusion in the west (leaving the way open for a Soviet dash to the Middle Eastern Oilfields) fails. As such, in a daring move to close the Atlantic, and thus the supply of men and materiel between America and her European allies, the Soviets invade, and seize, Iceland. American forces there are taken by surprise and are virtually wiped out. Only officer Lieutenant Mike Richards, a young US Air Force meteorologist in his twenties, and veteran US Marine Sergeant Smith, with Marines Rodgers and Garcia survive to escape, with a radio-communications set, into the Icelandic hinterland. After contacting NATO command through Stornoway in Scotland, the four, under Lt. Edwards' command, are eventually instructed to move across 100 miles of Iceland's countryside, crawling with Soviet troops, to a secluded bay to report on Soviet activity as a forerunner to a NATO invasion to liberate Iceland. Sergeant Smith speaks first.*

> 'I don't even have cards for the whole coastline. Damn. Look here, Lieutenant. The ridges and rivers on this rock come out from the center like the spokes on a wheel, y'see? That means we climb a lot, and these here ain't little hills. All the low places got roads, and sure as hell we can't follow no roads, right?' He shook his head.
>
> Edwards forced a grin. 'Can't hack it? I thought you Marines were in good shape.'
>
> Smith was a man who ran five miles every morning. He could not recall ever seeing this little Air Force wimp out doing roadwork. 'Okay, Mr. Edwards.

> They say nobody ever drowned in sweat. On your feet, Marines, we got orders for a little hike.' Rodgers and Garcia exchanged a look. 'Mister' was not exactly a term of endearment for an officer, but Smith figured that insubordination only counted if the officer *knew* he was being insulted. (Clancy 1985: 351–2)

What is also interesting about this example is that it would appear that people are sometimes impolite to others for self-gratification purposes and, further, it is indicative of impoliteness only *being* impoliteness if someone (not necessarily the intended recipient) understands the utterance is intentionally face threatening/damaging. Although, of course, for impoliteness to be genuinely issued, a hearer/receiver has to understand it for what it is (for it to be, in other words, successfully face damaging – hence the use of 'Stay Silent' as a possible defensive counter strategy – see Chapter 7). The point here is that at least some strategies for communicating impoliteness may inherently have the extra-linguistic goal of some degree of speaker satisfaction alongside the other, extra-linguistic goals they seek to achieve through the use of impolite linguistic behaviour. This view is further strengthened by the continuing use of, or even the triggering of the use of, impoliteness once car owners realise that their goal of having their indictment for parking illegally quashed, fails as is sometimes the case. Further research on this is clearly needed.

5.1.5 Seek disgreement/avoid agreement Culpeper (1996: 357)

There were no specifically clear examples of the *Seek disagreement* strategy as presented in Culpeper (1996: 357). However, as I have suggested elsewhere (Bousfield 1999), there is a 'flip side' to the *Seek disagreement* strategy, that of *Avoid agreement*. Such a strategy could be one variation or sub-strategy not explored by Culpeper (1996) for the *Seek disagreement* strategy. An example of *Avoid agreement* as a conflictive, impolite strategy can be seen in the following, taken from **Extract 3** of **The Clampers** data.

[13] ***Context:*** *As this extract begins S2 the owner of an impounded car, along with friend S3 has gone down to the council offices to take his personal belongings out of the impounded car – S2 has decided to let the council keep his car. S1, the council official, is asking S2 for proof of identification and asked him to sign a waiver declaring his intentions for the car. S3 does not speak in this section of the extract.*

1. S1: will you sign me a disclaimer I need a disclaimer signed as well
   S2: eh
   S3:

2. S1: you you're just going to totally disclaim the vehicle yeah
   S2: I don't want the
   S3:

3. S1: oohh come on
   S2: car fuck it you lot can keep the car *no there's no come on*
   S3:

4. S1: <indistinct>
   S2: *because you've towed the car off my own . blasted road where I'm*
   S3:

5. S1: indistinct>
   S2: *staying right twice not once but twice* that's two nearly three hundred
   S3:

6. S1: all I need is identification
   S2: pounds
   S3:

[…]

Note S2 clearly avoids agreeing with S1's phrase urging him to reconsider (Stave 3 *oohh .. come on*). The phrase *no there's no come on because you've towed the car off my own . blasted road not once but twice*, is an extended *avoidance of agreement* which is qualified with the reason as to (an account of) why he is indeed avoiding agreement. He is clearly angry over the loss of his car, for which he blames the council, and he wants to threaten the face of S1 (a council employee) because of it. The 'reason' or account he gives operates here as a booster to the impoliteness. Note, Brown and Levinson (1987) assume that giving a reason is a politeness strategy, though the CA literature suggests an account can be given to support a dispreferred response to an first pair part of an adjacency pair (see Chapter 8, below). However, here, the speaker is using the reason/account to explain why he is (a) so upset (which is an indirect, off-record criticism of (i) the whole concept of clamping in particular, and (ii) of his interactant in general as she works for the council – the body which has enforced the removal of his car – this is evidenced through his use of the personal pronoun contracted with the verb 'have': *you've* to include his interactant in those whom he blames), and (b) why he's being impolite (to paraphrase: he seems to be saying, 'your actions have driven me to it!'). As such, his utterance could be said to be one variation of Culpeper's (1996: 357) *Seek Disagreement* impoliteness output strategy.

5.1.6 Use taboo words – swear, or use abusive or profane language (Culpeper 1996: 358)

In the next extract I will discuss the use of taboo language. This excerpt is taken from **The Clampers, Extract 12.**

[14] ***Context:*** *It is 7.30 in the morning. Bailiff S1 is making his first call of the day to a female driver S2 who has repeatedly ignored parking ticket payment requests. Her husband S3 is also present. S1 has just knocked on S2's door and S3 has answered it.*

1. S1: Court bailiffs is she in
   S2:
   S3: yeah yeah at the moment why what's the
2. S1: we've got a court order been issued sir for non payment of
   S2:
   S3: problem
3. S1: fines on this vehicle … Harrow council have authorised removal of
   S2:
   S3:
4. S1: the vehicle for non-payment of fines if you can manage to get that sir
   S2:
   S3:
5. S1: she's now got a sum payable of three hundred and twenty one pounds
   S2:
   S3:
6. S1: twenty five and the vehicle will be going into court storage . once
   S2:
   S3:
7. S1: she's paid the fine she can go and collect her vehicle from the court
   S2:
   S3:
   <S2 pushes then hits S1>
8. S1: storage fali facility alright
   S2: *what the fuck you doing* excuse me .
   S3:
9. S1: the car is going he has a court order
   S2: what are you *fucking* doing
   S3:

<S2 hits S1 in mouth – S1 starts dialling on the phone>

10. S1: police please yeah
S2: really you want some *fucking* money right
S3:

11. S1: <indistinct>
S2: all you have to do is ask for the money you don't
S3: all you have to do is ask for the *fucking* money right

12. S1: you can't get in the car madam
S2: have to *fucking* take the car
S3:

13. S1:
S2: *piss off* <indistinct>
S3: Jackie come here come here

[...]

What is interesting here is not only the number of times the strategy of 'use taboo language' is used, but the various *ways* in which taboo language is used. S2 deploys 5 uses of the 'use taboo language' strategy (in just this short excerpt taken from a longer extract: two in staves 8–9: '*what the fuck* you doing excuse me . what are you *fucking* doing', one in stave 10: 'really you want some *fucking* money right', one in staves 11–12: 'all you have to do is ask for the money you don't have to *fucking* take the car' and one in stave 13: '*piss off*'). Her husband, S3 deploys the use taboo language strategy once in this excerpt (Stave 10: 'all you have to do is ask for the *fucking* money right'). The use of such taboo terms could be captured in the strategy *Use taboo words* – swear, or *use abusive or profane language* (Culpeper 1996: 358).

The above example clearly shows two ways in which the strategy of using taboo language / profane swear words, is regularly deployed in the data sets studied. Note, first the use of the phrase *piss off*, by S2 in stave 11. This, unlike the other taboo usages, was aimed directly at S1 and was deployed in such a way as to offend, on-record (within the context and all other things being equal), purposefully, and gratuitously, the face of S1. She is telling S1, in no uncertain terms, that she wishes him to leave her, and what she sees as her belongings (the car) alone. She is predominantly opting to use what Culpeper (1996) called 'positive impoliteness' (but 'negative impoliteness' in his terms, is also used, as we will see). Note as with the vast majority of impoliteness strategies, the overall *effect* is that the utterances of S2 are both, in Culpeper's original (1996) terms, positively and negatively impolite. She is negatively impolite because the overall command she is making throughout her utterances is for S1 to 'go away' – an impingement on his freedom of action (including his power, his right, and, indeed, his obligation to remove the vehicle). In the context in which such a command is delivered, note, the lexical choices she makes (not to mention the physical violence she inflicts on S1) adds a clear dimension of positive face attack in that she is showing extreme disapproval. As such this 'combined positive and negative face' strategy of impoliteness (a) creates the overall evaluation of the act of command to 'go away' as being one of impoliteness, and (b) further strengthens the argument that a division between the two types is superfluous.

However, not all instances of taboo swear words are used in this, direct way. For example, the instance of the phrase of *what are you fucking doing* in stave 9, effectively has the use of the word *fucking* operating as a 'booster' (cf. Holmes 1984), enhancing the face threat of the main challenge (see Sections 5.5.4 and 8.4.3). The taboo word *fucking* in *what are you fucking doing?* (like the immediately prior *what the fuck you doing* also in stave 8), plays the grammatical role of intensifier (e.g. Quirk et al. 1985: 438–9 and 450), amplifying or boosting the force of the challenge. From an interpersonal perspective it indicates an extremely negative attitude of the speaker towards the hearer. Holmes (1984: 363) makes the following point: 'Devices may reinforce one another, as when strong stress, lexical Boosters and repetition co-occur in one utterance'. The cumulative effect of using mutually reinforcing impoliteness strategies is to boost, or enhance, the impoliteness. It is worth noting here that the *Use taboo words* strategy (Culpeper 1996) does appear to be the one most likely to combine with other strategies though further research on this score is clearly needed. The combination of impolite strategies in this and other ways will be discussed in more detail and depth in Chapter 6 (Section 6.2.1, see also the discussion made in Culpeper et al. 2003).

5.1.7 Threaten/frighten – instil a belief that action detrimental to the other will occur (Culpeper 1996: 358)

As with utterances which attack aspects of face concerned with approval, belonging and solidarity, those which attack aspects face relating to freedom of action are many and varied throughout the corpus of extracts studied in this book. Rather than present every example, I present a few examples of each main type of impolite utterance within each of the data sets studied. Examples of impolite strategies which, primarily, attack the addressee's face relating to freedom of action can be found across the data sets. Note the following example, taken from **The Clampers, Extract 3.**

[15] ***Context:*** *S2 and S3 have arrived at Wembley pound later that day to take the possessions out of S2's car. S4 is one of the clamping officers at the pound. After telling the*

camera that he's decided to leave the car, cut his losses and take his possessions, S2 makes to leave the pound, with S3 and confronts S4 as he does so

[…]

25. S2: *touch my fucking new car and I'll bust your fucking head off*
    S4: jackanory

[…]

S2, in this example makes an abstract, but yet rather interesting threat to clamping officer, S4. It is highly unlikely that S4 will be able to tell that any given future car which he clamps and removes belongs specifically to S2, unless he sees S2 leave the car illegally parked. That said, the threat above (coupled with force boosting *taboo* language (cf. Holmes 1984)), nevertheless appears to be designed to frighten S4. Such phenomena could be captured within Culpeper's impolite linguistic output strategy *Frighten – instil a belief that action detrimental to the other will occur* (1996: 358). Indeed, such impolitenesses were common across most of the data sets studied – another example of which we can see in the following, taken from **Boiling Point, Extract 61.**

[16] ***Context***: *Restaurant owner, S1, berates S2 regarding a dish that S2 was supposed to have prepared by now. It is late. This comes as the restaurant has the Michelin cookery guide inspectors in. S1 is already tense when this situation arises.*

1. S1: <indistinct> now.concentrate you you're just <bleep>
   S2: <indistinct>
2. S1: <bleep>trying to fuck it up for everybody here
   S2: oui Gordon yes Gordon
3. S1: <indistinct> you know whose this for what's
   S2: yes Gordon yes Gordon
4. S1: that there what's that for I don't give a fuck
   S2: oui Gordon <indistinct>
5. S1: about that dickhead *concentrate on keeping your job*
   S2: oui Gordon oui
6. S1:
   S2: Gordon

End.

Note here how, in the co-text (see Section 6.1.1) of other, abusive impoliteness strategies, S1 threatens S2 in stave 5 with the thinly veiled and only marginally off-record: *concentrate on keeping your job*. The implication here, generated via flouts of the maxims of Manner and Relation (Grice 1975), is that S2 is in danger of being released, involuntarily, from service by S1 (i.e. being "fired"), if he does not conform to S1's exacting standards. We should note that it is the preceding co-text and the implicature generated that make this utterance impolite which could, otherwise, be considered to fit the definition of off-record *politeness* (cf. Brown and Levinson 1987). This type of utterance can be considered to be an indirectly issued sub-strategy of Culpeper's *Frighten – instil a belief that action detrimental to the other will occur* impolite linguistic output strategy (1996: 358). This strategy, which threatens the addressee's face relating not only to his freedom of action (negative face), as Culpeper (1996) would have, but there's also a strong element of disapproval running throughout the extract which is tantamount to an impolite criticism communicated in an off-record manner. Such occurrences are by no means confined to the high-stress exchanges in kitchen discourse. It occurs across all the data sets studied and its realisation ranges in style, ferocity and in/directness.

5.1.8 Condescend, scorn or ridicule – emphasize your relative power. Be contemptuous Culpeper (1996: 358)

Condescension, scorn or ridicule can be powerfully impolite, as the following example indicates. Taken from **Extract 2, The Clampers.**

[17] ***Context:*** *S1 is a tribunal officer for Southwark council. He hears and decides upon appeals concerning parking tickets. S2 and S3 are a husband and wife (respectively) who are appealing against a ticket they received. This extract is taken from the terminal stages of their appeal hearing.*

[...]

10. S1: I've finished Mr Culp . will you will you will you please leave the
S2: in
S3:

11. S1: room I'm not answering any further questions . do you want me
S2: this situation
S3:

12. S1: to press the buzzer will you please
S2:
S3: *well that's being babyish isn't it*

13. S1: leave the room
    S2: for what reason
    S3:

[…]

Here S3, in response to S1's veiled threat of *do you want me to press the buzzer* (Stave 11), responds with the condescending utterance of *well that's being babyish isn't it?* in stave 12. Such an utterance is captured within the strategy of *Condescend, scorn or ridicule – emphasize your relative power. Be contemptuous*, in Culpeper (1996: 358). It is worth noting here Culpeper at al's (2003) remark about this example in that the power being emphasised by S3 is moral and not authoritative power (such as that indirectly threatened by S1 in staves 11–12, *do you want me to press the buzzer*). The types of power which pertain in instances where impoliteness is deployed bears consideration for future research.

5.1.9 'Explicitly' associate the other with a negative aspect – personalise, use the pronouns 'I' and 'you' (Culpeper 1996: 358)

The following, taken from **The Clampers, Extract 8,** is very interesting.

[18] ***Context:*** *Two 'Clampers' proceed to clamp an illegally parked car. Just as they have finished, the car's driver, a workman who was doing a job for a local homeowner, returns to his car to find it clamped, and the clampers still there. S1 is 'Ray' the clamping supervisor, S2 is 'Ammett' Ray's van driver and clamping assistant, S3 is Passing Heckler, S4 is Returning Workman and owner of the clamped van.*

[…]

Edit: *Up to this point there has been a confrontation between the clampers and the returning van owner. Following this the owner called the pound, paid by credit card over the phone to have the clamp released and then there was a brief pause where the Clampers get confirmation of payment. S1 is just finishing his radio call from base giving him authorisation to remove the clamp.*

20. S1: okay cheers bye we're going to declamp it
    S4: it all seems a bit pointless

21. S1:
    S4: doesn't it they're paying him to drive round collecting money I

22. S1:
    S4: mean why not invest it in parking meters don't you think this is a bit

23. S1: = well you see I'm just doing a job but I've come along here
S4: stupid= *yeah well so was Hitler*

24. S1: and yeah well
S4: all I'm asking you as a person don't you think this is a bit stupid

25. S1: <exhalation> yes and no
S2:

[...]

In stave 23, S4's response to S1's claims that he is only doing his job is to associate, via the maxim of Relation (Grice 1975), S1 and his actions with Adolf Hitler. This is likely to be seen as impolite given the particular legacy and memory which Adolf Hitler left the world.[5] Such utterances could be captured, as variants, with the impolite output strategy, *Explicitly associate the other with a negative aspect – personalize* (sic), *use the pronouns 'I' and 'you'*. (Culpeper 1996: 358). Note however there is an issue, at least in this extract, with the use of the word *Explicitly* to describe the strategy. The associations that S4 is making between S1, S1's job and Adolf Hitler are not at all explicit, rather, they're more indirect (but no less face threatening for all that) amounting, essentially, to an *off-record impolite criticism* and a *dismissal* of S1's attempts to defend himself (see Chapter 7). Indirect /off-record utterances by their very nature are not explicit. As such, whilst not marked with those linguistic features as the use of personal pronouns which Culpeper would suggest are typical of the strategy, the association made here, is still face threatening, for all its indirectness. Note further, that although Culpeper originally cast this as a 'negative face' directed impoliteness strategy there is also a case to be made for the above example being seen as impoliteness directed against the want to be approved of ('positive face'). Associating the clamper with Adolf Hitler is, clearly, an attempt to communicate that the speaker *does not approve* of the clamper's actions as claiming one is just doing one's job does not excuse one from performing reprehensible acts. Beyond the by-now obvious issues with maintaining a distinct list of positive/negative impoliteness strategies, it may be that the wording here needs to be changed to accommodate the variations inherent in both this extract and in the following example taken from **The Clampers, Extract 1:**

[19] ***Context:*** *Ray and Miguel, clamping supervisor and assistant respectively have arrived to remove the clamp from a van. The van's owner is waiting for them. S1 is Ray, S2, the van's owner, S3 – Miguel – does not speak throughout this extract.*

5. Though, admittedly, this is dependent upon the political affiliations and preferences of each.

[…]

17. S1: can't park on a yellow line sir there's nothing I can do about it I
S2:

18. S1: simply work for the council=
S2: =*don't give me you just wear the uniform*

19. S1: I do wear I work for the council sir you need to
S2: *so you're as just as much to blame as*

20. S1: you you you you need to contact the council
S2: *everybody else as far as I'm concerned*

[…]

28. S1: I don't have to talk to you if you're going to be rude to me yeah I
S2:

29. S1: that's fine then sir I
S2: I don't really want to talk to you you're not going to do anything

29. S1: I'm really not
S2: about it are you *as far as wearing your uniform is concerned*

30. S1:
S2: *they were doing that when they were shoving the guys into the*

31. S1:
S2: *gas chambers in Germany wearing the uniform does not matter*

32. S1:
S2: *you're just as culpable as anybody else*

[…]

Note in staves 29 to 32, S2's comment to S1 that *as far as wearing your uniform is concerned they were doing that when they were shoving the guys into the gas chambers in Germany wearing the uniform does not matter you're just as culpable as anybody else*. These remarks are linked to and, ultimately, are the culmination of the earlier remarks which S2 made in staves 18–20 *don't give me you just wear the uniform* and *so you're just as much to blame as everybody else as far as I'm concerned*, which were made in response to S1's efforts to Abrogate (see Chapter 7, Section 7.2.1.3) responsibility for the van being clamped. Together, S2's utterances make for a powerful condemnation of S1's actions by, among other things, *associating* S1 with specific, highly negative actions taken by some members of the German political authorities during WWII. Again, if we were to retain a distinction, as in the previous example, a *strong* case could be made for the orientation of these comments towards attacking the recipient's 'positive face' as well as 'negative face'. The indication that the speaker does not approve of the recipient of the utterance, is again quite clear.[6] As a brief aside, examples like these indicate quite clearly why it is, indeed, difficult to discuss im/politeness 'strategies' individually out of context. It all depends upon what perlocutionary effects the speaker is aiming to achieve.

5.2 Sarcasm/mock politeness

Culpeper (1996:356) notes that use of sarcasm (which he equates with the term 'Mock Politeness') can also convey impoliteness. Sarcasm, in Culpeper's terms, is the performance of 'politeness strategies that are obviously insincere, and thus remain surface realisations.' (Culpeper 1996:356, see also Culpeper 2005). This appears to be close to Leech's conception of irony (1983:82, 142). An example of sarcasm can be seen in the following example taken from **The Clampers, Extract 8.**

[20] ***Context:*** *Two 'Clampers' proceed to clamp an illegally parked car. Just as they have finished, the car's driver, a workman who was doing a job for a local homeowner, returns to his car to find it clamped, and the clampers still there. After an impolitely charged exchange, the Clampers return to their van to leave whilst S4 phones the clamping fines office to pay his release fee. As he is dialling the numbers he finds something to say to the retreating clampers:*

S1 – 'Ray' the clamping supervisor.
S4 – Returning Workman and owner of the clamped van.

[...]

14. S1: I will do
S4: <sarcastically> *have a good day*

[...]

Here, S4 issues a heavily sarcastic utterance when he says *have a good day*. The full impact of the sarcasm is only apparent whilst listening to the audio of the exchange. Culpeper et al. (2003) have shown how tonal and other phonological qualities can be used to make some utterances intensely impolite which, on the surface, would appear to be polite (as might be the case with S4's utterance in the stave transcription above if the notation <sarcastically> were removed). A perhaps

6. Indeed, all impoliteness, however realised, could, at least theoretically, be seen to include, on at least some minor level, a specific disapproval of the recipient, the recipient's beliefs, actions, etc... in order for such impoliteness to be issued in the first place.

clearer example of sarcasm (without needing to *overtly* consider the tonal qualities), is found in the following example, taken from **Redcaps, Extract 53.**

[21] ***Context:*** *Following his unsatisfactory showing at the morning's barrack room inspection, Private Baxter (S2) has an appointment with the Company Sergeant Major (S1). S1 is reprimanding S2 about his failure to get a haircut.*

[…]

20. S1: PRESENT YOUR BODY in front of the barber sitting in the chair
    S2:
21. S1: with the rest of your body square and square to the front and be in the
    S2:
22. S1: position of attention HE'LL THEN CUT YOUR HAIR .. you then
    S2:
23. S1: pay him the Queen's shilling and then move out why did you fail to
    S2:
24. S1: do it are you got an attitude problem then why didn't you get it
    S2: no sir
25. S1: cut … COME ON THEN . SPEAK TO ME
    S2: the queue was very
26. S1: *OH DEAR UNFORTUNATELY you had to queue up*
    S2: long sir and I

[…]

Note S1's comments in stave 26 here when he says *OH DEAR UNFORTUNATELY you had to queue up.* In light of the co-text of S1's earlier comments I think it is safe to say that this utterance, a shouted interruption, is sarcastic in nature. It is hard to believe that, following his earlier comments to S2, S1 would suddenly become genuinely sympathetic to the excuse S2 was offering as to why he did not have a haircut. Indeed, the audio of the extracts confirms the sarcastic tone in which it was issued. As such, we can only interpret this as being *impolite.*

5.2.1 Is mock politeness always offensive?

Is mock politeness (sarcasm) always offensive? Logically we would perhaps suspect that it is. After all, Culpeper notes for mock politeness that, '… the FTA is performed with the use of politeness strategies that are obviously insincere, and thus remain surface realisations.' (Culpeper 1996: 356). However, what follows is an intriguing example of mock politeness that is far from being merely a surface realisation. Hypothetically, it requires two further levels of interpretation to arrive at the apparent meaning. This example is taken from **The Clampers Extract 7**.

[22] ***Context:*** *S2: Sandy, a clamping assistant is late for work. S1: Ray, her supervisor is in discussion with her about it as the rest of the clamping team is preparing for the day's work. Ray and Sandy are good friends.*

1. S1: good morning sandy mcleod I trusted you sandy OKAY CHARLIE
   S2:
2. S1: <indistinct>can you get ready to go please the buses are awaiting your
   S2:
3. S1: arrival thank you very much you're a schizophreniac this morning
   S2:
4. S1: aren't you one minute you're as miserable as sin the next minute
   S2:
5. S1: you're laughing
   S2: I know it's what happens when you're late it puts a
6. S1: don't be late then
   S2: dampener on everything I know I do apologise but
7. S1: I was in a good mood when I woke up this
   S2: the baby wasn't well
8. S1: morning but looking at you you're making me miserable is it a hug is
   S2:
9. S1: that what you need this morning sure
   S2: no no I'm fine I know your
10. S1: <indistinct> you look very sad you allright
    S2: hugs takes the breath out of me
11. S1: OKAY LET'S GET READY TO GO PLEASE … am I nice
    S2: yeah
12. S1: to you how much do you
    S2: *you're the best boss anyone could ever have*
13. S1: love me then do you know how much I love you *no come here*
    S2: no
14. S1: *Sandy do you know how much I love you .. from the insects in the*
    S2:
15. S1: *ground to the last cloud in the sky* …. ya bitch
    S2: you're so sweet

End.

Note here S1's comments in staves 12 to 13: *no come here Sandy do you know how much I love you .. from the insects in the ground to the last cloud in the sky*. This is a very interesting form of mock politeness or sarcasm. S1 is being mock polite/sarcastic to S2, this much is clear from his flouting of the maxims of Quantity, Quality and Manner (Grice, 1975), thus an implicature is formed. This implicature being that he is insincere which constitutes a face-attack. However, this is not, in itself, a *sincere* attack on S2's face as it is an all-too-obvious flout, or, to put it another way it is an '*ostentatious ostentatious-transgression*' (or a case of double ostentatiousness).

What happens can be characterised thus:

1. S1's insincere face enhancement becomes (through the insincerity), a face attack;
2. Because of the friendship pertaining between S1 and S2 (as part of the background/context), this face attack and the over-the-top ostentatious flout, is rendered a face enhancement of S2 (but one not carrying the original force conveyed by the surface utterance).

In short what we have here is 'mock sarcasm', that is 'mock-mock-politeness', which is, generally speaking a face enhancement for the intended recipient. Indeed, such a comment appears to re-iterate and strengthen the existing social bonds between the two. While banter (mock impoliteness) and sarcasm (mock politeness) are, in Leech's (1983: 142) terms, 'second order principles', this *hyperbolic* form of 'mock-sarcasm' is, arguably, a 'third order principle' designed to strengthen the social bonds between individuals. More research on this type of phenomenon is clearly needed.

Obviously, sarcasm, in order to be effective, requires something more than mock, or insincere, impoliteness; like all types, varieties and strategies it requires a specific context (see Chapters 6 and 7). Research in this area, and its implications for mock impoliteness, is clearly worthy of further study, but, as ever, with the constraints of time and space, such concerns, for the present text, will have to remain an intriguing and potentially productive area for future research. One further note needs to be made here. Culpeper (1996, 2005) following Leech considers Sarcasm/Mock Politeness to be a second order principle. Here, in Chapter 4 I listed this as a sub-variety to the tactic of off-record impoliteness. I did this for two reasons: (i) sarcasm/mock politeness, by its very nature, can never be directly 'expressed' and, as such, is an off-record tactic, (ii) my proposed model here explicitly allows for the mixing, or combination (joint-and-simulataneous realisation) of multiple im/politeness strategies for effect. As such, the model proposed here accounts for both first, second (and even 'third') order principles.

5.3 Withholding politeness

Culpeper points out that impoliteness may be realised through, 'the absence of politeness work where it would be expected.' (Culpeper 1996: 357). Indeed, as Culpeper (1996: 357) notes, Brown and Levinson would appear to agree with the face-threatening aspects and implications surrounding the withholding of politeness when they claim:

> [...] politeness has to be communicated, and the absence of communicated politeness may, *ceteris paribus*, be taken as the absence of a polite attitude.
>
> (Brown and Levinson 1987: 5)

Examples of withheld impoliteness are, by their very nature, hard to identify with any degree of certainty. Instances can only be clearly identified when an interactant in an exchange goes *on record* to withhold politeness which may be expected at a particular juncture. An example of this, on-record withheld politeness occurs in the following example, taken from **The Clampers, Extract 2.**

[23] ***Context:*** *S1 is a tribunal officer for Southwark council. He hears and decides upon appeals concerning parking tickets. S2 and S3 are a husband and wife (respectively) who are appealing against a ticket they received. This extract is taken from the terminal stages of their appeal hearing whereupon the tribunal officer, S1, has refused their appeal on the grounds that the prefers the council's evidence to that of the plaintiffs, S2 and S3. After a brief exchange of argumentation, S1 closes the conversational floor and requests that the plaintiffs leave. They are unhappy with both he decision and the fact that they have no further time or leave to argue their case.*

[...]

12. S1: will you please leave the room
S2: for what reason
S3: that's being babyish isn't it

13. S1: I've finished I've finished .. the hearing
S2: are you turning us out for what reason I'm
S3: give us <--Indistinct-->

14. S1: erm right I understand I mean people do get cross erm
S2: furious there's been no
S3:

15. S1: er Mr Culp well thank you very
S2: compassion at all I don't understand
S3:

16. S1: much for coming good day
S2: *I don't thank you at all*
S3:

End.

Note here the 'on-record' withholding of politeness where it may otherwise be expected. Generally speaking, when a greeting is given by one interlocutor to another, another greeting is, usually, forthcoming immediately afterwards. This is one of many adjacency pairs (cf. Schegloff and Sacks 1973), which, as an aspect of preference organisation within the field of conversational analysis, I discuss in greater depth in Chapter 8.

In staves 15–16, S2 goes on record to say that *I don't thank you at all.* In breaking the expectations of the adjacency pairs, in refusing to reciprocate thanks, S2's on record withholding of politeness is highly marked and, thus, interpretable as a form of impoliteness given the context. In the model outlined earlier (Chapter 4) I suggested that 'withhold politeness' is an off-record sub-tactic – this is because it is predominantly 'conspicuous by its absence', that is to say, when an interlocutor withholds politeness, it is difficult to say whether or not it is meant as impoliteness (hence, it is, predominantly, *off-record*). The example here, whilst rare, does serve as a good example of the variable nature of the strategies with regards to 'on' or 'off' record realisation. The distinctions between the varieties are, therefore, best viewed as scalar and non-discrete.

5.4 Strategies from Culpeper (1996) not realised in the corpus

There were a number of strategies predicted by Culpeper (1996) to be possible devices for conveying impoliteness that simply did not occur in any of the examples from the whole corpus here studied. These were, *Use obscure or secretive language – for example, mystify the other with jargon, or use a code known to others in the group, but not the target* (Culpeper 1996: 357); *Invade the other's space – literally (e.g. position yourself closer to the other than the relationship permits) or metaphorically (e.g. ask for, or speak about information which is too intimate given the relationship),* (Culpeper 1996: 358); and *Put the other's indebtedness on record* (Culpeper 1996: 358). Even though no clear or specific examples of these strategies appeared in the data taken from the data sets studied, this does not mean that such strategies will not occur in other examples within the discourses studied or in other data sets yet to be explored.

In addition to the above three strategies there were no, specific, utterance level instances of interactants deploying the *Make the other feel uncomfortable – for example do not avoid silence, joke or use small talk* strategy within any of the examples studied (Culpeper 1996: 358). However, there are two issues concerning this strategy. First, there may well be other data sets, or indeed other examples within the *types* of data sets here studied in which *Make the other feel uncomfortable* is deployed, as a strategy, at the level of the utterance (rather than as an effect, deliberate or otherwise, of other face threatening strategies being deployed) for the purposes of damaging the face of an interactant. Second, and perhaps most importantly, it was quite clear that making one's interlocutor feel uncomfortable is always achieved with successfully issued impoliteness. An example will clarify the point here, taken from **Soldiers To Be, Extract 37**.

[24] ***Context***: *Sergeant 'Tich' Lovall, S1 addresses all of the recruits following that morning's barrack room inspection.*

1. S1: but worse than not achieving the standard . you just have not even
   S2:
2. S1: tried . you have not bothered . I do not expect you to get it right . but I
   S2:
3. S1: do expect you to give me a hundred percent .. you have not done that
   S2:
4. S1: and I warned you right at the beginning . if you cannot motivate
   S2:
5. S1: yourself I will motivate you . simple . your life is shite . get fell in
   S2:
6. S1. outside now ..... GET OUTSIDE NOW
   S2.

End.

Here, Sergeant 'Tich' Lovall is remonstrating with a group of cadets who have performed, in his opinion, poorly during barrack room inspection. His rather critical comments of *but worse than not achieving the standard . you just have not even tried* (Stave 1) coupled with *you have not bothered* (Stave 2), start to accumulate with his later critical, warning comments that *I do expect you to give me a hundred percent .. you have not done that and I warned you right at the beginning . if you cannot motivate yourself I will motivate you* (Staves 2–4). The cumulative effect of these words together, which seem to be further exacerbated by the utterance *simple . your life is shite*, may not, on the surface, be operating to make the recruits feel uncomfortable in the way in which Culpeper envisaged the strategy would work. Nevertheless they do seem to be having that very effect upon them overall. In short, the cumulative effect of these individual criticism strategies (see Section 5.3.1 below), have the effect of making the recruits 'feel uncomfortable' for not achieving the standard which was expected of them. Many 'dressing down' activity type exchanges in military training discourse, and even criticisms in other discourses are done for this explicit purpose – making the recipient feel uncomfortable. With respects to the military training discourse, the recipient(s) will, therefore, take more care and attention, and put in more effort the next time that such a task is required of them. For military training purposes this makes for a more diligent, more efficient and more effective soldier all round, which is, quite clearly, the overall goal of all military training personnel with regards their charges. The fact that they choose to do so not only by patient and repeated teaching, but also by impoliteness containing instruction, may well have something to do with the fact that the latter tactic appears to foster 'common enemy syndrome' which operates to bond the recruits together into a protective, supportive group in antithesis to the instructors. In other discourses, the reasons for making the hearer feel uncomfortable are dependent on the context and the extra-linguistic goals of the participants. However, from the data sets here studied it appears that making one's interlocutors feel uncomfortable may be what impoliteness is all about. It may be that Culpeper's original definition (Culpeper 1996) is underspecified and in need of reconceptualisation. As it stands, this strategy is always an issue where impoliteness is successful.

5.5 Utterances not covered by Culpeper's (1996) strategies

Culpeper (1996) explicitly acknowledges there may well be other strategies for conveying impoliteness – ones that his model does not predict. This concept of potential, additional strategies shadows the acknowledgement of additional strategies being possible within the model of politeness as proposed by Brown and Levinson (1987). As Leech (1999) points out, Brown and Levinson's model is an open ended one. Indeed, in the data sets studied it is necessary to identify and adopt a few additional strategies in order to adequately and accurately describe what is taking place. I have already noted a few variants on the strategies suggested by Culpeper (1996), such as *Avoid Agreement,* an addendum to the *Seek Disagreement* strategy above, and the *Threaten* strategy, which I have termed a variant of the similar, but not wholly synonymous, *Frighten* strategy (Culpeper 1996: 358). However the adoption of other, additional, strategies showed themselves to be necessary in describing the impolitenesses that were occurring. These were the following:

5.5.1 Criticise – dispraise h, some action or inaction by h, or some entity in which h has invested face

Whilst Culpeper does not explicitly consider the concept of criticism as an impolite positive face threatening strategy, its existence is tacitly accepted when Culpeper's (1996) model draws interpretative power from Leech's (1983) Politeness Principle. For, as Leech (1983: 135) notes, the approbation maxim of the PP states: Minimise dispraise of other; Maximise praise of other. Logically, one mechanism by which an interlocutor may be impolite could be if the approbation maxim was broken intentionally to '*maximise* dispraise of other'. A criticism could, therefore, be powerfully impolite. Note the use of a criticism in the following extract, taken from **The Clampers, Extract 1.**

[25] ***Context:*** *Ray and Miguel, clamping supervisor and assistant respectively, have arrived to remove the clamp from a van. The van's owner is waiting for them. S1 is Ray, S2, the van's owner, S3 – Miguel – does not speak throughout this extract. Up to this point they have been arguing over the fact that S2's van has been clamped, the legality of that particular instance and the ethics of clamping in general. S1 has tried to keep the exchange limited to the incident at hand and has repeatedly informed S2 of the actions he needs to take in order for S2 to make these comments and complaints. He tries again as this fragment of the extract starts:*

[…]

20. S1: you need to contact the council and make your=
    S2: =I have just gone

21. S1:
    S2: down there and paid them and I have my form but that doesn't make

22. S1:
    S2: up for the time I've lost the inconvenience and the hassle and what is

23. S1: well I fully
    S2: basically government legalised extortion does it

24. S1: appreciate what you're saying but what I'm saying to you I can take
    S2: I'm sure you do I'm sure you hear it

25. S1: your notes I can take your notes on board but there's nothing I
    S2: ten times a day

26. S1: personally can do I simply work do my job for the council
    S2: just do your job

27. S1: I do my job for the coun *if you want me to explain then if you*
    S2: I don't care what you do

28. S1: *want be like that then I can walk away I don't have to talk to you if I*
    S2:

29. S1: *don't want to if you're going to be rude to me yeah*
    S2:

[…]

Here we see a criticism issued by the Clamper S1. In staves 27 to 28 he issues the utterance (which includes a false start), *if you want me to explain then if you want be like that then I can walk away I don't have to talk to you if I don't want to if you're going to be rude to me yeah,* which, as a counter strategy (see Chapter 7) is, if initially inarticulate, a criticism of S1's impolite, unsympathetic 'snub' issued in Stave 27: *I don't care what you do.*

However, the identification and classification of 'criticise' as a strategy will only take the analyst so far. It needs to be noted that not all forms of impolite criticism occur in this way within the data sets studied. Criticism, as a strategy, can either underlie other (verbalised) strategies, or can be a component part of other strategies. Where criticism is a component part of another strategy is where the 'Challenge' impolite strategy occurs (see below). We will see, in Chapter 6, the more dynamic aspects of where criticisms underlie other, verbalised, strategies. Here, suffice it to say, criticism appears to be a strategy of a very different order to some of the strategies found in Culpeper (1996).

5.5.2 Hinder/block – physically (block passage), communicatively (deny turn, interrupt)

As a strategy, the idea of being impolite through interruptions was initially touched upon by Culpeper (1996) but was not named. It is referred to as *hindering* in Bousfield (1999) but Culpeper et al. (2003) later adopted the term *blocking* in. While it could potentially be viewed as a variant of the *Invade the other's space* strategy (Culpeper 1996: 358), *hindering* or *blocking* an interactant is presented here as an individual strategy as its realisations are sufficiently different from the description of *Invade* as given by Culpeper (1996), in that:

> *Invade the other's space* – literally (e.g. position yourself closer to the other than the relationship permits) or metaphorically (e.g. ask for, or speak about information which is too intimate given the relationship). (Culpeper 1996: 358)

Invading the other's space, primarily affects, and plays upon, the relationship between the interlocutors, whereas *blocking* stops individuals from taking a turn on the conversational floor (see Sections 5.5.2 and 8.2) or from withdrawing from a conversational exchange (see Section 7.3.5) – in effect, blocking primarily affects the structural flow of the interaction and, hence, threatens the target's freedom of action as well as their need for approval in that it both stops the target from taking a turn and indicates that their views are not wanted, welcome or valued.

Examples of interactants physically *blocking* the passage of another do exist in my data. However, as the following prototypical example shows they are ambiguous at best. Example taken from **The Clampers, Extract 13.**

[26] ***Context:*** *S1 is a clamping supervisor and has received a direct order from the council to assist in the immediate removal of a clamped minicab. The council want the vehicle removed immediately as the driver S2 has threatened to cut the clamp off. However, S2 is preventing S1 and colleagues from removing the vehicle by refusing to get out of the car (The parking officials, on the one hand, are obliged to remove the vehicle especially if there is a threat of the car being illegally declamped (i.e. having the clamp cut off), on the other hand they are not allowed to remove any vehicle with a person, or animal, living or dead, who, or which, is inside it).*

1. S1: Chris can you phone the police to come to Doddington Grove please
   S2:
2. S1: he won't allow us to remove the vehicle you say you sent someone to
   S2: just
3. S1: the parking shop they've just
   S2: I've sent them to pay for the ticket
4. S1: gone just now well as far as we're concerned what we've received
   S2:
5. S1: from the parking shop is the fact that you said you were going to cut
   S2:
6. S1: the clamp off
   S2: someone must be playing pranks because I only made
7. S1:
   S2: one call and the woman said I should pay sixty eight pounds
8. S1: I'll just go and see if they've arrived there and made your payment
   S2:

9. S1: yeah .... hi Jean can you check if you've got a payment
S2: alright then

10. S1: coming in for this vehicle yet .. okay
S2:

Edit: *The police arrive.*

[...]

It is the fact that the vehicle owner refuses to leave his vehicle, rather than anything he says, specifically, in the explanatory extract, that is *hindering* the clampers by blocking their attempts to remove his vehicle. Whether his main aim, or even a peripheral aim of his, is to offend the face of the clampers is ambiguous at best. Again, because of the non-vocalised nature of *physically blocking* someone, clear unambiguous examples could only be seen when an interactant went on record to note that they were blocking someone. That said, it is not too hard to imagine a situation in which physically hindering someone could be construed as extremely impolite. Note the following example taken from a novel by author of counterfactual fiction, Harry Turtledove.

[27] ***Context***: *In the series of novels entitled 'World War' and their successors, 'Colonisation', Turtledove depicts a world in which technologically superior alien life forms, evolved from Lizards, invaded the Earth in 1942. By 1964 their conquest is far from complete but one of the many areas annexed and ruled by the Lizards, who call themselves, 'The Race', is China. The Chinese, despite being fractious, universally rankle under the Race's rule. The following is an extract taken from the final book in the Colonisation series, entitled 'Aftershocks' (p. 379) and describes a Lizard armoured fighting vehicle out on patrol as it unsuccessfully attempts to negotiate its way speedily along the overcrowded 'Hsia Hsieh Chieh' or Lower Slanting Street in Peking. The Chinese call the shorter-than-human Lizards, 'Little Scaly Devils', and in keeping with this Mindstyle this is how Turtledove's narrator refers to them when describing their actions in China.*

> The little scaly devils' machine tried to slide into a space just ahead. But a man on an oxcart squeezed in first. He had to lash the ox to make it move fast enough to get ahead of the armored vehicle. As soon as he found himself in front of it, he set down the whip and let the ox amble along at its own plodding pace. That did infuriate the scaly devils. Their machine let out a loud, horrible hiss, as if to cry, *Get out of the way!* The man on the oxcart might have been deaf, for all the good that did them.
> People ... laughed and cheered. The fellow on the oxcart took off his broad straw hat and waved it, acknowledging the applause. If the little scaly devils understood that, it probably made them angrier than ever. Unless they chose to get violent, they could do nothing about it. (Turtledove 2001: 379)

Here we can clearly see that the man on the oxcart specifically and gratuitously chose to physically *block*, or rather, *hinder* the passage of members of the alien *Race* for the purposes of offending their collective face, (whilst, no doubt, giving himself and the onlookers a sense of satisfaction).

On the other hand, interruptions and turn denials are a common occurrence of impoliteness, especially in the Army training data set as shown in this example, taken from **Redcaps, Extract 53.**

[28] ***Context:*** *Following his unsatisfactory showing at the morning's barrack room inspection, Private Baxter (S2) has an appointment with the Company Sergeant Major (S1). Baxter marches into the CSM's office as the extract starts.*

1. S1: go on get out GET OUT . when you arrive in my office
S2:
2. S1: ENSURE that your arms are locked into the side of your body
S2:
3. S1: and your thigh's <at a right angle>and you put your foot down in the
S2:
4. S1: position of ATTENTION with your feet at an angle thirty degrees to
S2:
5. S1: the rest of your body and left hand square to the front DO YOU
S2:
6. S1:UNDERSTAND if you don't march in right this time it'll
S2: YES SIR
7. S1: be A CONVICTION why *why are you*
S2: [S2 marches in and salutes]
8. S1: *in front of me now .. I'LL TELL YOU WHY* because you've failed to
S2:
9. S1: comply with two verbal orders *is that true or is that not true IT IS*
S2: sir
10. S1: *TRUE ISN'T IT* but what is the first one you have failed on Monday
S2:
11. S1: evening you were told to put your name in all your military items of
S2:
12. S1: clothing *did you do it . NO YOU DIDN'T .* WHY NOT
S2: no excuse sir

[…]

Note here that on no less than three separate occasions (staves 6–7: *why are you in front of me now .. I'LL TELL YOU WHY*, staves 8–9: *is that true or is that not true IT IS TRUE ISN'T IT* and 11: *did you do it . NO YOU DIDN'T*), in this segment from the extract alone, S1 first allocates, then impolitely denies turns to S2. These would appear to have been done, primarily, at the very least, for the purposes of damaging the face of S2. Thus noted here, I shall return to the concept of interruptions and turn denials for discussion in Chapter 8.

5.5.3 Enforce role shift

As an impolite output strategy this strategy operates by forcing the intended recipient out of one social and/or discoursal role and into another (see Chapter 7). This could be said to be, primarily, an attack upon negative face as it impinges on the recipient's freedom of action (though, their positive face is also an issue by virtue of the fact that, in being impolite to them, an interlocutor has taken issue with some action, stance, or situation of *h's* with which *s* does not approve. (See 'trigger events' Chapters 4 (Section 4.5.4) and 7 (Section 7.1.4)). Examples of this impolite strategy can be found in the following example, taken from **Extract 8, The Clampers**.

[29] ***Context:*** *Two 'Clampers' proceed to clamp an illegally parked car. Just as they have finished, the car's driver, a workman who was doing a job for a local homeowner, returns to his car to find it clamped, and the clampers still there. S1 is the clamper, S4 the vehicle's owner.*

[...]

Edit where the clampers get confirmation that the vehicle owner has paid the release fee. S1 is just finishing his radio call from base giving him authorisation to remove the clamp

20. S1: okay cheers bye we're going to declamp it
    S4: it all seems a bit pointless

21. S1:
    S4: doesn't it they're paying him to drive round collecting money I

22. S1:
    S4: mean why not invest it in parking meters *don't you think this is a bit*

23. S1: = well you see I'm just doing a job but I've come along here
    S4: *stupid=* yeah well so was Hitler

24. S1: and yeah well
    S4: *all I'm asking you as a person don't you think this is a bit stupid*

25. S1: <exhalation> yes and no
S2:

[...]

Note the enforcing of a role switch by S4 on S1 when he attempts to shift S1 out of his role of 'representative' and 'mouthpiece' for the local council, and enforce the role of 'private citizen', when he says in staves 22–23: *don't you think this is a bit stupid.* And, after initally failing he attempts it again in stave 24, when he explicitly indicates how, and in what role, he expects S1 to answer, when he says: *all I'm asking you as a person don't you think this is a bit stupid.* The identification of the offensive strategy 'enforce role switch' in stave 22 is only sustainable in the light of the co-text in S4's second turn in stave 24, when he makes the metapragmatic comment *I'm asking you as a person* to explicity clarify his intent. The dynamics of social and discoursal roles are also an issue in 'counter strategies', as we shall see (Chapter 7).

5.5.4 Challenges

Challenges are always issued in the form of a question. We can define the strategy thus: *Challenge – ask* h *a challenging question, question* h's *position, stance, beliefs, assumed power, rights, obligations, ethics, etc.* The *Challenge* strategy is discussed in Lachenicht (1980: 668–671), who draws upon the discussion in Labov and Fanshel (1977). Labov and Fanshel consider challenges to be requests for action or information which are critical (1977: 93).

Impolitely challenging an interactant is simultaneously, in Culpeper's (1996) terms, both 'positively' and 'negatively' face damaging. This is because of the two fundamental ways in which 'challenges' work, or rather, the two separate types of the Challenge strategy that exist as either (a) Rhetorical, or (b) Response Seeking.[7] The rhetorical aspects of challenges can cause '*negative face damage*' as they are equivalent to strong assertions that attempt to force the intended recipient to respond in a highly restricted and self-damaging way (see, Quirk et al. 1985. See also Chapter 8, this book, for further, in depth, elaboration of this point). Chal-

7. The differences between Rhetorical and Response-seeking Challenges are fuzzy and not at all clear. Response-seeking challenges often *appear* as rhetorical questions in their own right. However, the response that is sought in response-seeking challenges is there, merely, to force the responder to go *on record* to say what does not need to be said in order that the responder damages their own face in doing so. Often it is only the context and/or the response of the intended recipient, that can help us, as interlocutors and as analysts, decide which type of challenge has been issued. See Chapter 8 for a fuller discussion.

lenges also, in at least equal measure, can cause '*positive face damage*' as they all carry an underlying criticism (see Labov and Fanshel 1977: 93–96) of the intended recipient in some way. Examples of challenges in the data sets studied include the following, taken from **Extract 1, The Clampers.**

[30] ***Context:*** *Ray and Miguel, clamping supervisor and assistant respectively have arrived to remove the clamp from a van. The van's owner is waiting for them. S1 is Ray, S2, the van's owner, S3 – Miguel – does not speak throughout this extract.*

[…]

1. S1: hi there sir this yours
   S2: yeah it is yeah I'd like to er ask you why you
2. S1: why we clamped it you see
   S2: clamped it yeah there's nobody here for one
3. S1:
   S2: hundred and fifty yards it's not doing any offence I was in there
4. S1: well it is doing an offence let me stop you just there
   S2: getting my tools out when
5. S1: because it is doing an offence straight away parked on a yellow line
   S2:
6. S1: parked on a yellow line
   S2: what's wrong with a ticket it's extortion you
7. S1: can you
   S2: know it is it's government extortion it's absolutely outrageous
8. S1: can you just answer me one question can you see the yellow line
   S2:
9. S1: visibly under your car
   S2: …I live here *why is there a yellow line*
10. S1:
    S2: *anyway why do I have to park my car three hundred yards up the*
11. S1:
    S2: *road* it gets stolen broken into vandalised three times this year
12. S1:
    S2: already *why have you done it why do you make my life impossible*
13. S1: can I just say you you you can
    S2: *how am I supposed to work doing this* <----indistinct----->

14. S1: clearly see the yellow line on the road it's not a new yellow line its
    S2:

15. S1: been there for quite some time
    S2: *so why don't you just stop the ticket*

[…]

S2 issues no less than five challenges to S1. The first three (staves 8–9 and 10–11), challenges, *why is there a yellow line anyway, why do I have to park my car three hundred yards up the road, how am I supposed to work*, have some potential for just being predominantly 'incidentally' face-damaging utterances (i.e. the speaker is merely giving vent to personal vexation). However, two of the challenges, *why have you done it,* and *why do you make my life impossible,* are more clearly directed at S1 through the use of personalised pronouns ('why have *you* done it?' and 'why do *you* make my life impossible?'). It is more likely that these are impolite utterances, deployed predominantly to aggravate the face of S1. Additionally, the rhetorical nature of some of the questions, particularly the final two (staves 10–11) *why do you make my life impossible* and *how am I supposed to work doing this,* is part of a strategy to implicate, via the Maxim of Manner (Grice 1975), the impolite belief that S1 makes S2's life difficult. In this context these are, in Labov and Fanshel's terms (1977), requests for information which can only be heard as being critical. Indeed, as we will see in Chapter 8, the way in which the challenges are worded makes it difficult for the addressee to avoid self-damage if they are responded to in the way to which the original issuer (the 'challenger') expects. Interestingly, S1 opts not to answer the challenges here directly, but rather issues a relatively mild criticism of S2's decision to park where he did in the first place – the reason this is interesting is that Labov and Fanshel predict that '[t]he reply to a challenge is either a *defense* or an *admission*.' (Labov and Fanshel 1977: 98).[8] In effect, then, S2's response is a defensive one which points out the challenger's own infraction. Note however that this, 'defensive reply' sparks, or 'triggers' (see Section 7.2.1.3, below) another challenge in stave 13. Interestingly again, Labov and Fanshel (1977: 95) consider repeated requests of this nature to be an aggravated form of criticism (see also Section 6.2.1.1, for further discussion of the effects of repeating impolite and aggravating utterances). As we can see, such utterances can be sophisticated face attacks. I shall return to the discussion of 'Challenges' in Chapter 8, (Section 8.4.2 'Challenges, Questions, Tags and Conducivity'), below.

8. See Chapter 6, Section 6.2.1.

5.6 A more complex example of impoliteness

The following example shows us a very interesting, multi-level way in which face may be attacked through various means. The extract is taken from **Boiling Point, Extract 68**

[31] ***Context***: *S1, Restaurateur Gordon Ramsay talks to S2, Mark, about an error that he (Mark) has just committed with regards the timing of the meal which he is preparing.*

1. S1: what what we doing what we doing mark what did I say mark what
   S2:
2. S1: did I say well you've got the ticket on <it's standing on the shelf> [S1
   S2:
3. S1: picks up the 4 dishes prepared by S2 and throws them into the bin]
   S2:
4. S1: what did I say . what did I say after the starter
   S2: <erm> after the starters Gordon
5. S1: <indistinct> has gone away and where are the starters
   S2: yes Gordon
6. S1: have they gone yet .... *you fuck off downstairs . right now*
   S2:
7. S1: *dreamer*
   S2: yes Gordon

End.

Here we see what appears to be an instance where, again, what Culpeper (1996) would consider to be simultaneous 'positive' and 'negative' face threatening effects are being produced by positive and negative impolite face threatening strategies. We can see, in stave 6, that restaurant owner Gordon Ramsay impolitely instructs S2 to go down into the cellar with *you fuck off downstairs . right now*, where there are no cooking facilities and where S2 can be of limited use (at best) to the rest of the cooking staff. S1 would appear to be excluding S2 rather gratuitously, as the use of the profane term *fuck off* with *right now* appear both to contribute to, and further exacerbate, the face threat. On one level, the order to go both attacks S2's 'negative' face (by imposing upon his presumed desire to stay and perform his job) and his 'positive' face (it excludes him from the activity, and from the group of cooking staff. cf. *Exclude the other from an activity* (Culpeper 1996: 357)) and, further, implies that he is of little value. On another level, the command to leave is exacerbated by the positive impolite strategy realised through the use of *fuck off (Use taboo words – swear, or use abusive or profane language* (Culpeper 1996: 358)), and a 'negative' impoliteness strategy realised through the use of *right now* which seems to be operating as a maximiser, boosting (cf. Holmes 1984) the face threat. Such maximisers are opposite in terms of orientation to those of Brown and Levinson's (1987) polite minimisers (e.g. '*Could* you do me a *little favour, when you have time?*[9]), in that maximisers aim to increase the face threat of an utterance whilst minimisers aim to reduce it.

I have already noted above, the face threatening implications which *dreamer* (also in stave 6), has for the positive face of S2, as S1 impolitely implies S2's concentration is lacking. And I noted that such phenomena as these can be captured with recourse to the positive impoliteness, linguistic strategy of *Call h names, use derogatory nominations* (Culpeper 1996: 358). However, when considered in context, being issued in quick succession to the mixed faced strategies in *you fuck off downstairs . right now* which S1 has deployed here, then we can see that Ramsay's contributions in stave 6 are even more highly damaging to both aspects of S2's face here. These types of combinations of impolite, face damaging strategies, and others, which I have discussed here in brief will be dealt with in more detail and more depth in Chapter 6.

5.7 Other considerations

5.7.1 Mock impoliteness

As the unmistakable flip side to mock politeness (sarcasm), mock impoliteness (banter) makes for an interesting concept – one which, ostensibly, appears to offend the face of the intended recipient but, which, in practice, serves to strengthen social bonds between the producer and intended recipient (cf. Labov 1972), as the following example taken from **The Clampers, Extract 7**, shows.

[32] ***Context:*** *S2: Sandy, a clamping assistant is late for work. S1: Ray, her supervisor is in discussion with her about it. They are good friends.*

[...]

12. S1: to you how much do you
S2: you're the best boss anyone could ever have

13. S1: love me then do you know how much I love you no come here
S2: no

9. Thanks to Jonathan Culpeper for this example.

14. S1: Sandy do you know how much I love you .. from the insects in the
    S2:

15. S1: ground to the last cloud in the sky .... *ya bitch*
    S2: you're so sweet

End.

Note the instance of mock impoliteness by S1 in stave 15 when he says *ya* (you) *bitch*. Given the context in which this had been uttered, the co-text preceding the actual utterance and the fact that the two are friends then we can safely assume this utterance, despite being apparently an abusive term of address, is, in fact, *mock impoliteness* which further strengthens the social friendship pertaining between the two (given the discussion made under Section 5.2.1, in the context of *mock politeness/sarcasm*, above). Thus briefly acknowledged, I do not intend to return to the discussion of mock impoliteness in this book and as such it remains an area ripe for future research.

5.7.2 Shouting

Culpeper notes that '...shouting, for example, could be a means of conveying impoliteness' (1996: 358). In addition, Jay claims (1992: 97, 108) that a person who is shouting in anger is both making sure that the hearer is aware of his or her anger as well as invading the space of the hearer. This is unsurprising as shouting is louder than is absolutely necessary for efficient communication to take place. Shouting, in effect, flouts the maxim Manner (Grice 1975) with respect to volume, which creates an interpretable implicature. As such, it can, as Culpeper theorises, be used as a mechanism for conveying impoliteness. An implicature caused by shouting could be construed as the utterer being angry and/or wishing to convey an impolite attitude towards the intended recipient. As ever, context (see Chapter 7, below) plays a crucial part in the interpretation of impoliteness as derived from any specific strategy. An example from the data sets includes the following, taken from **Redcaps, Extract 49.**

[33] ***Context****: Recruit Perkins (S2) has arrived at the Royal Military Police Training College on his motorcycle. He has a knapsack on and is carrying his helmet. Unusually, the NCO greeting the recruits, S1, has not, initially, noticed his arrival and as this excerpt starts, S1 is inside the guardroom as S2 is attempting to enter.*

1. S1: who are you PERKINS . GET YOUR KIT
   S2: <Perkins sergeant>
2. S1: OFF OUTSIDE AND MARK . TIME ON THE DOORSTEP
   S2:

3. S1:
   S2: YOU MAGGOT

End.

Note, also, the following example which is taken from **Redcaps, Extract 48**.

[34] ***Context:*** *Female recruit, Janes, (S2), has just arrived at the royal military police training centre. She has been instructed by the NCO (S1) greeting the recruits to enter the guardroom by marching smartly in prior to her asking permission to sign herself in to the training centre. Her marching, at the first attempt, isn't what it could be. S1 shouts at her from outside the building.*

1. S1: WHAT WAS THAT JANES . GET YOURSELF OUT HERE
   S2:
2. S1: GIRL ......TRY AGAIN . LET'S TRY MILITARY MARCHING
   S2:
3. S1: SHALL WE
   S2:

End.

The shouting here seems to be combined with other strategies. In the case of Perkins (example [33] drawn from extract 49) above, S1 was combining shouting with the criticism that Perkins had not left his motorbike helmet and backpack outside the door and had not called 'time' on the doorstep. The fact that he had, in no way, any warning that this was what was required of him to start with, does not seem to matter to S1, or apparently to the military in general. In the second example, above, a female recruit to the Royal Military Police finds herself on the receiving end of a combined shout/sarcasm when S1 says *WHAT WAS THAT JANES? . GET YOURSELF OUT HERE GIRL ...... TRY AGAIN . LET'S TRY MILITARY MARCHING SHALL WE*. This is after she has tried a lacklustre attempt at military marching. One notes that, following the impolite shouted sarcasm (and implicit, off-record criticism) by S1, S2 marches in, in a much more 'military way' the second time. Combinations of impolite strategies will be discussed in more detail in the next chapter.

5.7.3 Emotive language vs. strategic impoliteness: The case of taboo language

At this point it needs to be noted that for taboo words to be considered impolite, they need *not* be directed directly at the addressee, or even be boosting another impoliteness strategy which is directed at the addressee (or some entity in which the addressee has invested face). As Jay (1992, 2000) notes (and as with all successfully deployed impoliteness) the very *use* of taboo words, phrases and forms may be considered impolite as the hearer(s) of taboo language may feel uncomfortable with its very use – *make h feel uncomfortable* is a strategy which goes hand in hand with impoliteness, (see the discussion in Section 5.2, above). However, the question of intent once again is raised. It is possible that hearers are uncomfortable with the use of taboo language, even if it is not directed at them personally, or directly at either aspect of their faces – and that may be the speaker's intent. Similarly, hearers of taboo language may feel uncomfortable even if there is no intention on the speaker's part to make the hearer(s) feel so. Impoliteness, as defined by Culpeper (1996), and as understood here, does not cover this. However, 'rudeness', understood here as the opposite of 'politic verbal behaviour' (cf. Watts [1989] 1992) would take such usage into account. In short, we must accept that not every instance of taboo usage is a case of linguistic impoliteness – there are some cases where taboo language (whether intended to offend or not) breaks social norms: rudeness can make the hearer feel uncomfortable.

Even where the use of taboo language includes the intent to cause face damage, the major issue with the *Use taboo language* strategy is that it is predominantly a symptom of emotive communication and is not linguistic impoliteness *per se*. As such it could be considered to have been inadequately described in Culpeper 1996. The instances of taboo usage in the examples throughout the data sets are virtually always emotive to some degree. However, as Culpeper et al. (2003) note, even taboo language which is not necessarily directed at the hearer can indicate a negative attitude towards the hearer or the hearer's actions; or can indicate anger and exasperation which, via the maxim of Manner (1975), can implicate that the speaker's current state of mind is the hearer's fault. An example of this can be seen in the following example, taken from **The Clampers, Extract 8.**

[35] ***Context:*** *Two 'Clampers' proceed to clamp an illegally parked car. Just as they have finished, the car's driver, a workman who was doing a job for a local homeowner, returns to his car to find it clamped, and the clampers still there.*

S1 – 'Ray' the clamping supervisor.
S4 – Returning Workman and owner of the clamped van.

[…]

Edit where the driver of the recently clamped vehicle returns

5. S1: no I'm afraid not .. did you not realise that you couldn't
   S4: <indistinct>
6. S1: park in here yeah = well there is a
   S4: well there ain't no signs up are there=

7. S1: sign up here on the fence that tells you that this whole bay is resident
   S4:

8. S1: parking only I'm afraid you have to have a voucher to park in this
   S4:

9. S1: area
   S4: *HOW ARE YOU SUPPOSED TO EARN A BLEEDING LIVING*

10. S1: well there's no point in
    S4: *IN THIS FUCKING COUNTRY EH*

11. S1: shouting at me yeah
    S2:

[…]

The pertinent section here is between staves 8 to 10. Note, that despite S4's usage of the personal pronoun *YOU* in Stave 8 and the apparent interrogative nature of the utterance, S4 was facing away from both clampers and was stamping around after throwing his toolkit down onto the road. His utterance of *YOU*, in context, was generic (*How are you* = 'How is anyone…') and the question was, at least primarily, a non-targetted expression of his displeasure at being clamped which was supported by his use of two instances of taboo language: *BLEEDING* and *FUCKING* in staves 9 and 10, and the fact that he was shouting (not to mention the paralinguistic evidence from the physical throwing of his toolkit and his emotively charged pacing). Note, however, S1's response to this generally emotive expression of anger in stave 10: *well there's no point shouting at me yeah*. S1's response appears to show that he has taken S4's utterances as being personally offensive – that, in effect, his face has been damaged or at least threatened by S4's emotive outburst. As such, even emotive outbursts, especially those involving taboo language use, could be considered to be face threatening by a hearer even if such face threat was not targeted at them, or intended as impoliteness. As noted, such instances may not be impoliteness, as it is understood here, but may be encapsulated within a consideration of 'rudeness' as the flip side to politic verbal behaviour (cf. Watts 1992).

Such emotive usages are to be differentiated from more strategic-oriented usages of taboo language. However, no single example of a 'cool headed', intended, *purely* strategic, or measured instance of usage is recognisably recorded throughout the corpus. This is most probably a functional aspect of the data used: After all, heated arguments make good television (see Culpeper 1998, 2005 for the link between 'impoliteness and entertainment'). Indeed, that may be the point, the very essence if you will, of taboo language usage: that it represents a social breakdown, a temporary, situational amelioration of Brown and Levinson's (1987) Model Person (who in the name of maintaining one's own face wants and needs, seeks to maintain the face wants and needs of one's interlocutors). Cool headed taboo usage, in context, could represent impoliteness *prima facia*. However, instances of this type were hard to clearly identify in my data sets. Indeed, the latest usage of 'cool-headed' taboo usage that I came across was in Michael Moore's book, *Stupid White Men*. Genre-label avoiding, this text can only really be described as a humorous-political, 21st century pamphlet. To the American Democratic Party, with whom he has become disillusioned, Moore gives the Democrats the following advice "If you can't clean up your act, fuck you and the donkey you rode in on." (Moore 2002: 226).

All this said, it should not be assumed that I consider that all 'hot' usages of impoliteness cannot be intentional. In light of Bandura's (1973) comments (see Section 4.5.4) regarding the futility of separating instrumental and hostile varieties of aggression, the realisation of taboo language as being "either" emotive expression "or" strategic face threat is perhaps misleading. It is probably best to view intstrumental and hostile varieties as being on a scale – though more research and consideration is clearly necessary.

The use of *profane, abusive and taboo language* is, perhaps unsurprisingly, a common feature of almost all of the data sets studied in this study (only in the 'Motorway Life' data set is it absent). However, we must note that the use of taboo language does not appear to be open for all participants, across all discourses, to use. Brown and Levinson (1987) assume that the greater the power of a particular participant, the less polite that participant has to be. By logical extension of this point, it would suggest that those with more power should have open to them a greater range of intentionally exacerbated face threatening linguistic strategies – however this does not appear to be the case across all discourses. Whilst in the army data sets and the kitchen discourse we do see those people who are in a power position using taboo language, we do not see those in power using it in the car parking or the police data sets. There could be one very good reason for this – the use of taboo language is seen, all other things being equal, as being socially unacceptable. Its use would indicate that (a) social and linguistic conceptualisations of im/politeness are not as separate (see Chapter 4) as the literature would suggest as, (b) individuals don't appear to cognitively or intellectually separate the two in conversation.[10] In short, the use of taboo language by a clamper to a private car owner, or a police officer to a member of the public, even one being arrested, could result in strict and heavy social – and even legal – repercussions for the taboo language using officer in question – whether it was predominantly strategically issued, or was predominantly the result of a

10. This, of course, is an area for future research and consideration.

temporary loss of emotive control. Despite its linguistic impoliteness role, taboo language can never lose the socially damaging effects that it has in the context of real-life conversation. Clearly research on taboo language needs to continue, but it also needs to consider the face wants of the participants and the social-linguistic interface of conceptualisations of im/politeness as lay users understand the notion(s). For the time being, in addition to the consideration it has been given by Culpeper (1996), a case could be made that *all* impoliteness could be construed as being an impingement on the Brown and Levinson (1987) notion of 'negative face' (the want to be unimpeded) of the hearer – in that they are forced cognitively to consider its effects. Ultimately, therefore, the retention of the dichotomy is unnecessary, as I have argued above.

5.8 Conclusion

> [...] people employ certain strategies [...] for reasons of expediency – experience has taught us that particular strategies are likely to succeed in given circumstances, so we use them. (Thomas 1995: 179)

Although, in the above quote, Thomas was concerned with politeness theories Culpeper et al. (2003) believe it is also true for impoliteness. In effect, instead of attending to the face needs of their interlocutors, impolite interactants seek to aggravate, attack and threaten face as a way of attaining their extra-linguistic goals (cf. Holmes and Marra 2002; Culpeper et al. 2003).

In this chapter I have described the results found when an existing model of impoliteness (Culpeper 1996, 2005) is taken and applied to the extracts in the data sets studied in this book. As we have seen, Culpeper's model fares well under such a test as most of the strategies identified by Culpeper (1996) also occur in the data sets studied. However, I think it fair to say that (a) at least some of the definitions of impolite strategies given in Culpeper (1996) need complementary and corrective reconceptualisations in order to 'tighten' them up, and (b) there would appear to be a great variety in what counts as an impolite 'strategy' in that, as I have shown, they are not all of the same order. Linguistic impoliteness is clearly many layered and multi modal.

Additionally, as I have shown, we have begun to see that it is difficult to talk about the realisation of individual impolite output strategies as defined by Culpeper (1996) without reference either to other impolite output strategies, or even of the ways of combining strategies (which is more properly the purview of the following chapter) for specific effects. There are very good reasons for this.

The individual strategies, whilst seemingly perfectly logical and attractive in theoretical form,

a. rarely, if ever, can be said to occur in isolation with just one unambiguous meaning when the context and co-text are taken into account.
b. often, if not always, attack, aggravate or otherwise threaten both the so-called 'positive' and 'negative' face aspects of the interactants (cf. Culpeper et al. 2003; and Thomas 1995). The dichotomy seems, therefore, unsustainable.

Taking such phenomena into account is a necessary part of presenting and understanding the data, and, as ever, natural data serves to be the testing bed in which theoretical models are tried. Such models, whilst intensely useful and crucial to the progress and development of thought, cannot truly stand alone without taking into consideration how the very discourses in which impoliteness is situated build up and pan out, for as Grimshaw points out that 'participants in conflict talk have the same resources available for that interaction as do all conversationalists' (1990: 10). Moving towards a consideration of the particular resources which interactants can and do deploy in conflictive, impolite containing exchanges is the aim of the following chapters (6, 7, and 8). Here I will show how interactants attempt to defuse, ameliorate, deflect or otherwise tone down the face damaging effects of impoliteness, how they, in effect, attempt to counter impoliteness. I will look at the ways in which impolite offensive and impolite defensive utterances draw from more than one strategy for specific effect(s); I will discuss the structure of conversations containing impolite exchanges, showing how interactants make moves to prepare the ground for impoliteness to occur and I will show how interactants attempt to manipulate both their interactants and the rules, expectations and conventions of conversational exchanges in order to more effectively deliver, or counter, impoliteness.

CHAPTER 6

The dynamics of impoliteness I

Dynamics at the utterance level

The classic approaches to politeness (e.g. Brown and Levinson 1987; Leech, 1983, 2005) and impoliteness (Culpeper 1996; Kienpointner 1997; Lachenicht 1980) have tended to concentrate upon the realisation of single strategies. Indeed, one criticism, often levelled at Brown and Levinson (1987), is that it really only deals with single strategies taken out of the context of ongoing discourse (see Blum-Kulka 1992; Thomas 1986; Werkhofer 1992). This, as Thomas (1986) points out, is a charge often levelled at those researchers who worked within the "philosophical" framework of Austin (1962), Grice (1975) and Searle (1969, 1979);

> The characteristic procedure is to discuss bits of 'ordinary' (or 'everyday') conversation, viewed as discrete acts of exchanges; and the discussion tends to be conducted with made-up examples ('data') enriched with intuitions of ill/well formedness (or 'naturalness'). The exchanges are represented with little or no description of particular situations of utterance, and indeed are neither essentially spoken nor written; rather, they are abstracted away from such particulars.
> (Dillon et al. 1985: 446)

It needs to be noted that the model proposed by Culpeper (1996, and to a lesser extent, Culpeper 2005), being an extension of Brown and Levinson's (1987) model which draws from Searle's (1969) theory of Speech Acts, inherited the problem of considering the single-strategy-out-of-context (for a fuller discussion of Culpeper's model and its development see Chapter 4, above). Though to be fair (in relation to Dillon et al.'s comments above), both Brown and Levinson, and Culpeper most certainly did *not* make use of made-up examples enriched with intuition. Furthermore (in relation to the present study) consideration of impoliteness strategies specifically within the context of extended discourse was not a central or even a peripheral aim of Culpeper's (1996) seminal paper. Indeed this limitation was later tacitly acknowledged and initial steps have been made to argue for the need to account for such phenomena (see Bousfield 2007a, 2008; Culpeper et al. 2003; Culpeper 2005). This is a central issue for this book and is dealt with in detail in some Chapter 7.

In the present chapter, then, and both complementing and drawing upon that which I discussed in the previous chapter, I continue to investigate how impoliteness is actually conveyed. As we saw in the discussion in Chapter 5, it is impossible to discuss the occurrence and realisation of impoliteness in the discourses here studied without noting the fact that participants tend to combine, or 'mix' together, impolite strategies within a single utterance. I am therefore taking up this point in examining such 'combined-strategy' phenomena. The combination of impoliteness strategies turned out to be predominant in the data discussed in this book – participants *rarely* used a single strategy in isolation. I will return to this point in Section 6.2, below.

To begin, however, I should note that the structure of this chapter will be the following: I begin by *suggesting* how impolite utterances can be 'prepared for' at the micro, 'turn-at-talk' level (see 6.1, Utterance 'beginnings', below); I then discuss the complex ways in which impolite utterances (cf. Culpeper 1996) can combine together for specific effect (see 6.2, Utterance 'middles', below) within a single utterance, or a turn at talk; and finally I discuss some possible features of the ending of impolite utterances (see 6.3 Utterance 'ends', below), where I will be making links between the concept of 'forcing feedback' for face-offensive purposes, and the concept of conducivity as discussed in Chapter 8 (Section 8.4, below).

6.1 Utterance 'beginnings'

Impoliteness does not spring from nowhere, and nor does it occur in pure, strict isolation. As we will see in the next chapter within extended discourses there are always antecedent events which trigger the onset of impoliteness. In this chapter, however, I discuss the beginnings of impolite utterances – the co-textual as well as the structural and pragmatic features which are often in place in order to 'prepare the ground' for impolite utterances to follow.

6.1.1 The co-text

Within interchanges of spoken discourse, I understand co-text (as an aspect of the wider, 'context' (see next chapter)) to be *primarily* those utterances, made by all participants having a bearing on the discussion which have preceded the present moment[1] and, to a lesser extent, to be those utterances which are (likely,

1. By 'moment' I mean, in an abstract sense, the point at which an interlocutor decides what it is that they are about to say.

or predicted) to follow the present moment – all within the discoursal/activity type in which the participants are currently engaged. As Mey puts it, the co-text concerns and refers to the environment within which occurs, 'conversation, that is […] linguistic interchanges between two or more partners' (Mey 2001: 134).

It is important to both define (if only briefly), and understand the concept of co-text here as I move, in this chapter, to consider (a) the preparation for, (b) the onset of, and (c) the realisation of impolite containing utterances, not to mention the potential for (d) post-utterance intensification of impolite face damage. I will discuss each of these in turn.

6.1.2 Preparing for impoliteness: 'Pre-impoliteness' sequences

As an aspect of the co-text of linguistic interchanges certain utterances can operate as precursors to some other utterance. Such utterances are well known within the literature of both Pragmatics and Conversation Analysis as 'Pre-sequences' (see Atkinson and Drew 1979; Levinson 1983; Merritt 1976 and Mey 2001, amongst others). The classical examples, a series of 'attention getters', taken here from Mey, (2001:144), include: 'Hey', 'You know something?' and 'Excuse me'. Mey notes (2001: 144; see also Levinson 1983: 346; and Sacks 1992: Vol. II), that after the initial groundwork has been prepared through pre-sequencing the real 'business at hand' can be dealt with. Pre-sequences which perform such preparatory groundwork, include, but are by no means limited to: *pre-invitations* ('What are you guys doing on Sunday?), *pre-requests* ('I'd like to ask you … ?'), *pre-announcements* ('I'd just like to say something'), and *pre-threats* ('You just watch it!') amongst others (see Levinson 1983: 345–356; Mey 2001: 144). While these are all structural phenomena, on an *interpersonal* and a *pragmatic* level it stands to reason that there could be a class of 'pragmatic pre-sequences' that can be considered 'preparation-to-perform-impolite' (*pre-impolite*) utterances. It does need to be stressed, at this point, that the *pre-impoliteness* sequences I describe here may, themselves, be both prototypically what we would consider to be polite as well as being impolite.[2] Note the following example, taken from **Extract 1, The Clampers.**

[36] ***Context:*** *Ray and Miguel, clamping supervisor and assistant respectively have arrived to remove the clamp from a van. The van's owner is waiting for them. S1 is Ray, S2 the van's owner and S3 is Miguel who does not speak throughout this extract.*

1. S1: hi there sir this yours
   S2: yeah it is yeah *I'd like to er ask you why you*

2. And for this reason they must be considered more *pragmatic* and less *structural* phenomena.

2. S1: why we clamped it you see
   S2: *clamped it* yeah there's nobody here for one

3. S1: well it is doing
   S2: hundred and fifty yards it's not doing any offence I was in there

4. S1:
   S2: getting my tools out when

[…]

This example, already partially discussed under 'Challenges' (see Section 5.5.4) above, represents a prototypical pre-sequence which operates as a *pre-impolite utterance*. Note, here, S1's utterance in stave 1: *I'd like to ask you why you clamped it.* To begin with, this, ostensibly, seems to be operating, structurally, as a *pre-request* (I'd like to *ask* you…), which is, typically, seen as being indirectly polite (cf. Brown and Levinson 1987; Leech 1983). However, when we consider the context (see Section 7.1. below), including the following co-text, we can see that the utterance simply cannot be operating, *in this context*,[3] as true, sincere politeness.

Considering the context: We must note that the van is parked on double yellow lines (which means: no parking, at any time, under British highway parking regulations) and the addressee of S2's utterance in stave 1, is a *bona fide*, clamping official employed specifically to enforce British highway parking regulations within the ward of London's Southwark council (where the van is illegally parked). In effect, S2, (a British van driver), in asking *I'd like to er ask you why you clamped it*, is flouting both Grice's (1975) maxim of quantity (it is *given information* why the van has been clamped – it is illegally parked), and, potentially, the maxim of manner (the very fact that S2 is asking suggests he is either taking, or about to take, an antithetical, questioning and challenging position to that of his addressee, the clamper, S1). The flout of these maxims generates a conversational implicature – that it is not *genuine* indirectness / politeness and, considering the *given knowledge* regarding illegal parking, it appears, therefore, to be a precursor to further, upcoming utterances which may be antithetical / challenging. As evidence supporting the comments just made, at this point we should note the guarded response to this precursor, which is given by S1, in stave 2: '*why we clamped it?*' This repetition of the wording of S2's immediately prior turn is significant. It is clearly operating as a guarded request for clarification. The reason it is a request for clarification is *precisely* because of the *given information* regarding the legality of parking on double yellow lines in Britain. This comment seems to have the illocutionary force of: *do you really want/need me to state out loud the legal reason*

3. See Section 7.1, below for a fuller discussion of context.

why you've been clamped (and thus, put on record your infraction which would, clearly, be face-threatening)? Indeed, S1's aborted turn in stave 2 of '*you see*' could indeed be seen as an attempt to state the *given knowledge* regarding parking (indeed, looking back to Section 5.5.4, we can see, in staves 7 and 13 of the longer version of this example [see example 30] that S1 attempts to, first politely (stave 7), then directly (stave 13), draw S2's attention to the double yellow line on the road – and thus attempts to refer to this *given knowledge*).

In terms of the co-text (and the continuing context) we should now note S2's utterance in staves 2 and 3: *yeah there's nobody here for one hundred and fifty yards it's not doing any offence*. This is an indirect complaint regarding the actions of clamper S1 and is thus an implied criticism – something that is a *potentially* impolite utterance (see Section 4.4, above). When we further note the temporal – sequential organisation of the two utterances made by driver, S2, together (more on this in the next chapter), we note that little, if any, time has been genuinely allocated to clamper, S1, to respond to the apparent 'pre-request' of *I'd like to ask you why you clamped it*, (it does not appear as if the conversational floor (see Section 8.2, below) was genuinely offered at the apparent transition relevant place). Thus, given the context, (especially, the *given background knowledge* and the clamper, S1's *societal role* (see Section 7.1.2.1, below)), and the co-text of the utterance, we can conclude on the balance of probabilities, that such an utterance is not a genuine *pre-request* but it is, nevertheless, a 'pre-impoliteness' that is, an utterance preparing the ground for the onset of the impolite utterances which follow. That it was recognised as such by clamper S1 appears to be evidenced through his guarded response, *why we clamped it*, in stave 2, to the pre-impoliteness.

Pre-sequences that, in addition to their structural role operate as *pre-impolite* utterances are not uncommon throughout the data sets studied in the present project. We can see an example in the following extract taken from **Soldiers To Be, Extract 21.**

[37] ***Context***: *A Room inspection. A male sergeant is inspecting the barrack room of a number of female recruits. S1 is the inspecting corporal, S3 'Daggert' a female recruit. S1 is inspecting the state of S3's clothing which is hung up in her locker.*

[…]

Edit: S1, the Sergeant, begins inspecting the clothing of another recruit, S3.

8. S1: so where . have you been washing your kit   in the
   S2:
   S3:   in the toilets sergeant

9. S1: fucking toilets . *right you people pin your ears back and listen to me*
   S2:
   S3:

10. S1: okay it is not acceptable to <stop > washing your kit . you will wash
    S2:
    S3:

11. S1: your kit people tell me that females are more hygienic than men . at
    S2:
    S3:

12. S1: the moment I find that very very hard to believe I can guarantee you
    S2:
    S3:

13. S1: the males over there have been taking their kit to the laundry . you
    S2:
    S3:

14. S1: people . so far are not impressing me . disgusting . alright your kit is
    S2:
    S3:

15. S1: in the locker but it is not fucking clean
    S2:
    S3:

End.

Note sergeant S1's *pre-announcement* in Stave 9: *right you people pin your ears back and listen to me*. In the context in which it is made, this conversationally structural *pre-announcement* (which is operating as an attention getter / attention focuser) also operates as a pragmatic *pre-impoliteness* utterance: Note the onset of impoliteness in staves 10–15 including, primarily, an overall criticism of the group's actions, which includes a negative comparison to another group (staves 11–12), the implication of negative beliefs (cf. Leech 1983) evidenced through the negative opinion of the female recruits with the use of the word *disgusting* (stave 14) and the usage of taboo language (stave 15: 'it is not *fucking* clean') to boost the above.

Such pre-impoliteness moves need not be so simply or neatly encapsulated within a single utterance. They can be constructed by being 'built up' over a short range of a few juxta-posed utterances. Note the following example taken from **Soldiers To Be, Extract 25.**

[38] ***Context:*** *Platoon Sergeant 'Tich' Lovall (S1) is about to send his recruits, who have finished A.F.S. – the first three weeks of their training, on to C.M.S.R. – the final eleven, and much more difficult, weeks of their basic training. The recruits are late for parade. Furthermore, Sgt Lovall feels the need to give recruit Downes (S2) a word of advice before sending him on. S3 is an unidentified member of the recruits. The time is a little after 7 a.m.*

[…]

5. S1:Downes **…** *come here* **………..***stand there* **.** *look at me* **.** *listen* **.** top
   S2:
6. S1:tip of the day when you get down to C M S R shut your fucking mouth
   S2:

[…]

In the above extract S1's summons of, and instructions to S2 to *come here, stand there, look at me* and *listen* all operate together to perform as an attention getting/focussing, pragmatic *pre-impoliteness* which serve to prepare the ground for the impoliteness contained in *when you get down to CMSR, shut your fucking mouth!*

One important concept to discuss here is that just as structural pre-sequences can be, from a *pragmalinguistic* perspective, prototypically or conventionally polite (e.g. 'Can I ask you … ?'), they can also operate as being prototypically or conventionally impolite also, they do not always need to operate *only* as *pre*-impolitenesses, as the following example taken from **Soldiers To Be, Extract 34** shows.

[39] ***Context:*** *A room inspection. S1 is the inspection sergeant, S2 is the recruit being inspected. S1 has discovered an improperly cleaned eating utensil.*

[…]

3. S1: what's that going to do to you when you have to survive in the field **…**
   S2:
4. S1: *ANSWER THE QUESTION HAYES* **.** WHAT'S THAT GOING TO
   S2:
5. S1: DO TO YOU WHEN YOU HAVE TO SURVIVE IN THE FIELD
   S2:

[…]

Note, in this instance, S1's 'pre-question' of *ANSWER THE QUESTION HAYES*, in stave 4, is, in itself, an impolite rebuke (a form of criticism, see Section 5.5.1, above) for Hayes not answering the previous question *what's that going to do to you when you have to survive in the field* in stave 3. In addition it is further boosted by a shout (see Section 5.7.2, above). The utterance, *ANSWER THE QUESTION HAYES* is itself impolite through the duality of shouting and it being a criticism for S2 not answering. Nevertheless it also serves to prepare the ground for further impoliteness. So impolite comments can also be preparatory to further impolite comments to follow.

In a similar vein pre-impolite utterances need not be prototypical pre-sequences. As we can see in the next example, they can be apparently polite interrogatives, taken from **Boiling Point, Extract 66.**

[40] ***Context***: *Gordon Ramsay, S1, talks to one of his kitchen staff, S2.*

1. S1: *what what were we discussing lunchtime* . *what were we talking about*
   S2:
2. S1: *lunchtime* . *what were we discussing* . automatically standing in the
   S2:
3. S1: front of the trays without being fucking told every goddamned day
   S2:

End.

Note, here, head chef, S1's three (*repeated* see Section 6.2.2, below), pre-impolite utterances in staves 1 and 2: *what what were we discussing lunchtime* . *what were we talking about lunchtime* . *what were we discussing*. All of these act as preparatory pre-cursors to the actual impoliteness in stave 2–3's: *automatically standing in the front of the trays without being fucking told every goddamned day*, which has two usages of 'taboo language' (cf. Culpeper 1996) and is an implied criticism (see Section 5.5.1, above).

We should note that, 'extra-linguistic' activities performed by participants can also operate as pre-impolite moves too. Consider the following example taken from **Boiling Point, Extract 64.**

[41] ***Context***: *Henry, S2, a Chef de Partie has overcooked the artichokes and, thus, held up another dish for another table. S1, the head chef and restaurateur chooses to talk to S2 about this.*

1. S1: <and you see> *you you yeah come on the path a minute on the path*
   S2:
2. S1: *[S1 physically manhandles S2 onto the path]* if you send me six
   S2:
3. S1: fucking main courses like that again and I I I'll I'll grab you by the
   S2:

4. S1: fucking scruff of the neck and throw you on the street do you
   S2:

5. S1: understand
   S2: yes Gordon

[…]

We can see, here, how head chef, S1, in stave 2 physically manhandles S2 onto the 'path' (an area leading from the cooking area proper, to the 'hot plate' countertop – where the food is placed to be collected by the waiters). The physical manhandling along with the preparatory comment *come onto the path a minute, yeah?* operate as pre-impoliteness moves, signalling the (potential for the) onset of the impolite utterance made by S1 in staves 2 to 5.

Finally, even complex, role-manipulating utterances can be described as having a certain preparatory role to the creation of impolite utterances. We saw the following example in Section 5.5.1 above, which I discuss here again in order to further explore some of the rich complexity of language exploited to enhance the impoliteness. This example is taken from **Extract 8, The Clampers**.

[42] ***Context:*** *Two 'Clampers' proceed to clamp an illegally parked car. Just as they have finished, the car's driver, a workman who was doing a job for a local homeowner, returns to his car to find it clamped, and the clampers still there. S1 is the clamper, S4 the vehicle's owner.*

[…]

Edit where the clampers get confirmation that the vehicle owner has paid the release fee. S1 is just finishing his radio call from base giving him authorisation to remove the clamp

20. S1: okay cheers bye we're going to declamp it
    S4: it all seems a bit pointless

21. S1:
    S4: doesn't it they're paying him to drive round collecting money I mean

22. S1:
    S4: why not invest it in parking meters *don't you think this is a bit*

23. S1: = well you see I'm just doing a job but I've come along here
    S4: *stupid=* all I'm ask yeah

24. S1: and yeah
    S4: well so was Hitler all I'm asking you as a person don't you think this

25. S1: well <exhalation> yes and no
S4: is a bit stupid

[…]

Again, in stave 22, we should note the enforcing of a role switch by S4 on S1 when he attempts to shift S1 out of his role of 'representative' and 'mouthpiece' for the local council, and enforce the role of 'private citizen', with the utterance: *don't you think this is a bit stupid.* Not only is this an initial attempt to enforce a role shift (see Section 5.5.3 above) it also acts as a preparatory utterance, which allows the continuation of impoliteness via subsequent role shifting in stave 23–24: *all I'm asking you as a person…*

All such utterances operate to prepare the ground or otherwise 'shape' the conversation in such a way as to allow the delivery of the impolite utterances following which are the devices that are primarily used to attack face.

6.2 Utterance 'middles'

Lachenicht, discussing aggravating language, notes that '[…] it is possible to combine more than one sub-strategy into an utterance' (1980: 635). Based on work I originally conducted for the present book, Culpeper et al. (2003) identify two non-mutually-exclusive ways in which impoliteness strategies pattern in a participant's turns. Other than Lachenicht (1980) and Culpeper et al. (2003), researchers into (im)politeness and aggravating or aggressive language have largely ignored the phenomena of combining strategies.[4] There are, as we will see, a number of more subtle ways in which impoliteness strategies can pattern based on the two identified and discussed in Culpeper et al. (2003).[5]

6.2.1 Simple vs. complex impoliteness

The first thing to note is the definitional difference to be made between the 'simple' (single) realisations of an impoliteness strategy (cf. Culpeper 1996) in real-life

4. Though see Muntigl and Turnbull's section on 'act combinations' (1998) for a promising, early start on combining argument illocutions.

5. At this point it needs to be noted that in building upon, expanding, and further enhancing the argument made in Culpeper et al. (2003), which I do throughout my discussion, I necessarily draw upon some of the work which I did for that paper, both individually, and in conjunction with my co-authors.

discourse, and, what I have termed, the 'complex' (combined) (co-)realisation of impoliteness strategies, within a single utterance, or turn-at-talk.

Simple or single utterance realisation is what Brown and Levinson (1987) and Culpeper (1996) deal with in their models. It is important to note here, however, that this was done more for ease of reference rather than for an insistence that this was the norm in interactional exchanges – a point which seems to have been misunderstood by those criticising these approaches for adopting a 'single-turn-at-talk-out-of-context' approach. Indeed, while he analysed two whole interactions, detailed description of the extended discourses was never an aim, nor an explicit issue, within Culpeper's (1996) explicitly exploratory paper on impoliteness. Note that the description of the impoliteness framework in Culpeper (1996) tended to focus on single 'strategies' *only* as a means of exposition and discussion, not as an insistence that the strategies where discrete entities, (indeed, the same must be stressed for my presentation of 'strategies' throughout this book). Note also that Brown and Levinson were looking for *specific* politeness strategies and were not, *at that stage*, particularly interested in how such strategies co-occured in extended interaction. This said, they never claimed that such strategies could not combine.

As seen in the previous chapter, it is *exceptionally* hard to identify, in context, an impolite utterance which operates as, and only as, a single impoliteness strategy (cf. Culpeper 1996). No clear examples existed in my data sets and, as I have discussed the individual strategies in the previous chapter, I will not dwell further on the possibility here.

6.2.1.1 *Complex: Repeated utterance realisation*

In this case, one particular strategy is used repeatedly in order to form a parallelism. That is, a word, a phrase, grammatical structures, intonational contours, or indeed any single feature or set of features, (or a variation-on-the-theme of a word, phrase, grammatical structure, intonational contour, or any single feature) which constitutes a pragmatic strategy can be used repeatedly (usually, but not exclusively, in juxtaposition) to form a parallelism (a perceptually prominent pattern where some features are held constant and others may vary). In the following example we see one participant repeatedly using the 'challenge' strategy, in **The Clampers, Extract 1.**

[43] ***Context:*** *Ray and Miguel, clamping supervisor and assistant respectively have arrived to remove the clamp from a van. The van's owner is waiting for them. S1 is Ray, S2, the van's owner, S3 – Miguel – does not speak throughout this extract.*

1. S1: hi there sir this yours
   S2: yeah it is yeah I'd like to er ask you why you

2. S1: why we clamped it you see
   S2: clamped it yeah there's nobody here for one

3. S1: well it is doing
   S2: hundred and fifty yards it's not doing any offence I was in there

4. S1: well it is doing an offence let me stop you just there
   S2: getting my tools out when

5. S1: because it is doing an offence straight away parked on a yellow line
   S2:

6. S1: parked on a yellow line
   S2: what's wrong with a ticket it's extortion

7. S1:
   S2: you know it is it's government extortion it's absolutely outrageous

8. S1: can you can you just answer me one question can you see the yellow
   S2:

9. S1: line visibly under your car
   S2: …I live here *why is there a yellow line*

10. S1:
    S2: *anyway why do I have to park my car three hundred yards up the*

11. S1:
    S2: *road* it gets stolen broken into vandalised three times this year

12. S1:
    S2: already *why have you done it why do you make my life impossible*

13. S1:
    S2: *how am I supposed to work doing this*

[…]

Note here how the series of repetitions in staves 9 to 13, is issued rapidly by S2, with minimal gaps between each of the challenges (see the discussion of 'Challenges' in Section 5.5.4 above). Holmes (1984: 355), discussing the modification of illocutionary force, points out that 'repetition itself serves as a rhetorical device to increase the force of the repeated speech act'. Clearly, in this case, repetition of the challenges serves to *boost*, and thereby to exacerbate the threat to S1's face. As in the example here, repetition can also 'hog' the conversational floor (see Sections 8.2 and 8.3 below), imposing upon the other participant's face. The key point about the rapid repetition (the parallelism) of impoliteness strategies relates to interpersonal effect: it increases the imposition upon the addressee and/or emphasises the negative attitude of the speaker towards the hearer. In other words, it can boost, or enhance, impoliteness.

However, repetition need not only occur juxtaposed within single conversational turns. Repetition can, and does, occur across turns seemingly despite how the intended recipient responds. In the following example of military training discourse, S1, the training sergeant, is investigating who has cut a recruit's hair resulting in an illegal haircut. S1 has his suspicions and calls in all eight recruits of one barrack room. S1 concentrates his questions on S2, the recruit he suspects is responsible for cutting the other recruit's hair. Up to this point S1 has discovered that S2 did indeed cut the recruit's hair after he (S2) had initially tried to lie his way out of trouble and then, once discovered, explain his way out of trouble. Again, note the italicised sections depicting repeated strategies in this example taken from **Soldiers to Be, Extract 23.**

[44] ***Context****: S1 sergeant 'Tich Lovall' is investigating who has cut a recruit's hair resulting in an illegal haircut. S1 has his suspicions and calls all eight recruits of one barracks room in. S1 concentrates his questions to S2: recruit Downes, S3: recruit Harris and S4: recruit Andrews – the three recruits he suspects who are indeed responsible for cutting the other recruit's hair. Up to this point he has asked recruit Downes (who he suspects is the ring leader) if he cut Newson's hair.*

[…]

21. S1: that question *you know all the rules you know all the*
    S2: yes I did sergeant

22. S1: *regulations you know what we expect and you know what you can*
    S2:

23. S1: *and can't do don't you* *you know everything don't you*
    S2: no sergeant no

24. S1: because you're a wide boy aren't you the
    S2: sergeant no sergeant ….

25. S1: regulation haircut in this place is a number two on sides and a
    S2:

26. S1: number four on top .. because that's the rules *do you know all*
    S2: sergeant

27. S1: *the rules* *do you know what you're doing*
    S2: no sergeant no sergeant

28. S1: it's as simple as this you are now on an official platoon sergeant's
    S2:

29. S1: warning ...... you have got . seven days to sort yourself out
S2: sergeant

30. S1: *do you understand what I'm saying to you* *do you*
S2: yes sergeant

31. S1: *understand why I'm saying it to you* *do you understand*
S2: yes sergeant

32. S1: *what you have done wrong* *do you understand what you*
S2: yes sergeant

33. S1: *have to do to improve yourself and your performance to put it*
S2:

34. S1: *right* seven days .... get away
S2: yes sergeant ..

End.

Here, there are three *separate* types of repeated strategies here. The first, across the first three staves (staves 21–24) could be viewed as instantiations of the 'sarcasm' (cf. Culpeper 1996, 2005) impoliteness strategy. The first of which are repeated in juxtaposition: *you know all the rules you know all the regulations you know what we expect and you know what you can and can't do* with the last repetition of the 'sarcasm' strategy coming after S2's denial: *you know everything don't you.* Interestingly here, the sequence of repetitions, as a device for boosting the sarcasm, seems to culminate within, and be summed up by the pragmatic propositional content of this final repetition. The claim that the hearer, S2, 'knows everything', can *only* be highly sarcastic. It is, quite literally, impossible to 'know everything' and thus the sarcasm is obvious and therefore marked. This final statement seems to be the quintessential summing up of the preceding, building sarcasm, the effect, of course, being to heighten the force of the impoliteness (for further, more-detailed discussion of this example, see Section 8.4.8 below).

The second set of repetitions occurs in staves 26 to 27. Here we see repeated, over two turns, the strategy of 'Challenge' with *do you know all the rules* and *do you know what you are doing*. In both cases S1 ostentatiously breaks the maxim of quantity (Grice 1975) as it is clear from S2's actions and from within the co-text of S1's own utterances up to this point that S2 neither knows all the rules nor is he sure of what he is doing. In relation to S1's own preceding comments, and the two repeated strategies here, this double transgression, by S1, of the maxim of quantity (Grice 1975) can be construed as being impolite.

Finally, in the last five staves (30–34), S1 deploys a repetitive combination of utterances which, again, encompasses the 'Challenge' impolite strategy. The utterances: *do you understand what I'm saying to you, do you understand why*

I'm saying it to you, do you understand what you have done wrong and *do you understand what you have to do to improve your performance to put it right* cumulatively have a powerful impolite illocutionary force and perlocutionary effect. Not only is the strategy of 'Challenge: ask a challenging question', repeated, but the repetitive use of the expression *do you understand* is also highly face threatening to S2. It impinges on S2's face as it forces a very specific and thus tightly controlled set of responses from S2 (see *post-intensifying interrogatives – forcing feedback*, Section 6.3.1, and see also Chapter 8, 8.4 below). Furthermore, as in the previous example, these strategies clearly 'hog' the conversational floor in the way they are repeated (see Sections 8.2 and 8.3, below). It further impinges upon S2's face (above and beyond that caused by being *impolitely challenged*) as the way in which these last (repeated 'Challenge' strategy) utterances are said (cf. Grice's 'maxim of manner', 1975) adds a strong element of the impoliteness strategy of *condescension* (cf. Culpeper 1996) which suggests a way of talking which is reminiscent of the way in which adults talk to wayward children.

In the following example, *Chef de Partie*, S2 has overcooked the artichokes and, thus, has held up a dish for serving when everything else is ready. Restaurateur and chef S1 chooses to talk to S2 about this, in the example taken from extract **Boiling Point, Extract 64.**

[45]

1. S1: <and you see> you you yeah come on the path a minute on the path
   S2:

2. S1: [S1 physically manhandles S2 onto the 'path'] if you send me six
   S2:

3. S1: fucking main courses like that again and I I I'll I'll grab you by the
   S2:

4. S1: fucking scruff of the neck and throw you on the street do you
   S2:

5. S1: understand   you're not just fucking up with table two there
   S2:   yes Gordon

6. S1: we're sending six main courses <bleep> and we've had all the lamb
   S2:   yes Gordon

7. S1: back and all the fucking fillet back for you why .... *can you cook an*
   S2:

8. S1: *artichoke*   yeah *can you cook an artichoke* ..
   S2:   yes Gordon   yes Gordon

9. S1:	how old are you		*twenty four and you can't cook*	
S2:		twenty four Gordon		
10. S1:	*an artichoke*		you you can cook it	
S2:		yes Gordon		yes Gordon
11. S1:	like what like a <fucker>			
S2:				

[...]

What is particularly interesting here is the fact that the repeated strategy of 'Challenge: ask challenging question' is, unlike the instances we have seen before, virtually identical in both realisations in terms of both form as well as propositional content. In staves 7–8 we see S1 challenge S2 with *can you cook an artichoke?*. S2's answer, also in stave 8, of *yes Gordon*, is simply met with an initial *yeah*[6] and then, crucially, is followed with the identical-to-the-first-challenge *can you cook an artichoke* (stave 8). It is perhaps unsurprising that S2 took a full one-second pause before answering this second challenge given the response to his last answer. S2 may well have been taken aback by such use of impolite repetition as its use is likely to engender a sense of confusion over precisely what it is that S1 wants him (S2) to say or would, at least find acceptable. Not only is the strategy repeated, but the lexical items, indeed, the very self-same syntactic structure is also repeated making for an intense, highly charged impolite utterance which together form the impolite belief (Leech 1983:81) that S2 cannot cook. A further issue being that even with the other instances of repeated impoliteness strategies, (where there appears to be a clear desire on the part of the speaker to make the FTA exacerbated in order to heighten the face damage), there does also seem to be confusion over whether the questions are purely sarcastically impolite challenges, genuinely information seeking, or something in between. It is the uncertain status of these, which cause the communication problems with S2. However, it may be safe to say that what has happened in this instance is that all pretence of information seeking has virtually been abandoned. S1 clearly heard S2's answer to *can you cook an artichoke*, we know this as he said *yeah* in response to *S2's yes Gordon*, but to then repeat the exact same 'Challenge' of *can you cook an artichoke* indicates that, in S1's opinion, (a) S2's answer is unsatisfactory and (b) S2 cannot, in point of fact, correctly cook an artichoke despite, (c) being a well trained and experienced Chef de Partie. In fact S1 was to later say to the camera that S2's gaffe of overcooking the artichokes was nothing really

6. Note the interesting pragmatic effects of this expression. Despite its traditional 'agreement' properties, Muntigl and Turnbull (1998: 228) consider that its use can be an oppositional marker.

to worry about. Given S1's reputation, if he really believed S2 could not cook an artichoke he may well be within his rights to end S2's employment forthwith. The fact that he pressured S2 in this way indicates that he was intensely unhappy that S2 made such a fundamental mistake as overcooking artichokes. The global aim, one suspects, is to teach S2 (and indeed the listening kitchen staff who are operating in the discourse role of 'authorised bystanders', see Section 7.1.2.1, below) the folly and consequences of making such basic errors – hence the impoliteness is instrumental. But as we can see repeated usage of one particular strategy can be a powerful tool in further exacerbating the force of impolite utterances.

6.2.1.2 *Complex: Combined utterance realisation*

The second complex way in which impolite utterances are realised in these data sets is where a particular utterance, or turn at talk, combines two or indeed more different impolite (super-)strategies. This, essentially, means that one utterance performs two, or more, strategies simultaneously. As noted (in Section 6.2.1.1) above, Brown and Levinson (1987: 17) resist the idea that strategies can be mixed in terms of face. As we will see, Brown and Levinson's position here is not sustainable in light of the evidence of real-life discourse.

Combining strategies need not be oriented towards just one specific aspect of face. A clear example of combined impolite utterance realisation, which attacks face (both positive and negative in Brown and Levinson's (1987) terms) can be seen in this example taken from **The Clampers, Extract 12**.

[46] ***Context:*** *It is 7.30 in the morning. Bailiff S1 is making his first call of the day to a female driver S2 who has repeatedly ignored parking ticket payment requests. Her husband S3 is also present. S1 has just knocked on S2's door and S3 has answered it.*

1. S1: Court bailiffs   is she in
   S2:
   S3:   yeah   yeah at the moment why what's the problem
2. S1: we've got a court order been issued sir for non payment of fines on
   S2:
   S3:
3. S1: this vehicle ... Harrow council have authorised removal of the vehicle
   S2:
   S3:
4. S1: for non-payment of fines if you can manage to get that sir she's now
   S2:
   S3:

5. S1: got a sum payable of three hundred and twenty one pounds twenty
   S2:
   S3:

6. S1: five and the vehicle will be going into court storage . once she's paid
   S2:
   S3:

7. S1: the fine she can go and collect her vehicle from the court storage fali
   S2:
   S3:

8. S1: facility alright <S2 arrives and pushes then hits S1>
   S2: *what the fuck you doing* excuse me . *what are you*
   S3:

   <S2 hits S1 in mouth – S1 speed dials on his phone>
9. S1: the car is going he has a court order
   S2: *fucking doing* really you want
   S3:

10. S1: <into phone> police please yeah
    S2: some fucking money right
    S3:

[…]

Here, in staves 8–9, S2 (the female car owner) combines the strategy of 'Challenge: ask a challenging question' with the strategy of 'use taboo words' to make *what the fuck you doing*. This particular strategy combination is repeated, albeit in slightly different grammatical form with the *what are you fucking doing* utterance immediately afterwards.

In the example here, whilst the taboo word *fuck(ing)* plays the grammatical role of intensifier (e.g. Quirk et al. 1985: 438–9 and 450), amplifying or boosting the force of the challenge, on an interpersonal level it also marks the extremely negative attitude of the speaker towards the hearer. As Holmes (1984: 363) argues, 'Devices may reinforce one another, as when strong stress, lexical boosters and repetition co-occur in one utterance'. The cumulative effect of using mutually reinforcing impoliteness strategies is to boost the impoliteness.

It needs to be noted here, however, that there are, in fact, *three* separate types of combined strategy realisation in total. The first, we have seen in the above example, with one type of strategy (usually *taboo usage*) being used to *boost*, intensify, or further exacerbate, the impoliteness of the main strategy. The second is where different impolite strategies follow one another in quick succession, usually (but not limited to being) a juxtaposition, and the third is where an otherwise 'single' strategy, in context, effectively 'wraps up' two or more strategies within a single utterance. That is, one utterance performs two, or more, different impolite strategies *simultaneously*. Note the following example taken from **Soldiers To Be, Extract 45.**

[47] ***Context***: *S1 is the inspecting Sergeant Major who has come to check the recruits' turnout and confidence. After a brief pep talk, telling the recruits to relax, he begins his final inspection before they go onto the final phase of drill instruction. S2 is recruit James South. S1 has just chastised the recruit in line before recruit South for poor turnout, he then turns to South.*

1. S1: go on
   S2: private South er wishing to join the-er second light infantry ..
2. S1: *you're a bit of a space cadet you* aren't you
   S2: frommm Sheffield sir
3. S1: right now start again and let's be more confident in what
   S2: yes sir
4. S1: you're saying do not flap
   S2: pri private South wishing to join the second
5. S1: relax a bit .. okay apart from that not
   S2: light infantry . from Sheffield sir
6. S1: a bad turnout at all
   S2:

End.

Note here the utterance, by S1, in stave 2: *you're a bit of a space cadet*. The assertion here, in the context in which it is uttered, is operating both as an instantiation of the *Call h names, use derogatory nominations* strategy (cf. Culpeper 1996) and as an instance of the *Criticism* strategy (see Section 5.5.1, above). Compare this method of combining strategies with the following example, taken from **Soldiers To Be, Extract 30.**

[48] ***Context***: *Burma platoon, the female recruits on field exercise, have spent a cold, rough night outside. The temperature has dropped and they are exhausted. Early in the morning the NCOs inspect the recruits' kit. They do not like what they find. S1 is a corporal inspecting the recruits' kits. S2 and S3 are also corporals assisting S1. They have split up and are 'motivating' the recruits individually and as a team. Other speakers, who will be included in the staves as and when they contribute, are recruits.*

Edit: *Corporal S1 questions recruit S12 on her ability to keep her kit waterproof. He picks up on the fact that the plastic bin liner she is using is full of holes.*

[…]

46. S1: that's its waterproof bag is it this here this here's going
S12: yes corporal

47. S1: to stop it getting soaking wet this bag here the one with the hole in
S12:

48. S1: the end there the one that isn't fastened at the top as a matter of fact
S12:

49. S1: the one that isn't actually a bag . it's actually . a black necklace of
S12:

50. S1: some sort because it isn't a bag is it so all your kit now if
S12: no corporal

51. S1: it was raining out here would just be ss laying there getting soaking
S12:

52. S1: wet and then this kit you've got on would be getting soaking wet
S12:

53. S1: then we're going to go up the hill and do section attacks all
S12:

54. S1: afternoon and you're going to get soaking wet and then I'll say right
S12:

55. S1: okay you've worked hard today get back in your area get changed
S12:

56. S1: into your dry kit OHH no you can't because yours is already fucking
S12:

57. S1: soaking . but not that it matters because you're a minger anyway
S12:

58. S1: because you've got all that dirty kit on because there's nothing in
S12:

59. S1: your bloody clean kit is there . IS THERE *your admin is*
S12: no corporal

60. S1: *so far up your hoop lady I can actually see it coming out of your*
S12:

61. S1: *mouth . waste of space* pack your kit
S12:

End.

In the above example, S1's utterance in staves 59 to 61, can in point of fact, be seen to be two, juxtaposed, instantiations of two separate impoliteness linguistic output strategies. Note the first one in staves 59–60: *your admin is so far up your hoop lady I can actually see it coming out of your mouth*, a hyperbolic criticism (conveyed via the expression of some rather impolite beliefs (cf. Leech 1983)) of S12's inability to keep her spare kit clean and dry. This is then followed by the elided expression of S1's 'impolite beliefs' concerning S12, in stave 60: *waste of space*, which, simply put, suggests that S12 is not a good soldier (in S1's eyes).

Such varied ways of combining impolite phenomena abound in all the data sets studied. Additionally, as I noted above, these complex various ways in which impolite strategies can pattern are not mutually exclusive. Note the following, as one example among many, from **Soldiers To Be, Extract 33.**

[49] ***Context***: *A room inspection. S1 is the inspecting corporal, S2 is the recruit being inspected. S1 has just inspected S2's training shoes. He has picked them up out of S2's locker and has now turned round to ask S2 a question.*

1. S1: turn around . what's that on the bottom of there why's
S2: <dried mud corporal>

2. S1: it on there . PUT YOUR FUCKING FEET TOGETHER WHEN YOU
S2:

3. S1: TALK TO ME why's it on there no excuse . *fucking right*
S2: <no excuse>

4. S1: *you've no excuse you're just fucking fat and idle* aren't you
S2:

End.

In the last two staves, alone, S1 uses (a) the tactic of repetition via the taboo word *fucking* (staves 3 and 4), both instances of which are operating as boosters, amplifying the face damage of (b) the impolite strategies in, both, [*you're*] *right you've no excuse* (staves 3–4: a criticism) and in *you're just fucking fat and idle* (stave 4: the expression of impolite beliefs (cf. Leech 1983). Further note, how (c) these latter two strategies are realised 'hard-and-fast' together, in juxtaposition, to combine one after the other. And we should further note that they all operate, together, to express, on an interpersonal level, the negative attitude held by S1 towards the addressee, S2.

There is no claim that the complex patterning of impolite linguistic phenomena shown here is the only way in which intentionally impolite exacerbated face threats can occur. Indeed, how impoliteness patterns in other types of data set, within other discourses (and even in other activity types to the ones discussed) is a critical and pressing area for future research on impoliteness.

6.3 Utterance 'ends'

Having seen some of the most significant ways in which impoliteness can pattern in complex ways within utterances, it is now worth considering how when utterances or turns-at-talk end, can aid in the delivery, and interpretation of impoliteness.

6.3.1 Post-intensifying interrogatives: Forcing feedback

Consider the following example taken from **Boiling Point, Extract 64.**

[50] ***Context***: *Henry, S2, another Chef de Partie has overcooked the artichokes and, thus, held up another dish for another table. S1 chooses to talk to S2 about this.*

1. S1: <and you see> you you yeah come on the path a minute on the path
   S2:
2. S1: [S1 physically manhandles S2 onto the 'path'] if you send me six
   S2:
3. S1: fucking main courses like that again and I I I'll I'll grab you by the
   S2:
4. S1: fucking scruff of the neck and throw you on the street *do you*
   S2:
5. S1: *understand*
   S2: yes Gordon

[…]

We should note the device, used in stave 4, by chef S1 to force feedback from staff member S2: *do you understand?* This is what I have termed a post-intensifying interrogative and is closely linked to the phenomena I discuss in Chapter 8 (Section 8.4.3, *Challenges, Questions, Tags and Conducivity*) below.

In context, the utterance: *if you send me six fucking main courses like that again and I I I'll I'll grab you by the fucking scruff of the neck and throw you on the street* is already impolite as it is, as it combines (see above) two instances of 'taboo language' (cf. Culpeper 1996: 358) which are boosting the 'threat/frighten' strategy (cf. Culpeper 1996: 358, see Section 5.3 above, also) of being thrown out on the street (and presumably losing his job). However, when further combined with the interrogative *do you understand*, (which forces feedback from the target of the impoliteness, S2), the impoliteness in the utterance becomes even more damaging. The face threat is *intensified* by the 'post-strategic' interrogative. Whilst I have noted the concept here, for the sake of completeness within the concepts discussed in this section and this chapter, I will return to discuss the use of post-intensifying interrogatives in Chapter 8, under the use of questions and conducivity (Section 8.4.2), below. In short, what I mention here, is merely one way of explaining what occurs, in an impoliteness sense, with these forms of tag question.

6.4 Conclusion

Within this chapter, we have seen the dynamics of impoliteness primarily at the utterance level, though, of course, it is virtually impossible to discuss such phenomena without discussing the wider discourse, or context, in which the impoliteness occurs. I have suggested some possibilities for how impolite utterances can be prepared for, that is, how the conversational 'ground' can (potentially) be prepared for the onset and delivery on impoliteness; we have also seen how impolite strategies can co-occur in significant and complex ways within a turn, for additional face damaging effects, and I have touched upon (but will return to in more depth in Chapter 8) how utterances can boost their impoliteness yet further, by forcing participant feedback. It is worth noting that (a) just how prevalent are preparatory impolite utterances; and (b) how frequent the patterning of such complex strategies is, remain areas for future consideration. Indeed, ascertaining the effectiveness of post-intensifying interrogatives in other types of conflictive discourses, whether certain strategies are more likely to be combined or repeated (or combined and repeated), and what the cumulative effects of such tactics are, also remains as future considerations.

Thus noted, I now turn to the dynamics of impoliteness at the discoursal level, that is, how impoliteness is deployed, communicated and countered across extended discourse.

CHAPTER 7

The dynamics of impoliteness II

Dynamics at the discoursal level

In Chapter 6 I discussed how individual impolite utterances began, how they were formulated, and how they ended. In this chapter I look at how impoliteness is deployed and dealt with across extended discourses. First, as I look at how impolite exchanges begin – I briefly discuss how context relates to impoliteness, and I look at the types of phenomena that are responsible for triggering the onset of impoliteness. Secondly, I look at patterns of impoliteness and reactions to it across exchanges. Finally, I look at how impolite-containing, conflictive discourses may come to resolution. I believe that research into such patterns provides some of the richness of context necessary for identifying and analysing impoliteness. That said, just what exactly is 'context' and more importantly for us here, how does it relate to, and shape, the creation and perceptions of impoliteness?

7.1 Discourse 'beginnings'

7.1.1 Context: Defining the activity type

A central understanding of pragmatic theory which bears stating here is that language is not used in a vacuum but is, in fact, used in specific situations by individual interactants for functional purposes. Context includes such concepts as the physical, social and psychological background in which language is used (see Brown and Yule 1983: 36–46; Crystal 1991: 79; Halliday and Hasan 1989: 5–9; Levinson 1983: 23). It is therefore apparent that we need a mechanism by which we can begin to understand the context in which participants within a speech event operate. Levinson (1979) suggests adopting what he terms 'Activity Types'. Drawing from prototype theory for both his approach and terminology, Levinson (1979: 368) defines an activity type as being:

> A fuzzy category whose focal members are goal-defined, socially constituted, bounded, events with constraints on participants, setting and so on, but above all on the kinds of allowable contributions. Paradigm examples would be teaching, a

> job interview, a jural interrogation, a football game, a task in a workshop, a dinner party, and so on. (Levinson 1979: 368)

So Levinson sees the individual's use of language as shaping the event. As Thomas says:

> The pragmaticist [Levinson] tries to show how speakers use language to change the situation they find themselves in. (Thomas 1995: 189)

While I agree, I would go further than this and note that whilst language shapes the situation, the situation shapes the language. Within both the army and police data sets, the particular roles that some interactants have within a speech event are rigidly and traditionally enforced – that is, the participants are constrained, to a greater extent, by their context, than the participants of the car-parking (though of course the clampers are more constrained than the private car owners), kitchen (again, the staff are more constrained in their language use than is the restauranteur), or person-to-person data sets, but, those selfsame participants (with a limited set of options) do, still, try to change the type of speech event in which they find themselves. Note the following example, taken from **Soldiers To Be, Extract 32.**

[51] ***Context***: *Recruit Wilson, S2, is finding the training hard. She is short and finds it hard to keep up with the rest of the platoon on march. Furthermore, once back at camp she falls asleep in class and is disciplined for it. She decides to PVR – that is, she decides to take Premature Voluntary Release – from the army. She calls on the platoon sergeant, S1, who takes a rather interesting tack in order to encourage her to stay.*

[…]

12. S1: you're being paid to learn and if you've got any I'll tell you what if this was
    S2:

13. S1: civvy street and you were caught sleeping what would happen tell me
    S2:

14. S1: you wouldnae get sacked you'd get a written warning
    S2: *I'd get sacked*

15. S1: well that's exactly what's going to happen here you're getting a written
    S2:

16. S1: warning and I'm going to annotate that into your report and any<indistinct>
    S2:

17. S1: you're in front of the company commander and the next step is civvy street
    S2:

18. S1: do you understand me get away .. EH don't just turn away you fall out turn
    S2:
19. S1: to the right sharply and assume you're calling time
    S2: ONE TWO
20. S1: THREE ONE
    S2:

End.

Note S2's response, in stave 14, above to S1's challenge. By saying *I'd get sacked*, S2 may be attempting to short-circuit the speech event of the 'dressing down' which she finds herself in and may be attempting to pre-empt a release from army service[1] – her stated aim for the speech event in this case. It is interesting to note that her attempt to avoid the 'dressing down' was not entirely successful as S1 directly contradicts her in stave 14: *you wouldnae get sacked you'd get a written warning well that's exactly what's going to happen here.*

Even though her specific face want – to be released from army service, and her general face want – to avoid criticism, have both failed here, it is significant in this case that she used her limited linguistic freedom in this situation in an attempt to change the context of the speech event (and thus, attempted to change the speech event itself to one which attended to her desire to leave). This limited-capability manipulation may be captured within Levinson's (1979) activity types and, as such, may well be a step forward in helping us account for such phenomena. But how do we describe an activity type? Thomas (1995: 189–190) provides the following suggestions for the features that could constitute an activity type:

- The Goals of the Participants
- Allowable Contributions
- The degree to which Gricean maxims are adhered to or are suspended
- The degree to which the interpersonal maxims are adhered to or are suspended
- Turn-taking and topic control
- The manipulation of pragmatic parameters

I shall discuss what each of these features mean for impoliteness research, in turn.

1. Her wish to be released from the army is stated, both by the narrator of the scene, and by the recruit in question personally (note the contextual information above). She eventually *does* take PVR (Premature Voluntary Release) from the British Army to work in a coffee shop.

The goals of the participants. These are the goals of the individuals rather than the goals of the event. In the above example, recruit S2's main goal was to be released from the army. S1's goals were to attempt to keep S2 in the army, to train all army recruits (including S2) to the same standard, and to ensure S2 knew her 'lapse' (in falling asleep) was an infraction. In most military 'dressing downs' the local goals of the recruits are often to (a) get the event over with as quickly as possible, and (b) to reduce, as much as possible, the inevitable face damage they are going to suffer. For the NCO trainers of the recruits, the main local goals are often to ensure that (a) the recruit understands what the infraction is for which they are being remonstrated with, and that (b) the recruit does not commit the infraction again. Interestingly, the general, global goals of both recruit and trainer are to ensure that the recruit is trained to an acceptable standard before passing out as a full member of the military.

Allowable contributions. Thomas (1995: 190) notes that some interactions are characterised by social or legal constraints on what participants may say. Within the data sets here studied, this is a primary consideration. Despite their power, the rights they have and the obligations they are under to enforce national and vehicular parking laws, respectively, police and clamping officers may not directly offend the faces of their interactants through the use of certain impolite linguistic output strategies, such as *Use Taboo Language*, without the risk of censure. Likewise army recruits (indeed, all military individuals ranked lower than their interlocutors) have a limited set of linguistic options open to them, generally, when talking to their superiors. No more so does this appear the case than in situations where impoliteness is a significant feature.

The degree to which Gricean maxims are adhered to or are suspended. In army training, for example, one may not expect the Gricean (1975) maxims to be broken any more so than (or even to the same level as), 'normal' everyday conversation – blunt speaking, unmitigated by concerns for the face wants of the recruits, appears to typify army training discourse. In police-to-public encounters, one may not be surprised, for example, for a suspect to violate one or more of the maxims if they are, indeed, guilty of that for which they are a suspect, and do not want to face legal repercussions. But, by the same token, if they are innocent, one would expect them to largely adhere (within normal expectations of use) to the maxims.

The degree to which the interpersonal maxims are adhered to or are suspended. In every one of the data sets here discussed at least one participant in every extract does not adhere to Leech's (1983) interpersonal maxims, specifically the Politeness Principle (PP) (see Section 4.2.1.1, above). However, while the expectation that they will be broken in some way may exist within 'dressing down' activity types, this may not be the case with, for example, an 'informal, on-street, complaint' about a ticket received (an individual may not be talking to the individual who ticketed him, or may be making a general, but polite, protest at being clamped). In short, while some activity types would presume the interpersonal maxims will be broken, for effect, some which *can* result in impoliteness, do not presume this, (rather they anticipate it may be a possibility).

Turn-taking and topic control. As we will see in the next chapter, the degree to which an individual can exploit turn-taking norms in order to control the interaction, to establish his, or her, own agenda, to successfully manage the activity type and achieve their goals is an important and significant area for impoliteness. Socio-legal constraints emplaced on the interactants by their social and discoursal roles in the situation at hand significantly affect the way in which turn-taking and topic control can be exploited, as we will see.

The manipulation of pragmatic parameters. Like all of these concepts, how, and to what extent, the participants can manipulate the pragmatic parameters of the speech event (the social distance; their powers, rights, obligations, the size of the face threat, how the face threat is delivered or managed), are all dependant upon the socio-discoursal roles each participant has. In most cases within the data sets of the current research project, the roles both constrain, and allow, certain manipulations of the pragmatice parameters to take place. The most obvious, of course, is the manipulation of expectations of politeness where it may be considered, at least, a theoretical possibility (the aforementioned politely delivered protest as part of an informal, on-street, complaint).

However, while a valuable 'way in' to studying and understanding how impoliteness is used and countered, much of what Levinson describes through Activity Types only really relates to the co-text (see Chapter 6, Section 6.1.1, above) in which the participants' utterances are made. That said, when we consider other factors, then we can see that Activity Types can help set the context for such utterances to occur. Of these other types of factors, I will first discuss the roles of the participants who are involved in the linguistic interchange.

7.1.2 Context: The interactants (their powers, rights, obligations and roles)

Consideration of the powers, rights, and obligations (cf. Brown and Levinson 1987) of the participants in any speech event, or activity type, is of crucial importance when we consider the use of, or countering of, impoliteness.

7.1.2.1 *Roles in discourse*

The role of participants can be divided into 'social' and 'discoursal' varieties. It is important, Thomas points out (1986: 92), not to confuse the two concepts. However, the two do, often, go hand in hand, as we will see.

Social roles

The social role of an individual is vitally important. Social role generally refers to the social relationship obtaining between one participant and another in a linguistic exchange. Social roles in the data sets studies include: **The Clampers** and **Parking Wars** – Parking Attendant, Legal Adjudicator, Vehicle Pound Administrator, Local Government Officer, Private Vehicle Owner, Neighbour. **Soldiers to Be** and **Redcaps** – Training NCOs, Officers, Recruits. **Boiling Point** – Restaurant-owner-and-Chef, Maitre-de, Waiter, Commis Chef, Chef de Partie, Chef. **Motorway Life** and **Raw Blues** – Police Officer, Suspect, Trainee, Private Citizen.

While I am aware of the distinction to be made across many different subtypes of social role (societal, intepersonal, etc.) which refer to interactants in a linguistic interchange, the overt definition and explanation here, is not needed (though is an area for future consideration). The social roles of the participants in an interaction imply power, rights and obligations of the participants. The applicability of considering social roles with regards to impoliteness I have already mentioned above (see Chapter 5, 'enforce role shift' 5.5.3, above), and to which I will return in Section 7.2.1.3 'Abrogation', below.

Discourse roles I: Producers of talk

The discourse role refers to the relationship between the participants and the message. Thomas identifies a number of different types of individual who produce 'talk' (summarised from Thomas 1986: 111–138).

Speaker – Unless otherwise indicated the speaker is assumed to be speaking on his/her own authority. Can be reclassified, upon indication, as follows:
Author – The originator of an illocutionary act.
Mouthpiece (the individual operates within a surrogate role) – not directly identified with the authority, but represents the author behind the illocutionary act. Not held responsible for the illocutionary act.
Spokesperson (the individual operates within a surrogate role) – may be a member of the group that authorised the message.
Reporter – Has no mandate from the author & does not represent the author, but has "self-selected" to report an illocutionary act.

Discourse roles II: Receivers of talk
Likewise, Thomas identifies a number of different types of individual who receive 'talk' (summarised from Thomas 1986). To begin she differentiates between the two main types of hearer, thus: (a) **Addressee**: The person to whom the utterance is directed, *versus*, (b) **Hearer**: Not directly addressed, but legitimately present at a speech event.

She further subdivides the classification of **Addressee** into "Real" versus. "Ostensible" addressees.
Real: Within earshot and is intended to hear the utterance and recognise it for what it is and to whom it is directed.
Ostensible: The purported addressee, to whom the utterance is ostensibly addressed – works best when the ostensible addressee cannot possibly understand what is going on – (e.g. If I was to ask the family dog if my wife has fed her, when my wife is present).

Thomas further notes a distinction between **Addressees** vs. **Audience**: The distinction, Thomas admits, is slight. The main difference being that audiences have no/reduced speaking rights. Both are active participants in a speech event. For example, jurors have no speaking rights, but all arguments are directed at the jury. Failure of argumentation by the legal counsel could lead to loss of liberty, property or life (extreme cases), etc. for the defendant.

The types of 'hearer' which Thomas defines, are: **Bystanders** and **Overhearers**.

Bystanders: Bystanders are known to be in earshot but not sanctioned. They are not the target of the speaker's message but may, nevertheless, affect the way s/he speaks.

Overhearer: Not known to be in earshot and not sanctioned – as a rule the speaker does not realise the overhearer is there and, therefore, the overhearer does not affect the way the speaker delivers the utterance. (Adapted, and modified from Thomas 1986.)

Consideration of the social and discoursal roles of the participants in linguistic interchanges which contain impoliteness is crucial. Without considering the roles of the participants, then we may not gain a full appreciation of the way in which impoliteness is handled or dealt with. Note the following example taken from **Soldiers to Be, Extract 26.**

[52] Context: S1 the drill sergeant has just received a platoon of guards recruits. They are performing poorly at drill. He singles out one recruit (S2) for his poor performance.

1. S1: *hey . are you on a fucking Sunday outing are you .... eh* *well*
   S2: <no sergeant>
2. S1: *what do you think you're doing waltzing around .... if I see not getting er*
   S2:
3. S1: *not moving your arms short and sharp I'll lock you up* not a problem not
   S2:
4. S1: bother me you'll be moving short and sharp when you get down there
   S2:
5. S1: *there's a lot of you as well a lot of you are being idle* right you've got to
   S2:
6. S1: start yeah making these bodies move short and sharp it's not happening
   S2:
7. S1: at the minute
   S2:

End.

An individual's social role implies certain rights, certain powers, and certain obligations. In this example, drill sergeant S1 singles out recruit S2 for a specific purpose. This could be interpreted as being an instance whereby S1's impolite remarks in staves 1–3 are indirectly referring to the fact that S2 is not performing assigned tasks the way in which a soldier (which is recruit, S2's, social role) is obliged. More than this, S1 is, apparently, singling out S2 for impolite, *taboo* and *sarcasm* boosted *criticism* (see Chapter 5, Section 5.5.1), as a way of informing the whole squad, who are *bystanders* to the linguistic interchange, that they have not been operating to the requirements of their social roles as soldiers. That this is the case is evidenced in stave 5, where S1 enforces a discoursal role shift on the squad-as-bystanders, to the squad-as-direct-addressees with the utterance *there's a lot of you as well a lot of you are being idle* which helps strengthen the implication of impolite beliefs about the squad's activities and abilities as soldiers.

In this next example, taken from **Boiling Point, Extract 65,** Gordon, S1, has physically hauled Owen, S2 and another chef, Henry, along the 'path' to stand near to Mark. This is at the front of the kitchen where all of the staff may see what transpires.

[53]

1. S1: I've just filled out err Mark I've just filled out a form for <paying everyone's
   S2:

2. S1: salaries> do you know what I've put him down as a Chef de
   S2: <indistinct>
3. S1: Partie yeah . you know what he is . he's a Chef de Partie as well . [turns to
   S2:
4. S1: Henry] *you are from now on a Commis and you* [hits Owen] *are a fucking*
   S2:
   [points at each]
5. S1: *Commis* don't like that give me your notice and fuck off . *Commis* . *Commis*
   S2:
6. S1: now fuck off . yeah and young man if you can't stand the salary not enough
   S2:
7. S1: money do you know what you can do write your fucking notice and fuck
   S2:
8. S1: right off . with pleasure .. when I turn on some fucker I wash my fucking
   S2:
9. S1: hands clean . okay Commis feel happy now less stressed .. want
   S2: oui Gordon
10. S1: a little cry Chef de Partie .. Mark .. Mark .. Chef de Partie
    S2: no Gordon ......
11. S1: .... a Chef de Partie ....<indistinct> ay ay I don't give a fuck if you go
    S2:
12. S1: do you know that .. I'll never miss dickheads . never . never ever ever ever
    S2:

End.

Interestingly there are a number of role related issues to do with the way in which impoliteness is being issued. Like the above example, the rest of the watching kitchen staff are (at least potentially) operating as receivers of the exchange, within discoursal roles of *bystanders*. The message that follows acts as a potential warning to them. The impoliteness against the *direct* addressees is being constructed, in part, by the enforcement of new social roles upon them – each of them are being demoted from a role in the kitchen as a *Chef de Partie* (a medium ranked member of the cooking staff), to being a *Commis Chef* (the lowest of the cooking staff within a kitchen). Interestingly, the fact that S1 has the power (as the restaurant owner, and their employer) to demote the two direct addressees, here, is by no means a mitigating factor for the FTA of demotion (as Brown and Levinson (1987) might suggest). In fact it is one of the essential pre-conditions for such a speech act to be successfully delivered.

In the final example, an impolite utterance *about* an individual who was assumed not to be within earshot implies a certain role for the subject of the comment. The example is taken from **Motorway Life, Extract 71.**

[54] ***Context***: *S1, PC Justine Jackson has stopped on the motorway to talk to two pedestrians who are new-age travellers. S2 is the man, S3 is his pregnant girlfriend. They have quite clearly just walked onto the motorway from the off-ramp and, indeed, are still on it. As S1 pulls up to a stop, S2 and S3 attempt to carry on walking, away from the police car.*

1. S1: wait a minute wait a minute where you going
   S2: just going to go ring a mate up
   S3:

2. S1: why where where have you come from
   S2: to ger get him to give us a lift
   S3:

3. S1: because you're on the motorway here you know it's covered by
   S2: Bristol
   S3:

4. S1: motorway regulations and you're not allowed to be a pedestrian on the
   S2: yeah aye
   S3:

5. S1: motorway
   S2: well we're going to go ring him up and tell him to give us a lift anyway
   S3:

6. S1: right it's a thousand pound fine as well
   S2: cos we can't get one anyway . .
   S3:

7. S1: [S1 turns to get a notebook out of the police car] right and no I haven't
   S2: is it?
   S3: *hasn't she got better things to do with her time …*

8. S1: got better things to do than this is my job this is what I do alright at the end
   S2:
   S3: right

9. S1: of the day you're of no fixed abode at the moment you're committing an
   S2:
   S3:

10. S1: offence I can lock you up . alright so don't be funny and make snide rem
    S2:
    S3: right
11. S1: remarks to your boyfriend because you're very lucky you're not going to
    S2:
    S3:
12. S1: the police station
    S2:
    S3:

End.

Here, in this situation, S3's comment about S1 'behind-her-back' (quite literally – as the police officer had her back turned) indicates that S3 assumed that the officer was out of earshot and that her *sotto voce* comment would, therefore, be unheard. However, the fact that the officer (S1) heard it, indicates that S1 was operating in the discoursal role of an *overhearer*. The comment, derisory *about* S1, was not meant to be heard *by* S1. Beyond the implications for roles, here, this example indicates that offence can be taken from derisory comments even if face damage was not *directed at* the person offended. S3 had clearly intended her comment to be interpreted, by S2, as being offensive about S1, but she had not intended S1 to hear it.

Common across the data sets used in this study is a consideration of the socio-discoursal roles of all the participants. The impolite implications behind how participant roles are referred to, changed, switched, and indeed enforced is clearly an area for further, future consideration. This is especially important considering the central importance of *both* social, as well as discoursal roles in implying power, rights and obligations of an interactant. Sufficed to say at this stage that the time and location sensitive nature of all utterances even tends to subsume certain elements of an individual's Power, Rights and Obligations within a given speech event as the following example, which deals with social roles, shows. The example is taken, not from my corpus of data sets, but from an American comedy show 'Third Rock from the Sun'. I have used this example only for clear explanatory purposes. The show centres upon a group of 4 non-human space aliens who are masquerading as human beings in order to observe human society. One, 'Dr Dick Allbright', poses as a physics lecturer at a local college. He has a long suffering (human) secretary called 'Nina'. Nina is friends with the alien posing as Dick Allbright's sister and calls round to the Allbright's 'family' home one evening to invite Allbright's sister out for a drink. After being shown in by Dr Allbright's sister, who then hurries off to get ready for an evening out, Nina steps into the front room in which Dr Allbright is reading. He has just finished his mug of coffee when he notices Nina's arrival:

Dick Allbright: (*Holding mug up in the air*): Ah Nina! Get me another cup of coffee will you?
Nina (*Indignant*): You can get your own coffee, Dr Allbright!

Clearly, the imposition of Nina having to make Dr Allbright's coffee can only be mitigated when both are at work in normal working hours – to extract both from the time and location of work and assume that Dr Allbright's rights and power still force an obligation on Nina is clearly erroneous, as Nina's all-too-human reaction shows. Dr Allbright did not understand why Nina would not get him another coffee (he is, after all, an alien and her boss) but the imposition, in the particular time and location, was not one which Nina was willing to accept. Note that not all aspects of power, rights and obligations were subsumed – Nina still referred to Dick, deferentially, as 'Dr Allbright'. He is still, outside of work time and work space, a Doctor after all (or at least she believes him to be), but outside of work he is no longer her work-superior, especially in a social-home setting. Essentially, there is a clash of schemata here. As such, his request, whilst perfectly normal in a work setting, is unsupported by the considerations of power, rights and obligations that normally obtain between them and, actually, this request comes across as an unintentional (but, for the audience, amusing) FTA here.

7.1.3 Other aspects of the context: Given, background knowledge

As Gabrielatos (2001) notes, apart from knowledge of language, the context and the participants' roles, producers and receivers in a linguistic interchange need to make use of background knowledge relevant to the situation in order to interpret the messages of producers. In this example, taken from **Extract 1, The Clampers,** we can see the significance of given, background, knowledge.

[55] ***Context:*** *Ray and Miguel, clamping supervisor and assistant respectively have arrived to remove the clamp from a van. The van's owner is waiting for them. S1 is Ray, S2, the van's owner.*

1. S1: hi there sir this yours
   S2: yeah it is yeah *I'd like to er ask you why you clamped it*
2. S1: why we clamped it you see
   S2: yeah there's nobody here for one hundred and fifty yards

[…]

As discussed earlier, it is given, background knowledge for all British drivers on UK roads that double yellow lines mean that parking is prohibited at all times. That S2 specifically asks S1 the reason why S2 has had his vehicle clamped while it is parked on double yellow lines, breaks the contextual expectations of the situation. This violation is what signals that *can I ask you why you clamped it* is, potentially, not operating as a polite (pre-)request, but is a potential pre-impoliteness. Thus noted, as I have discussed this, above, I will not dwell on it further here.

The dynamism of context

What is of specific interest to a chapter dealing with the dynamics of impoliteness is the *dynamic* potential of context. As van Dijk notes:

> A first property of context to be emphasised is its 'dynamic' character. A context is not just one possible world-state, but at least a sequence of world-states. Moreover, these situations do not remain identical in time, but *change*. Hence a context is a COURSE OF EVENTS. Such a course of events has, [...] an initial state, intermediary states and a final state. (van Dijk 1977: 191–192).

This is of central importance to us here because the context within a specific linguistic exchange can change as the discourse progresses. Note the following example, taken from **Redcaps, Extract 50.**

[56] ***Context***: *The Redcap recruits have a room inspection. S1 is a sergeant, S2 is recruit McKee. McKee has previously been signed onto the sick roll with a head cold from which he is still suffering*

9. S1: .. one step forward MARCH what's wrong with your locker
   S2: [Steps forward]
   [sergeant notices footwear in locker]
10. S1: this morning McKee .. get your respirator out .... WHAT ARE YOU
   S2:
11. S1: DOING SHOWING ME YOUR SLIPPERS McKEE
   S2: er corporal green
12. S1:
   S2: says that I'm to show my slippers in my locker for every inspection
13. S1: =WHY
   S2: sergeant= erm when I'm asked by the inspecting . erm officer sergeant
14. S1: that's about right isn't it
   S2: I'm supposed to reply I am slipper McKee

15. S1: McKee going sick with a shagging cold
S2: sergeant

End.

Note here, how the activity type changed from being a *Barrack-Room inspection* to being an *informal 'Dressing Down'* following the triggering situation (see below) of non-military items of kit in a military clothing locker. The dynamism of the Activity Types is not just an occurence in military training discourse. Note the following example from **The Clampers, Extract 17.**

[57] ***Context:*** *Ticketer, S1, is working Meadow Garth Road at 8.30 a.m. The road is adjacent to a primary school and parents often 'illegally' park while dropping their children off. S2 is a mother being ticketed, S3 is another mother and S4 is the school's headmistress.*

1. S1: yes madam
S2: Excuse me are you the traffic warden who's been specially asked to come
S3:
S4:

2. S1:
S2: along and er check up on the s um cars who are parking with the school
S3:
S4:

3. S1: no madam one one at a time ladies one I can
S2: you just happened to turn up here
S3: your job is
S4: this is not on because we have a disp[ensation]

4. S1: only talk to one okay absolutely right madam and
S2: you're
S3: to give out tickets go to Holdsden that's a big problem in Holdsden allright
S4:

5. S1: right can I ask you a question where is this car parked:.... wait two
S2:
S3:
S4: look

6. S1: seconds answer <her> question first where is this car parked
S2:
S3:
S4: no no

[...]

Note how the Activity Type in which S1 was engaged (question and answer session with a member of the public) soon moves, from staves 3-to-5 onwards, with *this is not on* and *your job is to give out tickets go to Holdsden*, into an 'on-street complaint'. Clearly, (and at the risk of being too generic), the fact that contexts are dynamic, they move from one course of events to another, is something that all studies of discourse, not just studies of impoliteness, need to consider.

The above examples primarily refer to the change from one existing state, to another. They do not cover the 'initial states', which trigger the impolite containing Activity Types, nor do they consider the 'final states', how the conflict is resolved. I turn to such considerations now.

7.1.4 Triggering impoliteness: The 'offending event' (Jay 1992)

Impoliteness does not exist in a vacuum and it does not in normal circumstances just spring from 'out of the blue'. The contexts in which impoliteness appears and is utilised strategically must have been previously invoked, that is, with all other things being equal, the interactant who utters impoliteness must have felt sufficiently provoked at some point prior to actually delivering the impoliteness. As we noted in Culpeper et al. (2003: 1547) episodes in which impolite confrontation occur centre around some sort of initial dispute, that is, they consist of 'general disagreements in interaction which are displayed by the occurrence of some sort of opposition to an antecedent event' (Corsaro and Rizzo 1990: 26). Essentially impoliteness is triggered by what is perceived to be a threat to some aspect of the impoliteness utterer's face. What I will discuss in this section then is the type of phenomena that can be seen to be triggering impoliteness.

As I noted in Section 4.5.4, above, Jay (1992, 2000)[2] discusses 'cursing' (which he defines (1992: 9) as wishing harm[3] on someone), including the phenomena that can trigger such language. As noted, he listed the following two major considerations, each with major elements, which can operate as 'triggers' resulting in aggressive language behaviour as a response:

> *The Offender:* (Age; Sex; Status; Ethnic Group; Physical Appearance; Social-Physical Setting; Self as Wrongdoer; Non-Human Wrongdoer),
>
> *The Event:* (Behaviour; Language; (Perception of) Intentionality; Damage (or Cost)).

2. I am grateful to Jonathan Culpeper for originally bringing these texts to my attention.

3. Here I am interpreting 'Harm' to mean mental, psychological and emotional harm as well as physical harm.

These Jay views as constituting the most important elements of the 'Offending Event' (1992, 2000). Jay notes that the major elements are not static and will not always trigger the same type of aggressive linguistic response. They both can and do vary from situation to situation, that is, they're wholly dependent upon the context.

As an example of an 'offending event' resulting in impoliteness as a response, note the following taken from *Soldiers To Be*

[58] ***Context***: *S1 the drill sergeant has just received a platoon of guards recruits. They are generally performing poorly at drill. S1 singles out one recruit, S2, for his exceptionally poor performance. S2 seems to be out of step with the other recruits.*

1. S1: hey . *are you on a fucking Sunday outing are you* ...eh?
   S2: <no sergeant>

[...]

Here, by reference to Jay's model, we can see that S2's poor drill performance appears to be operating as an *Offending Event* based, primarily, on his combined EVENT-BEHAVIOR which leads him into becoming an OFFENDER (Jay 1992) in S1's eyes.[4] It is this offending event which *triggers* the impolite response from S1 that we can see in stave 1, namely: *Hey, are you on a fucking Sunday outing are you, eh?* This appears to be not only a sarcastically (Culpeper 1996: 356–357; 2005: 60–63) impolite question, via flouts of Grice's (1975–1989) maxims of quantity (where the addressee is – on an army parade ground practicing drill – is already known to the addresser), manner (it is a sarcastic, non-genuine question) and possibly, relation (Sunday outings and military training appear to have nothing in common), it also combines (see Section 6.2.1.2 above) with the linguistic impoliteness strategy *use taboo language* (Culpeper 1996) where the word *fucking* is acting as a 'booster' to the *sarcasm* (see Section 5.2 above for a discussion of this phenomenon). Taken together, the combination through the expression of *taboo-boosted sarcasm* forms the more global strategy of being an impolitely expressed *criticism* (cf. see Section 5.2 and, Culpeper 2005; Culpeper et al. 2003). Such occurrences are not limited to the army training data. Note the example below, taken from *Boiling Point*.

[59] ***Context***: *Restaurateur Gordon Ramsay, S1, berates, Owen, S2 who has dropped some dishes in the busy kitchen*

4. As we can see, Jay's salient elements of the 'Offending Event' are probably best seen as points or reference rather than as discrete categories. The salient elements can combine within Offending Events to become 'triggers' to the expression of cursing, or, importantly for us here, the communication of impoliteness.

1. S1: oh *come on donkey* who was that get a grip Owen
   S2: me Gordon ...... yes Gordon

[...]

Here speaker 2's actions of accidentally dropping the dishes seem to have allowed speaker 1 to view speaker 2 as performing an offending event through reference to EVENT-BEHAVIOR. Essentially, this is a similar situation to the one discussed in [3] above. The use of the conventionalised dysphemism (Bolinger 1980: 72–73) *donkey* as a term of abuse falling into the category of *call h names* (Culpeper 1996) is the impolite response to the triggering 'offending event' of Owen accidentally dropping the dishes. So, in summary, we can now see how, in response to an offending event performed by interactant 'A', feelings of frustration, anger, annoyance, or similar, could be triggered in an interactant 'B' resulting in the issuing of an impolite 'response' to the triggering event. Of course, this is not to suggest *in any way whatsoever* that impoliteness is the only possible response to an offending event. There are many possible responses to offending events – as I explore throughout the rest of this chapter, below. I should note two additional things: Firstly, (i) it is not by any means the case that responses (impolite or otherwise) to a response-triggering Offending Event come hard and fast after the actualisation of the Offending Event. Responses to Jay's (1992) 'Offending Events' can come after a single situation, or can be the proverbial 'final straw that broke the camel's back' in that the offending event can be the final element of a wider, cumulatively offensive sequence of events which are separated from the present moment in space and time. Therefore, it is perhaps wise to refer to the phenomena here not as 'Offending *Events*' (which suggests single, *in situ* occurrences) but rather as 'Offending *Situations*' from this point onwards. Secondly, (ii) the combination of EVENT-BEHAVIOR as forming an Offending Situation is not the only format that such 'impoliteness triggers' take in the data sets here studied. Whilst the salient element EVENT either singly or combined with the element BEHAVIOR was often implicated, the precise make-up of impolite triggering offending situations took many forms. Here we should note that, given S1's impolite response, below, the element of BEHAVIOR combines with the PHYSICAL APPEARANCE of S5's goods (Speaker's negative evaluation of Hearer's goods is a positive face threat. See Brown and Levinson 1987: 66) and with the STATUS of S5 in S1's eyes to form an offending situation which triggers impoliteness. Note the following:

[60] ***Context***: *Burma platoon, the female recruits on field exercise have spent a cold, rough night outside. The temperature has dropped and they are exhausted. Early in the morning the NCO's inspect the recruits' kit. They do not like what they find. S1 is a corporal inspecting the recruits' kits. S2 and S3 are also corporals assisting S1. They have*

split up and are 'motivating' the recruits both individually and as a team. They have been inspecting recruit after recruit and have been finding infractions. In this exchange Speaker 5 (S5) is the second recruit to be singled out. Her kit, whilst laid out on the ground, is unclean and in a state of disarray.

[…]

[S1 picks up and inspects items of S5's kit]

14. S1: *FUCKING HELL* .... you might as well not bother coming along had you ..
    S5:
15. S1:*everything is minging* did you just like not bother last night you just think *ah*
    S5:
16. S1:*sod it I'm nearly finished can't be bothered six weeks I'm a trained soldier*
    S5:
17. S1: *or something* ...... <gestures that he expects an answer> *no*
    S5: no corporal
18. S1: *you're not are you*
    S5:

[…]

Following the 'offending situation' made by speaker 5's BEHAVIOR (or lack of it in failing to clean her kit and keep it organised (cf. PHYSICAL APPEARANCE as an offending situation (Jay 1992)) prior to the EVENT of the kit inspection, speaker 1 also makes reference to speaker 5's STATUS. This suggests it is also implicated in the offending situation which has triggered the impolite utterance in stave 14, *use taboo language* (Culpeper 1996) with *FUCKING HELL* which also, via a flout of Grice's (1975) maxim of manner, implicates the impolite belief that the state of S5's equipment is unacceptable and, thus, has shocked S1. With S1's turn in stave 15, of *everything is minging*[5] this appears to be the impolitely expressed belief (see Leech 1983: 81) that her kit and equipment is in an unacceptable state and, as such, it appears to be operating as a *criticism* (see Culpeper et al. 2003). Finally, S1's turn is staves 15–18 of *ah sod it I'm nearly finished can't be bothered six weeks I'm a trained soldier or something* is the expression of impolite beliefs, via S1's hypothetical representation and assessment of S5's point of view and direct thoughts (See Holt 2007) that S5 (in S1's eyes) considers her status to be superior to what it actually is. It appears, therefore, that the salient elements of

5. *Minging* (the first 'g' is pronounced as a voiced nasal or velar plosive phoneme (dependent upon British English accent) as opposed to a voiced palato-alveolar affricate [ʤ]) is a pejorative British English colloquialism. It refers to the filthy, dirty, ugly, unkempt and/or other distasteful characteristics of the subject being described.

the offending situations that can trigger the issuing of impoliteness are not to be considered as discrete 'stand-alone' elements, but rather as elements which can and do combine to become impolite 'triggers'.

By and large, in *The Clampers* and *Parking Wars* data sets, such initial triggers to impoliteness were often just one participant's vehicle being the recipient of a parking ticket (indictment) or a clamp, or the vehicle being towed away. In the Kitchen data, *Boiling Point*, and the Military (*Redcaps* and *Soldiers to Be*) and Police training (*Raw Blues*) data sets, the triggering event for impoliteness was the perception, by a superior, of a subordinate's infraction. In the Police activities data (*Raw Blues* and *Motorway Life*) the triggering event was often the result of a stop and search, an arrest, or of police questioning. In other cases it was simply the actions of, or comments made by, another participant which triggered the impoliteness.

In effect what causes the onset of impolite containing utterances by a particular interlocutor is virtually any (at least, perceived) aggressive, antecedent, event (intentional or otherwise) which offends, threatens or otherwise damages the face of the interlocutor.

7.2 Discourse 'middles'

Thus far, I have looked purely at impolite responses to offending situations. What I have not yet fully considered is that any given response to an offending situation could itself be seen as a *further* triggering, offending situation, which could, in turn, lead to feelings of frustration or anger in the/an other interlocutor which could, in turn, lead to the expression of a new impolite utterance, and so on and so forth. Locher (2004: 29, 174, 211, 309, 317–318 & 328) discusses how, in argument sequences, interlocutors can 'propel each other along' whereby *responses* to what is considered here an *offending situation* can also be, themselves, considered as *offending situations.* To put it another way, when impoliteness is triggered, the impoliteness expressed, communicated and understood could trigger the expression and communication of impoliteness in response, and so on.

In the next section then, I will be discussing the myriad dynamic ways in which impoliteness and other forms of face-threatening behaviour can be realised across the whole discourse once the 'antecedent event' or 'offending situation' has triggered the onset of such linguistic phenomena.

7.2.1 Choices when faced with an offending event[6]

Thomas (1986: ii) states that ' […] naturally-occurring interaction [...] far from being "cooperative" in the everyday (i.e. social-goal sharing) sense of the word is "confrontational" or "gladiatorial"'. Impoliteness, of course, is one way of being 'confrontational' or 'gladiatorial', but it is only one side of the battle: it takes two to have a fight. As Culpeper et al. (2003) note, research on both politeness and impoliteness has tended to overlook what the recipient of an offending event such as a face threat or a face attack does in response.

7.2.1.1 *Respond vs. do not respond*

Analysis of the data sets indicates that when a recipient of an utterance perceives an initial offending event, or a mid-discourse strategic impoliteness act, that is, an exacerbated face threatening act (FTA) has been performed, they have two choices open to them: they can choose either to respond or not to respond (i.e. Stay Silent).

Choosing not to respond

There is one major consideration for any researcher here. This is the sheer difficulty of analysing and interpreting any given 'silence'. Staying Silent may signal any number of phenomena, or intended participant aims, within a conversational exchange. For example, defending one's own face is one such possible reason for Staying Silent in the face of an impolite attack. Other reasons include being offensive, that is, refusing to speak when an expectation to speak exists, as noted by Thomas (1995: 175), but perhaps more so, if the expectation to be polite exists as noted by Culpeper (1996: 357). Other reasons include (a) the participant not hearing the content of the utterance of one's interlocutor; (b) accepting the FTA; or (c) simply not having understood the content of the utterance of one's interlocutor, amongst others.

Staying Silent may indicate cognitive thinking time in shaping how one wants to respond; it may even indicate that the individual who is Staying Silent is simply 'struck dumb' or 'lost for words' given their interlocutor's utterance turn. It may even indicate that the individual Staying Silent simply hasn't got anything to

6. It needs to be noted, at this point, that I draw upon, and (re)elaborate on the points, concepts and overall discussion we made in Culpeper et al. (2003). The work discussed here is based on earlier drafts of this chapter, and the input of my co-authors for the aforementioned paper. As the authors of this paper, we decided, for reasons of space and expediency, to present only the initial, basic ideas upon which I now (re)elaborate and present with a wider set of examples.

say on the subject. Indeed, there are as many reasons to Stay Silent as there are contexts in which conversation can take place. As such, it has been my task to analyse and interpret 'silences' by deciding, from a conversation analysis point of view – by what comes after a silence – whether such silences are of significance to impoliteness and, if so, how so. In short, one has had to choose those instances of silence which are strategically played for some aspect of face importance. In sum, choosing not to respond to a face attack presents particular problems for both the other participants in the original speech event and the researcher, who must depend solely on contextual factors in interpreting the meaning of the silence. The other participants, however, do not seem to be limited with the constraints of the analyst. Some interlocutors do assign meaning to silences and (re)act accordingly. Therefore, the problem with Staying Silent, whether strategic or enforced for whatever reason, is the riskiness of the strategy as the following example shows, taken from **Redcaps, Extract 53.**

[61] ***Context***: *Following his unsatisfactory showing at the morning's barrack room inspection, Private Baxter (S2) has an appointment with the Company Sergeant Major (S1). Baxter marches into the CSM's office as the extract starts.*

[…]

7. S1: why why are you in front of me now .. I'LL TELL YOU WHY because
   S2:

8. S1: you've failed to comply with two verbal orders is that true or is that not
   S2:

9. S1: true IT IS TRUE ISN'T IT but what is the first one you have failed on
   S2: sir

10. S1: monday evening you were told to put your name in all your military items
    S2:

11. S1: of clothing did you do it . NO YOU DIDN'T . WHY NOT
    S2: no excuse sir

12. S1:NO EXCUSE you don't walk in my office and say no excuse and <unclear>
    S2:

13. S1: off the top of my head you ensure that if you're given a verbal order you
    S2:

14. S1: CARRY OUT that instruction do you understand= and the second
    S2: =YES SIR

15. S1: offence what's the second offence which you failed to comply with
    S2: failed

16. S1: =WHY . THE REST OF YOUR SQUAD . had a haircut
S2: to get a haircut sir=

17. S1: THE REST OF YOUR SQUAD . paraded yesterday . we've got a camp
S2:

18. S1: barber to come in and do you from town to save you running down to the
S2:

19. S1: town and paying civilian prices downtown ALL YOU HAVE TO DO IS
S2:

20. S1: PRESENT YOUR BODY in front of the barber sitting in the chair with the
S2:

21. S1: rest of your body square and square to the front and be in the position of
S2:

22. S1: attention HE'LL THEN CUT YOUR HAIR..you then pay him the Queen's
S2:

23. S1: shilling and then move out why did you fail to do it are you got an attitude
S2:

24. S1: problem then why didn't you get it cut ... COME ON THEN
S2: no sir

25. S1: SPEAK TO ME OH DEAR UNFORTUNATELY
S2: the queue was very long sir and I

26. S1: YOU HAD TO QUEUE UP
S2:

[...]

What has happened here is that, in stave 24 Baxter, the recruit (S2) has effectively been penalised for choosing not to respond. However, the reasons for his choice of employing the Stay Silent option here are very interesting. Note staves 7 to 11 earlier in the extract. Baxter, S2, is asked direct questions in the form of impolite challenges, by S1. However, any attempts to answer are denied through repeated usage of the impolite *Hinder: interrupt strategy* (see Section 5.5.2, and Section 7.2). We can see this clearly with the extended utterance of S1 over staves 7–11 (note the emboldened utterances): *why why are you in front of me now .. I'LL TELL YOU WHY because you've failed to comply with two verbal orders is that true or is that not true IT IS TRUE ISN'T IT but what is the first one you have failed on monday evening you were told to put your name in all your military items of clothing did you do it . NO YOU DIDN'T . WHY NOT*

In no less than three cases here S1 first Challenges S2 and then denies S2 the conversational floor (I will return to this example for further, in depth discussion of this point in Chapter 8, Section 8.4). It is only when S1 issues the Challenge *WHY NOT* that S2 is allowed to answer. Given the overall strategy that S1 had been producing here, of following a Challenge strategy with a Hinder strategy, it is perhaps unsurprising that S2 chose to opt for the strategy of Staying Silent in stave 23 when challenged with *then why didn't you get it cut...* This has been done, presumably, in an attempt to reduce the face damage of attempting to speak when a turn has not been allocated. The problem here then being that his silence provokes the response *COME ON THEN SPEAK TO ME* which is an implied criticism of S2's silence combined with an explicit shout. Ultimately then, this strategic use of Stay Silent fails here, in this instance, as S2's forced response of the *queue was very long sir and I* is met immediately with derision, sarcasm, shouting, criticism and a turn denial with: *OH DEAR UNFORTUNATELY the queue was very long*. Thus his explanatory utterance, given while being forced to speak, ended up being a trigger for further face damage to occur.

It is necessary to note here that while Staying Silent sometimes backfires, as in the above example, it does have the potential to be successful. This is obviously why it is used. In strategic terms, Staying Silent appears to be deployed as a way of attempting to save face, as we saw above. In this extract, taken from Soldiers to Be extract 30, the recruits have been taken on a field exercise. They have been away one night and are now being subjected to a spot check of their weapons, equipment and all other items of kit. S2, the corporal has discovered that S1 had not fully filled up her water canteen when she had the opportunity to do so the evening before. S2, the corporal takes what water is left in S1's water canteen and pours it over S2's head. After an initial reaction to step back she merely stands still and *submits* to the drenching. Taken from **Soldiers To Be, Extract 30.**

[62] ***Context***: *Burma platoon, the female recruits on field exercise have spent a cold, rough night outside. The temperature has dropped and they are exhausted. Early in the morning the NCOs inspect the recruits' kit. They do not like what they find. S1 is a corporal inspecting the recruits' kits. S2 and S3 are also corporals assisting S1. They have split up and are 'motivating' the recruits individually and as a team. Other speakers, who will be included in the staves as and when they contribute, are recruits.*

[...]

45. S1:
S2: what are you going to do now .... you're going to dehydrate aren't
S3:
S11:

46. S1:
  S2: you harvey . . harvey you're going to dehydrate aren't you . make sure
  S3:
  S11:

47. S1:
  S2: it's full
  S3:
  S11:

[…]

Here we see recruit Harvey, S1, opt to 'Stay Silent' on no less then three occasions when she is asked a direct question by the corporal, S2, and where an answer is clearly expected to be forthcoming from her. Her first instance of Staying Silent occurs immediately after the 'Challenge' *what are you going to do now* in stave 45. Her decision not to answer does, initially, provoke a second impoliteness from S2 when he points out the impolite belief detrimental to S1 that *you're going to dehydrate* (stave 45–46). It is impolite as it was S2 who poured away the remainder of S1's water and, thus, her dehydration is his fault at least in part. This is followed by the post-impoliteness-intensifying interrogative tag (see Bousfield 2007b, Section 6.3.1, above, and Section 7.4 below) *aren't you Harvey*. Again, S2 opts to Stay Silent. This provokes a third *verbal* impoliteness (not including the initial drenching) from S2 of *Harvey you're going to dehydrate* followed by another post intensifying interrogative tag of *aren't you*. Once again, S1 opts to *Stay Silent*. This time she merely provokes the non-exacerbated FTA order of *make sure it's full*, before S2 *withdraws* (cf. Vuchinich 1990. See also Section 7.3, "Discourse Ends" below.) from the speech event. In effect, despite initially provoking further impolite attacks, S1's overall strategy of Staying Silent in the face of such exacerbated FTAs, (presumably as an attempt to stave off the prospect of self-damaging face utterances, such as the hypothetical, *I'm going to dehydrate*, which implicitly indicates a 'self-criticism' with the explicit 'action detrimental to herself'), ensures a good defence of her face as, in effect, corporal S2 simply reverts to non-impolite, implied, military style orders and subsequently *withdraws* (see 7.3, below).

Whilst I have acknowledged its other possible uses, I have been discussing *Stay Silent* as a possible way of saving or defending one's own face in light of an exacerbated FTA. Such strategic moves I term as 'defence/counter' strategies and I will discuss verbalised response-types (as opposed to the Stay Silent type) of this phenomenon in more depth in the Section 7.2.1.3, below.

Choosing to respond

Participants who choose to *respond* to the impoliteness act have a further theoretical set of choices open to them: they can either *accept* the face attack or they can attempt to *counter* it.

7.2.1.2 *Counter vs. accept*

In accepting the face attack, the recipient may, for instance, assume responsibility for the impoliteness act being issued in the first place or they may agree with the impolite assessment contained within the exacerbated FTA. Thus, repeated, strong and personalised complaints (i.e. an impoliteness act) might be met with an apology, and similarly a criticism (i.e. also an impoliteness act) may be met with an agreement. Note that this option involves increased face damage to the responder. It needs to be noted here that even Staying Silent, as discussed above, may well be an example of an individual accepting the face attack of the exacerbated, impolite, FTA.

The alternative option, to *counter* the face attack, involves a set of strategies that can be considered in terms of whether they are *offensive* or *defensive.*

7.2.1.3 *Offensive vs. defensive*

Counter strategies can be usefully classified into two groups: those offensive strategies which primarily counter face attack with face attack, and those defensive strategies which primarily defend one's own face or that of a third party. Of course, these strategy groups are not mutually exclusive: defensive strategies may, intentionally or incidentally, also be offensive (i.e. they damage an interactant's face in the process of saving one's own). It should be noted that my discussion here encompasses counter strategies to all kinds of potential face damage – intentional, incidental and accidental. In opting to counter a perceived, antecedent, FTA, participants may opt for an offensive or a defensive stance.

Offensive counter strategies are those which are typified by researchers such as Culpeper (1996) or Lachenicht (1980) (see also Chapter 4, Section 4.1, above). How one responds can lead to a 'pairing' effect. An impolite offence may be met with an impolite defence as a counter, to provide an offensive-defensive (OFF-DEF) pairing. Conversely, an impolite offence may be met with an impolite offence as a counter, to provide an offensive-offensive (OFF-OFF) pairing.

The OFF-OFF pairing, as the name suggests, involves offensive strategies primarily countering face attack with face attack; this is the pattern referred to by Harris et al. (1986). Such offensive counter strategies are, of course, the impoliteness strategies of researchers like Culpeper (1996) or Lachenicht (1980).

However, such OFF-OFF pairings were rarely realised in this data for a number of very good reasons. The first reason being that few of the interactants in my data were in the same social or power positions as their interlocutors. Nowhere is this more true than in the Kitchen, Military and Police training data sets. Even in the discourses in which such OFF – OFF strategic pairings arose – this being, primarily, within the car parking disputes in **The Clampers** and **Parking Wars** – it would appear that, all other things being equal, one main global aim of the clampers or council officials was to resolve the conflictive discourse in the most expedient manner possible and get back to the task at hand, namely of de-clamping, receiving payments, issuing tickets or deciding the outcome of appeals. This would suggest a more equal power relationship (than that in the Army and Police training or Kitchen data sets) with more fluidity to the negotiation and re-negotiation of participant rights, obligations and socio-discoursal roles. Secondly, the deployment of an offensive counter to an offensive utterance often does nothing to move the conflict towards a peaceable resolution and can result in a *standoff* (see Section 7.3.5 below).

However, this said, offensive counters in my data included the following example taken from **The Clampers, Extract 8**.

[63] ***Context***: *Here two 'Clampers' have clamped an illegally parked car. Just as they have finished, the car's driver, a workman who was doing a job for a local homeowner, returns to his car to find it clamped, and the clampers still there.*

8. S1: you have to have a voucher to park in this area
   S4: *HOW ARE YOU*

9. S1:
   S4: *SUPPOSED TO EARN A BLEEDING LIVING IN THIS FUCKING*

10. S1: *well there's no point in shouting at me yeah I never asked*
    S4: *COUNTRY EH*

11. S1: *you to park here yeah* I'm simply trying to help you if you don't want me
    S4:

12. S1: to help you then I don't need to help you yeah yeah
    S4: yeah just give me that please

13. S1:
    S4: and go away

[…]

Here we see the initial offensive impoliteness being countered with and offensive utterance. The initial utterance issued by S4, *HOW ARE YOU SUPPOSED TO EARN A BLEEDING LIVING IN THIS FUCKING COUNTRY EH?* is an indirect challenge to the clamper, coupled with an expression of anger combined with two instances of taboo usage. The response elicited by this outburst is the clamper's, *Well there's no point shouting at me yeah, I never asked you to park here yeah.* This is an offensive linguistic output operating as a counter utterance and comprising a direct criticism of both the driver's challenge and his expression of anger and irritation (not to mention also being of his choice of parking place).

Defensive strategies primarily counter face attack by defending one's own face; these are essentially the 'denials' to which Labov (1972) refers. As I will illustrate below, such strategies seek to deflect, block or otherwise 'manage' the face attack of the impoliteness to reduce or remove the face damage.

Abrogation (role-switching as a defence)
I have alluded to role switching as a defence, above, (Section 7.1.2.1). By far the most frequent counter strategy made by parking officials in **The Clampers** and **Parking Wars** data sets is what I term 'abrogation'. Abrogation is a defensive strategy which attempts to avoid responsibility for the 'triggering' action(s) that have caused the opposing interlocutor to issue a face damaging utterance in the first place. Due to the intrinsically personal nature of threats to face, the way in which abrogation works as a counter strategy is by the utterer attempting to deny personal responsibility for the offending, trigger situation which has caused him or her to become the focus of another's exacerbated (impolite) face threatening acts. In the data here, this involves attempting to bring about a switch in social roles from being addressed in the role of private citizen to that of a public servant, and/or a switch in discourse roles, where an interactant emphasises that they are merely acting in a representative role, such as a 'mouthpiece', and not as 'author' (see 7.1.2.1 above). In effect, abrogation by social role switching is like saying, 'I'm not to blame, I'm just following orders!' whilst abrogation by discoursal role switching is like saying 'Don't shoot the messenger!' An example of abrogation through explicit social role switching and implicit discoursal role switching can be seen in the following example to illustrate enforced role switching as a form of attack. Clearly, there can be a complex interplay of role switching in confrontational data, as one interactant attempts to outmanoeuvre another: This example is taken from **Extract 8, The Clampers**.

[64] ***Context:*** *Two 'Clampers' proceed to clamp an illegally parked car. Just as they have finished, the car's driver, a workman who was doing a job for a local homeowner, returns to his car to find it clamped, and the clampers still there. S1 is the clamper, S4 the vehicle's owner.*

[...]

Edit where the clampers get confirmation that the vehicle owner has paid the release fee. S1 is just finishing his radio call from base giving him authorisation to remove the clamp

20. S1: okay cheers bye we're going to declamp it
    S4: it all seems a bit pointless doesn't
21. S1:
    S4: it they're paying him to drive round collecting money I mean why not
22. S1: = *well you see*
    S4: invest it in parking meters don't you think this is a bit stupid=
23. S1: *I'm just doing a job* but I've come along here and
    S4: yeah well so was Hitler all I'm asking
24. S1: yeah well <exhales> yes and no
    S4: you as a person don't you think this is a bit stupid

[…]

Here, in stave 22 with *well you see I'm just doing a job*, S1 attempts to switch back into, or rather re-inforce, his social role of 'public servant: clamping official' and, hence, hide behind his occuptional obligation to clamp illegally parked vehicles, and thus abrogate any responsibility for the incidental face damage the trigger event (being clamped) may have caused S4.

Dismiss: make light of face damage, joke
The defensive counter strategy here works by dismissing the face attack as inconsequential and/or non-damaging as in this extract **Parking Wars, Extract 72.**

[65] **Context**: *A small group of local residents have organised a demonstration against the busyness of a local road which is used as a 'rat run' for a local industrial estate and is also used as an 'overflow car park' for a local train station. One driver (S2) and his family (S3 and S4) have become stuck in the traffic jam caused by the demonstration. They have parked in the car park of a local public house and have returned to the scene – ostensibly to enter the public house. A confrontation, including the threat of physical violence, ensued, but was offset earlier by S1 (The organiser of the demonstrators). The linguistic exchange continued.*

[…]

10. S1: I'm trying to save the environment I live in *yeah*? *good*!
    S2: yeeeah
    S3:
    S4: you are a nutcase

End.

In this example, S1 responds with the comment *yeah good*, to the impolite, derogatory nomination (cf. Culpeper 1996), which also expresses impolite beliefs about S1, which S4 utters in stave 10 with *you are a nut case*. The 'off-hand' *yeah good* dismisses the face threat of S4's impoliteness by making light of the face damage.

Ignore the face attack (whether explicit or implied)
One way in which this defensive counter strategy is achieved is through allowing the interactant issuing the face attack to 'let off steam'. Army recruits have noted (in '**Redcaps**') that during a 'dressing down' (or 'a bollocking' as they sometimes call it) the best thing to do is to respond positively to whatever the officer or senior NCO says, take heed of the meaning, but just let the rest go over your head. This, while apparently appearing to conform to the 'accept' option above, as a part of a strategy of submitting to one's opponent's position, is also an instance of expressing surface agreement – a variant of the *ignore the face attack* strategy. An explicit example of which can be seen in the following extract, **Parking Wars, Extract 74.**

[66] ***Context****: A town where residents and students live side by side. A dispute has arisen between one resident, S1, and one student, S2, over one parking space. They are discussing an incident which occurred earlier.*

1. S1: why is it that you get out of the car with this attitude [raises his hands]
   S2: [sighs and
2. S1: no no you've been seen doing it yes with this
   S2: shakes head] have I really
3. S1: attitude and your language is foul so it's foul
   S2: phew right let me just turn that one around
4. S1: oh right
   S2: on you you were the one who has been shouting and swearing at me
5. S1: *Ah aye aye*
   S2: I haven't been <indistinct> you know that I've got everybody on my side
6. S1: *yes* *yes*
   S2: and all you neighbours went out <and say the same thing> and all your local
7. S1: *yes yes yes*
   S2: <people> that have lived here for a long time

[…]

Note here how S1 makes moves to counter S2's overall criticism of him by using surface, or insincere, agreement in stave 5 *Ah aye aye*, stave 6 *yes* and *yes* and stave 7 *yes yes yes*.

Yet another variant of this counter strategy is when the *implied* face attack is ignored. This is particularly clear in cases of sarcasm, where the surface meaning is accepted, rather than the implied sarcastic barb. In this example, the same extract as given for 'sarcasm' (see Section 4.1.4, above), S4 has returned to his car to find that S1 has just clamped it. After S4 has demonstrated his anger, he snatches the penalty ticket and other details away from S1, and tells him to 'go away'. S1 has just returned to his van, taken from **Extract 8, The Clampers**.

[67]

14. S1: *I will do*
S4: . . <sarcastically> have a good day

[…]

Here, S1 replies only to the surface meaning of S4's sarcastic utterance. This strategy may also be offensive at the same time as being defensive, given that it is such a blatant misunderstanding of S4's meaning.

Offer an account – explain

This defensive countermove is used as an attempt to introduce new and potentially mitigating facts concerning the triggering event which has caused one's interlocutor to be impolite in the first place. Offering an account, explaining one's actions, in effect, may help to reduce the face damage of the impoliteness received by, for example (but not limited to), having it retracted, or showing it to be erroneously issued in the first place. We can see an example of an attempted 'account' as a defensive move in the following, taken from **Soldiers To Be, Extract 23.**

[68] ***Context***: *S1 sergeant 'Tich Lovall' is investigating who has cut a recruit's hair resulting in an illegal haircut. S1 has his suspicions and calls all eight recruits of one barracks room in. S1 concentrates his questions to S2: recruit Downes, S3: recruit Harris and S4: recruit Andrews – the three recruits he suspects who are indeed responsible for cutting the other recruit's hair. Up to this point he has asked recruit Downes (who he suspects is the ring leader) if he cut Newson's hair. Downes has said three times that he did not do so. Sergeant Lovall has his doubts.*

1. S1: I'm going to ask you once more ..who cut . Newson's hair who
S2: Andrews sir
S3:
S4:

2. S1: what's your name who cut . his hair
S2: Andrews sergeant
S3:
S4: Andrews sergeant

3. S1: Harris did you cut all of his hair okay
S2:
S3: Harris
S4: top half of it sergeant yeah

4. S1: so who cut the other bit so what were you doing here
S2:
S3:
S4: Downes sergeant

5. S1: then Downes ssss keep your hands still
S2: *er there was er we had lunch* sorry
S3:
S4:

6. S1: I asked you if you had cut Newson's hair you said no
S2: sergeant so <indistinct> not all of
S3:
S4:

7. S1:
S2: it sergeant
S3:
S4:

[…]

Note, here, stave 5. With: *er there was er we had lunch*, S2 attempts to defend against the impolite challenge of S1's *so what were you doing here then, Downes?* That this is impolite, in context, is evidenced through the fact that Downes, the addressee, has denied any responsibility, or part, in the illegal haircut of the unnamed recruit's hair. The fact that S1, the sergeant, asks S2, Downes, what he was doing, (*after* S2 has denied doing anything and following implication by Downes' fellow recruits), is, both, a criticism and a challenge, and is thus, in my view, impoliteness. It is interesting to note that S2's attempts at an explanation were truncated. This is a common occurrence across the army training data set when individuals try to account for their actions in a way which is not an immediate admission of responsibility.

Plead

This is a *theoretical* defensive option. As a countermove to impoliteness, there were no identifiable utterances which were instances of 'pleading' in the data sets studied. However, this is not to say that such a defensive move would not, or could not, occur in other examples from these types of data sets, or indeed, in other data sets. The main reason it is discussed here is that there is a clear example if an individual pleading in response to the non-impolite, but nevertheless, face-threatening act of having her car towed away. When an interactant pleads, they are damaging *their own* positive face, in order to avoid the perceived threat of greater face damage. Pleading is characterised by the copious use of politeness strategies and deference which *may* also conspire to make the offender look odious for not retracting or mollifying the face attack. In the example below, the clamper, S1, is currently assisting in the removal of an illegally parked vehicle. As the offending vehicle is being lifted onto the back of the removal truck, S2, the car's owner returns. She becomes distraught almost immediately. Taken from **The Clampers, Extract 20**.

[69] ***Context:*** *Clamper S1 is currently assisting in the removal of an illegally parked vehicle. As the offending vehicle is being lifted onto the back of the removal truck, the car's owner, a woman, returns. She becomes distraught almost immediately.*

1. S1: sorry madam
   S2: *oh..oh please don't* oh this has never happened to me before
2. S1: unfortunately madam we can't I don't have the authority to put the vehicle
   S2:
3. S1: back down on the floor once it's off the floor madam I don't have
   S2: *oh please*
4. S1: the authority .. do you know where Wembley pound is that's where it's
   S2: no-o *oh please*
5. S1: going I can't I can't drop it madam I don't have the authority
   S2: *don't do it to me* <cries>

[…]

Opt out

Here the participant opts out as a counter strategy. Examples in the data sets studied include instances where an interactant goes *on record* to indicate that they are 'opting out' of the conversation, as in the following example. Here S1, a disgruntled driver at an appeals hearing, has just been informed that his appeal has been unsuccessful, despite his claims that the traffic warden who indicted him has falsified her records. S2, the adjudicator, has already gone on record to say that he prefers the traffic warden's evidence over S1's. Taken from **Extract 16, The Clampers.**

[70] ***Context:*** *S1 is a driver who has received a ticket and is appealing against it. S2 is the adjudicator. S1 insists that the ticketing officer used unfair means to ticket him and has fabricated her pocket book notes.*

[...]

21. S1: so you're quite happy that this woman perjured herself in writing
    S2: *I'm not*

22. S1:
    S2: *saying anything more Mr Langarth* and that is the end of the proceeding

23. S1: so you are happy you're happy that she perjured
    S2: *I'm not saying anything*

24. S1: herself
    S2: *I I'm not making any further comment* thank you .. If you'll be kind enough

25. S1:
    S2: to wait in the foyer

End.

What is interesting, and what may already be apparent, is the fact that there appears to be a much more limited set of defensive strategies that are open, *generally*, to participants in Army or Police training discourses, or the Kitchen discourse, than in the Car Parking discourse. This, quite clearly, concerns matters to do with the particular social roles, including the rights, powers and obligations of the participants within these discourses. What appears to happen in Army training discourse, is that recruits opt for one of: *Stay Silent*, *Account*, or *Ignore Face Attack*, and they often *submit* to the opposing position as a way of *accepting* the face damage in the utterance in order to offset greater face damage if they try to defend against it. Recruits, in the extracts studied, *never* respond to impoliteness offensively. This is not to say that this would never happen in other instances outside of the extracts of the data set – however, if, and when, it happens, the repercussions of an army or even police recruit responding to offensive impoliteness with an offensive counter (OFF-OFF), being, technically, insubordination, would, almost undoubtedly, be rather severe. Indeed, this limited capability of 'defence and response', seems to be true, also, for the Kitchen data set, again, because of the power imbalance between the head chef/restaurateur, on the one hand, and member of the cooking staff on the other. This said, however, we should note the following, interesting, example, taken from **Boiling Point, Extract 63.**

[71] ***Context***: *Restaurant owner and head chef Gordon Ramsay, S1, again berates Owen, S2, a Chef de Partie, who has caused a delay in preparing some a dish.*

1. S1: what's going on here you .... what is going on what about <indistinct>
   S2:
2. S1: fucking foie gras.eh you arsehole.you lost it again.you lost it again.what's
   S2:
3. S1: your big deal . why don't you fuck off home then go on fuck off home then
   S2:
4. S1: eh arsehole . why don't you fuck off home then .. why don't you fuck off
   S2:
5. S1: home .. why are you fucking it up
   S2: I don't want to Gordon <indistinct>
6. S1: have you lost it well fucking wake up dickhead
   S2: no Gordon yes Gordon
7. S1: what's the big deal <why isn't there any fucking foie gras> do you
   S2: ....
8. S1: want to go home and cry to mummy again . are you a big fucking wuss
   S2: no Gordon no
9. S1: guy puts himself in the shit fucks the kitchen stands there bubbling
   S2: Gordon ..
10. S1: like a fucking baby ...... *have you any bite back as a guy*
    S2: sorry Gordon ....
11. S1: *have you any bollocks you* *have you fuck as far as I'm*
    S2: yes Gordon
12. S1: *concerned they're in your arsehole*
    S2: <oui Gordon>

[...]

Here, in staves 10 to 11, by uttering *have you any bite back as a guy? Have you any bollocks, you?* S1 actually berates S2 for not having the confidence to respond offensively (or even to attempt a defensive turn) to his earlier impolite utterances. Given the context of S1's no nonsense reputation, even a defensive move, made at the wrong time, could potentially cause the speaker to lose his job. This threat appears to overhang the staff of *Ramsay's* all the time. In light of this, S2 really has 'nowhere to go', that is, he has no options open to him to even try to limit the face damage he is suffering. Even his acceptances of the face damage (which elicit an *apology* in stave 10 with *sorry Gordon*), rather than accepting face damage to limit future damage, actually operates to further trigger more impoliteness from S1.

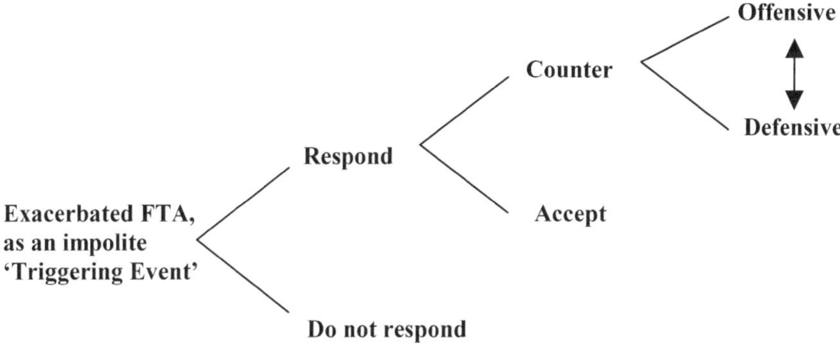

Figure 3. A summary of response options

At this point it may be possible to summarise the options thus far described in Figure 3, which is modified from the original we presented in Culpeper et al. (2003).

Note the scalar representation of the Offensive – Defensive response option on the right of Figure 3. This is to represent the fact that offensive counter strategies have the secondary effect of defending the face of the responder; likewise, some defensive strategies may, intentionally or incidentally, have the effect of offending the face of the addressee as well. Furthermore, it is clear that offensive and defensive counter phenomena can be combined (see Section 6.2.1.2, above). However, the model above is not in fact the best way of describing what happens. I will return to this point later in this chapter (Section 7.4).

7.2.2 When things aren't 'pair' shaped?

Apparently, not every example of defensive counterwork can be seen clearly as a pairing of the OFFENSIVE-DEFENSIVE utterances as shown above. Indeed, given the very valid criticisms laid at the door of those who only consider discoursal pairs (such as Dillon et al. 1985), it is neither safe, nor advisable to just consider the OFF-DEF and OFF-OFF pairs. It *appears* that participants who choose to counter long strings of impoliteness (such as a repetitive, or highly complex strings of combined impoliteness strategies) with defensive strategies tend to orient their direct defensive responses to only a few aspects of the impolite, exacerbated FTAs. In this example, S1 (a car owner) has stopped his car to heckle S2 (a traffic warden), who has just ticketed him for illegal parking. Taken from **The Clampers, Extract 11.**

[72] ***Context:*** *A gentleman, S1, driving a car has stopped to heckle at ticketer S2 as he goes about his business. It is late in the day. S1, a non-native speaker of English, is leaning out of his car and is gesturing emphatically at S2.*

1. S1: one day you're going to get a lot of problems and you create the problems
   S2:
2. S1: we don't create the problems ban the bloody cars all over London and we
   S2:
3. S1: have no worries you give us authority to put them <indistinct> and then
   S2: *yeah* *all right all right I agree with you*
4. S1: you come and give us a ticket bar the cars take the cars
   S2: *all right I agree with you sir*
5. S1: off London do it today not tomorrow
   S2: *yeah to many c* *yup too many cars yeah too*
6. S1: don't give us this bloody headache all the time
   S2: *many cars on the road*
7. S1:
   S2: *yeah too many cars* . anyway you gonna shift

End.

Note here the apparent lack of synchronisation between S1's accusations and S2's responses, particularly towards the end where the repeated *yeah too many cars* does not seem to address S1's immediately prior discourse. Culpeper et al. (2003) argue that it would seem that S2 has moved away from the basic pairings of *direct* (OFF-OFF and OFF-DEF) pairings. They argue here that S2's responses betray the fact that he is operating on 'automatic pilot' whilst S1 issues a string of connected impoliteness strategies and as Culpeper et al. (2003) note, *anyway*, in stave 7, marks S2's shift back to serious business. But is this *all* that is going on here? Considering the complex way in which *both* defensive *and* offensive strategies may be combined we can see that it, arguably, only *seems* that S2's discourse has moved away from S1's. While S2's responses do indeed seem to betray the fact that he is operating on some form of 'automatic pilot', his *repeated* use of 'insincere agreement', even where it is not wholly appropriate to the immediately prior discourse at hand, is in fact operating as the defence strategy of allowing S1 to "let off steam", to, in effect, get his anger and his issues off his chest. He does this by giving positive-sounding back channels, in the form of his 'agreements' (actually *insincere agreements*) which encourages S1 to run his course of complaints and impolitenesses. Thus it could be argued that S2 is combining the two strategies of 'allow interactant to let off steam' and 'express insincere agreement' through his repetitive use of the insincere agreements as positive and encouraging sounding back channels. The point to be made here is that the pairings of OFF-DEF are, *basically*, still in operation here.

In the final example within this section, I aim to show a much more complex case than those I have hitherto discussed. Please note, the overall direction of the discussion below is taken from Culpeper et al. (2003), and I should further note that Jonathan Culpeper, one of my co-authors, played a key and central role in the analysis of this example. S1's car has been towed to the car pound, after it was clamped for being illegally parked. Previously, S1 refused to pay the release fee, stating that he preferred to spend his money on a new vehicle. He has returned to the pound to take his belongings out of the car. As he leaves, he strongly threatens S2 (a clamper), taken from **Extract 3, The Clampers.**

[73] ***Context:*** *As this extract begins S2, the owner of an impounded car, along with friend S3 has gone down to the council offices to take his personal belongings out of the impounded car. S2 and S3 from this extract have arrived at Wembley pound later that day to take the possessions out of the car. S4 is one of the clamping officers at the pound. After telling the camera that he's decided to leave the car, cut his losses and take his possessions, S2 makes to leave the pound, with S3, and confronts S4 as he does so*

[…]

25. S2: touch my fucking new car and I'll bust your fucking head off
S4: *jackanory*

26. S1: yeah ?!? yeah <bleeped> just cos you've got a fat
S4: *yeah! yeh! full of it aren't you eh*

27. S2: <belly> anyway
S4: *hey fit in your mouth quite easily really wouldn't it eh*

28. S2: <indistinct> <laughing to S3>
S4: <chuckles and shakes head>

End.

On the face of it, S2's response, *jackanory*, looks like a defensive strategy, which might be formulated as the *Dismiss: make light of face damage, joke* defensive counter strategy (see Section 7.2.3, above). *Jackanory* is an intertextual reference to a children's television programme in which fictitious stories were read out. S2 implies that S1's threat is the stuff of children and fiction – it carries no weight. Whilst this strategy does indeed *dismiss* the impoliteness act, it also belittles the speaker's attempt in producing it. 'Belittle the other' is a negative impoliteness strategy (cf. Culpeper 1996: 358). So, simultaneously S2 *appears* to be offensive. Clearly then, this does not fit the pairs suggested by either Labov (1972) or

Harris et al. (1986). Looking at S2's responses *full of it aren't you eh* and *it'd fit in your mouth quite easily wouldn't it*, the situation becomes even more complex, since we begin to see a pattern characteristic of 'mock' impoliteness or ritualistic banter. Labov (e.g. 1972: 340) points out that strong ritualistic insults are outrageously bizarre and obviously untrue, and Eder (1990: 75) suggests that in ritual insulting participants 'continually challenge each other to come up with a better, more clever response to an accusation or insult'. These aspects fit S2's responses: he engages in mock impoliteness. On the other hand, S2's impoliteness is not obviously untrue (S2 appears to be overweight) or clever: he engages in 'genuine' impoliteness. Contrary to Labov (1972), who suggested it was important that all parties considered the insults to be untrue in ritualistic banter, Kochman (1983) (see also Eder 1990, for further evidence) argues that the key to doing ritualistic banter lies in taking insults – even true, personal insults – in a non-serious way. In this example, we (Culpeper et al. 2003) argue that S2 practices a much more global defensive strategy than the others discussed. His utterances may constitute more of a particular Activity Type (Levinson [1979] 1992), that of Ritualistic Banter, and in so doing reduce the impact of S1's impoliteness. At the same time, S2 shows off his considerable linguistic dexterity. Finally, we should note one contextual factor that may have facilitated the occurrence of this particular interaction, namely, that S1 is walking away from S2. Most of the talk occurs when they are several metres apart – clearly, a safer situation for more risky communicative strategies.

I conclude this section with one brief point. It needs to be acknowledged that in other discourses other impoliteness patterns may well emerge, as well as other defensive strategies. Such an observation leads to an area for future research and consideration.

7.3 Discourse 'ends'

Thus far, little attention has been given by researchers of (im)politeness to how the discourse is resolved. Vuchinich (1990), working in the field of conflict terminations, provides an interesting set of options for the conclusion of conflictive arguments that the researcher, dealing with impoliteness, can adopt. Vuchinich (1990) identifies 5 types of conflict termination: (1) Submission To Opponent, (2) Dominant Third Party Intervention, (3) Compromise, (4) Stand-Off, and (5) Withdrawal. I shall discuss each of these in turn (in Sections 7.3.1 to 7.3.5) below.

7.3.1 Submission to opponent

With this type of resolution one participant "gives in" and accepts the opponent's position. Instances of this type of impolite discourse resolution are common throughout many of the data sets studied here, especially the military training data. Note the following example, not unrepresentative, taken from **Soldiers To Be, Extract 38**.

[74] ***Context****: A second room inspection. S1 is the inspection sergeant, S2 is the recruit being inspected. S1 has returned to recruit S2, Hayes, who he had inspected during the morning whereupon S1 had earlier discovered an improperly cleaned eating utensil (a fork). He returns during the afternoon to inspect S2's eating utensils. The fork seems to be fine, but the knife isn't. S3, an attending corporal begins to contribute to the discussion from stave 4 in response to a comment by S2.*

1. S1: look along the blade of that knife what can you see how much
   S2: food sergeant
2. S1: did you use these this morning do you think that
   S2: a lot . sergeant yes sergeant
3. S1: food is fresh on there this morning or do you think it's been there for quite
   S2:
4. S1: a long time ..
   S2: possibly sergeant
   S3: *possibly* .. so you *possibly* went to breakfast
5. S1:
   S2: oh I went to breakfast this morning .. corporal
   S3: this morning did you corporal
6. S1: *that's*
   S2: yes yes corporal
   S3: so that could *possibly* be from breakfast or most definitely
7. S1: *disgusting isn't it*
   S2: yes corp sergeant
   S3:

End.

Note, in stave 7, that after a series of 'acceptances' of S1 and S3's positions, S2 finishes with another 'acceptance' which seals his *submission* to the position, and comments, made by his interlocutors. As implied, 'accepting' the FTA of an opponent's antecedent event is one aspect of, generally, *submitting*. While *submission* was a common occurrence in military and police training discourses, as well as the kitchen discourse, it was less common, in one respect, to the car parking data. From one perspective, almost every private vehicle driver has to submit to the fact that they have received, and must pay, a financial parking penalty of some description (some appeals are successful, however). On another level, where the clampers are taken to task over the ethics of ticketing or clamping, the drivers are less *submissive*.

7.3.2 Dominant third party intervention

An ongoing-conflict between participants is "broken-up" by a third party – usually having some power over the participants. There are few examples of this type of resolution activity in the data sets here studied. One example can be seen in the following extract. As this extract begins, police officer, S1, as part of a roleplay exercise, has already intervened to separate S2, a West Indian woman and S3 an impolite language using English Caucasian man. Taken from **Raw Blues, Extract 59**.

[75] ***Context***: *A police roleplay exercise in which the recruits have to deal with a racially charged scenario. In this scenario a white man is supposed to be angry because he thinks a woman's West Indian husband has taken his parking space. Racial abuse which causes distress is an offence under British law and the police can arrest an individual if they can prove that racial abuse has, in fact, caused such distress. S1 is the police recruit, S2 the West Indian woman distressed by the abuse, S3 is the individual suspected of causing offence.*

Edit: *After speaking with S2, The police recruit approaches S3.*

7. S1: I appreciate that sir she's
S3: I can't get in my parking space no you don't appreciate it

8. S1: <you're being abusive>
S3: ignorant fucking West Indians doing my head in

9. S1: there you've caused this lady distress and
S3: no no listen I've been I've been casting

10. S1: fine <I'm arres->
S3: my opinion that's what I think they're fucking ignorant they're all

11. S1: <indistinct> sir sir *I'm actually placing you under arrest* this is
S3: ignorant what for

12. S1: what I'm saying to you please I'm placing you under arrest under section er
S3:

13. S1: four ay of the public act of the public public order act okay
S3:

End.

Within this extract we see that, as the hypothetical exchange between man, S3 and woman, S2 has been broken up, then third party, S1 (the police officer) consolidates his intervention and resolution of the impolite discourse by 'arresting' S3.

It need not be 'traditional' authority figures who become third party interventionists. Note the following, highly interesting, example, taken from **Extract 72, Parking Wars.**

[76] ***Context***: *A small group of local residents have organised a demonstration against the congestion on a local road which is used as a 'rat run' for a local industrial estate. It is also used as an 'overflow car park' for a local train station. One driver and his family have become stuck in the traffic jam caused by the demonstration. They have parked in the car park of a local public house and have returned to the scene – ostensibly to enter the public house. They become involved in a discussion with the demonstrators. S1 is the leading demonstrator, S2 is her husband, S3 is the driver of the vehicle who had been caught up, S4 is his wife. Other members of the demonstration and the family do not contribute to the talk exchange. The scene starts as S2, who has been exchanging words with S3 and S4, swipes S3 across the face with a rolled up piece of paper. S3 responds by grabbing S2 and attempting to punch him as S2 tries to twist away.*

1. S1: Oy Oy <indistinct shouting> you don't live here . we do . go away . tell you
   S2: < indistinct shouting >
   S3: < indistinct shouting >
   S4: < indistinct shouting >
2. S1: what . call the police ... Freddie this is our . for god's sake you'll ruin the
   S2:
   S3:
   S4:
3. S1: whole thing get over the road get over the road GET .
   S2: <it wasn't me> he grabbed hold of me he started it
   S3: <I never
   S4:
4. S1: OVER THE ROAD . you you you're all on camera all on camera darling
   S2:
   S3: started it he hit me>< indistinct argumentation >
   S4: < indistinct argumentation >

[...]

Note, here, S1's comments to husband, S2 in staves 2-to-4: *Freddie this is our . for god's sake you'll ruin the whole thing get over the road .. get over the road .. GET . OVER THE ROAD*. Effectively, (and incidentally after a little trouble), she successfully intervenes in the 'sub-conflictive-exchange' between S2 and S3 which was turning violent. The fact that she herself was a participant in the wider impolite exchange, and she, herself, had used negative face oriented bald on record impoliteness in stave 1: *you don't live here . we do. go away*. Not strictly speaking a neutral third-party participant, S1, nevertheless, was not *directly* involved in the fisticuffs which started as the extract began. She is, in effect, a third party who is championing S2 (her husband) and in doing so, attempts to intervene to stop the imminent violence. She succeeds, and couples her third party intervention with a forced withdrawal upon her husband.

Of course, not every attempt at intervention by a third party is successful in resolving the situation. Note the following example taken from **The Clampers, Extract 17.** (Note the whole extract is rendered here to contextualise the attempted interventions in stave 3 (with S4 arriving to intervene) and staves 3-to-4 (with S3 arriving to intervene).

[77] ***Context:*** *Ticketer, S1, is working Meadow Garth Road at 8.30 a.m. The road is adjacent to a primary school and parents often 'illegally' park while dropping their children off. S2 is a mother being ticketed, S3, another mother and S4 is the school's headmistress.*

1. S1: yes madam
   S2: Excuse me are you the traffic warden who's been specially asked to come
   S3:
   S4:
2. S1:
   S2: along and er check up on the s um cars who are parking with the school
   S3:
   S4:
3. S1: no madam one one at a time ladies one I can
   S2: you just happened to turn up here
   S3: your job is
   S4: this is not on because we have a disp[ensation]
4. S1: only talk to one okay absolutely right madam and
   S2: you're
   S3: to give out tickets go to Holdsden that's a big problem in Holdsden allright
   S4:
5. S1: right can I ask you a question where is this car parked:.... wait two
   S2:
   S3:
   S4: look

6. S1: seconds answer <her> question first where is this car parked
S2:
S3:
S4: no no you

7. S1: okay then I don't need to answer
S2:
S3:
S4: don't need to answer that question because

8. S1: your questions it's on a double yellow line obstructing an emergency
S2:
S3:
S4: I excuse me

9. S1: exit right
S2:
S3:
S4: you do not know the history of this place we have personal dispensation

10. S1: can you show me in your windscreen where it
S2:
S3:
S4: for our parents when they're dropping their children off

11. S1: says you have a dispensation for the local council
S2:
S3:
S4: well that is I'm sorry the local council

12. S1: well
S2:
S3:
S4: it's all recorded you go to the local council and get information before

13. S1: you you one at a time ladies one at a time
S2: the school is trying <indistinct> the council
S3: <-------------indistinct--------------->
S4: issuing parking tickets to my parents

14. S1: who wants to speak to me first ladies I mean take your pick cos you can
S2: makes no
S3:
S4: this is my chi<indistinct>

15. S1: queue up if you want I've only got one set of ears you know what I mean
S2:
S3:
S4:

16. S1: well I am trying to be but I've only got one
S2: it's nice to see you being so responsive the council
S3:
S4:

17. S1: set of ears we'll start with you madam <to S4> I work for tee ef em
S2: has made no attempt to respond
S3: excuse me excuse me you
S4:

18. S1: parking okay I did the first time I met you okay where's your car
S2:
S3: are a parking attendant alright act like one okay shut up and act like a
S4:

19. S1: madam you've just answered my question I'm going to go and issue
S2:
S3: parking attendant I'm not driving I'm not driving
S4:

20. S1: tickets good bye you did I gave it to
S2:
S3:
S4: excuse me I haven't got your number

21. S1: you just now that's your problem madam it's there
S2:
S3:
S4: I did not write it down

22. S1: on show for you <shrugs>
S2:
S3: your collar's covering it your
S4: I well I can't read it

23. S1:
S2:
S3: collar's covering it
S4:

End.

Note here how the intervention by third (and fourth) parties S3 and S4 does absolutely nothing to resolve the situation. Indeed, their intervention is the very trigger for impoliteness to ensue as they exacerbate the already tense situation. This is, quite clearly, as a result of the fact that, despite protests to the contrary on the behalf of S4, neither S3, nor S4 have any power over the other participants within this general context or specific activity type.

7.3.3 Compromise

Compromise occurs where the participants negotiate (a) concession(s) – a position between the opposing positions that define the dispute. We should make no mistake that a compromise is a form of denying (*parts of*) an opposing position and can lead to the termination of the conflict, if agreed upon by all parties. This said no clear instances of compromise positions occurred within any of the data sets here studied. Off camera, the narrator informs us that the dispute in example [66] which is over a parking space between neighbours ends in a compromise (the student agrees not to park in the retired gentleman's parking space on the days the gentleman and his wife go shopping). The only possible attempt at producing a compromise position can be seen in the following example, taken from, **The Clampers, Extract 8.**

[78] ***Context:*** *Two 'Clampers' proceed to clamp an illegally parked car. Just as they have finished, the car's driver, a workman who was doing a job for a local homeowner, returns to his car to find it clamped, and the clampers still there.*

Edit *where the Clampers get confirmation. S1 is just finishing his radio call from base giving him authorisation to remove the clamp.*

[…]

20. S1: okay cheers bye we're going to declamp it
    S4: it all seems a bit pointless doesn't

21. S1:
    S4: it they're paying him to drive round collecting money I mean why not invest

22. S1: = well you see I'm
    S4: it in parking meters don't you think this is a bit stupid=

23. S1: just doing a job but I've come along here and
    S4: yeah well so was Hitler all I'm asking you as a

24. S1: yeah *well <exhalation> yes and no*
    S4: person don't you think this is a bit stupid

25. S1: yes to the extent yes to the extent that we know
S4: you know they mean your your cars are parking on the main roads

[…]

Note here how S1's move to produce a compromise (which also operates as a, primarily defensive, counter move), in stave 24: *Well <exhalation> yes and no* which he attempts to qualify with an *account*, ultimately fails as S4 interrupts S1 immediately. No other instances of successful, or attempted compromise were made. This may well be due to the nature of the Activity Types in which the interactants were engaged as well as the differences in such contextual phenomena as the power, the rights and the obligations of the interactants (in that, for example, Clampers are *obliged* to ticket, clamp and remove vehicles and are simply not allowed to 'let off' any driver who has not paid the penalty. Interestingly, even when this becomes clear, it does not, necessarily follow that these, so-called 'mitigating' circumstances, remove the face threat inherent in being clamped, ticketed and/or towed away. Thus, impoliteness, from vehicle owners can still ensue).

7.3.4 Stand-off

The conflict continues (theoretically, indefinitely) with neither party submitting. In practice, a "Standoff" usually occurs when the topic changes, usually after both parties realise the opponent is not going to submit or compromise. An example of a *Stand-Off* (which is combined with a withdrawal) can be seen in the following example, taken from **The Clampers, Extract 1.**

[79] ***Context:*** *Ray and Miguel, clamping supervisor and assistant respectively have arrived to remove the clamp from a van. The van's owner is waiting for them. S1 is Ray, S2, the van's owner, S3 – Miguel – does not speak throughout this extract.*

[…]

25. S1: nothing I personally can do I simply work do my job for the council
S2: *just do your job* *I don't*

26. S1: I do my job for the coun if you want me to explain then if you want be
S2: *care what you do*

27. S1: like that then I can walk away I don't have to talk to you if I don't want to if
S2:

28. S1: you're going to be rude to me yeah I that's fine then
S2: *I don't really want to talk to you you're*

29. S1: sir I I'm really not
S2: *not going to do anything about it are you* as far as wearing your

30. S1:
S2: uniform is concerned they were doing that when they were shoving the guys

31. S1:
S2: into the gas chambers in Germany wearing the uniform does not matter

32. S1: that's right I clamped your car sir
S2: you're just as culpable as anybody else

33. S1: and I won't dispute that fact that I clamped your car
S2: *well end of conversation*

34. S1: well that's fine by me if you don't want to talk we don't have to talk
S2:

End.

Note here, how S2, apparently, made a number of moves to *withdraw* from the conflictive discoursal interchange (in staves 25, 25-to-26, 28 and then, explicitly, in 33), but the clamper, S1, rather interestingly turned this into a *Stand Off.* This may be due to the potentially face damaging consequences of S2's attempts to *withdraw linguistically* after he has had his own say – it is, potentially, a snub (cf. Culpeper 1996: 357) – and S1's response in staves 33-to-34 of *well that's fine by me if you don't want to talk we don't have to talk* has the appearance of a defensive counter move indicating that no loss of personal face, or impolite face damage, has been suffered by S1. It is this defensive counter-response that indicates the exchange ends in a *stand off* which is then coupled with, shortly afterwards, a *withdrawal.*

What is perhaps interesting is that no instances of stand off occurred in the extracts from the Military, the Police, or the Kitchen data – some other resolution (where the resolutions were known, see Section 7.4, below), occurred. This may well be as a result of the roles and power relations, (which are much more concrete), that obtain between the conversational participants in those discourses.

7.3.5 Withdrawal

With *withdrawal* one opponent withdraws from communicative conversational activity, or physically leaves the area. We can see instances of this throughout the data sets studied. Note the following example, taken from **Parking Wars, Extract 73.**

[80] ***Context**: A car has illegally parked in a bus lane. The driver, S1, who had left his female partner in the car approaches S2, the ticketing officer, to discuss the parking ticket.*

1. S1: <indistinct> what and you < indistinct>
   S2: I'm afraid you're parked in an active bus lane sir
2. S1: with the lady in the car you lot are <fucked up> fucking pussy off .. and you
   S2: no there's no there's no there's
3. S1: pussy off .. fuck you [initially walks to car then returns proffering his ticket]
   S2: no time there's no .. thankyou sir
4. S1: write your badge number on there write your badge number on there
   S2: sorry
5. S1: it's already on the ticket <fuck you> pussy off
   S2: it's already on the ticket sir
6. S1: <you fucker> [S1 gets in car and roars away]
   S2:

End.

Note, here, how it was driver, S1, (the sole producer of impolitenesses in this extract), who was the one to *withdraw*. In army training data when recruits *withdraw* they must, first, require permission to do so, and must *withdraw* correctly, note the following example taken from **Soldiers To Be, Extract 32.**

[81] ***Context**: Recruit Wilson, S2, is finding the training hard. She is short and finds it hard to keep up with the rest of the platoon on march. Furthermore, once back at camp she falls asleep in class and is disciplined for it. She decides to PVR – that is, she decides to take Premature Voluntary Release – from the army. She calls on the platoon sergeant, S1, who takes a rather interesting tack in order to encourage her to stay.*

[…]

16. S1: warning and I'm going to annotate that into your report and any <indistinct>
    S2:
17. S1: you're in front of the company commander and the next step is civvy street
    S2:
18. S1: do you understand me get away .. EH don't just turn away you fall out turn
    S2: [turns]
19. S1: to the right sharply and assume you're calling time
    S2: ONE TWO THREE ONE

End.

Note in stave 18 where S1 orders S2 to withdraw, S2 attempts to do so without following formal protocol. The rebuke (cf. *criticism* above, Section 5.5.1) she receives is swift, and effective – she 'calls time' in order to facilitate her *withdrawal.*

Such marked and signalled *withdrawal,* is not required by those who are 'trainers' in military training discourse as the following example shows, from **Soldiers To Be, Extract 35.**

[82] ***Context:*** *A room inspection. After inspecting corporal S1 has inspected a room he decides to address all of its occupants as to his impressions on their general state of presentation.*

1. S1: FOR A MONDAY MORNING THAT IS ABSOLUTELY DIABOLICAL
   S2:
2. S1: YOU HAVE GOT SO MUCH WORK TO IMPROVE IT'S
   S2:
3. S1: UNBELIEVABLE . YOU'VE HAD ALL WEEKEND . AND WHAT
   S2:
4. S1: HAVE YOU BEEN DOING . PROBABLY DOWN THE NAAFI
   S2:
5. S1: VISITING ALL YOUR LITTLE FRIENDS . OR TRYING TO CHAT THE
   S2:
6. S1: GIRLS UP . IT'S NOT GOOD ENOUGH [storms out slamming the door]
   S2:

End.

Here we see corporal, S1, combine an extended *criticism* of the recruits with *shouting* (cf. Culpeper 1996: 358). Together they seem to be boosting S1's negative attitude towards the addressees and S1 uses a diminutive (stave 5: little friends) and an expression of an impolite belief (stave 5: *trying to chat the girls up* ... *trying* implies the possibility that they were unsuccessful, the whole thing together implies via flouts of the maxims of manner and, possibly, quantity (in terms of necessary volume), that they were being frivolous in their actions and not performing their duties correctly).

7.4 Other considerations

Of course, it should be obvious from the few examples discussed here that conflict terminations, like any conscious conversational strategy, can be combined with other strategies. In the previous example, from example [80] (Section 7.3.5, above), it may be fair to say that the overall decision to withdraw, by S1, was combined with expressions of extreme negative attitude, as evidenced by the taboo language usage, and by an implicit attempt to threaten the clamper (S1's: write your number on there – implies that S1 is going to make a complaint about S2 to S2's superiors – this is an indirect, implied attempt to *threaten/frighten*).

As such, the model set out in Figure 3 above, while not wholly accurate, does still give a good representation of the types of options that are open to the participant within an impolitely charged linguistic exchange. Of course, terminations need not only combine with impolite strategies, they may also combine with other types of conflict termination strategies. Note the following example whereby S2, in submitting to her interlocutor's position, also withdraws from the exchange. Taken from **Soldiers To Be, Extract 32.**

[83] ***Context***: *Recruit Wilson, S2, is finding the training hard. She is short and finds it hard to keep up with the rest of the platoon on march. Furthermore, once back at camp she falls asleep in class and is disciplined for it. She decides to PVR – that is, she decides to take Premature Voluntary Release – from the army.*

[…]

18. S1:do you understand me get away .. EH don't just turn away you fall out turn
    S2: [turns]
19. S1:to the right sharply and assume you're calling time
    S2: ONE TWO THREE ONE

End.

Note here how S1 insists that S2 submit to his (authoritatively backed) order. The fact that she has not done so, could be seen, in context and co-text, to be an implied criticism. S2, in stave 19, *submits* to his position and *withdraws* in the same, combined, action.

It needs to be noted at this point that not every instance of a situation in which impoliteness occurred was identifiable as having a conflict termination of a specific sort. The editing processes used in the production of the television documentary serials from which the extracts were taken, meant the resolution which was taken, was not shown to the viewing public.

7.5 Conclusion

Within this chapter I have discussed the significance of considering the wider discoursal context in which impoliteness occurs. Further, I have discussed the

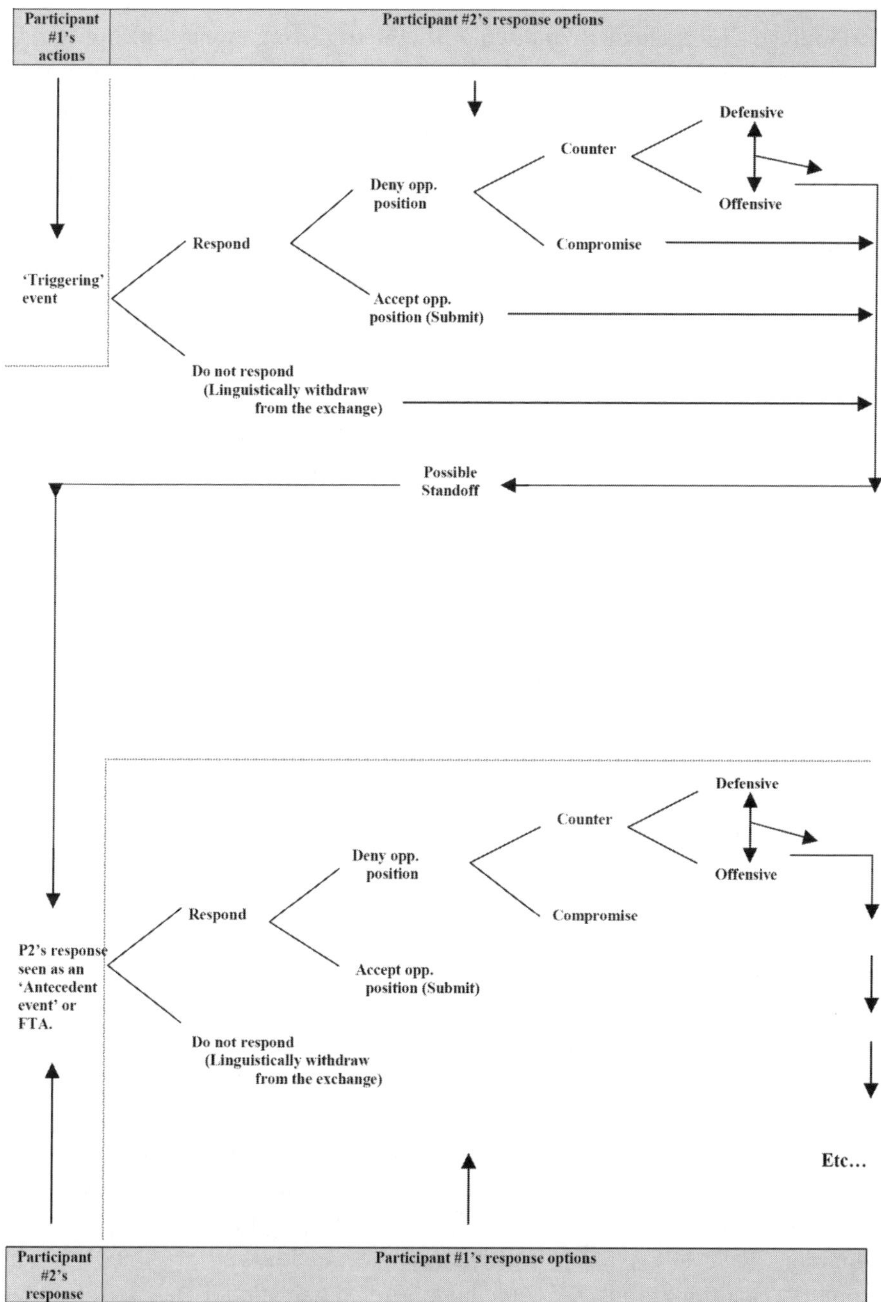

Figure 4. Summary of response options (extended)

'beginnings' of impoliteness in discourse – the triggering events which give rise to conflictive illocutions; I have discussed the 'middles' of impoliteness in discourse – the options which appear to be open to interlocutors in interaction; and I have discussed the 'ends' of impoliteness in discourse – the resolution of impolite discourses. On the basis of what we have seen it may be possible to expand upon the summary made by Culpeper et al. (2003: 1563) as presented in Figure 3, above, to incorporate all the factors discussed. The model of options could be extended to that shown in Figure 4.

Note here in Figure 4 how we can now see a fuller range options open to participants: Following an impoliteness act, an exacerbated FTA, or some other, face-threatening, offending event (Jay 1999, 2000)/situation or 'antecedent event' (Corsaro and Rizzo 1990), the target has the option of choosing *Respond*, or *Do not respond* (effectively, linguistically withdraw from the exchange (Vuchinich 1990)).

Now, in responding, the participant has the option of choosing to *Deny the opposing/opponent's position,* or of *accepting the opponent's position* (Vuchinich 1990, see submission). In denying the opposing position, the participant has the option of attempting to counter the offending, triggering event, or of fielding a *compromise* to it (Vuchinich 1990); in attempting to counter, the participant has the option of using one or a combination of offensive (cf. Culpeper 1996; Kienpointer 1997; Lachenicht 1980) or defensive (Culpeper et al. 2003) strategies.

The offensive and/or defensive counter strategy used by the participant may result in a form of resolution (if one's participant decides to withdraw in the face of the counter strategies deployed) or may result in a *standoff* (Vuchinich 1990) as the addressee (the original perpetrator of the impoliteness act; the exacerbated FTA or the 'antecedent event'), may consider the impolite-counter utterance to be, itself, an impoliteness act; an exacerbated FTA, or an 'antecedent event'. This would then, with the turn given back to the original participant, lead to yet another set of choices, and so on, and so forth. Of course, dominant *third party intervention* (Vuchinich 1990), not represented on the ostensibly two-party Figure 2 above may short circuit the entire procedure at any point.

Admittedly, the above model-as-summary of response options is not perfect. For one thing, some of the 'resolution' choices may not successfully terminate any given exchange. For another, Vuchinich's (1990) 5 types of conflict termination don't seem to explicitly or satisfactorily deal with the role of apologies in conflict resolution.[7] *Apologies* could be subsumed under 'offer an account/explanation' or 'plead' or construe an entirely separate defensive counter-strategy. The

7. I would like to express my thanks to an anonymous reviewer who brought this issue to the forefront of my attention.

complex nature of apologies and the subsequent, required discussion to fully account for them in relation to impoliteness and impolite-laden conflict and resolution are, for reasons of space alone, beyond the scope and scale of the current study. Therefore, the model-as-summary of response options I have postulated here is one which must be subject to trial and revision in relation to data sets of differing discourse types.[8] Thus acknowledged, I would argue that the current model is nevertheless a good way of understanding the basic decision making processes that participants may go through within the context and the constraints of the linguistic exchange in which they are engaged.

8. Impoliteness, Conflict Resolution and Apologies together remain an area ripe for future research.

CHAPTER 8

The dynamics of impoliteness III

Exploiting the rules of the turn taking system

In the previous chapters we have seen something of the dynamics of impoliteness work which interactants can and do use in certain types of discourses. Beyond, merely, the strategic realisation of impolite offensive behaviour (Chapter 5), we saw in Chapter 6, that interactants can and do 'mix and match' impolite offensive (and to a lesser extent, defensive) strategies both (a) within a single utterance and, (b) within a single conversational turn (note, I do not consider these terms to be synonymous: see Section 8.2, below). Additionally, in Chapters 6 and again in 7 we saw that interactants can and do *combine, repeat* or otherwise deploy strategies, even across multiple turns, in creatively complex ways for specific face-threatening effects. Furthermore, in Chapter 7 we saw how impolite, linguistically aggressive exchanges are triggered, develop and are, ultimately, resolved.

In all these chapters thus far I have consciously avoided overt and extended recourse to the rules (cf. Sacks et al. 1974) and theoretical background of Conversation Analysis (CA). This is because manipulation of the features and 'rules' of CA can in fact be construed as constituting yet another distinct way over and above what has already been shown in which impoliteness, and counter-impoliteness, can be realised in conversation.

Indeed, as I will show in this chapter, manipulation and exploitation of the turn-taking rules; of speaker expectations; and of the socio-situational norms that pertain to everyday speech, can aid in the delivery of highly effective impolite utterances. More specifically, I examine speakers' sophisticated usage of (a) (dis)preferred seconds to first pair parts for a deeper understanding and appreciation of the expectations and uses of such (dis)preferred second turns; (b) as well as the uses and abuses of interruptions, and (c) the way in which turn allocations and possession of the interactional floor pertain to the communication of impolite utterances. In this way we may gain a greater understanding of how sophisticated conversational interactants use impoliteness and how they may defend themselves against it.

The other main reason that impoliteness which is created by exploitation of CA features is treated as a separate chapter from the phenomena I discussed in Chapters 5 and 6, is that, the phenomena which were discussed in the two previous chapters largely deal with the deployment and use of specific 'strategies' (cf. Brown and Levinson 1987; Cashman 2006; Culpeper 1996, 2005; Culpeper et al. 2003; Lachenicht 1980), whereas the phenomena I discuss in this chapter deal with the manipulation and exploitation of the understandings and expectations of how the very structure and sequencing of conversation work.[1]

The aim in this chapter then is to identify how exploitation of the conversational structure of the chosen discourses can create, or contribute to, the production of impoliteness work alongside, and infused with, the complex deployment of the conversational strategies that we have already seen in Chapters 5 through 7. The sophisticated usage of the phenomena I discuss here could be construed as impolite 'tactics' to stand alongside and support the impolite strategies of researchers like Culpeper (1996).

I should note, here, that some of the concepts I explore here (e.g. Interruptions, which closely follow the 'Hinder: linguistically' strategy discussion from Chapter 5, above; and Conducivity, which closely follows the post interrogatives I mentioned in brief in Chapter 6, Section 6.3.1), I have already discussed, or touched upon, in earlier chapters. Such phenomena, where they appear for discussion in this chapter, are mentioned for a sense of completeness and will be cross-referenced to the earlier discussions. Some repetition may be necessary to put the argument of the chapter into its proper context.

8.1 Impoliteness and the turn-taking system

Sacks et al. (1974: 12) make an early claim that there is a conversational rule: overwhelmingly, there is one and only one interactant speaking at a time in two-party, or in multi-party talk. They further extended this argument into the rule: 'no gap, no overlap' in two-to-multi-party talk. What is meant by this, (and to which we can add the above), is that the change from one speaker to the next is orderly and without undue pauses, or silences.

1. Of course, while the many transgressions and manipulations discussed herein could be, in an analyst's eyes, (re)constructed and pieced together as 'strategies', this would, however, be a purely analyst's understanding and label. It would not be a lay interactant's understanding. This would, furthermore, be harking back to the era in which 'strategy-spotting' in texts, (in which utterances were taken out of context) was considered cutting edge research for politeness work – an era we left some 15 years ago. While I have, necessarily, identified some relevant strategies within the data sets studied (in context), I need to point out that a return to this era of 'strategy spotting' is not an aim of mine.

Silverman (1998: 103), building upon, and drawing from Sacks (1992) and Sacks et al. (1974) identifies the main features of conversation organised sequentially

1. People talk one at a time
2. Speaker change recurs
3. Sequences that are two utterances long and are adjacently placed may be 'paired activities'
4. Activity can be required to occur at appropriate places
5. Certain activities are chained

However, Sacks was quick to point out that the 'rules' of CA should not be applied in any mechanistic sense to expectations of how conversation is, or will be structured. Indeed, Silverman (1998: 108), reports that Sacks was very aware of the dangers of doing so. While researchers such as Goffman have argued that the 'one-at-a-time' character of conversation is the conceptual basis for work on turn-taking (Goffman 1971), this is not necessarily true with impolite discourse. Note the following example, amongst many, which is taken from **Parking Wars, Extract 74.**

[84] ***Context****: A town where residents and students live side by side. A dispute has arisen between one resident, S1, and one student, S2, over one parking space. They are discussing an incident which occurred earlier.*

[…]

8. S1: you annoyed me they way you spoke to my wife as far as I'm
   S2: does it really matter

9. S1: concerned don't do it again please don't
   S2: I didn't speak to your wife in any er crude way at all the only thing I said to

10. S1: do it again please don't do it again
    S2: your wife was are you threatening me and she said

11. S1: how can an old lady like that threaten you . for goodness' sake .
    S2: no I'm not

12. S1: what's the matter with you I think I
    S2: I didn't mean threatening in the way by way of

13. S1: think you've got a problem you . I think you've su you've really got a
    S2: hitting I meant

14. S1: problem
    S2: yeah

[…]

Note here that in staves 8, 9, 10, 12, 13 and partially in 14, both speakers S1 and S2 are speaking simultaneously. Such a phenomena, contrary to Sacks et al.'s claim, is common within some of the data sets studied within this book (The Clampers, Parking Wars), but is not so common in others (Soldiers To Be, Redcaps, Raw Blues, Boiling Point). This, clearly, concerns matters to do with speaker rights, participant powers, and interactant's obligations which are built upon interlocutor's particular social and discoursal roles. Without dwelling too long on an old position here one should note the claims from such researchers as Meltzer et al. (1971) who argue, 'A primary justification for why conversation should proceed in this [one-at-a-time] fashion is that simultaneous talk would not permit much communication'. One assumes this would be the case as, according to Jefferson, simultaneous talk '[…] is potentially unhearable' (Jefferson 1973; cited in Edelsky 1981: 397).

Haviland, transcribing an unruly political discussion at Jteklum Cabildo, 1982, in (what purports to be) Zincantec Tzotzil presents us with the following transcription:

```
1     a;    ((unintelligible))
      [
2     b;    ((unintelligible))
      [
3     c;    ((unintelligible))
      [
4     d;    ((unintelligible))
      [
5     e;    ((unintelligible))
      [
6     f;    ((unintelligible))
      [
7     g;    ((unintelligible))
      [
8     h;    ((unintelligible))
      [
9     I;    ((unintelligible))
      [
10    j;    ((unintelligible))
      [
11    k;    ((unintelligible))
```

(Haviland 1997: 548–9)

'Representing' no fewer than 11 adult Zincantec men shouting simultaneously during a politically, and presumably emotionally charged dispute settlement, Haviland notes that his audio recording was unable to provide even evidence of the known speakers at the event, let alone what each individual speaker actually said. However, he notes that:

> The fact that no single voice on the audiotape of this event is intelligible to this transcriber should not, of course, suggest that the participants themselves were unable to distinguish or attend to what the others were saying.
>
> (Haviland 1997: 549)

It should be clear, therefore, that the 'one-at-a-time' nature of talk suggested by Sacks et al. and adopted by others, is at best an *expectation* of orderly communication but is not by any stretch of the imagination a necessary prerequisite or 'rule'.

It is perhaps best, then, to view simultaneous talk as one of a possible multitude of linguistic occurrences which may be either (1); moves which may be supportive or confrontational with regards the current turn's speaker; or (2) moves which may simply be symptomatic of a specific locutor's gambit, combative or otherwise, for the floor. But herein lies an issue. What do we mean by 'floor' and 'turn'? The terms, so often used freely and even interchangeably by certain CA analysts (cf. Mehan 1978, see below), have to be more clearly defined for the researcher of im/politeness to be able to show, with any degree of accuracy, how speakers utilise, exploit and manipulate both turns, and bids for/allocations of the floor in discourses containing impoliteness.

8.2 Considering the concepts of 'turn' and 'floor' with respect to impoliteness

Mehan (1978) describes the interactant who holds or is taking a turn as, quite simply, the one who is speaking. This seems a little imprecise as one does not necessarily need to be taking a turn on the floor in order to make an utterance. Back channels, supportive interruptions and the like are all instances of a locutor who is 'speaking' yet not taking a turn on the floor. Mehan's position, like that of many researchers over the years, has often confused the issue of turns and floors, and indeed has often confused the two terms and rendered them as being virtually synonymous. Edelsky (1981) and Mey (2001) (see also Hayashi 1996) more precisely define the two terms 'turn' and 'floor'.

Edelsky (1981: 403) defines a 'turn' as '... an on-record "speaking" (which may include non-verbal activities) behind which lies an intention to convey a message that is referential and functional.' By contrast 'the floor' in Edelsky's terms is defined (1981: 405) as '...the acknowledged what's-going-on within a psychological time/space'.

Mey, on the other hand, succinctly defines the floor as being '[...] the right to speak' (Mey 2001: 135), and defines a turn as being the utterance made by a speaker once one person has relinquished the floor and the speaker takes it. It would appear that we may adopt definitions which combine these views. A turn, (or *turn-at-talk*), then, could be defined as an utterance (a) by which a participant aims to achieve goals, or aims, or otherwise convey a message; and (b) by which the participant takes, or holds, the floor (or, indeed, *attempts* to take or hold the floor). A new turn starts when speaker change upon the floor occurs. For the floor, we may adopt Mey's position, being, the right to speak which is qualified with, and by, an understanding of the context, including such features as the participants' rights, powers, obligations and socio-discoursal roles, and the activity type in which all are engaged. These are the definitions which I use throughout the present study.

Edelsky argues (1981: 406) that it is possible for a participant to take a turn without having the floor. Evidence of this can be seen throughout many of the extracts presented in this book, with clear examples seen in example [84] in Section 8.1, above. This I would argue is relatively uncontroversial even when applied to non-impolite discourse types. In the same vein and following on from Edelsky's position, above, it would therefore follow that it may also be possible for a participant to have been allocated the floor, but of opting not to take a turn. One would, in effect, be *Staying Silent* (see the broader discussion made earlier in Section 7.2.1.1, *Choosing not to respond*, above) or of opting for the 'don't do the FTA' superstrategy in Brown and Levinson's (1987) terms. Adding here to the discussion made in Section 7.2.1.1, above, as it applies directly to the argument, I should like to note that for Tannen (1985) silence can express, in Brown and Levinson's terms, both positive and negative politeness, and can be the extreme manifestation of indirectness; it can be communicative, they argue, without saying the wrong words or being negative. Therefore, it follows that, in contexts, and discourses in which impoliteness plays a central role, silence can surely be realised in a fashion that mirrors Tannen's (1985) position, in that it could simultaneously express both negative and positive *im*politeness – again, if further proof is needed, this challenges the distinction between these aspects of face as being dichotomous. This is not to say, of course, that silence need actually be, or that I consider it always is, communicative. Jaworski (1993), on the power of silence, indicates that it can be both communicative and non-communicative, and where communicative, it can be both positively and negatively charged, (see 'withholding politeness' Section 5.3, above. See also Culpeper's strategy of 'withholding politeness where it may be expected' 1996: 357; also see Thomas 1995: 175).

This means then that we can further refine our definition of 'floor' a little more clearly. A floor would, context permitting, include (a) the right, (b) the expectation and (c) possibly even the obligation, to speak. Additionally we must also consider that the definition of floor could also include, context permitting, (d) the right to be heard, and (e) even the expectation, and possibly (f) even the obligation (upon others) that your turn will be heard and considered.

A point which we need to bear in mind when considering impoliteness which both manipulates and exploits such phenomena is that while 'turn' and 'floor' are clearly linked, these two concepts are nevertheless fundamentally, discrete phenomena. Additionally, *despite* the definition above, when we consider impolite discourses we should remember that just because one has the right to speak, then this does not necessarily mean one has the right to be considered, given attention to or even to be heard. Likewise, just because one person in a given context may have the right to have their views heard, considered and even acted upon, does not necessarily mean that that person will actually take the opportunity to air their views.

Within the data sets studied for this research project, there are, quite clearly, instances where a turn is being taken, for the purposes of issuing impoliteness work, but the floor is either (a) not necessarily available to the speaker, or (b) has been denied outright. Examples from the data sets include (again pertinent sections *italicised*): Taken from **The Clampers, Extract 1.**

[85] ***Context:*** *Ray and Miguel, clamping supervisor and assistant respectively have arrived to remove the clamp from a van. The van's owner is waiting for them. The exchange, to this point, has centred around S2's impolite comments regarding the ethics of clamping in general and of S1's role and culpability in clamping in particular.*

[…]

20. S1: you need to contact the council and make your=
    S2: as I'm concerned =I have just gone down

21. S1:
    S2: there and paid them and I have my form but that doesn't make up for the

22. S1:
    S2: time I've lost the inconvenience and the hassle and what is basically

23. S1: well I fully appreciate what you're saying
    S2: government legalised extortion does it

24. S1: but what I'm saying to you I can take your notes I can take your notes on
    S2: I'm sure you do I'm sure you hear it ten times a day

25. S1: board but there's nothing I personally can do I simply work do my job for
    S2: just do your job

26. S1: the council I do my job for the coun if you want me to explain then if you
    S2: I don't care what you do

[…]

Note here the competitive nature of the talk. S1 attempts to gain the floor with his failed turn in stave 20 and after taking a turn in staves 20–23 and further attempts in staves 24 to 26, S2 takes a turn when the floor is not his to take.[2] He, in effect, 'speaks out of turn'. The main point to be made here is that the non-ratified, 'out-of-turn', turn-taking which S2 indulges in here *contributes* to the realisation of impoliteness. It is not to be considered the impoliteness itself, rather, it is merely one mechanism by which the communication of impolite face-threatening utterances are being supported, in that it serves to (a) Propagate the Activity Type of 'on-street, informal, complaint', (b) indicate that S2 does not have S1's face wants at heart (see stave 26), and (c) allow the impoliteness in stave 25 *just do your job* to be delivered without waiting for a Transition Relevant Place (hereafter TRP). In short, such non-ratified turn-taking can contribute to an atmosphere of conflict within the linguistic interchange.

However, the phenomena of turns taken without the availability of the floor only really occurs, within my data, in the car-parking disputes data, and not in the military training data set, the police training data, nor in the kitchen data set. This concerns matters to do with participant roles in the discourses whereby the power relations implied by certain roles indicate that usually one participant has significantly more applicable (in that context) power than another. What does tend to occur more in the army training, police training and kitchen data sets, than in the car parking data, are instances of the floor being available, even belonging to a specific individual, but, either, (a) the turn is not taken, or (b) the turns being denied. Note the following example taken from **Redcaps, Extract 52.**

[86] ***Context****: The female recruits are having a room inspection. S1 is the inspecting sergeant, S2 is recruit Williams who is being inspected.*

1. S1: Williams is it   what have you done with those trousers this
   S2:   yes sergeant ....
2. S1: morning Williams . I don't know what they're used to at Winchester but
   S2:
3. S1: that wouldn't even PASS PLAYSCHOOL .... show them all correctly
   S2:

2. Hence the necessity for considering the prospect of simultaneously produced turns (as opposed to one-at-a time). S2 is taking a turn while S1, technically, has the floor in that he is taking his turn regarding, and relating to, the 'acknowledged what's going on'. S1, therefore, in holding the floor, has the right to be heard and S2's 'out-of-turn' turns run the risk of transgressing this right to be heard and, thus, run the risk of being considered impolite by impinging on, at least, S1's face relating to the want or desire to be free from imposition.

4. S1: pressed tonight along with your jumper . look over your left shoulder ..
S2:

5. S1: look at your . epaulets .. you haven't pressed them have you .. you slept
S2:

6. S1: in your jumper last night didn't you Williams THAT'S WHAT
S2: no sergeant

7. S1: IT SHAGGING WELL LOOKS LIKE . look across your left shoulder again
S2:

8. S1: what's that ...... WHAT IS IT .. no wrong look again WHAT'S
S2: <indistinct>

9. S1: THAT FLUFF . WHAT'S IT DOING THERE WILLIAMS
S2: fluff sergeant

[S2 has apparently become disoriented. She is swaying on her feet by this stage.]

10. S1: .... WELL WHAT'S IT DOING THERE WILLIAMS ...... SPEAK TO
S2:

11. S1: ME GIRL .... SPEAK TO ME you should take a seat Williams
S2: <indistinct>

[…]

Note here, staves 8, 9, 10 and 11. In stave 8, S1 asks a question of S2, *what's that ......*, which, in effect, makes the floor available to her, but she does not take her allocated turn on the floor, in effect, she fails to respond after a three second pause which precipitates a chained re-iteration of the question asked, only louder and more forcefully, with, *WHAT IS IT ...* In effect, her silence is seen as a dispreferred second which allows S1 a repetition of the original question (see Section 8.4.8, below for a fuller discussion of this phenomenon).

In staves 9, 10 and 11, S2, apparently becoming disoriented, possibly due to the stress of being the target S1's FTAs, refuses to take her turn on the available floor no less than 3 times. After a question followed by a 2 second pause: *WHAT'S IT DOING THERE WILLIAMS....*, a chained question followed by a 3 second pause *WELL WHAT'S IT DOING THERE WILLIAMS ......* and a bald instruction followed by a 2 second pause *SPEAK TO ME GIRL ....*, S2 only answers after the chained bald instruction is re-iterated in stave 11, *SPEAK TO ME.* The refusals to take a turn may have been defensive moves against the aggressive impoliteness of the sergeant, or may simply have been an inability to answer due to her disorientation. Refusing to take a turn on an available floor is a relatively common defensive occurrence within the army training data. (As we saw in Chapter 7,

Section 7.2.1.3, above). This phenomena also occurs in the kitchen data, as the following example, taken from **Boiling Point, Extract 63**, shows.

[87] ***Context***: *Restaurant owner and head chef Gordon Ramsay, S1, berates Owen, S2, a Chef de Partie, who has caused a delay in preparing vegetables for a dish.*

1. S1: what's going on here you **........** what is going on what about <indistinct>
S2:
2. S1: fucking foi gras **.** eh you arsehole **.** you lost it again **.** you lost it again what's
S2:
3. S1: your big deal **.** why don't you fuck off home then go on fuck off home then
S2:
4. S1: eh arsehole **.** why don't you fuck off home then **..** why don't you fuck off
S2:
5. S1: home **..** why are you fucking it up
S2: I don't want to Gordon <indistinct>

[…]

This example is particularly interesting. In staves 1 to 5 S1 asks no less than 11 impolite questions of S2 before S2 chooses to answer, thus: (1) *what's going on here you* **........** *(2) what is going on (3) what about <indistinct> fucking foi gras* **.** *(4) eh you arsehole* **.** *(5) you lost it again* **.** *(6) you lost it again (7) what's your big deal* **.** *(8) why don't you fuck off home then go on fuck off home then (9) eh arsehole . (10) why don't you fuck off home then* **..** *(11) why don't you fuck off home* **..**

In each case, as denoted by the varied pauses of between fractions of a second (0.5 seconds) and 4 seconds long, in S1's speech, S1 is clearly allocating the floor to S2. S2 is, however, refusing to take a turn on the available floor, clearly as a set of repeated defensive moves[3] against the exacerbated FTAs embedded in the questions from S1. It is only after the last, chained and re-iterated, *why don't you fuck off home* **..** by S1 in stave 5 that S2 answers with *I don't want to Gordon*.

There are, of course, instances where the floor is available to a locutor, but the turn which is allocated is denied and rescinded the moment the locutor concerned attempts to take a turn on the floor. I have already discussed the phenomena by reference to the **Redcaps, Extract 53** in Sections 5.2 as example [21] and 7.2.1.1 (Choosing not to respond) as example [61] above, and, as such I will not dwell overlong on the points already made, except to point out that S1 manipulates the turn-taking system by 'running roughshod' over TRPs as a way of (a) supporting his impolite beliefs about S2, (b) maintaining his power and indirectly reminding

3. See Chapter 7.

S2 of his social role, by (c) contributing to the atmosphere of the speech event by propagating the Activity Type of a 'formal dressing down'. How he does this is through turn taking manipulation, as we can see below.

1. ***STAVE 7–8:*** *why why are you in front of me now? . I'LL TELL YOU WHY because you've failed to comply with two verbal orders*
2. ***STAVE 8–9:*** *is that true or is that not true? IT IS TRUE ISN'T IT*
3. ***STAVE 9–10:*** *but what is the first one you have failed on? Monday evening you were told to put your name in all your military items of clothing*
4. ***STAVE 11:*** *did you do it? . NO YOU DIDN'T .*
5. ***STAVE 11:*** *WHY NOT ? (S2 allowed to take turn)*
6. ***STAVE 24–25:*** *then why didn't you get it cut? ... COME ON THEN . SPEAK TO ME!*

8.3 Interruptions

I take (successful) interruptions to be instances whereby a participant in a linguistic interchange self selects and takes a turn at a place in the conversation other than at a TRP and, moreover, who successfully attains the floor with this turn. Hutchby (1992) (see also Bilmes 1997) analyses interruption in argument sequences in American talk radio. Although, as Hutchby notes, interrupting (in Western culture) is often seen as a sign of dominance, hostility and therefore, potentially, impoliteness, it should be noted that this need not always be the case. Indeed, the type of confrontation talk analysed by Hutchby shows positive aspects:

> Interruption has a positive dimension ('we have to do this to save the world'); it provokes resistance strategies on the part of the radio listener which are not disruptive of a speaker's topical line, and the professional radio program maker uses interruption as a way of being in control without being rude or aggressive.
> (Hutchby 1992; cited in Ulijn and Li 1995: 598–599)

As such, it needs to be noted here that it would be wrong to assume that all interruptions are, by their very nature, hostile. Not every instance of interruption in the data sets studied has been considered significant for impoliteness work.

Where interruptions are significant they can be classified as being instantiations, or varieties of the *Hinder: linguistically*, impoliteness output strategy (see 5.5.2, above). Other than the outright impoliteness of the strategy, as discussed in Section 5.5.2, above, interruption can be used in a impoliteness-support role. Note the following exchange: Taken from **The Clampers, Extract 17**.

[88] ***Context:*** *Ticketer, S1, is working Meadow Garth Road at 8.30 a.m. The road is adjacent to a primary school and parents often 'illegally' park while dropping off their children. S2 is a mother being ticketed, S3, another mother, and S4 is the school's headmistress. By this point the conversation has been already been argumentative and conflictive.*

[…]

16. S1: well I am trying to be but I've only got one
S2: it's nice to see you being so responsive the council
S3:
S4:

17. S1: set of ears *we'll start with you madam* <to S4> I work for tee ef em
S2: has made no attempt to respond
S3: excuse me excuse me you
S4:

18. S1: parking okay I did the first time I met you okay where's your car
S2:
S3: are a parking attendant alright act like one okay shut up and act like a
S4:

19. S1:
S2:
S3: parking attendant
S4:

[…]

The 'impolite-supportive' interruption here comes in stave 17. Note how S1 interrupts S2 who after self-selecting at a Transition Relevant Point was taking a valid turn on the floor. S1 interrupts S2, apparently intentionally, and attempts to hand the floor, and the following turn, to S4 who has been trying to make a point for some time. There is a strong possibility that, perhaps along with a genuine desire to progress the discussion, there was, coupled with this desire, an intent by S1 to 'snub' S2. This is evidenced from the following discourse. As I have already discussed above, S3's response to this impoliteness (S1 interrupting S2 to allocate a turn to S4). S3 self-selects a turn with *excuse me excuse me you are a parking attendant* … to berate S1 for his behaviour here, incidentally, interrupting S4's turn on the floor in the process. This latter interruption should not be construed as impolite, as the intent to cause open insult to S4 does not appear to be an aim of S3. Indeed, as Goldberg (1990) convincingly argues, people interrupt by using a relationally neutral act such as co-operation or a rapport oriented act, for instance camaraderie. While power oriented interruptions are interpreted as rude and impolite, rapport-oriented interruption can express open empathy, affection, solidarity and concern. In effect, what is happening here with S3's interruption of S1 in stave 17, is that she is, in effect, using S1's tactic against him – to interrupt S1 for impolite purposes while supporting S2's position, turn and face.

Clearly this kind of 'impolite-supporting' interruption may only occur in cases of more than two party talk as it requires the interrupter to support one speaker at the direct cost to face of another. Furthermore, of the 76 extracts analysed this is the only example in which a supportive utterance could be said to be being used impolitely, against a third party. As such this rare phenomenon will necessarily remain an area for future research in impoliteness.

8.4 Impoliteness, preference organization and conducive questions

It is the main contention of the remaining sections of this chapter that pragmatic manipulation and exploitation of the turn-taking rules (see Sacks et al. 1974), of speaker expectations, and of the socio-situational norms that pertain to everyday speech can aid in the delivery of highly effective intentionally face damaging utterances. More specifically, this paper seeks (a) to examine how speakers can support the issuing of intentionally unmitigated or exacerbated face threatening utterances through sophisticated usage of (dis)preferred seconds to first pair parts; and (b) a deeper understanding and appreciation of the expectations and uses of such (dis)preferred second turns. In this way we may gain a greater understanding of how sophisticated conversational interactants use impoliteness and how they may defend themselves from it.

The aim here, then, is to identify just how exploitation and manipulation of the conversational structure of the chosen discourses can create, or contribute to, the production of impoliteness work alongside the combined deployment of impoliteness strategies, evidence of which has already been noted by Culpeper et al. (2003: 1560–1562). The sophisticated use of the phenomena I discuss here could be construed as being impolite discoursal 'resources' which can be incorporated with the impolite tactics (on/off-record) and strategies of Cashman (2006), Culpeper (1996, 2005), and those discussed in Chapter 5 of this book.

8.4.1 Preference organization

Preference organization, as an aspect of the model of adjacency pairs (cf. Schegloff and Sacks 1973), was first suggested by Sacks et al. (1974), and was further developed by Pomerantz (1984) amongst others (see also Levinson 1983, for a good overview). As Sacks et al. (1974) note, adjacency pairs constrain what the next speaker may properly do. That is, given a specific first pair part, a specific second pair part is the preferred response (see also, Levinson 1983: 303–307; Mey 2001: 149–153; Silverman 1998: 105). Such paired activities occur in various forms: Greetings are usually followed by greetings; questions by answers; summonses by responses; initiations by responses, assessments by agreements, and so on. The pairs that interest us most here, and upon which I will concentrate this discussion, are both assessments and (dis)agreements, and questions and answers.[4] This is because in the data sets studied, these are the ones most obviously exploited for impolite, face threatening purposes.

As Silverman (1998: 105) points out, with all adjacency pairs, (assessments and agreements, and questions and answers included), the two parts together are relatively ordered – i.e. given a specific 'first', the appropriate 'second' should be done. In effect, the first turn (in a pair) constitutes a 'slot' for the second and sets up an expectation about what this slot may 'properly' contain (Silverman 1998: 98–99). Of course the fact that something *may* properly happen once a slot has been created, does not mean it *will* happen. An interlocutor may make an alternative linguistic choice. As Levinson points out,

> Alternative second parts to first parts of adjacency pairs are not generally of equal status; rather some second turns are PREFERRED and others DISPREFERRED. The notion of preference is not intended as a psychological claim about a speaker's or hearer's desires, but as a label for a structural phenomenon very close to the linguistic concept of markedness. (Levinson 1983: 332–333)

Pomerantz, looking at some features of preferred/dispreferred turn shapes with assessments and responses, agrees with Levinson. She argues (1984: 54) that a first speaker's assessment of someone or something known to the recipient routinely invites a subsequent second assessment, with which the recipient can (non-equivalently) agree or disagree with the first speaker. As we will see, however, impoliteness can enter the picture whether such expectations are fulfilled (with a preferred response), or not (with a dispreferred response).

8.4.2 A pragmatic approach to preference organization

First though, what needs to be noted at this point is an issue with Sacks et al's (1974) position on preference organization. They, like other researchers (Levinson

4. There is no claim however, that impoliteness may only occur when these two types of adjacency pairs are utilised or manipulated. Whether, and to what extent either, (a) these types of adjacency pairs in other discourses; or (b) other types of adjacency pairs in these or other discourses, can be exploited for impolite purposes, remain areas for future consideration.

1983 (332–334: see quotation above); Pomerantz 1984; Silverman 1998), consider preference organization to be a purely formal/structural phenomenon. Taylor and Cameron (1987: 114) however directly dispute this position, claiming that it is inappropriate to, "maintain the early ethnomethodological claim that [preference is] purely formal, with no basis in the truly psychological or functional sense of 'preference'." When we consider the possible combination of preference organization with conduciveness in questions (as we will see in Section 8.4.6, below), as well as the effect which context, and other factors have on the talk exchange in which (dis)preferred pairs are produced, then it would seem that there may be in operation two closely linked but nevertheless discrete aspects of preference. These are what I here term as: 1st order, or *structural* preference (following the CA specialists' terminology and understanding), and a 2nd order, 'socio-cognitive'[5] or, for want of a better phrase, *sociopragmatic* aspect of preference (which indicates a broadly *pragmatic* understanding of the phenomenon in that it embraces the non-CA-specialist usage of preference).

Quite often the two are virtually indistinguishable. Indeed, Brown and Levinson (1987), despite being firmly pro-structural in their approach to preference organization, do not see the division which is apparent within their own words when they consider the concept's applicability to politeness. Discussing preference organization they note that,

> The preferred type of response is usually more frequent also, but the term 'preference' refers to the structural disposition, to the fact that conversational organization conspires to make it easier to use the preferred type of turn, not to participants' wishes [...] If one asks what determines which kinds of response are preferred vs. dispreferred, in this structural sense corresponding to unmarked vs. marked in form respectively, a large part of the answer must lie in face considerations (Heritage 1984a, 1984b: 268). (Brown and Levinson 1987: 38)

Brown and Levinson qualify the above comments by noting that the preferred response to an assessment, for example, is an agreement, '[...] because disagreement is an FTA;' (Brown and Levinson 1987: 38). The main issue which needs to be noted here is that face considerations are not structural concerns, but rather are concerns which are socially and thus psychologically rooted and driven. Indeed, the existence of a *sociopragmatic* level existing alongside the *structural* level of preference is either explicit or implicit in many researchers' positions. Owen (1983: 151) and Hayashi (1996: 230) both see preference as a reflection of what the speaker wants to do. Owen observes that, 'once we begin to talk of preferences as

5. Indeed, as we will see, this aspect of 'Preference' may benefit from research which considers further subdivision into discrete, but linked 'psychological' and 'social' varieties.

"on the part of" either participant, we are surely close to dealing with motivations, wants, or some other similar notion' Owen (1983: 151).

Despite Levinson's insistence (1983: 332) that 'preference' is not intended as a psychological claim but as a label for a structural phenomenon, he does go on to suggest that there is a correlation between both the content and the sequential position of such turns with the tendency to produce them in preferred or dispreferred format. If we are assuming a purely structural conceptualisation of preference organization then it could be argued that the preferred response to a question would be, quite simply, an answer – any type of answer, whether expected or unexpected, correct or incorrect, truthful or false. However, as we can see from Table 5, below, Levinson assumes that the preferred second to a question first pair part would be an 'Expected Answer', and likewise, a dispreferred second would be an 'Unexpected Answer'.

To begin, we must as pragmaticists consider an answer to a question to be an utterance which relates (even via (i) contextualised exploitation of Grice's (1975) maxim of relation (cf. Mooney 2004), or (ii) by reference to Sperber and Wilson's (1986) theory of relevance, or some other approach to implicit meaning in context) to the question asked, in a meaningful, contextualised and communicative way. An answer cannot be simply *anything* that follows a question. If this were so, then this aspect of CA would, at least theoretically, have the potential of being forced to operate outside of the concept of communication on occasion. If we are to consider 'expectations' to answers then, clearly, we're looking at the psychological and the social considerations – the psycho/social (or socio-cognitive if you prefer) *expectations* – of the participants within the discoursal context in which the question is asked. After all, expectations of answer could suggest, at the very least, the following:

Table.5. Correlations of content and format in adjacency pair seconds (*Pairs* discussed in this sub-section are in **bold**) (see Levinson 1983: 336)

Preference Organization					
First Pair Parts:					
	Request	Offer/Invite	**Assessment**	**Question**	Blame
Second Pair Parts:					
Preferred	Acceptance	Acceptance	**Agreement**	**Expected Answer**	Denial
Dispreferred	Refusal	Refusal	**Disagreement**	**Unexpected Answer**	Admission

(a) Interlocutors are psychologically expecting a *specific* (*type* of) answer, not just *an* answer. This would, therefore, preclude the possibility of preference organization being *just* a formal, structural phenomenon when considered in context. Indeed, if we are to accept the 'expected-unexpected' preference organization structure of the 'Question-Answer' pairing (as depicted in Figure 5), then we must, necessarily, acknowledge the context in which such questions are asked and, further, we must acknowledge that an answer is only an answer *to* the question put. When considered out of context the 'Question-Answer' pairing as depicted by Levinson is (arguably) only sustainable with closed-questions (requiring a 'yes/no' answer).

(b) In context, an expected answer may well depend upon the conduciveness, or the controlling nature (see Woodbury 1984: 199) of the actual question. This potential link, or co-dependency, of conduciveness and preference organization is explored below.

Despite her position regarding the purely structural approach to preference organization, Pomerantz echoes Brown and Levinson's (1987: 1987) position regarding preference as relating to politeness[6] and face considerations when she suggests preference includes such notions as sociability, support and solidarity (Pomerantz 1984: 77). Once again, one should note that such phenomena are both psychologically and/or socially driven. Sociability, support, solidarity and face considerations are not purely structural phenomena (though, of course, they do have some structural aspects to them). As such the positions of Taylor and Cameron (1987), supported by the positions of Hayashi (1996), Owen (1983) and, implicitly, Pomerantz (1984: 77), predict (indeed, insist upon) a level of preference which *does* account for such phenomena – in short, we must at the very least, begin to accept the possibility of a *sociopragmatic* aspect or level of preference being in operation alongside the *structural* aspect or level in all types of conversation. To do so is especially useful when we consider both impoliteness in general and the concept of conduciveness within certain question forms in particular (see Section 8.4.3 below).

Understanding that there may be more than one aspect or level to preference organization and how these might be conceptualised is all very well, but how do we define and explain the overall concept in depth? Levinson considers preference organization to be 'very close to the concept of markedness.' (1983: 333). Additionally, Comrie states that,

6. When Brown and Levinson (1987: 38) talk about preference organization and face considerations, they are clearly talking about preference organization and *politeness*, as they confine their own treatment of face consideration primarily to the concept of politeness and do not consider impoliteness in great depth (Eelen 2001).

> The intuition behind the notion of markedness in lingustics is that, where we have an opposition between two or more members […], it is often the case that one member is felt to be more usual, more normal, less specific than the other (in markedness terminology it is unmarked, the others marked).
> (Comrie 1976: 114)

Comrie goes on to point out that, '… unmarked categories tend to have less morphological material than marked categories,' and '… there is a greater likelihood of morphological irregularity in unmarked forms'. (Comrie 1976: 114). Levinson sees the parallel between markedness and preference organization as quite apt,

> […] because in a similar way preferred (and thus unmarked) seconds to different and unrelated adjacency pair first pair parts have less material than dispreferreds (marked seconds), but beyond that have little in common (cf. "irregular"). In contrast, dispreferred seconds of quite different and unrelated first pair parts (e.g. questions, offers, requests, summonses, etc.) have much in common, noteably components of delay and parallel kinds of complexity. (Levinson 1983: 333)

Indeed, Pomerantz (1984: 64 & 75) echoes the views of markedness, delay (e.g. silent pauses, or fillers, such as 'erm…' or 'um…' before answering), and complexity with respects to dispreferred seconds to assessments:

> […] when agreements are invited by initial assessments, disagreements that are proferred regularly are performed in turns and sequences that exhibit the following features: (1) the inclusion of delay devices prior to stated disagreements like silences, hesitating prefaces, requests for clarification, and/or (2) the inclusion of weakly stated disagreement components, that is, partial agreements/partial disagreements. (Pomerantz 1984: 75)

Just why this is important will become apparent when I discuss the final two examples in Section 8 below. Before that, in constructing the overall argument of this section, it seems wise to consider the concept of conducivity in relation to questions and to impoliteness.

8.4.3 Challenges, questions, tags and conducivity

Following Culpeper et al. (2003) I have been advancing the discussion surrounding the impolite usage of 'Challenges' which is made by Lachenicht (1980) who draws from the discussion in Labov and Fanshel (1977). This has, so far, been formulated thusly: 'Challenge' linguistic impoliteness strategy, that is, *Challenge* – ask *h* a challenging question, critically question *h*'s position, stance, beliefs, assumed power, rights, obligations, ethics, previous actions, etc. Here, Culpeper et al. (2003: 1559), still following the positive/negative dichotomy on face, point out that *Challenging* an interactant, in an impolite way, is 'negatively' face oriented. Advancing the discussion further now, it is now worth noting that challenges can, in point of fact, be both 'positively' and 'negatively' face orientated (though, of course, the Brown and Levinson dichotomy on face is now questionable, as we've seen in the discussions made in Chapters 4 and 5). This is essentially because of the undercurrent of criticism (which would be seen as a face threatening act oriented at 'positive' face) pertaining to challenges (Labov and Fanshel (1977)). We can see now that there are two fundamental ways in which challenges 'work', or rather, the two separate *types* of the Challenge strategy that exist: Impolite, face-threatening challenges can now be defined as being either (1) *Rhetorical Challenges* – that is, challenges that do not require an answer but which merely 'activate' in the minds of the interlocutors what the given 'answer' actually is. Thus, one controls one's interlocutor into actively thinking about the impoliteness thereby increasing the (chances of) face damage being inflicted; or (2) *Response Seeking Challenges* – that is, challenges that *do* require an answer but an answer which is 'controlled' to the extent that, ultimately, the answer is face-damaging to the individual uttering it. I expound upon these types of challenge further, here:

8.4.3.1 *Rhetorical challenges*

The rhetorical type of challenge has already been discussed (Culpeper et al. 2003: 1559–1560), in relation to an example, partially rendered here again, from **Extract 1, The Clampers**.

[89] ***Context:*** *Ray and Miguel, clamping supervisor and assistant respectively have arrived to remove the clamp from a van. The van's owner is waiting for them. S1 is Ray, S2 is the van's owner. Miguel does not speak throughout this extract.*

[...]

8. S1: yellow line visibly under your car
   S2: ... I live here *why is there a yellow line*

9. S1:
   S2: *anyway why do I have to park my car three hundred yards up the road* it gets

10. S1:
    S2: stolen broken into vandalised three times this year already *why have you*

11. S1:
    S2: *done it why do you make my life impossible how am I supposed to work*

12. S1: can I just say you you you can clearly see the yellow line on the
    S2: *doing this* <----indistinct----->

13. S1: road it's not a new yellow line its been there for quite some time
    S2: *so why don't you just*

14. S1:
    S2: *stop the ticket*

[…]

Re-iterating, very briefly and for the purpose of completeness, the points made earlier (Section 5.5.4) and from Culpeper et al. (2003: 1559–1560) the issuing of no less than 5 challenges – *why is there a yellow line anyway why do I have to park my car three hundred yards up the road why have you done it, why do you make my life impossible,* and *how am I supposed to work doing this* – are all questions which, by the nature[7] in which they have been delivered, have little or no expectation of a response. They are impolite rhetorical challenges that are partly giving vent to the speaker's anger and frustration and partly attacking the challenge-using interactant's interlocutors. The face damage to the intended recipient comes about as it is implicit that the recipient: (a) is expected to stay and listen to the vented frustration (impinging on the hearer's freedom of action), and (b) is being blamed by the speaker for the speaker being angry in the first place (impinging on the recipient's desire for approval as an implied criticism). Furthermore, in relation to point (b), above, whilst it seems, on one level, that S1 (Ray) takes the brunt of a criticism which is not aimed primarily at him, but, rather, at some anonymous institution behind him,[8] we must remember that, on another level, S1, in working *for* the council has invested a portion of his face *in* the council. After all, Goffman (1967) defined 'face' as:

> The showing that individuals give for themselves, their religion, *their job*, their family *or other group to which they belong.* (Goffman 1967: 5–6, my emphasis)

To take a broader example: Imagine I was to purposefully insult, not interactant 'A' him/herself directly, but rather interactant A's spouse, children, job, car, house, and/or family pet direct to (or, knowingly, in front of) interactant A. By virtue of the fact that (all other things being equal, I'd expect, at least) as interactant A has "invested" expectations of face in said spouse, children, job, car, house, and/or family pet, then I'm being intentionally offensive, or, 'impolite' to A.

7. The very rapid tempo allows the speaker to 'railroad' over TRPs by immediate self-selection.

8. Thanks to Richard J. Watts for pointing this out to me.

8.4.3.2 *Response seeking challenges*

Response seeking challenges operate somewhat differently from rhetorical challenges, for the very obvious reason that a response is invited, expected or even enforced (power relations and context permitting). Response seeking challenges can be further defined as one of two sub-types. *Type (i) response seeking challenges*[9] which allow the intended addressee (at least the semblance of) a chance to explain, or account for, their actions, beliefs, appearance, etc. Where such Challenges are used impolitely, the recipient is given the option of offering an *Account* or an *Explanation* (as a defensive counter strategy, Culpeper et al. 2003) for the event that precipitated the impolite challenge in the first place. Such phenomena as type (i) response seeking challenges can be seen in the following example, taken from **Soldiers to be, Extract 33.**

[90] ***Context****: A room inspection. S1 is the inspecting corporal, S2 is the recruit being inspected. S1 has just inspected S2's training shoes. He has picked them up out of S2's locker and has now turned round to ask S2 a question.*

1. S1: turn around . what's that on the bottom of there *why's*
S2: <dried mud corporal>
2. S1: *it on there* . PUT YOUR FUCKING FEET TOGETHER WHEN YOU
S2:
3. S1: TALK TO ME *why's it on there* no excuse fucking right you've no
S2: <no excuse>
4. S1: excuse you're just fucking fat and idle aren't you
S2:

End.

S1's challenge in staves 1–2, and 3, has the necessary undercurrent of criticism required of challenges (cf. Labov and Fanshel (1977)), but in this case the challenge is response seeking – the addressee, S2 is given (at least the semblance of) a chance to respond to the challenge issued. This type of challenge is contrasted from the second type available to conversational participants, the *type (ii) response seeking challenge*. The second type of response seeking challenge is that of the 'Verbal Trap'. The response which may be offered to a verbal trap type of challenge is simply an exercise in accepting a form of face damage as the respondent will self-inflict face damage irrespective of the/any response given. I will clarify this point by referring an example of a 'verbal trap' challenge in **Extract 50, Redcaps.**

9. Not all 'type (i) challenges' need necessarily be impolite. Rather it is one type of utterance which can be used for impolite purposes, as ever, with the context permitting.

[91] ***Context***: *The Redcap recruits have a room inspection. S1 is the inspecting sergeant, S2 is recruit McKee.*

1. S1: *McKee where should your cap badge be in relation to your beret on your*
   S2:
2. S1: *head* SO WHY'S IT NEAR
   S2: a quarter of an inch above the left eye sergeant
3. S1: ROUND YOUR EAR **.** break ranks and get it sorted McKee
   S2:

[...]

Note that the challenge by S1 in stave 1 of *McKee where should your cap badge be in relation to your beret* **.** *on your head* is not a rhetorical challenge – it is genuinely seeking a response. The use of the modalised question in *where should* in stave 1 (as well as S1's next turn (stave 2–3) outburst) indicates via presupposition that the cap is not, currently, where it ought, correctly, to be – it is therefore a request for information which can only be heard, in this context, as being critical (cf. Labov and Fanshel 1977:93). While this is, therefore, an implied criticism in itself, it also operates as a precursor to further impoliteness when the verbal trap is sprung. The issue here is that, as it is apparent to both of the interlocutors that the cap badge is not correctly positioned, the response seeking challenge is a verbal trap. S2, recruit McKee, simply could not have provided any relevant response which would not have provoked the next, this time rhetorical, impolite challenge from S2 in staves 2 to 3: *SO WHY'S IT NEAR ROUND YOUR EAR?* In short, S2 is trapped into 'inviting' further face damage with a strategy which, has an 'IF.... THEN...' type of structure in that IF he answers THEN the verbal trap 'springs shut' to damage his face.

It is worth noting, as I believe these extracts show, that the differences between types (i) and (ii) response-seeking challenges; and indeed, the differences between Rhetorical challenges, and Response-seeking challenges, are fuzzy and not at all clear. Often it is only the context and/or the response of the intended recipient, that can help us as interlocutors and as analysts decide which type of challenge has been issued and what its function may be.

8.4.4 Conducivity in questions

As I have already suggested above, questions have the *potential* to be one of the most effectively utilised linguistic devices for both the construction of, and issuing of impoliteness (context, as ever, permitting). In every case where this is true, the questions used for impolite offensive linguistic output are conducive. Conducive questions are defined by Quirk et al. (1985: 83) as indicating, '…that the speaker is predisposed to the kind of answer he (sic) has wanted or expected.'

Quirk et al. (1985: 808) also state that questions with a negative orientation are *always* conducive. I am again drawing from the linguistic interchange in The Clampers, Extract 8. As before, I am adding further layers to the analysis originally presented in Culpeper et al. (2003) in order to illuminate my argument and more fully explicate the role and function of impoliteness in society.

[92] ***Context:*** *Two clampers proceed to clamp an illegally parked car. Just as they have finished, the car's driver, a workman who was doing a job for a local homeowner, returns to his car to find it clamped, and the clampers still there.*

S1 – 'Ray' the clamping supervisor.
S2 – 'Ammett' Ray's van driver and clamping assistant.
S3 – Passing Heckler.
S4 – Returning Workman and owner of the clamped van.

Edit *where the Clampers get confirmation of the fine having been paid. S1 is just finishing his radio call from base giving him authorisation to remove the clamp when S4 begins speaking.*

[…]

20. S1: okay cheers bye . we're going to declamp it
S4: it all seems a bit pointless doesn't

21. S1:
S4: it they're paying him to drive round collecting money I mean why not invest

22. S1: = well you see I'm just
S4: it in parking meters *don't you think this is a bit stupid*=

23. S1: doing a job but I've come along here and
S4: yeah well so was Hitler all I'm asking you as a

24. S1: yeah well <exhalation> yes and no
S4: person *don't you think this is a bit stupid*

[…]

Quirk et al. (1985: 809) note that, '[i]f a negative question has assertive terms, it is biased towards a positive orientation'. Woodbury (1984) too, observes the same function. The question asked in stave 22, and repeated in stave 24 of *don't you think this is a bit stupid*, which includes the assertive term of *is*, is conducively oriented towards the receipt of a positive, 'yes' answer. The implication for impoliteness here is that if the *yes* answer is forthcoming then S4 will have successfully manipulated S1 into making a self-damaging admission.

However, we should note that, when this admission is not forthcoming following stave 22, it is re-iterated in stave 24. What is interesting here is the way in which it is answered. It is answered as a 'weak' form of disagreement[10] (Pomerantz 1984), which includes both a prototypical agreement and a prototypical disagreement form, by S1, in stave 24, with: *yes and no.* Quirk et al. (1985: 809) note that such questions as the one discussed above are similar in effect to certain types of tag question, to which I now attend.

8.4.5 Tag questions, conducivity and impoliteness

Quirk et al. (1985: 810) point out that '[m]aximum conduciveness is expressed by … a tag question appended to a statement.' Additionally, Woodbury argues that:

> Tag questions are formally similar to one another in that they all consist of declarative sentences followed by tags. The declarative sentence contains one or more propositions that the tag portion of the question invites the hearer to affirm or deny. (Woodbury 1984: 203)

Quirk et al. (1985: 810) suggest that if the statement is positive, then the tag is generally negative, and vice versa. They further suggest that tag questions comprise of four basic types dependent on the polarity of the statement (and, hence, tag) and the nuclear tone of the tag (either rising or falling):

POSITIVE STATEMENT + NEGATIVE TAG

RISING TONE ON TAG	FALLING TONE ON TAG
(i) He likes his JOB, DOESn't he?	(iii) He likes his JOB, DOESn't he?

NEGATIVE STATEMENT + POSITIVE TAG

RISING TONE ON TAG	FALLING TONE ON TAG
(ii) He doesn't like his JOB, DOES he?	(iv) He doesn't like his JOB, DOES he?

(Adapted from Quirk et al. 1985: 811)

Tags with rising tones invite verification, while tags with falling tones invite confirmation of the statement and have the force of an exclamation rather than a genuine question (Quirk et al. 1985: 811). In this respect (i) and (ii) above are genuine questions which have neutral expectations with regards the answer they

10. A weak form of disagreement, (in this case a compromise), which incorporates both agreement and disagreement forms is a type of defensive strategy that is less likely to offend the hearer (as a by product of action) than a strong disagreement.

expect (they are not conducive, merely seeking verification of the statement), whereas (iii) and (iv), embody a positive and a negative expectation, respectively, with regards to the answers they seek to elicit (they conducively expect answers in agreement with the statement). One example of the conducive effects of a POSITIVE STATEMENT + NEGATIVE TAG can be seen in the following example, **Soldiers To Be, Extract 45**.

[93] ***Context***: *S1 is the inspecting Sergeant Major who has come to check the recruits' turnout and confidence. After a brief pep talk, telling the recruits to relax, he begins his final inspection before they go onto the final phase of drill instruction where they will be assessed in all areas by the commanding officer. S2 is recruit James South. S1 has just chastised the recruit in line before recruit South for poor turnout, he then turns to South.*

1. S1: go on
   S2: private South er wishing to join the-er second light infantry .. frommm
2. S1: *you're a bit of a space cadet you aren't you*
   S2: Sheffield sir *yes sir*

[…]

In commenting on S2's indecision here we should note, the form of S1's question in stave 2, with a falling tone on the tag:

2. S1: *you're a bit of a space cadet, aren't you*
   S2: *yes sir*

Or to put it another way:

S1: [Declarative Assessment], [Negative Tag] = [Expectation of a…
S2: …positive answer]

The conducive, or, in Woodbury's (1984) terms, the controlling nature of the [declarative assessment] + [tag question] with falling tone invited a positive answer from S2 that was, indeed, forthcoming. In constructing his impoliteness in this way, S1 *increases* the potential for face damage to S2 by 'inviting', that is, coercing S2 to self-face damage by agreeing with the impolite assessment in the declarative: *you're a bit of a space cadet.*

This is not the only way in which tags are used conducively with declarative assessments to produce impoliteness in the data sets studied. Quirk et al. also note (1985: 812) that a further, less common type of tag question exists in which both statement and question are positive. Its tag typically has a rising tone. They say (1985: 812) that we may, therefore, add a fifth, less usual type of tag question to the earlier four types:

POSITIVE STATEMENT + POSITIVE TAG
RISING TONE ON TAG
So he likes his JOB, DOES he (Adapted from Quirk et al. 1985: 812)

According to Quirk et al. (1985: 812), the effect of this type of construction may be one of 'sarcastic suspicion':

Soldiers To Be, Extract 21.

[94] ***Context***: *A Room inspection. A male sergeant is inspecting the barrack room of a number of female recruits. S1 is the inspecting corporal, S2 'Daggert' a female recruit. S1 is inspecting the state of S2's clothes which he believes are not clean.*

1. S1: *you've been doing your laundry have you* how often
   S2: yes sergeant

[…]

It may be 'sarcastically contradictory':

Soldiers To Be, Extract 30.

[95] ***Context***: *Burma platoon, the female recruits on field exercise have spent a cold, rough night outside. The temperature has dropped and they are exhausted. Early in the morning the NCO's inspect the recruits' kit. They do not like what they find. S1 is a corporal inspecting the recruits' kits. S2 and S3 are also corporals assisting S1. They have split up and are 'motivating' the recruits individually and as a team. Other speakers, who will be included in the staves as and when they contribute, are recruits.*

Edit: *Corporal S1 questions recruit S12 on her ability to keep her kit waterproof. He picks up on the fact that she is using a plastic bin liner that is full of holes.*

[…]

46. S1: *that's its waterproof bag is it* this here this here's going
    S12: yes corporal
47. S1: to stop it getting soaking wet this bag here the one with the hole in
    S12:
48. S1: the end there the one that isn't fastened at the top as a matter of fact
    S12:
49. S1: the one that isn't actually a bag . it's actually . a black necklace of
    S12:

50. S1: some sort because it isn't a bag is it
S12: no corporal

[…]

It may be simply, just plainly 'sarcastic':

Soldiers To Be, Extract 22.

[96] ***Context:*** *S1, a sergeant is inspecting the male barrack room. S2 is a young male recruit. S1 dislikes what he sees in the room of eight recruits before turning to, and on, S2.*

[…]

4. S1: you're having a fucking laugh aren't you what did you do last
S2: no sergeant
5. S1: night then apart from fuck all
S2: ironed my kit and done my boots…… .
6. S1: *You ironed your kit did you* and you done your fucking boots
S2: yes sergeant
7. S1: yeah really [inspects boots] *you done those did you* [inspects boots] get
S2: sergeant ……. yes sergeant ……
8. S1: outside the fucking office now
S2: sergeant

[…]

It may also be 'scolding':

Redcaps, Extract 47.

[97] ***Context***: *Training sergeant, S1 is greeting trainee Military Police Personnel (Redcaps) at the main door as they arrive. S2 is a guardsman (Guards' regiments in some circles being considered finer than others) who, fresh out of basic training, has applied to be a military policeman. As he arrives at the Royal Military Police Training College he meets S1. S2 is in civilian clothes but as he sees S1 (in uniform) waiting by the front door, he steps up smartly, comes to attention and salutes.*

1. S1: who are you guardsman morris
S2: er guardsman morris colour sergeant yes
2. S1: *you've turned up in jeans to the royal military police training centre*
S2: sergeant
3. S1: *have you* with a girlie chain around your SHAGGING NECK
S2: yes sarn't <yes

4. S1: get that chain off now .... I expect better from a guardsman
   S2: sergeant> [---------------fumbles with chain------------]

[…]

In addition to the coerced responses elicited by the conducive questions above, tag questions, like all forms of questions, can be rhetorically issued. Note the following example taken from **Soldiers To Be, Extract 33.**

[98] ***Context:*** *A room inspection. S1 is the inspecting corporal, S2 is the recruit being inspected. S1 has just inspected S2's training shoes. He has picked them up out of S2's locker and has now turned round to ask S2, who is facing away from his locker in the position of attention, a question.*

1. S1: turn around . what's that on the bottom of there why's
   S2: <dried mud corporal>
2. S1: it on there . PUT YOUR FUCKING FEET TOGETHER WHEN YOU
   S2:
3. S1: TALK TO ME . why's it on there no excuse . fucking right
   S2: <no excuse>
4. S1: you've no excuse *you're just fucking fat and idle aren't you*
   S2:

End.

Here the context and co-text of S1's tag question in stave 4: *you're just fucking fat and idle* + *aren't you* [declarative assessment] + [negative tag with falling intonation] tends to suggest that the question was rhetorical in nature. S2's admission of having *no excuse* (stave 3) for not properly cleaning his training shoes, in the face of S1's response-seeking challenge (see above), *why's it on there* (staves 1–2 and again in 3,) tends to support the view that the question *you're just fucking fat and idle aren't you* is rhetorical. This is because it is simply re-formulating given information (in that he has admittedly been inefficient with regards to the cleaning of his training equipment, coupled with the visually obvious fact that S2 is a slightly larger-than-average-sized individual), albeit as an impolitely expressed assessment of S2 by S1. The fact that the [assessment] + [negative polarity tag question] usually predisposes an answer in agreement with the assessment does not significantly diminish the impolite face threat simply because the question is rhetorical. Indeed, Quirk et al. (1985) note that the force of rhetorical questions is the same as in strong assertions. The unspoken, unneeded agreement of S2 to S1's assertion that S2 is *fat* and *idle*, is on record and 'hangs in the air'. When we consider the illocutionary boosting effect (see Holmes (1984)) through the use of the taboo word *fucking*, which is combined with the expression of impolite beliefs (Leech 1983) which act as a criticism, then we can clearly see that the impolitely communicated face damage in an otherwise rhetorical tag question remains somewhat undiminished in this example.

8.4.6 Conducivity and preference organization

If we consider the effects which conducivity (Piazza 2002; Quirk et al. 1985), or the coercively controlling nature of questions (Woodbury 1984), can have in relation to preference organization (Levinson 1983; Pomerantz 1984; Sacks et al. 1974), then we can begin to see more clearly how such phenomena are used together for impolite purposes. Consider the following:

(i) Preference Organization (see Levinson 1983: 336):

First Pair Part:	**Preferred Response**	**Dispreferred Response**
Question:	Expected Answer	Unexpected Answer
Assessment:	Agreement	Disagreement

(ii) Conducive Questions (See Quirk et al. 1985: 809):

Negative oriented question with assertive terms expects a Positive Answer
[Declarative assessment + tag] expects an answer …
… in agreement with the Declarative

If we *combine* these two phenomena, then the preference organization of, at least, a Negatively Oriented Conducive Question should now be clear:

Table 6. Preference organization of conducive negative oriented questions

First Pair Part	Preferred Response to Second Pair Part	Dispreferred Response to Second Pair Part
Conducive Question with a negative orientation	Expected: A positive answer	Unexpected: A negative answer

When we consider Assessments and the Conduciveness inherent in certain Tag questions, then the preference structure appears to be:

Table 7. preference organization of **positive** assessments with **negative tag** questions

First Pair Part	Preferred Response to Second Pair Part	Dispreferred Response to Second Pair Part
Positive Assessment with a Negative Tag	Expected: A positive answer	Unexpected: A negative answer

And, likewise, vice versa:

Table 8. Preference organization of **negative** assessments with **positive tag** questions

First Pair Part	Preferred Response to Second Pair Part	Dispreferred Response to Second Pair Part
Negative Assessment with a Positive Tag	Expected: A negative answer	Unexpected: A positive answer

First pair parts which are positive assessments with positive tags (in being sarcastically suspicious; sarcastically contradictory; sarcastic; or scolding) are always, in the data-sets studied, either rhetorical in nature, or are 'verbal trap' questions in that however answered they operate as presages to further, more extreme impoliteness in the following turn(s). What constitutes a 'preferred' answer to such first pair parts is perhaps difficult to predict beyond the interlocutor being in agreement with the pragmatic, and not necessarily the surface meaning of the (either sarcastic, or critical) assessment. This type of 'preference' will be further discussed and explained in Section 8.4.8, below.

8.4.7 Impoliteness, conducive questions, and 'first order' (structural) preference use

We've already seen something of the way in which conducive questions set-up an expectation of what the answer will be, e.g. **Extract 45, Stave 2**: *you're a bit of a space cadet, aren't you* with the answer *yes sir*. As suggested above in example [93], and now stated explicitly, the same phenomena has been covered from two different angles. Not only is the *yes* answer coerced through conduciveness, but it is further predicted by the 'rules' of preference organization of Sacks et al. (1974) and echoed by Levinson (1983) and Pomerantz (1984).

Of course, the use of negatively oriented questions and question-tags is not the only way in which questions can be used either by being conducively impolite, or by use of verbal response traps. By setting up inferred expectations of what an answer to a specific positively oriented question[11] may be, a locutor asking a question, can, also set up that answer to be self face damaging. This is a tactic that occurs in the car-parking data set, the army training data set and the kitchen data set. Note the following examples. Taken from **Boiling Point, Extract 62**:

11. Positively oriented questions can be, from a conducive point of view, somewhat more neutral in their expectations with regards to answers than negatively oriented questions.

[99] ***Context***: *Restaurateur Gordon Ramsay, S1, berates, Owen, S2 who has dropped some dishes in the busy kitchen. He then turns, in Stave 3, to 'Dan' a senior member of his kitchen staff in an apparent attempt to include him in the conversation.*

1. S1: oh come on donkey who was that get a grip Owen
   S2: me Gordon ...... yes Gordon
2. S1: are you in a daze you are you in a daze fucking dreamer ...
   S2: no no Gordon ..
3. S1: Dan yeah the most expensive person on the pass eh . and he's sort
   S2:
   S3: oui Gordon
4. S1: of standing there like a fucker y'know . he's actually I mean *how good do*
   S2:
5. S1: *you actually think you are* . *bottom line* .. *ho-o-w good do you think you are*
   S2:
6. S1: *bottom line seriously* .. *do you think you're shit hot*
   S2: <indistinct> *no Gordon*

End.

Note here the danger inherent in the open questions which S1 asks of S2 in staves 4 to 6: *how good do you actually think you are?* . *bottom line?* .. *ho-o-w good do you think you are? bottom line? Seriously!* .. as well as in the closed-class *'yes-no'* question in stave 6: *do you think you're shit hot?* S1, in a position of power as the Restaurateur, employer and chief trainer of S2 is uniquely in a position to tell S2, honestly, how skilled at being a chef S2 actually is. By asking S2 these response seeking questions in this context, S1 is clearly setting up a 'preferred response verbal trap' in that just how to handle the open-class, 'wh-' question is the issue for S2. Had S2 responded with any form of positive, self-promotion, however honest about his own abilities as a chef, there may be very good reason for S1 to fear may have used his position of power to issue a blistering impolite attack upon S2 given other instances linguistic aggression used by S1.

Similarly, should S2 have responded with a preferred 'yes' to the final question (cf. Sacks et al. 1974), this would not only be seen as immodest, and therefore as a breech of the PP maxim of modesty (cf. Leech 1983: 81), which would be potentially face-damaging, but it could *also* have prepared the ground for a blistering face attack from S1 (i.e. the higher you set yourself up, the higher you have to fall[12]). By admitting *no Gordon,* S2 does indeed self-face damage (by apparently admitting he is not an excellent or a '*shit hot*' (which is a British colloquialism for 'excellent') chef), but he reduces the potential for further face-damage in subsequent turns from S1. This said S2 clearly risks face damage whether he answers *yes* or *no* here.

What is apparent from these and similar examples is that the very structure of the interrogative used and/or the very structure of conversation with an expectation of specifically preferred answers embedded through specific questions actually seems to imply face-damage before the question is even answered (if indeed it ever is). Defensive moves against such impolite attacks can often merely reduce the implied face threat rather than eradicate it, and even a refusal to respond with a preferred or dispreferred answer does not always seem to fully remove the face-damage. This is the use, and management of preference organization in a 'first' order, or *structural*, way.[13]

8.4.8 Second order or sociopragmatic preference: 'Preferring the dispreferred'

We've just seen how preferred answers can be, potentially, very face damaging for the answerer. But, there do seem to be instances whereby the structurally preferred second is not really expected, or indeed sought, by the question asker, but rather, a structurally 'dispreferred' second is; primarily for the purposes of continuing the impolite face-damaging exchange. This is using preference organization in a 'second' order, or sociopragmatic way.

I have already noted how the conduciveness of a given question seems to indicate a specific preference for the answer, but, because of the ongoing nature of some discourses, the questioner would seem, not only to prefer a dispreferred response, but also to require one. Note the following example taken from **Soldiers to Be, Extract 23.**

[100] ***Context**: S1 sergeant 'Tich Lovall' is investigating who has cut a recruit's hair resulting in an illegal haircut. S1 has his suspicions and call all eight recruits of one barracks room in. S1 concentrates his questions to S2: recruit Downes, S3: recruit Harris and S4: recruit Andrews – the three recruits he suspects who are indeed responsible for cutting*

12. Thanks to Jonathan Culpeper for, amongst many other things, this axiomatic clarification of the point being made.

13. At this point in needs to be noted that although there are, in my view, different 'layers', or 'facets' to preference organization, to separate them is, in actuality, artificial. The distinction is made here, in this chapter is purely for the purposes of discussion and exposition.

the other recruit's hair. Up to this point he has asked recruit Downes (who he suspects is the ring leader) if he cut Newson's hair. Downes has stated three times that he did not do so. Sergeant Lovall has his doubts. By the time this section of the extract starts, Sgt Tich Lovall has discovered through barrack room interrogation that S2, recruit Downes, was indeed responsible for the illegal haircut despite Downes initially denying that he was solely responsible. The rest of the barrack room has been dismissed and Downes has just been ordered by S1 into the Sergeant's office. He enters just as this extract begins.

[…]

15. S1: Downes .. stand there . get your feet together ….. three times ………. three
    S2:

16. S1: times……look at me when I'm speaking to you three times …. what do you
    S2:

17. S1: think that tells me about you   why are you lying
    S2:   that erm I'm a liar sergeant

18. S1: Downes
    S2:   because I was not responsible for what happened to his hair I

19. S1:   irrespective of your intention I asked you did you
    S2: tried to make it better as I

20. S1: cut his hair   that was the question wasn't it   what is the answer to
    S2:   erm   sergeant

21. S1: that question   *you know all the rules you know all the*
    S2:   yes I did sergeant

22. S1: *regulations you know what we expect and you know what you can and can't*
    S2:

23. S1: *do don't you*   *you know everything don't you*
    S2:   *no sergeant*   *no sergeant*

24. S1: *because you're a wide boy aren't you*   the regulation haircut in
    S2:   *no sergeant ..*

25. S1: this place is a number two on sides and a number four on top .. because
    S2:

26. S1: that's the rules   do you know all the rules   do you know
    S2:   sergeant   no sergeant

27. S1: what you're doing   it's as simple as this you are now on an
    S2:   no sergeant

28. S1: official platoon sergeant's warning …… you have got . seven days to
    S2:

29. S1: sort yourself out do you understand what I'm saying to you
S2: sergeant yes

30. S1: do you understand why I'm saying it to you do you
S2: sergeant yes sergeant

31. S1: understand what you have done wrong do you understand
S2: yes sergeant

32. S1: what you have to do to improve yourself and your performance to put it
S2:

33. S1: right seven days .... get away
S2: yes sergeant .. [S2 leaves]

End.

Note that in staves 21–24 S1 asks the question you know all the rules you know all the regulations you know what we expect and you know what you can and can't do don't you? Clearly, the negative tag, don't you embeds the expectation that the four assessments in the utterance will be agreed with and, thus, sets up an expectation that the answer will be the preferred 'Yes'. However, as we see in stave 28, the answer given is, *no sergeant*. Note also that this 'dispreferred' *no* answer does not exhibit any of the normal, dispreferred markers suggested by Levinson (1983), or Pomerantz (1984). Despite not receiving a 'preferred' answer, S1 continues: *you know everything don't you*. Again the negative tag, *don't you* attached to the assessment embeds the expectation that the answer will be in agreement with the assessment, and, thus, that it will be 'Yes'. However, the second response by S2 in stave 28, is, again, the dispreferred: *no sergeant*. S1 further presses with *because you are a wide boy aren't you*. Despite the negative tag, which, again, would bias the answer towards agreement with the rather impolite assessment, and thus expects the preferred 'Yes', we once again receive the dispreferred response, from S2 in stave 29 of *no sergeant*. So what, precisely, is going on? It is not as if we can ascribe the structurally 'dispreferred' behaviour of S2 to any notion of personality, situational context, or other extra-conversational factors because interestingly (in staves 26 to 27 and 29 to 33), S1 asks six questions of S2 which receive self-damaging structurally preferred answers. So what has occurred in staves 21–24? There appear to be two interesting factors at work here.

First, there is a clash of expectations. Where the extract is concerned in staves 21–23, the initial assessments either have an implicit sarcastic undercurrent or are explicitly sarcastic: *you know all the rules you know all the regulations you know what we expect and you know what you can and can't do don't you?* in staves 21–23 is not explicitly sarcastic. Strictly speaking recruits *are* required to learn, to know and to bear in mind all the rules and regulations of army life and are expected to infer what is expected of them by their superiors and, thus, are expected to know what they 'can and can't do'. However, as S2 is still only a recruit, and is, thus, still learning, then the above assessments are critical reminders that the recruit has not, yet, in Sergeant S1's opinion, learnt all these aspects of army life. *You know everything, don't you* (stave 23) is an explicitly sarcastic assessment with a conducively negative tag. It is highly unlikely, given both the context (including being involved in the activity type of a dressing down for giving an illegal haircut), and common sense, that one individual human being could literally *know everything*. Thus, the coerced answers of *no sergeant* in both of the above cases are in agreement with the pragmatic, rather than the literal surface meaning of the sarcastic assessments. The final derogatory assessment of *because you are a wide boy*[14] *aren't you* is not sarcastic, but is, rather, an insultingly impolite assessment of S2, by S1. The reason why S2 answered with the structurally 'dispreferred' answer of *no sergeant*, despite predictions in the literature to the contrary, is very interesting.

Brown and Levinson (1987), Levinson (1983), Pomerantz (1984) and Sacks et al. (1974), amongst others, have all noted one kind of complexity where two different kinds of conversational expectations work in opposing directions. There is (at least) one case in which expectations of structurally preferred answers are most often transgressed. Assessments by a speaker that are self-deprecations (Pomerantz 1984: 64), or self-denigrations (Levinson 1983: 338) are not expected to be agreed with.[15] In direct contrast to the normal structural view of preference organization the preferred response to a self-deprecatory assessment, therefore, is a disagreement and the dispreferred response is an agreement. This, Levinson (1983: 338) claims, is because an independent principle of a different order to preference organization is in operation – namely 'a norm enjoining the avoidance of criticism.' (cf. Leech's (1983: 81), PP 'Maxim of Approbation'). According to this norm, Levinson argues (1983) a respondent should therefore avoid agreeing with a self-deprecatory remark by an interlocutor. It is this latter principle which generally takes precedence (Levinson 1983: 338) over structural preference organization. If we reverse part of this principle, or rather, propose an independent principle of self-preservation in conflictive discourses, then as a self-defensive

14. 'Wide Boy' is a vernacular British colloquial term of insult, specifically for males (no 'Wide Girls' exist), for a cocksure individual who considers himself to be above the law, always right in deed or thought, and of deserving respect and admiration because of this attitude.

15. This, I feel, is the strongest argument, thus far, for concluding that preference organization is NOT purely a structural phenomenon, but, rather, includes a pragmatic *functional* level consisting of the psychological and social factors of the participants. After all, a purely structural understanding, devoid of psychological or social factors, should be completely unaffected by whether an assessment was self-deprecatory or not.

counter move a respondent, 'A' may feel that disagreeing with an impolite, deprecatory assessment made by 'B', about 'A', would be *a* preferred course of action.

Second, there appears, in this example at least, to be a *sociopragmatic preference* for the *structurally dispreferred* answer. Sacks et al. (1974) and Silverman (1998), amongst other researchers, have noted that the absence of a preferred second is instantly noticeable. In the event of not receiving the desired response, (of, in effect, receiving a structurally dispreferred second), to a first pair part, the floor is provided back to the original speaker for use by presenting a 'limited' further turn. This further turn is 'limited' as it usually allows a form of re-iteration of the initial first – which would again embed an expectation of a specific preferred answer which, if not forthcoming, sets up a further limited turn, and so on, and so forth, theoretically, *ad infinitum*. This can have the effect of setting up a *chaining* of 'impolitenesses', all of (a) the same, or of (b) a similar type, as is the case here in the above extract. An additional factor at work here is the very real possibility that the questioning interlocutor, in the above case, S1, is setting up the questions in order to 'pragmatically prefer' the 'structurally dispreferred' answers of *no sergeant*, for the very reason that he can, indeed, maintain open the re-iterated chain of impolite questions which, when realised together as a form of *repetition*, have a greatly increased face-damaging weight. In effect, the answers which S1 conducively elicits from S2 by the use of these sophisticated conversational tactics conspire to make it possible for him to (re-)produce impolite utterances across the discourse.

So, as I have shown, by giving structurally dispreferred seconds one risks leaving open the route of questioning and, thus, one risks maintaining the discoursal requirements for impoliteness to be, at least, more easily issued. If, however, a participant gives a structurally preferred second, where there is little or no expectation of it (i.e. if the interlocutor psychologically prefers a structurally dispreferred second in order to keep open the conduit of impolite *challenges*) then one can 'short-circuit' the offensive, impolite line of questioning and you must change tack or it halts the flow. Note the following example taken from **The Clampers, Extract 1** (see also Culpeper et al. (2003)).

[101] ***Context:*** *Ray and Miguel, clamping supervisor and assistant respectively have arrived to remove the clamp from a van. The van's owner is waiting for them. S1 is Ray, S2, the van's owner.*

1. S1: hi there sir this yours
   S2: yeah it is yeah I'd like to er ask you why you clamped it
2. S1: why we clamped it you see
   S2: yeah there's nobody here for one hundred and fifty yards

[…]

29. S1: sir I I'm really not
S2: not going to do anything about it are you as far as wearing your

30. S1:
S2: uniform is concerned they were doing that when they were shoving the

31. S1:
S2: guys into the gas chambers in Germany wearing the uniform does not

32. S1: *that's right I clamped your*
S2: matter you're just as culpable as anybody else

33. S1: *car sir and I won't dispute that fact that I clamped your car*
S2: *well end of*

34. S1: well that's fine by me
S2: *conversation*

[…]

Here, in stave 32, S1 gives the preferred answer *that's right I clamped your car sir and I won't dispute that fact that I clamped your car* to an implied question from the very start of the exchange (*was it you who clamped my car?*). As Sacks et al. (1974) have shown, adjacency pairs do not, necessarily have to be 'adjacent' but rather, the second turn to a first pair part may be delayed by several turns. In effect, the timing of the answer is key here, to S1's management of S2's impoliteness. The answer in staves 32–33 *that's right I clamped your car sir and I won't dispute that fact that I clamped your car* constitutes a form of insertion sequence. By answering the earlier (implied) question here, he avoids responding to the face damaging effects of being compared to a Nazi (implied in *as far as wearing your uniform is concerned they were doing that when they were shoving the guys into the gas chambers in Germany wearing the uniform does not matter you're just as culpable as anybody else*). Indeed, the very reluctance of S1 to engage directly, by providing preferred answers, with this implied question (amongst others), led to the escalation of the discourse which contained impoliteness. When S1 finally gives S2 a structurally 'preferred' response, S2, with no further conduit for impoliteness open, immediately opts to end the conversation with the utterance *well end of conversation.*

8.5 Conclusion

Within this chapter I have explored the role of some aspects of the classic turn taking system (Sacks et al. 1974), with regards to impoliteness. The concepts of conducivity in questions, and preference organization have been considered in relation to the creation of impoliteness. It should be noted that the additions to, and (re)conceptualisations of, certain aspects of the turn taking system made in this chapter in no way act to disprove the classic model. Rather they provide a complement to it. Indeed complements and revisions to the model were implicitly foreseen by Sacks et al. (1974):

> It is certainly the case that the proposed model is in several respects incorrect or insufficient. But however this particular model may be defective, we believe our discussions support the claim that the appropriate model for turn-taking in conversation will be this SORT of model. (Sacks et al. 1974: 725)

It is perhaps unsurprising that the classic model of turn-taking (Sacks et al. 1974), and its developments (Pomerantz 1984) are 'insufficient' where impoliteness is concerned, for as Pomerantz notes:

> [...] the institutionalized design features of preferred/dispreferred actions are both inherently structured and actively used so as to maximize co-operation and affiliation and to minimize conflict in conversational activites.
> (Pomerantz 1984: 55)

Pomerantz, like Brown and Levinson (1987: 38–40), sees turn-taking as being intrinsically linked to considerations of face, and so it is, but as the above quotation indicates, there is a fundamental bias, where face is concerned and considered in academic writing, towards politeness (cf. Eelen 1999, 2001). That the turn taking system could be applicable to impoliteness, and in what way, is quite simply overlooked. Clearly, the role of CA features, in how they are manipulated and exploited *pragmatically* either to issue or manage impoliteness is an area which would benefit significantly from future research, despite what conversation analysts might think about the way in which pragmaticists use their tools of enquiry.

CHAPTER 9

Conclusion

In this chapter, I first summarise and review the book, as discussed in Chapters 2–7. I then discuss some of the limitations to the study, raising further questions for research into impoliteness, which leads into the final section of this book – identifying areas for future research.

9.1 A general summary of the book

What I hope I have achieved throughout this book is a thorough investigation and analysis of the use of impoliteness within a small number of discourses which, when we consider the powers, rights, obligations and/or overall roles of the participants which the discourses contain, differ in some respects, and are similar in others. I have attempted to understand how participants can manage impoliteness both offensively and defensively in extended instances of spoken discourse. I have done this by widening my research beyond the traditional, and limiting, 'strategisation' of the phenomena of im/politeness.

Very broadly, I have looked at, and sought to move towards an understanding of how impolite discourses are triggered and how they proceed, sequentially, on a turn by turn basis; how this sequencing of impoliteness contributes to (the management of) impoliteness; how interactants may manipulate or exploit conversational expectations for impolite purposes and how impolite discourses may come to some sort of conclusion. I have also considered several contextual aspects under which impoliteness is issued, and countered, within the discourses studied.

9.2 Reviewing the research questions

In Chapter 1, in discussing the existing research that underpins the concept of impoliteness, I attended to the core research question for any study of impoliteness: *What is impoliteness?* By considering the concepts of intention and aggression (see Sections 4.5.3 and 4.5.4), I produced a working definition and understanding of the concept of impoliteness for use throughout the book. I define impoliteness (Section 4.5.2, above) as being the opposite of politeness, in that, rather than seeking to mitigate face-threatening acts (FTAs), impoliteness constitutes the issuing of intentionally gratuitous and conflictive verbal face-threatening acts (FTAs) which are purposefully performed unmitigated, in contexts where mitigation is required, and/or, with deliberate *aggression*, that is, with the face threat exacerbated, 'boosted', or maximised in some way to heighten the face damage inflicted.

In Chapter 4, I began by looking at the general, overarching research question *How is impoliteness used in conflictive exchanges?* and *What is the nature and role of impoliteness in interactional communication?* Here I began by, amongst other things, testing the model set out in Culpeper (1996) to ascertain its usefulness in accounting for impoliteness in the discourses used throughout this book. Here I noted that, although adequate as a first-step model of analysis, Culpeper (1996) was limited in the types, and scope, of impolite utterances for which it could account. Clearly, these research questions could only be attended to by considering a number of sub-questions. One of these, *How is impoliteness actually realised in interactive communication?* was, itself, found to be broad following the findings of Chapter 5. The findings, which include the fact that some impolite utterances consist, in Culpeper's (1996) terms, of 'combined' strategies led to considering the question *How can impoliteness strategies be combined?* In Chapter 6, I discovered in the discourses studied that such 'strategies' can combine in a number of ways. One notes that acts oriented towards both positive and negative face can and do combine; that combining impolite acts can occur through repetition, simultaneous goal pursuance, or even a combination of these two concepts and, as such, the maintenance of the positive-negative face dichotomy appears questionable (see Chapters 3 and 4). Additionally, in considering other aspects of the question *How is impoliteness actually realised in interactive communication?* and noting the counter-impoliteness responses of individuals to singly and combined impoliteness utterances, I considered the question *How can impoliteness be countered?*

In Chapter 7, we saw within the examples from the data sets studied that there were a number of sophisticated linguistic acts, or 'strategies' that are available to interactants which are oriented, primarily, towards the defence of one's own face when threatened or attacked by impoliteness. However, in considering *Are the countering strategies offensive or defensive?* I noted that they can be either primarily offensive, or primarily defensive or something in between. Indeed, I noted that the strategies, or utterance acts, used to counter impoliteness are in actuality scalar with respects to the 'purely' offensive – 'purely' defensive polar positions.

In considering the impolite counter strategies, I noted that the defensive options identified in Chapter 7, are not equally available to all across all the data sets. This led me to consider *What defence strategies are available to interactants within a given situational context?* Interestingly, in some of the discourses studied (the Military Training, Kitchen, Police Data sets), the defensive options available are somewhat limited to certain, usually low-in-power, interactants than in other (Clampers, Parking Wars) data sets. This led to considering the slightly wider question, *What are the communicative options available to interactants when faced with impoliteness?* An interesting observation is that the power of interactants does not automatically endow the right to be face threatening, or impolite, on another interactant in some of the discourses studied (Clampers, Parking Wars, Police data sets), indeed rather the opposite is the case as it appears to constrain the type and strength of the face threats they can produce. Similarly, in considering this research question, it was intriguing to note that in some discourses (military training, especially) some low power interactants were not only 'limited' in their defensive counter impoliteness options, but were denied the possibility of defensive responses altogether. This was as a result of both context (including their interactants' roles, power, rights and obligations), and sophisticated linguistic tactics (see Chapter 8) on behalf of their interlocutors. These sophisticated linguistic tactics, which I discussed in the previous chapter, included the exploitation and manipulation of interactants' expectations in conversation.

In considering attempts to counter impoliteness, I noted that, under certain conditions, the act of countering, itself, could lead to further impolite attacks. This lead to the question *What triggers impolite face attack?* which I introduced in Chapter 4 and explored in 7. I also explored how the linguistic exchanges proceeded by considering the question *How does the discourse build up and pan out, throughout the discourse?* which I discussed throughout Chapters 6, 7 and 8. All these together led to the question *What are the dynamic phenomena typifying discourses which contain active impoliteness?* I believe, for the data sets studied, I have answered this question throughout Chapters 6, 7 and 8. In order to avoid unnecessary repetition, I would refer the reader of this book to those chapters.

9.3 The limitations to the present study

There are a number of limitations to the present study which require consideration here. Essentially, this study represents my current thinking within a process of ongoing research. Therefore, the book is perhaps best viewed as a report on research in progress – designed not only to inform and argue, but to generate debate through the responses, reactions and extensions that the work here detailed will, hopefully, attract. More specifically, the present study is limited to a relatively small number of extracts representing a relatively small number of data sets. As such, wider generalisations are neither easy, nor advisable to make lightly. Indeed, I would expect and welcome comprehensive extensions and reconceptualisations to the data-driven (proto-)model here suggested as the field continues to expand and as researchers scrutinise new types of discourse and interactional activities.

Given the research background underpinning the study of impoliteness I have been forced to discuss impolite 'strategies' almost as if they were unproblematically discrete, identifiable entities across all discourses at all times. This, clearly, is not the case. Even moves by researchers such as Muntigl and Turnbull (1998) to avoid the discussion of strategies, opting to discuss somewhat broader 'acts', simply shifts the focus, and does not entirely solve the issue – their 'argument-acts' could be seen to be strategies by a different name. In actuality, to separate and identify interactant utterances, in context, as 'component strategies' is a heuristic exercise that runs *contra* to the non-modular nature of pragmatics. The very fact that there is a prolific combination of impolite 'strategies' in the data sets studied indicates that discussion of component strategies is, in one respect, an erroneous undertaking. However, the discussion of such strategies has been made purely for ease of exposition and exploration of points to be made. It is, essentially, a rhetorical device – not an insistence that interactants 'pick and mix' strategies consciously within a simplistic, non-dynamic context. In short, it is a convenient way of discussing interactant aims, local and global, within the particular complex, multi-contextual and pragmatically dynamic linguistic exchanges being considered.

Beyond mentioning it in brief in Section 5.2 above, I have not discussed in adequate length and detail, the role of *mock impoliteness*. Intuitively, it could be seen to be (and has been seen as) a device for strengthening group bonds through humorous and insincere face threatening linguistic interchanges (cf. Labov 1972; Leech 1983). Given the nature of my data it should be unsurprising that I have not devoted a large amount of time and effort in the identification and analysis of mock impoliteness. Banter (cf. Leech 1983), typically used to maintain or reinforce in-group cohesion, is a function that is not common to the examples from the data sets discussed here. Future research is clearly needed.

Two main areas not considered in this book, are (i) gender differences in the use and management of impoliteness, and (ii) the significance of prosody in the delivery, and/or countering, of impoliteness.

With regard to the former, study into 'gender and impoliteness' is an area ripe for future development building on the promising strides already made by such researchers as Mills (2003, 2005) and Mullany (2008). For the present study, as most (but not all) of the interactants in the discourse types here discussed were male, or were in settings which are traditionally seen to be, for want of a better phrase, 'a male preserve' (e.g. Army Training setting), the social, interactional and linguistic norms pertaining to the discourse types are likely to be more obviously 'male' in their actuality. As such a gender oriented exploration of impoliteness based on the data sets explored simply could not be meaningfully made here. Thus, the study of gender and impoliteness remains a tantalising and, I expect, fruitful line of academic inquiry.

With regard to the latter, as Culpeper et al. (2003) note, 'No utterance can be spoken without prosody, and it is therefore desirable at some point to include this dimension of speech in pragmatic analysis.' They go on to note that accounting for prosody adds the dimension of considering *how* what is said *is* said, to (orthographic representations of) *what* has been said. In this respect, it could be argued that they are more closely considering Grice's (1975) maxim of manner than has hitherto been the case. In making a move towards considering the role of prosody to the expression of impoliteness, Culpeper et al. (2003), who concentrate only 'The Clampers' data, note,

> There appear to be three main ways in which speakers exploit the 'attitudinal' role of intonation in this interaction to express impoliteness. Firstly, the force of a speech act is related to the choice of pitch contour. [...] Secondly, there are related discoursal issues; for example, signalling whether something is 'open' (non final), or 'closed' (final) – exploited here to bring a conversation to an end and thereby block the hearers' wishes. We can account for these meanings largely in phonological terms – in terms of choice of intonational category, such as rising vs. falling tone. Thirdly, there are global prosodic parameters – matters of phonetic realisation rather than phonological choice – such as high pitch and extreme loudness over an utterance or series of utterances, which can be seen as an invasion of auditory space, or the strategic denial of pitch concord, which can be seen as a prosodic means of increasing the distance between interlocutors. (Culpeper et al. 2003: 575)

The findings here do provide a good starting point, and, indeed Culpeper (2005) observes that prosody plays an important role in discourses other than in car-parking disputes when he explores its use in exploitative television games shows:

> Prosodic aspects play a central role in communicating offense in *The Weakest Link*. One intriguing issue is whether one could have understood the utterances as "impolite" without the prosody. In other words, is prosody just a "contextual aid" to meaning generation and understanding? (Culpeper 2005: 68)

Of course, whether this applies equally to other discourse types, such as army / police training, or kitchen data, remains to be seen and is, therefore, an area ripe for further research.

9.4 Areas for future research

In the course of this book I have mentioned some areas for further research consideration. I conclude by briefly discussing those areas which, in my view, are of critical and pressing importance. To begin, the limitations I have identified above help us to see areas in which future research might take place. Exploring the impoliteness of other extracts and other data sets will help us to broaden, refine, test, complement and thus strengthen the claims and findings made here throughout this book.

Additionally, an 'informant-led' study to ascertain a more precise definition of not only what 'strategies' or 'acts' are considered impolite (and the perception of the degree of offensiveness of the different impoliteness 'strategies'), but of what impoliteness *is* actually understood to be, would clearly be of benefit for future studies in the area of interactional communication. In a similar vein, a quantitatively based research project exploring which types of impoliteness are considered more face damaging than others, within certain and different contexts, would also be of benefit to studies of human linguistic interaction in general, and not just to studies concerned with the concept of 'face'.

The link between the concept of 'rudeness' and impoliteness, as the theoretical counterparts to Politic Verbal Behaviour (cf. Watts 1992) and politeness, would clearly benefit from future research. Further, such studies would provide support to those, primarily postmodern approaches to im/politeness which aim to more accurately reflect exactly how *lay users* the a language view im/politeness.

As is clear from the research questions considered above, one of the major considerations of the present book has been to broaden the scope of previous studies of both politeness (cf. Brown and Levinson 1987) and impoliteness (cf. Culpeper 1996; Lachenicht 1980), which, as Culpeper et al. (2003) (amongst others) have noted have tended to focus rather too narrowly on single lexically or grammatically-based strategies. If intention is a factor that distinguishes impoliteness from politeness, as argued in Culpeper et al. (2003), Culpeper (2005) and, further, here (see Chapter 4) then we need a richer understanding of an interactant's behaviour including their prosody, and of the discoursal context, in order to more confidently infer user intentions. It is for this reason that I here in this book, as I began to do in Bousfield (2007a), and as we explored within Culpeper et al. (2003) examine patterns of impoliteness both within and across exchanges.

Grimshaw (1990) points out that 'participants in conflict talk have the same resources available for that interaction as do all conversationalists' (1990: 10). Similarly, Thomas (1995: 179) concludes that the claim for politeness theories is that 'people employ certain strategies [...] for reasons of expediency – experience has taught us that particular strategies are likely to succeed in given circumstances, so we use them.' I have been able to show that some of the ways in which certain resources or 'strategies' are used by participants, is to communicate impoliteness. As I hope I have shown here, this extends to include participant expectations of conversational structure and the conduciveness of some question forms (see Chapter 8). While I have made a start in exploring the communicative properties of manipulating and exploiting schematically expected structures, there is clearly much more to be said about the turn-taking aspects of impoliteness.

With regard to counter-impolite strategies, whether they are predominantly defensively or offensively oriented (or something more equal) in other types of discourse remains to be seen. This is an area ripe for further consideration.

In addition to the areas mentioned, there are issues to do with the classical model (Brown and Levinson 1987) which, when considering impoliteness, could benefit from further research. Culpeper et al. (2003: 1576) note that,

> What the underlying dimensions of [the] impoliteness strategies are is little understood. What is clear is that an impoliteness framework is not simply a mirror-image of a politeness framework, such as Brown and Levinson's (1987). How one orders strategies for degree of impoliteness is not known. As with politeness, there appears to be no simply correlation with directness.

As such, the correlation between (i) im/politeness, (ii) in/directness, and (iii) on-/off-record utterances, remains intriguing and future research should be carried out here.

These are all just some of the areas that we need to consider, explore and interrogate in the future. There will, inevitably, be others not mentioned here also. All in all, despite recent attempts to move impoliteness to the centre of academic scrutiny, much remains to be done.

References

Apostel, L. 1979. "Persuasive communication as metaphorical discourse under the guidance of the conversational maxims." *Logique et Analyse 22*: 265–320.

Apostel, L. 1980. "De l' intérrogation en tant qu' action." *Langue Française 52*: 23–42.

Arndt, Horst and Richard Janney. 1985. "Politeness revisited: Cross-modal supportive strategies." *International Review of Applied Linguistics 23*: 281–300.

Atkinson, Maxwell M. and Paul Drew. 1979. *Order in the court: The organization of verbal interaction in judicial settings.* London: Macmillan.

Austin, John. L. 1962. *How to do things with words.* Oxford: Clarendon Press.

Austin, Paddy. 1990. "Politeness revisited – the dark side." In *New Zealand ways of speaking English,* Allen Bell and Janet Holmes (eds.), 277–293. Philadelphia: Multilingual Matters.

Bandura, A. 1973. *Aggression: Social learning analysis.* Englewood Cliffs, N.J.: Prentice-Hall.

Bavelas, J., B., L. Edna Rogers, and Frank E. Millar. 1985. "Interpersonal Conflict." In *Handbook of Discourse Analysis 4: Discourse Analysis in Society,* T. A. van Dijk (ed.), 9–26. London: Academic Press.

Beebe, Leslie, M. 1995. "Polite fictions: Instrumental rudeness as pragmatic competence." *Linguistics and the Education of Language Teachers: Ethnolinguistic, Psycholinguistics and Sociolinguistic Aspects*, 154–168. Georgetown University Round Table on Languages and Linguistics. Georgetown: Georgetown University Press.

Berkowitz, Leonard. 1993. *Aggression: Its Causes, Consequences and Control.* Temple University Press.

Billig, Michael. 2001. "Humour and hatred: The racist jokes of the Ku Klux Klan." *Discourse and Society 12*: 291–313.

Bilmes, Jack. 1997. "Being Interrupted." *Language in Society 26*: 507–531.

Björkqvist, Kaj, Karin Österman, and Ari Kaukiainen. 2000. "Social Intelligence – Empathy = Aggression?" *Aggression and Violent Behaviour 5* (2): 191–200.

Blum-Kulka, Shoshana. 1987. "Indirectness and politeness in requests: Same or different?" *Journal of Pragmatics 11*: 131–146.

Blum-Kulka, Shoshana. 1992. "The metapragmatics of politeness in Israeli society." In *Politeness in language: Studies in its history, theory and practice*, Richard J. Watts, Sachiko Ide and Konrad Ehlich (eds.), 255–280. Berlin and New York: Mouton de Gruyter.

Bolinger, Dwight. 1980. *Language: The Loaded Weapon. The Use and Abuse of Language Today.* London and New York: Longman.

Bollobas, E. 1981. "Who's afraid of irony? An analysis of uncooperative behaviour in Edward Elbee's Who's afraid of Virginia Woolf?" *Journal of Pragmatics 5*: 323–334.

Bousfield, Derek. 1999. *"They need strangling!" Impoliteness in the B.B.C. television series 'The Clampers'.* Unpublished M.A. dissertation. Lancaster University, UK.

Bousfield, Derek. 2004. *Impoliteness in Interaction.* Unpublished PhD thesis. Lancaster University, UK.

Bousfield, Derek. 2006. "The Grand Debate: Where Next for Politeness Research?" *Culture, Language and Representation*. Vol. III: 9–17.

Bousfield, Derek. 2007a. "Beginnings, Middles and Ends: Towards a biopsy of the dynamics of impoliteness". *Journal of Pragmatics 39* (12): 2185–2216.

Bousfield, Derek. 2007b. "Impoliteness, preference organization and conductivity". *Multilingua 26* (1/2): 1–33.

Bousfield, Derek. 2008. "Impoliteness in the struggle for power". In *Impoliteness in Language*, Derek Bousfield and Miriam Locher (eds.). Mouton de Gruyter. Berlin.

Bousfield, Derek. 2010. "Researching impoliteness and rudeness: Issues and definitions." In *Interactional Pragmatics*, Miriam Locher and Sage Lambert Graham (eds.), 101–134. Berlin: Mouton de Gruyter.

Bousfield, Derek and Miriam Locher (eds.) 2008. *Impoliteness in Language*. Berlin: Mouton de Gruyter.

Brenneis, Donald and Laura Lein. 1977. "'You fruithead': A sociolinguistic approach to children's dispute settlement." In *Child discourse*, Susan Ervin-Tripp and Claudia Mitchell-Kernan (eds.), 49–65. New York: Academic Press.

Brown, Penelope and Stephen C. Levinson. 1978. "Universals in language usage." In *Questions and Politeness*, E. N. Goody (ed.). Cambridge: Cambridge University Press.

Brown, Penelope and Stephen C. Levinson. [1978] 1987. *Politeness: Some universals in language usage*. Cambridge: Cambridge University Press.

Brown, Gillian and George Yule. 1983. *Discourse Analysis*. Cambridge: Cambridge University Press.

Brown, R. and Gilman, A. 1989. "Politeness theory and Shakespeare's four major tragedies." *Language in Society 18 (2)*: 159–212.

Camras, L. A. 1977. "Facial expressions used by children in a conflict situation." *Child Development 48*: 1431–1435.

Cashman, Holly R. 2006. "Impoliteness in children's interactions in a Spanish/English bilingual community of practice." *Journal of Politeness Research 2*: 217–246.

Chen, Rong. 2001. "Self politeness: a proposal." *Journal of Pragmatics 33*: 87–106.

Clancy, Tom. 1985. *Red Storm Rising*. ROC.

Comrie, B. 1976. *Aspect: An Introduction to the study of Verbal Aspect and Related Problems*. Cambridge: Cambridge University Press.

Corsaro, William, A., and Thomas A. Rizzo. 1990. "Disputes in the peer culture of American and Italian nursery-school children." In *Conflict Talk: Sociolinguistic Investigations of Arguments and Conversations*, Allen D Grimshaw (ed.), 21–66. Cambridge: Cambridge University Press.

Corliss, R. L. 1981. "What determines a pragmatic implication?" *Southern Journal of Philosophy 19*: 37–48.

Craig, Robert, Karen Tracy, and Frances Spisak. 1986. "The discourse of requests: Assessment of a politeness approach." *Human Communication Research 12*: 437–468.

Crystal, David. 1991. *A dictionary of Linguistics and Phonetics*. London: Blackwell.

Culpeper, Jonathan. 1994. *Characterisation in the stylistic analysis of dramatic texts*. Unpublished PhD thesis, Lancaster University.

Culpeper, Jonathan. 1996. "Towards an anatomy of impoliteness." *Journal of Pragmatics 25:* 349–367.

Culpeper, Jonathan. 1998. "(Im)politeness in drama." In *Exploring the language of drama: From text to context*, Jonathan Culpeper, Mick Short and Peter Verdonk (eds.), 83–95. London: Routledge.

Culpeper, Jonathan. 2002. *Personal Communication.*

Culpeper, Jonathan. 2005. "Impoliteness and *The Weakest Link*." *Journal of Politeness Research 1* (1): 35–72.

Culpeper, Jonathan, Derek Bousfield, and Anne Wichmann. 2003. "Impoliteness revisited: With special reference to dynamic and prosodic aspects." *Journal of Pragmatics 35* (10/11): 1545–1579.

de Kadt, E. 1998. "The concept of face and its applicability to the Zulu language." *Journal of Pragmatics 29*: 173–191.

Derriennic, J. 1972. "Theory and ideologies of violence." *Journal of Peace Research 9*: 361–373.

Dillon, G, L,. L. Coleman., J. Fahnestock, and M. Agar. 1985. Review Article. *Language 61* (2): 446–460.

Durkheim, E. 1915. *The elementary forms of religious life*. London.

Edelsky, Carole. 1981. "Who's got the floor?" *Language in Society 10*: 282–421.

Eder, Donna. 1990. "Serious and playful disputes: Variation in conflict talk among female adolescents." In *Conflict Talk: Sociolinguistic investigations of arguments and conversations*, Allen D. Grimshaw (ed.), 67–84. Cambridge: Cambridge University Press.

Eelen, Gino. 1999. *Ideology in politeness: A critical analysis*. Unpublished PhD thesis. Antwerp, Holland.

Eelen, Gino. 2001. *A critique of politeness theories*. Manchester: St. Jerome Publishing.

Eggins, S. and D. Slade. 1997. *Analysing Casual Conversation*. London and Washington: Cassell.

Ehlich, Konrad. 1992. "On the historicity of politeness." In *Politeness in language. studies in its history, theory and practice*, Richard J. Watts, Sachiko Ide and Konrad Ehlich (eds.), 71–108. Berlin and New York: Mouton de Gruyter.

Escandell-Vidal, Victoria. 1996. "Towards a cognitive approach to politeness." *Language Sciences 18* (3–4): 629–654.

Fish, Adrian. 1999. *Careless lives cost words: Catch 22: The Uncooperative Principle, Ritualised Conflict and Subversion.* Paper given at the Pragmatics and Stylistics Research Group. 19th May 1999. Lancaster University, UK.

Fitzpatrick, Edward Augustus. 1945. *Universal Military Training*. London, New York: McGraw-Hill.

Fraser, Bruce. 1990. "Perspectives on politeness." *Journal of Pragmatics 14*: 219–236.

Fraser, Bruce. 1999. *Whither Politeness?* Plenary paper given at the International Symposium on Linguistic Politeness, Chulalongkhorn University, Bangkok, Thailand, 7–9 December 1999.

Fraser, Bruce and William Nolen. 1981. "The association of deference with linguistic form." *International Journal of the Sociology of Language 27*: 93–109.

Gabrielatos, Costas. 2001. "Inference: Procedures and Implications for ELT." Updated version of Gabrielatos, Costas. 1999. "Inference: Procedures and Implications for TEFL." *TESOL Greece Newsletter* 63–64. See *www.gabrielatos.com/Inference.htm*

Goffman, Erving. 1967. *Interaction ritual*. Chicago: Aldine Publishing.

Goffman, Erving. 1971. *The Presentation of Self in Everyday Life*. Penguin Books.

Goldberg, J. A. 1990. "Interrupting the discourse of interruptions." *Journal of Pragmatics 14*: 883–903.

Goldhamer, Herbert. 1974. *The Soviet soldier: Soviet military management at the troop level.* New York: Crane, Russak.

Goode, E. 1978. *Deviant Behaviour: An interactionist approach.* New Jersey: Prentice Hall.

Goodwin, Charles and Marjorie Harness Goodwin. 1990. "Interstitial argument." In *Conflict Talk: Sociolinguistic investigations of arguments and conversations*, Allen D. Grimshaw (ed.), 85–117. Cambridge: Cambridge University Press.

Grice, H. Paul. 1975. "Logic and conversation." In *Speech Acts* [Syntax and Semantics 3], Peter Cole and Jerry Morgan (eds.), 41–58. New York: Academic Press.

Grice, H. Paul. 1978. "Further notes on logic and conversation." In *Pragmatics* [Syntax and Semantics 9], Peter Cole (ed.). New York: Academic Press.

Grice, H. Paul. 1981. "Presupposition and Conversational implicature." In Peter Cole (ed.), *Radical Pragmatics,* 183–198. New York: Academic Press.

Grice, H. Paul. 1989. *Studies in the Way of Words.* Cambridge, MA: Harvard University Press.

Grimshaw, Allen, D. (ed.), 1990. *Conflict Talk: Sociolinguistic investigations of arguments and conversations.* Cambridge: Cambridge University Press.

Gu, Y. 1990. "Politeness phenomena in modern Chinese." *Journal of Pragmatics 14* (2): 237–257.

Gumperz, J. J. 1992. "Contextualization and understanding." In *Rethinking context: Language as an interactive phenomenon*, A. Duranti and S. Goodwin (eds.), 229–252. Cambridge: Cambridge University Press.

Halliday, M. A. K. and R. Hasan. 1989. *Language, Context and Text: Aspects of language in a social-semiotic perspective.* Oxford: Oxford University Press.

Harris, Sandra. 2001. "Being politically impolite: Extending politeness theory to adversarial political discourse." *Discourse and Society 12* (4): 451–472.

Harris, Linda, Kenneth Gergen and John Lannaman. 1986. "Aggression rituals." *Communication Monographs 53*: 252–265.

Haugh, Michael. 2006. "Emic perspectives on the Positive-Negative politeness distinction." *Culture, Language and Representation*. Vol. III: 17–26.

Haviland, John, B. 1997. "Shouts, Shrieks, and Shots: Unruly political conversations in indigenous Chiapas." *Pragmatics 7* (4): 547–573.

Hayashi, Takuo. 1996. "Politeness in conflict management: A conversation analysis of dispreferred message from a cognitive perspective." *Journal of Pragmatics 25*: 227–255.

Hawley, Patrick. 2002. "What is said." *Journal of Pragmatics 34*: 969–991.

Held, Gudrun. 1992. "Politeness in linguistic research." In *Politeness in Language: Studies in Its History, Theory and Practice,* Richard J., Watts, Sachiko Ide, and Konrad Ehlich (eds.), 131–153. Berlin: Mouton de Gruyter.

Held, Gudrun. 1995. *Verbale Hoflichkeit. Studien zur linguistischen Theoriebildung und empirischen Untersuchung zum Sprachverhalten fanzsosischer und italienischer Jugundlicher in Bitt- und Dankessituationen.* Tubingen: Gunter Narr.

Hillbrand, Marc, and Reuben T. Spitz. 1999. "Cholesterol and aggression." *Aggression and Violent Behavior 4* (3): 359–370.

Holmes, Janet. 1984. "Modifying Illocutionary Force." *Journal of Pragmatics 8*: 345–365.

Holmes, Janet, and Meredith Marra. 2002. "Over the edge? Subversive humour between colleagues and friends." *Humour 15* (1): 1–23.

Hurst Tatsuki, Donna. 2000. "If my complaints could passions move: An interlanguage study of aggression." *Journal of Pragmatics 32*: 1003–1017.

Hutchby, Ian. 1992 "Confrontation talk: Aspects of 'interruption' in argument sequences on talk radio." *Text 12* (3): 343–371.

Hydén, Margareta. 1995. "Verbal Aggression as Prehistory of Woman Battering." *Journal of Family Violence 10* (1): 55–71.

Janney, Richard and Horst Arndt. 1992. "Intracultural tact versus intercultural tact." In *Politeness in Language: Studies in Its History, Theory and Practice,* Richard J. Watts, Sachiko Ide, and Konrad Ehlich (eds.), 21–41. Berlin: Mouton de Gruyter.

Jary, Mark. 1998. "Relevance theory and the communication of politeness." *Journal of Pragmatics 30*: 1–19.

Jaworski, Adam. 1993. *The Power of Silence: Social and Pragmatic Perspectives.* London: Sage.

Jay, William. 1992. *Cursing in America: a psycholinguistic study of dirty language in the courts, in the movies, in the schoolyards and on the streets.* Philadelphia: John Benjamins.

Jay, William. 2000. *Why we curse: A neuro-psycho-social theory of speech.* Philadelphia and Amsterdam: John Benjamins.

Jefferson, Gail. 1973. "A case of precision timing in ordinary conversation: Overlapped tag-positioned address terms in closing sequences." *Semiotica 9*: 47–96.

Jucker, Andreas. 1988. "Relevance theory and the communication of politeness." *Multilingua 7*: 375–384.

Kasher, Asa. 1976. "Conversational Maxims and Rationality". In *Language in focus,* Asa Kasher (ed.), 197–216. Dordrecht: Reidel.

Kasher, Asa. 1977. "What is a theory of use?" *Journal of Pragmatics 1* (2): 105–120.

Kasher, Asa. 1986. "Politeness and rationality." In *Pragmatics and Linguistics. Festschrift for Jacob Mey*, J. D. Johansen and H. Sonne (eds.), 103–114. Odense: Odense University Press.

Kasper, Gabriele. 1990. "Linguistic Politeness. Current research issues." *Journal of Pragmatics 14*: 193–218.

Kemp, Graham. 2001. "Definitions of International Aggression: Lessons for cross-cultural research." In *Cross-cultural Approaches to Research on Aggression and Reconciliation,* J. Martin Ramirez and Deborah S. Richardson (eds.), 51–58. New York: Nova Science.

Kiefer, F. 1979. "What do the conversational maxims explain?" *Linguisticae Investigationes 3* (1): 57–74.

Kienpointner, Manfred. 1997. "Varieties of rudeness: Types and functions of impolite utterances." *Functions of Language 4*, 2: 251–287.

Kotthof, Helga. 1993. "Disagreement and concession in disputes: On the context sensitivity of preference structures." *Language in Society 22*: 193–216.

Labov, William. 1972. *Language in the inner City: Studies in the black English vernacular.* Oxford: Blackwell.

Labov, William and David Fanshel. 1977. *Therapeutic Discourse: Psychotherapy as conversation.* New York: Academic Press.

Lachenicht, L. G. 1980. "Aggravating language: A study of abusive and insulting language." *International Journal of Human Communication 13* (4): 607–688.

Lakoff, R. 1973. "The logic of politeness; or, minding your p's and q's." In *Papers from the Ninth Regional Meeting of the Chicago Linguistics Society,* 292–305. Chicago Linguistics Society.

Lakoff, Robin. 1989. "The limits of politeness." *Multilingua 8*: 101–129.

Lauer, Paul. 1996. *Linguistic Politeness in letters of complaint.* Unpublished MA dissertation. University of Reading, UK.

Lee-Wong, S.-M. 1999. *Politeness and Face in Chinese Culture.* Frankfurt: Peter Lang.

Leech, Geoffrey N. 1983. *Principles of Pragmatics.* London: Longman.

Leech, Geoffrey N. 1999. Personal Communication.

Leech, Geoffrey N. 2003. "Towards an anatomy of politeness in communication." *International Journal of Pragmatics 14*: 101–123.

Leech, Geoffrey N. 2005. "Is there an East-West divide in Politeness?" *Journal of Foreign Languages* 6: 3–31.

Leech, Geoffrey N. 2007. "Politeness: Is there and East-West divide?" *Journal of Politeness Research: Language, Behaviour, Culture 3* (2): 167–206.

Leech, Geoffrey N. and Jennifer Thomas. 1990. "Language, Meaning and Context: Pragmatics." In *An Encyclopedia of Language*, Collinge (ed.), 173–206. London: Routledge.

Lein, Laura and Donald Brenneis. 1978. "Children's disputes in three speech communities." *Language in Society 7*: 299–323.

Levinson, Stephen C. 1979. "Activity types and language". *Linguistics 17* (5/6): 365–399.

Levinson, Stephen C. 1983. *Pragmatics*. Cambridge: Cambridge University Press.

Levinson, Stephen C. 1992. "Activity types and language". In *Talk at work*, Paul Drew and John Heritage (eds.), 66–100. Cambridge: Cambridge University Press.

Liu, Runquing. 1986. *A Dream of Red Mansions*. Unpublished MPhil dissertation. Lancaster University, UK.

Locher, Miriam. 2004. *Power and Politeness in Action: Disagreements in Oral Communication*. Berlin: Mouton de Gruyter.

Locher, Miriam and Derek Bousfield. 2008. "Impoliteness and Power in Language." In *Impoliteness in Language*, Derek Bousfield and Miriam Locher (eds.), 1–13. Berlin: Mouton de Gruyter.

Marshall-Hasdell, Dennis. 1994. "Soviet Military Reform: The Training System". *Royal Military Academy Sandhurst Conflict Studies Research Centre: 12.*

Mao, L. R. 1994. "Beyond politeness theory: "Face" revisited and renewed." *Journal of Pragmatics 21* (5): 451–486.

Matsumoto, Y. 1988. "Reexamination of the universality of face: Politeness phenomena in Japanese." *Journal of Pragmatics 12* (4): 403–426.

Mehan, H. 1978. "Structuring School Structure." *Harvard Educational Review 48* (1): 32–64.

Mehan, Hugh. 1990. "Rules versus relationships in small claims disputes." In *Conflict Talk: Sociolinguistic investigations of arguments and conversations*, Allen D. Grimshaw (ed.), 160–177. Cambridge: Cambridge University Press.

Meltzer, L., W. Morris and D. Hayes. 1971. "Interruption outcomes and vocal amplitude: Explorations in social psycho-physics". *Journal of Personality and Social Psychology 18*: 392–402.

Merritt, M. 1976. "On questions following questions (in service encounters)." *Language in Society 5* (3): 315–357.

Mey, Jacob, L. 2001. *Pragmatics: An Introduction (2nd Edition)*. London: Blackwell.

Mills, Sara. 2003. *Gender and politeness*. Cambridge: Cambridge University Press.

Mills, Sara. 2005. "Gender and impoliteness." *Journal of Politeness Research 1* (1): 263–280.

Mooney, Annabelle. 2004. "Cooperation, violations and making sense." *Journal of Pragmatics 36*: 899–920.

Moore, Michael. 2002. *Stupid White Men: And other sorry excuses for the nation!* Penguin Group.

Mullany, Louise. 2008. "'Stop hassling me!' Impoliteness, power and gender identity in the professional workplace." In *Impoliteness in Language*, Derek Bousfield and Miriam Locher (eds.), 231–251. Berlin: Mouton de Gruyter.

Muntigl, Peter and William Turnbull. 1998. "Conversational structure and facework in arguing." *Journal of Pragmatics 29*: 225–256.

O'Driscoll, Jim. 1996. "About face: A defence and elaboration of universal dualism." *Journal of Pragmatics 25* (1): 1–32.

Owen, Marion. 1983. *Apologies and remedial interchanges: A study of language use in social interaction*. Berlin: Mouton.

Ochs, E. 1979. "Transcription as Theory". In *The Discourse Reader*, A. Jaworski and N. Coupland (eds.), 1999. London and New York: Routledge.

Penman, Robyn. 1990. "Facework and politeness: Multiple goals in courtroom discourse." *Journal of Language and Social Psychology 9*: 15–38.

Pérez de Ayala, Soledad. 2001. "FTAs and Erskine May: Conflicting needs? – Politeness in Question Time." *Journal of Pragmatics 33*: 143–169.

Piazza, Roberta. 2002. "The pragmatics of conducive questions in academic discourse." *Journal of Pragmatics 34* (5): 509–527.

Pomerantz, Anita. 1984. "Agreeing and disagreeing with assessment: Some features of preferred/dispreferred turn shapes". In *Structures of social action*, M. Atkinson and J. Heritage (eds.), 57–101. Cambridge: Cambridge University Press.

Pratt, M. L. 1977. *Toward a Speech Act Theory of Literary Discourse*. Bloomington: Indiana University Press.

Pratt, M. L. 1981. "The ideology of speech-act theory." *Centrum*: 5–18.

Pyysiainen, Ikka. 2002. "Ontology of culture and the study of human behavior." *Journal of Cognition and Culture 2*: 167–182.

Quirk, Randolph, Sidney Greenbaum, Geoffrey Leech and Jan Svartvik. 1985. *A comprehensive grammar of the English language*. London: Longman.

Rifaat, A. 1979. *International Aggression: A study of the legal concept, its development and definition in international law*. Stockholm: Almqvist and Wiksel International.

Rudanko, Juhani. "Aggravated impoliteness and two types of speaker intention in an episode in Shakespeare's Timon of Athens." *Journal of Pragmatics 38* (6): 829–841.

Sacks, Harvey. 1992. *Lectures on conversation* (Vol. I. and II). Oxford and Cambridge: Blackwell.

Sacks, Harvey, Emanuel Schegloff and Gail Jefferson. 1974. "A simplest systematics for the organization of turn-taking for conversation." *Language 50*: 697–735.

Sampson, G. 1982. "The economics of conversation: Comments on Joshi's paper." In *Mutual Knowledge*, N. V. Smith (ed.). London, New York: Academic Press.

Scollon, Ron and Suzanne Wong Scollon. 1995. *Intercultural Communication*. Oxford: Blackwell.

Searle, John R. 1969. *Speech Acts*. Cambridge: Cambridge University Press.

Searle, John R. 1979. "The classification of illocutionary acts." *Language in Society 5*: 1–24.

Schegloff, Emanuel and Harvey Sacks. 1973. "Opening up closings." *Semiotica 8*: 289–327.

Silverman, D. 1998. *Doing Qualitative Research: A Practical Handbook*. London: Sage.

Skolnich, J. 1968. *The politics of protest*. New York: Simon and Schuster.

Slugoski, B. R. 1985. *Grice's theory of conversation as a social psychological model*. Unpublished PhD thesis, University of Oxford.

Spencer-Oatey, Helen. 1992. *Cross-cultural politeness: British and Chinese conceptions of the student-tutor relationship*. Unpublished PhD thesis, Lancaster University.

Spencer-Oatey, Helen. 1993. "Conceptions of social relations and pragmatics research." *Journal of Pragmatics 20*: 27–47.

Spencer-Oatey, Helen. 2000. "Rapport management: A framework for analysis." In *Culturally speaking: Managing rapport through talk across cultures*, Helen Spencer-Oatey (ed.), 11–46. London and New York: Continuum.

Spencer-Oatey, Helen. 2002. "Managing rapport in talk: Using rapport sensitive incidents to explore the motivational concerns underlying the management of relations." *Journal of Pragmatics 34*: 529–545.

Spencer-Oatey, Helen. 2005. "(Im)Politeness, face and perceptions of rapport: Unpackaging their bases and interrelationships." *Journal of Politeness Research 1* (1): 95–119.

Spencer-Oatey, Helen. 2007. "Theories of identity and the analysis of face." *Journal of Pragmatics 39* (4): 635–786.

Spencer-Oatey, Helen and Wenying Jiang. 2003. "Explaining cross-cultural pragmatic findings: Moving from politeness maxims to sociopragmatic interactional principles (SIPs)." *Journal of Pragmatics 35*: 1633–1650.

Sperber, Dan and Deirdre Wilson. 1986. *Relevance: Communication and Cognition*. Oxford: Blackwell.

Sperber, Dan and Deirdre Wilson. 1995. *Relevance: Communication and Cognition*. Second Edition. Oxford: Blackwell.

Spielberger, C. D., E. H. Johnson, S. F. Russell, R. Crane, G. A. Jacobs and T. J. Worden. 1985. "The experience and expression of anger: Construction and validation of an anger expression scale." In *Anger and hostility in cardiovascular and behavioural disorders*, N. A. Chesney and R. H. Rosenman (eds.), 159–187. New York: McGraw-Hill.

Straus, M. A. and R. J. Gelles. 1990. *Physical Violence in American Families: Risk Factors and Adaptations to Violence in 8,145 Families*. New Brunswick, NJ: Transaction Publishers.

Strawson, P. F. 1990. "Review, Paul Grice, Studies in the Way of Words." *Synthese 84* (1): 153–161.

Tannen, Deborah. 1985. "The Place of Silence in an Integrated Theory of Communication." In *Perspectives on silence*, Deborah Tannen and Muriel Saville-Troike (eds.), 3–18. Norwood, NJ: Ablex.

Tannen, Deborah. 1990. "Silence as conflict management in fiction and drama: Pinter's *Betrayal* and a short story 'Great Wits'." In *Conflict Talk: Sociolinguistic investigations of arguments and conversations*, Allen D. Grimshaw (ed.), 260–279. Cambridge: Cambridge University Press.

Tannen, Deborah and Muriel Saville-Troike. 1985. *Perspectives on silence*. Norwood, NJ: Ablex.

Taylor, Talbot, J. and Deborah Cameron. 1987. *Analyzing conversation*. Oxford: Pergamon Press.

Tedeschi, J. T., R. Smith and R. C. Brown. 1974. "A re-interpretation of research on aggression." *Psychological Bulletin 81*: 540–562.

Terkourafi, Marina. 1999. "Frames for politeness: A case study." *Pragmatics 9*: 97–117.

Terkourafi, Marina. 2008. "Toward a unified theory of politeness, impoliteness and rudeness." In *Impoliteness in Language*, Derek Bousfield and Miriam Locher (eds.), 45–74. Berlin: Mouton de Gruyter.

Thomas, Jenny. 1986. *The Dynamics of Discourse: A Pragmatic Analysis of Confrontational Interaction*. Unpublished PhD thesis, Lancaster University, UK.

Thomas, Jenny. 1995. *Meaning in interaction*. London and New York: Longman.

Tracy, Karen. 1990. "The Many Faces of Facework." In *Handbook of language and social psychology*, Howard Giles and William P. Robinson (eds.), 209–226. Chichester: Wiley.

Turner, Ken. 1996. "The principal principles of pragmatic inference: Politeness." *Language Teaching 29* (1): 1–13.

Turner, Ken. 1999. *Wx = D(S,H) + P(H,S) + Rx*. Paper given at the International Symposium on Linguistic Politeness, Chulalongkhorn University, Bangkok, Thailand, 7–9 December 1999.

Turner, Ken. 2000. "Review of Asa Kasher (1998)". *Linguistics 38* (1): 199–205.

Turtledove, Harry. 2001. *Colonization: Aftershocks*. New York: Hodder and Staughton General.

Ulijn, Jan M. and Xianglin Li. 1995. "Is interrupting impolite? Some temporal aspects of turn-taking in Chinese-Western and other intercultural business encounters." *Text 15* (4): 589–627.

Van der Dennan, J. M. G. 1980. *Problems in the concepts and definitions of aggression, violence and some related terms*. Groningen: Rijksuniversiteit.

van Dijk, Teun. 1977. *Text and Context*. London: Longman.

Vuchinich, Samuel. 1990. "The sequential organization of closing in verbal family conflict." In *Conflict talk: Sociolinguistic investigations of arguments and conversations*, Allen D. Grimshaw (ed.). Cambridge: Cambridge University Press.

Watts, Richard J. 1989. "Relevance and relational work: Linguistic politeness as a political behaviour." *Multilingua 8* (2–3): 131–166.

Watts, Richard J. 1991. *Power in family discourse*. Berlin and New York: Mouton de Gruyter.

Watts, Richard J. [1989] 1992. "Linguistic politeness and politic verbal behaviour." In *Politeness in language: Studies in its history, theory and practice*, Richard J. Watts, Sachiko Ide and Konrad Ehlich (eds.), 43–69. Berlin and New York: Mouton de Gruyter.

Watts, Richard, J. 2003. *Politeness*. Cambridge: Cambridge University Press.

Werkhofer, K. T. 1992. "Traditional and modern views: The social constitution and the power of politeness". In *Politeness in Language: Studies in its History, Theory and Practice*, Richard J. Watts, Sachiko Ide and Konrad Ehlich (eds.). Mouton de Gruyter.

Winslow, D. 1999. "Rites of passage and group bonding in the Canadian airborne." *Armed Forces and Society 25* (3): 429–458.

Woodbury, Hanni. 1984. "The strategic use of questions in court." *Semiotica 48* (3/4): 197–228.

Xie, Chaoqun. 2003. "Review of Gino Eelen (2001)." *Journal of Pragmatics 35*: 811–818.

Yllö, Kersti. 1993. "Through A Feminist Lens: Gender, Power and Violence" In *Controversies in Family Violence*, R. Gelles and D. Loseke (eds.), 47–62. Thousand Oaks, London, New Delhi: Sage Publications.

Index

Pragmatics & Beyond New Series

A complete list of titles in this series can be found on *www.benjamins.com*

199 **HOFFMANN, Christian R. (ed.):** Narrative Revisited. Telling a story in the age of new media. *Expected October 2010*

198 **LIMBERG, Holger:** The Interactional Organization of Academic Talk. Office hour consultations. xiv, 393 pp. + index. *Expected September 2010*

197 **DEDAIĆ, Mirjana N. and Mirjana MIŠKOVIĆ-LUKOVIĆ (eds.):** South Slavic Discourse Particles. 2010. ix, 166 pp.

196 **STREECK, Jürgen (ed.):** New Adventures in Language and Interaction. vi, 269 pp. + index. *Expected July 2010*

195 **PAHTA, Päivi, Minna NEVALA, Arja NURMI and Minna PALANDER-COLLIN (eds.):** Social Roles and Language Practices in Late Modern English. 2010. viii, 241 pp.

194 **KÜHNLEIN, Peter, Anton BENZ and Candace L. SIDNER (eds.):** Constraints in Discourse 2. 2010. v, 180 pp.

193 **SUOMELA-SALMI, Eija and Fred DERVIN (eds.):** Cross-Linguistic and Cross-Cultural Perspectives on Academic Discourse. 2009. vi, 299 pp.

192 **FILIPI, Anna:** Toddler and Parent Interaction. The organisation of gaze, pointing and vocalisation. 2009. xiii, 268 pp.

191 **OGIERMANN, Eva:** On Apologising in Negative and Positive Politeness Cultures. 2009. x, 296 pp.

190 **FINCH, Jason, Martin GILL, Anthony JOHNSON, Iris LINDAHL-RAITTILA, Inna LINDGREN, Tuija VIRTANEN and Brita WÅRVIK (eds.):** Humane Readings. Essays on literary mediation and communication in honour of Roger D. Sell. 2009. xi, 160 pp.

189 **PEIKOLA, Matti, Janne SKAFFARI and Sanna-Kaisa TANSKANEN (eds.):** Instructional Writing in English. Studies in honour of Risto Hiltunen. 2009. xiii, 240 pp.

188 **GILTROW, Janet and Dieter STEIN (eds.):** Genres in the Internet. Issues in the theory of genre. 2009. ix, 294 pp.

187 **JUCKER, Andreas H. (ed.):** Early Modern English News Discourse. Newspapers, pamphlets and scientific news discourse. 2009. vii, 227 pp.

186 **CALLIES, Marcus:** Information Highlighting in Advanced Learner English. The syntax–pragmatics interface in second language acquisition. 2009. xviii, 293 pp.

185 **MAZZON, Gabriella:** Interactive Dialogue Sequences in Middle English Drama. 2009. ix, 228 pp.

184 **STENSTRÖM, Anna-Brita and Annette Myre JØRGENSEN (eds.):** Youngspeak in a Multilingual Perspective. 2009. vi, 206 pp.

183 **NURMI, Arja, Minna NEVALA and Minna PALANDER-COLLIN (eds.):** The Language of Daily Life in England (1400–1800). 2009. vii, 312 pp.

182 **NORRICK, Neal R. and Delia CHIARO (eds.):** Humor in Interaction. 2009. xvii, 238 pp.

181 **MASCHLER, Yael:** Metalanguage in Interaction. Hebrew discourse markers. 2009. xvi, 258 pp.

180 **JONES, Kimberly and Tsuyoshi ONO (eds.):** Style Shifting in Japanese. 2008. vii, 335 pp.

179 **SIMÕES LUCAS FREITAS, Elsa:** Taboo in Advertising. 2008. xix, 214 pp.

178 **SCHNEIDER, Klaus P. and Anne BARRON (eds.):** Variational Pragmatics. A focus on regional varieties in pluricentric languages. 2008. vii, 371 pp.

177 **RUE, Yong-Ju and Grace ZHANG:** Request Strategies. A comparative study in Mandarin Chinese and Korean. 2008. xv, 320 pp.

176 **JUCKER, Andreas H. and Irma TAAVITSAINEN (eds.):** Speech Acts in the History of English. 2008. viii, 318 pp.

175 **GÓMEZ GONZÁLEZ, María de los Ángeles, J. Lachlan MACKENZIE and Elsa M. GONZÁLEZ ÁLVAREZ (eds.):** Languages and Cultures in Contrast and Comparison. 2008. xxii, 364 pp.

174 **HEYD, Theresa:** Email Hoaxes. Form, function, genre ecology. 2008. vii, 239 pp.

173 **ZANOTTO, Mara Sophia, Lynne CAMERON and Marilda C. CAVALCANTI (eds.):** Confronting Metaphor in Use. An applied linguistic approach. 2008. vii, 315 pp.

172 **BENZ, Anton and Peter KÜHNLEIN (eds.):** Constraints in Discourse. 2008. vii, 292 pp.

171 **FÉLIX-BRASDEFER, J. César:** Politeness in Mexico and the United States. A contrastive study of the realization and perception of refusals. 2008. xiv, 195 pp.

170 **OAKLEY, Todd and Anders HOUGAARD (eds.):** Mental Spaces in Discourse and Interaction. 2008. vi, 262 pp.

169 **CONNOR, Ulla, Ed NAGELHOUT and William ROZYCKI (eds.):** Contrastive Rhetoric. Reaching to intercultural rhetoric. 2008. viii, 324 pp.

168 **PROOST, Kristel:** Conceptual Structure in Lexical Items. The lexicalisation of communication concepts in English, German and Dutch. 2007. xii, 304 pp.

167 **BOUSFIELD, Derek:** Impoliteness in Interaction. 2008. xiii, 281 pp.

166 **NAKANE, Ikuko:** Silence in Intercultural Communication. Perceptions and performance. 2007. xii, 240 pp.

165 **BUBLITZ, Wolfram and Axel HÜBLER (eds.):** Metapragmatics in Use. 2007. viii, 301 pp.

164 **ENGLEBRETSON, Robert (ed.):** Stancetaking in Discourse. Subjectivity, evaluation, interaction. 2007. viii, 323 pp.

163 **LYTRA, Vally:** Play Frames and Social Identities. Contact encounters in a Greek primary school. 2007. xii, 300 pp.

162 **FETZER, Anita (ed.):** Context and Appropriateness. Micro meets macro. 2007. vi, 265 pp.

161 **CELLE, Agnès and Ruth HUART (eds.):** Connectives as Discourse Landmarks. 2007. viii, 212 pp.

160 **FETZER, Anita and Gerda Eva LAUERBACH (eds.):** Political Discourse in the Media. Cross-cultural perspectives. 2007. viii, 379 pp.

159 **MAYNARD, Senko K.:** Linguistic Creativity in Japanese Discourse. Exploring the multiplicity of self, perspective, and voice. 2007. xvi, 356 pp.

158 **WALKER, Terry:** *Thou* and *You* in Early Modern English Dialogues. Trials, Depositions, and Drama Comedy. 2007. xx, 339 pp.

157 **CRAWFORD CAMICIOTTOLI, Belinda:** The Language of Business Studies Lectures. A corpus-assisted analysis. 2007. xvi, 236 pp.

156 **VEGA MORENO, Rosa E.:** Creativity and Convention. The pragmatics of everyday figurative speech. 2007. xii, 249 pp.

155 **HEDBERG, Nancy and Ron ZACHARSKI (eds.):** The Grammar–Pragmatics Interface. Essays in honor of Jeanette K. Gundel. 2007. viii, 345 pp.

154 **HÜBLER, Axel:** The Nonverbal Shift in Early Modern English Conversation. 2007. x, 281 pp.

153 **ARNOVICK, Leslie K.:** Written Reliquaries. The resonance of orality in medieval English texts. 2006. xii, 292 pp.

152 **WARREN, Martin:** Features of Naturalness in Conversation. 2006. x, 272 pp.

151 **SUZUKI, Satoko (ed.):** Emotive Communication in Japanese. 2006. x, 234 pp.

150 **BUSSE, Beatrix:** Vocative Constructions in the Language of Shakespeare. 2006. xviii, 525 pp.

149 **LOCHER, Miriam A.:** Advice Online. Advice-giving in an American Internet health column. 2006. xvi, 277 pp.

148 **FLØTTUM, Kjersti, Trine DAHL and Torodd KINN:** Academic Voices. Across languages and disciplines. 2006. x, 309 pp.

147 **HINRICHS, Lars:** Codeswitching on the Web. English and Jamaican Creole in e-mail communication. 2006. x, 302 pp.

146 **TANSKANEN, Sanna-Kaisa:** Collaborating towards Coherence. Lexical cohesion in English discourse. 2006. ix, 192 pp.

145 **KURHILA, Salla:** Second Language Interaction. 2006. vii, 257 pp.

144 **BÜHRIG, Kristin and Jan D. ten THIJE (eds.):** Beyond Misunderstanding. Linguistic analyses of intercultural communication. 2006. vi, 339 pp.

143 **BAKER, Carolyn, Michael EMMISON and Alan FIRTH (eds.):** Calling for Help. Language and social interaction in telephone helplines. 2005. xviii, 352 pp.

142 **SIDNELL, Jack:** Talk and Practical Epistemology. The social life of knowledge in a Caribbean community. 2005. xvi, 255 pp.

141 **ZHU, Yunxia:** Written Communication across Cultures. A sociocognitive perspective on business genres. 2005. xviii, 216 pp.

140 **BUTLER, Christopher S., María de los Ángeles GÓMEZ GONZÁLEZ and Susana M. DOVAL-SUÁREZ (eds.):** The Dynamics of Language Use. Functional and contrastive perspectives. 2005. xvi, 413 pp.

139 **LAKOFF, Robin T. and Sachiko IDE (eds.):** Broadening the Horizon of Linguistic Politeness. 2005. xii, 342 pp.

138 **MÜLLER, Simone:** Discourse Markers in Native and Non-native English Discourse. 2005. xviii, 290 pp.

137 **MORITA, Emi:** Negotiation of Contingent Talk. The Japanese interactional particles *ne* and *sa*. 2005. xvi, 240 pp.

136 **SASSEN, Claudia:** Linguistic Dimensions of Crisis Talk. Formalising structures in a controlled language. 2005. ix, 230 pp.

135 **ARCHER, Dawn:** Questions and Answers in the English Courtroom (1640–1760). A sociopragmatic analysis. 2005. xiv, 374 pp.

134 **SKAFFARI, Janne, Matti PEIKOLA, Ruth CARROLL, Risto HILTUNEN and Brita WÅRVIK (eds.):** Opening Windows on Texts and Discourses of the Past. 2005. x, 418 pp.

133 **MARNETTE, Sophie:** Speech and Thought Presentation in French. Concepts and strategies. 2005. xiv, 379 pp.

132 **ONODERA, Noriko O.:** Japanese Discourse Markers. Synchronic and diachronic discourse analysis. 2004. xiv, 253 pp.

131 **JANOSCHKA, Anja:** Web Advertising. New forms of communication on the Internet. 2004. xiv, 230 pp.

130 **HALMARI, Helena and Tuija VIRTANEN (eds.):** Persuasion Across Genres. A linguistic approach. 2005. x, 257 pp.

129 **TABOADA, María Teresa:** Building Coherence and Cohesion. Task-oriented dialogue in English and Spanish. 2004. xvii, 264 pp.

128 **CORDELLA, Marisa:** The Dynamic Consultation. A discourse analytical study of doctor–patient communication. 2004. xvi, 254 pp.

127 **BRISARD, Frank, Michael MEEUWIS and Bart VANDENABEELE (eds.):** Seduction, Community, Speech. A Festschrift for Herman Parret. 2004. vi, 202 pp.

126 **WU, Yi'an:** Spatial Demonstratives in English and Chinese. Text and Cognition. 2004. xviii, 236 pp.

125 **LERNER, Gene H. (ed.):** Conversation Analysis. Studies from the first generation. 2004. x, 302 pp.

124 **VINE, Bernadette:** Getting Things Done at Work. The discourse of power in workplace interaction. 2004. x, 278 pp.

123 **MÁRQUEZ REITER, Rosina and María Elena PLACENCIA (eds.):** Current Trends in the Pragmatics of Spanish. 2004. xvi, 383 pp.

122 **GONZÁLEZ, Montserrat:** Pragmatic Markers in Oral Narrative. The case of English and Catalan. 2004. xvi, 410 pp.

121 **FETZER, Anita:** Recontextualizing Context. Grammaticality meets appropriateness. 2004. x, 272 pp.

120 **AIJMER, Karin and Anna-Brita STENSTRÖM (eds.):** Discourse Patterns in Spoken and Written Corpora. 2004. viii, 279 pp.

119 **HILTUNEN, Risto and Janne SKAFFARI (eds.):** Discourse Perspectives on English. Medieval to modern. 2003. viii, 243 pp.

118 **CHENG, Winnie:** Intercultural Conversation. 2003. xii, 279 pp.

117 **WU, Ruey-Jiuan Regina:** Stance in Talk. A conversation analysis of Mandarin final particles. 2004. xvi, 260 pp.

116 **GRANT, Colin B. (ed.):** Rethinking Communicative Interaction. New interdisciplinary horizons. 2003. viii, 330 pp.

115 **KÄRKKÄINEN, Elise:** Epistemic Stance in English Conversation. A description of its interactional functions, with a focus on *I think*. 2003. xii, 213 pp.

114 **KÜHNLEIN, Peter, Hannes RIESER and Henk ZEEVAT (eds.):** Perspectives on Dialogue in the New Millennium. 2003. xii, 400 pp.

113 **PANTHER, Klaus-Uwe and Linda L. THORNBURG (eds.):** Metonymy and Pragmatic Inferencing. 2003. xii, 285 pp.

112 **LENZ, Friedrich (ed.):** Deictic Conceptualisation of Space, Time and Person. 2003. xiv, 279 pp.

111 **ENSINK, Titus and Christoph SAUER (eds.):** Framing and Perspectivising in Discourse. 2003. viii, 227 pp.

110 **ANDROUTSOPOULOS, Jannis K. and Alexandra GEORGAKOPOULOU (eds.):** Discourse Constructions of Youth Identities. 2003. viii, 343 pp.

109 **MAYES, Patricia:** Language, Social Structure, and Culture. A genre analysis of cooking classes in Japan and America. 2003. xiv, 228 pp.

108 **BARRON, Anne:** Acquisition in Interlanguage Pragmatics. Learning how to do things with words in a study abroad context. 2003. xviii, 403 pp.

107 **TAAVITSAINEN, Irma and Andreas H. JUCKER (eds.):** Diachronic Perspectives on Address Term Systems. 2003. viii, 446 pp.

106 **BUSSE, Ulrich:** Linguistic Variation in the Shakespeare Corpus. Morpho-syntactic variability of second person pronouns. 2002. xiv, 344 pp.

105 **BLACKWELL, Sarah E.:** Implicatures in Discourse. The case of Spanish NP anaphora. 2003. xvi, 303 pp.

104 **BEECHING, Kate:** Gender, Politeness and Pragmatic Particles in French. 2002. x, 251 pp.

103 **FETZER, Anita and Christiane MEIERKORD (eds.):** Rethinking Sequentiality. Linguistics meets conversational interaction. 2002. vi, 300 pp.

102 **LEAFGREN, John:** Degrees of Explicitness. Information structure and the packaging of Bulgarian subjects and objects. 2002. xii, 252 pp.

101 **LUKE, K. K. and Theodossia-Soula PAVLIDOU (eds.):** Telephone Calls. Unity and diversity in conversational structure across languages and cultures. 2002. x, 295 pp.

100 **JASZCZOLT, Katarzyna M. and Ken TURNER (eds.):** Meaning Through Language Contrast. Volume 2. 2003. viii, 496 pp.

99 **JASZCZOLT, Katarzyna M. and Ken TURNER (eds.):** Meaning Through Language Contrast. Volume 1. 2003. xii, 388 pp.

98 **DUSZAK, Anna (ed.):** Us and Others. Social identities across languages, discourses and cultures. 2002. viii, 522 pp.

97 **MAYNARD, Senko K.:** Linguistic Emotivity. Centrality of place, the topic-comment dynamic, and an ideology of *pathos* in Japanese discourse. 2002. xiv, 481 pp.

96 **HAVERKATE, Henk:** The Syntax, Semantics and Pragmatics of Spanish Mood. 2002. vi, 241 pp.

95 **FITZMAURICE, Susan M.:** The Familiar Letter in Early Modern English. A pragmatic approach. 2002. viii, 263 pp.

94 **McILVENNY, Paul (ed.):** Talking Gender and Sexuality. 2002. x, 332 pp.

93 **BARON, Bettina and Helga KOTTHOFF (eds.):** Gender in Interaction. Perspectives on femininity and masculinity in ethnography and discourse. 2002. xxiv, 357 pp.

92 **GARDNER, Rod:** When Listeners Talk. Response tokens and listener stance. 2001. xxii, 281 pp.

91 **GROSS, Joan:** Speaking in Other Voices. An ethnography of Walloon puppet theaters. 2001. xxviii, 341 pp.

90 **KENESEI, István and Robert M. HARNISH (eds.):** Perspectives on Semantics, Pragmatics, and Discourse. A Festschrift for Ferenc Kiefer. 2001. xxii, 352 pp.

89 **ITAKURA, Hiroko:** Conversational Dominance and Gender. A study of Japanese speakers in first and second language contexts. 2001. xviii, 231 pp.

88 **BAYRAKTAROĞLU, Arın and Maria SIFIANOU (eds.):** Linguistic Politeness Across Boundaries. The case of Greek and Turkish. 2001. xiv, 439 pp.

87 **MUSHIN, Ilana:** Evidentiality and Epistemological Stance. Narrative Retelling. 2001. xviii, 244 pp.

86 **IFANTIDOU, Elly:** Evidentials and Relevance. 2001. xii, 225 pp.

85 **COLLINS, Daniel E.:** Reanimated Voices. Speech reporting in a historical-pragmatic perspective. 2001. xx, 384 pp.

84 **ANDERSEN, Gisle:** Pragmatic Markers and Sociolinguistic Variation. A relevance-theoretic approach to the language of adolescents. 2001. ix, 352 pp.

83 **MÁRQUEZ REITER, Rosina:** Linguistic Politeness in Britain and Uruguay. A contrastive study of requests and apologies. 2000. xviii, 225 pp.

82 **KHALIL, Esam N.:** Grounding in English and Arabic News Discourse. 2000. x, 274 pp.

81 **DI LUZIO, Aldo, Susanne GÜNTHNER and Franca ORLETTI (eds.):** Culture in Communication. Analyses of intercultural situations. 2001. xvi, 341 pp.

80 **UNGERER, Friedrich (ed.):** English Media Texts – Past and Present. Language and textual structure. 2000. xiv, 286 pp.

79 **ANDERSEN, Gisle and Thorstein FRETHEIM (eds.):** Pragmatic Markers and Propositional Attitude. 2000. viii, 273 pp.

78 **SELL, Roger D.:** Literature as Communication. The foundations of mediating criticism. 2000. xiv, 348 pp.

77 **VANDERVEKEN, Daniel and Susumu KUBO (eds.):** Essays in Speech Act Theory. 2002. vi, 328 pp.

76 **MATSUI, Tomoko:** Bridging and Relevance. 2000. xii, 251 pp.

75 **PILKINGTON, Adrian:** Poetic Effects. A relevance theory perspective. 2000. xiv, 214 pp.

74 **TROSBORG, Anna (ed.):** Analysing Professional Genres. 2000. xvi, 256 pp.

73 **HESTER, Stephen K. and David FRANCIS (eds.):** Local Educational Order. Ethnomethodological studies of knowledge in action. 2000. viii, 326 pp.

72 **MARMARIDOU, Sophia:** Pragmatic Meaning and Cognition. 2000. xii, 322 pp.

71 **GÓMEZ GONZÁLEZ, María de los Ángeles:** The Theme–Topic Interface. Evidence from English. 2001. xxiv, 438 pp.

70 **SORJONEN, Marja-Leena:** Responding in Conversation. A study of response particles in Finnish. 2001. x, 330 pp.

69 **NOH, Eun-Ju:** Metarepresentation. A relevance-theory approach. 2000. xii, 242 pp.

68 **ARNOVICK, Leslie K.:** Diachronic Pragmatics. Seven case studies in English illocutionary development. 2000. xii, 196 pp.

67 **TAAVITSAINEN, Irma, Gunnel MELCHERS and Päivi PAHTA (eds.):** Writing in Nonstandard English. 2000. viii, 404 pp.

66 **JUCKER, Andreas H., Gerd FRITZ and Franz LEBSANFT (eds.):** Historical Dialogue Analysis. 1999. viii, 478 pp.

65 **COOREN, François:** The Organizing Property of Communication. 2000. xvi, 272 pp.

64 **SVENNEVIG, Jan:** Getting Acquainted in Conversation. A study of initial interactions. 2000. x, 384 pp.

63 **BUBLITZ, Wolfram, Uta LENK and Eija VENTOLA (eds.):** Coherence in Spoken and Written Discourse. How to create it and how to describe it. Selected papers from the International Workshop on Coherence, Augsburg, 24-27 April 1997. 1999. xiv, 300 pp.

62 **TZANNE, Angeliki:** Talking at Cross-Purposes. The dynamics of miscommunication. 2000. xiv, 263 pp.

61 **MILLS, Margaret H. (ed.):** Slavic Gender Linguistics. 1999. xviii, 251 pp.

60 **JACOBS, Geert:** Preformulating the News. An analysis of the metapragmatics of press releases. 1999. xviii, 428 pp.

59 **KAMIO, Akio and Ken-ichi TAKAMI (eds.):** Function and Structure. In honor of Susumu Kuno. 1999. x, 398 pp.

58 **ROUCHOTA, Villy and Andreas H. JUCKER (eds.):** Current Issues in Relevance Theory. 1998. xii, 368 pp.

57 **JUCKER, Andreas H. and Yael ZIV (eds.):** Discourse Markers. Descriptions and theory. 1998. x, 363 pp.

56 **TANAKA, Hiroko:** Turn-Taking in Japanese Conversation. A Study in Grammar and Interaction. 2000. xiv, 242 pp.

55 **ALLWOOD, Jens and Peter GÄRDENFORS (eds.):** Cognitive Semantics. Meaning and cognition. 1999. x, 201 pp.

54 **HYLAND, Ken:** Hedging in Scientific Research Articles. 1998. x, 308 pp.

53 **MOSEGAARD HANSEN, Maj-Britt:** The Function of Discourse Particles. A study with special reference to spoken standard French. 1998. xii, 418 pp.

52 **GILLIS, Steven and Annick DE HOUWER (eds.):** The Acquisition of Dutch. With a Preface by Catherine E. Snow. 1998. xvi, 444 pp.

51 **BOULIMA, Jamila:** Negotiated Interaction in Target Language Classroom Discourse. 1999. xiv, 338 pp.

50 **GRENOBLE, Lenore A.:** Deixis and Information Packaging in Russian Discourse. 1998. xviii, 338 pp.

49 **KURZON, Dennis:** Discourse of Silence. 1998. vi, 162 pp.

48 **KAMIO, Akio:** Territory of Information. 1997. xiv, 227 pp.

47 **CHESTERMAN, Andrew:** Contrastive Functional Analysis. 1998. viii, 230 pp.

46 **GEORGAKOPOULOU, Alexandra:** Narrative Performances. A study of Modern Greek storytelling. 1997. xvii, 282 pp.

45 **PALTRIDGE, Brian:** Genre, Frames and Writing in Research Settings. 1997. x, 192 pp.

44 **BARGIELA-CHIAPPINI, Francesca and Sandra J. HARRIS:** Managing Language. The discourse of corporate meetings. 1997. ix, 295 pp.

43 **JANSSEN, Theo and Wim van der WURFF (eds.):** Reported Speech. Forms and functions of the verb. 1996. x, 312 pp.

42 **KOTTHOFF, Helga and Ruth WODAK (eds.):** Communicating Gender in Context. 1997. xxvi, 424 pp.

41 **VENTOLA, Eija and Anna MAURANEN (eds.):** Academic Writing. Intercultural and textual issues. 1996. xiv, 258 pp.

40 **DIAMOND, Julie:** Status and Power in Verbal Interaction. A study of discourse in a close-knit social network. 1996. viii, 184 pp.

39 **HERRING, Susan C. (ed.):** Computer-Mediated Communication. Linguistic, social, and cross-cultural perspectives. 1996. viii, 326 pp.

38 **FRETHEIM, Thorstein and Jeanette K. GUNDEL (eds.):** Reference and Referent Accessibility. 1996. xii, 312 pp.

37 **CARSTON, Robyn and Seiji UCHIDA (eds.):** Relevance Theory. Applications and implications. 1998. x, 300 pp.

36 **CHILTON, Paul, Mikhail V. ILYIN and Jacob L. MEY (eds.):** Political Discourse in Transition in Europe 1989–1991. 1998. xi, 272 pp.

35 **JUCKER, Andreas H. (ed.):** Historical Pragmatics. Pragmatic developments in the history of English. 1995. xvi, 624 pp.

34 **BARBE, Katharina:** Irony in Context. 1995. x, 208 pp.

33 **GOOSSENS, Louis, Paul PAUWELS, Brygida RUDZKA-OSTYN, Anne-Marie SIMON-VANDENBERGEN and Johan VANPARYS:** By Word of Mouth. Metaphor, metonymy and linguistic action in a cognitive perspective. 1995. xii, 254 pp.

32 **SHIBATANI, Masayoshi and Sandra A. THOMPSON (eds.):** Essays in Semantics and Pragmatics. In honor of Charles J. Fillmore. 1996. x, 322 pp.

31 **WILDGEN, Wolfgang:** Process, Image, and Meaning. A realistic model of the meaning of sentences and narrative texts. 1994. xii, 281 pp.

30 **WORTHAM, Stanton E.F.:** Acting Out Participant Examples in the Classroom. 1994. xiv, 178 pp.

29 **BARSKY, Robert F.:** Constructing a Productive Other. Discourse theory and the Convention refugee hearing. 1994. x, 272 pp.

28 **VAN DE WALLE, Lieve:** Pragmatics and Classical Sanskrit. A pilot study in linguistic politeness. 1993. xii, 454 pp.

27 **SUTER, Hans-Jürg:** The Wedding Report. A prototypical approach to the study of traditional text types. 1993. xii, 314 pp.

26 **STYGALL, Gail:** Trial Language. Differential discourse processing and discursive formation. 1994. xii, 226 pp.

25 **COUPER-KUHLEN, Elizabeth:** English Speech Rhythm. Form and function in everyday verbal interaction. 1993. x, 346 pp.

24 **MAYNARD, Senko K.:** Discourse Modality. Subjectivity, Emotion and Voice in the Japanese Language. 1993. x, 315 pp.

23 **FORTESCUE, Michael, Peter HARDER and Lars KRISTOFFERSEN (eds.):** Layered Structure and Reference in a Functional Perspective. Papers from the Functional Grammar Conference, Copenhagen, 1990. 1992. xiii, 444 pp.

22 **AUER, Peter and Aldo DI LUZIO (eds.):** The Contextualization of Language. 1992. xvi, 402 pp.

21 **SEARLE, John R., Herman PARRET and Jef VERSCHUEREN:** (On) Searle on Conversation. Compiled and introduced by Herman Parret and Jef Verschueren. 1992. vi, 154 pp.

20 **NUYTS, Jan:** Aspects of a Cognitive-Pragmatic Theory of Language. On cognition, functionalism, and grammar. 1991. xii, 399 pp.

19 **BAKER, Carolyn and Allan LUKE (eds.):** Towards a Critical Sociology of Reading Pedagogy. Papers of the XII World Congress on Reading. 1991. xxi, 287 pp.

18 **JOHNSTONE, Barbara:** Repetition in Arabic Discourse. Paradigms, syntagms and the ecology of language. 1991. viii, 130 pp.

17 **PIÉRAUT-LE BONNIEC, Gilberte and Marlene DOLITSKY (eds.):** Language Bases ... Discourse Bases. Some aspects of contemporary French-language psycholinguistics research. 1991. vi, 342 pp.

16 **MANN, William C. and Sandra A. THOMPSON (eds.):** Discourse Description. Diverse linguistic analyses of a fund-raising text. 1992. xiii, 409 pp.

15 **KOMTER, Martha L.:** Conflict and Cooperation in Job Interviews. A study of talks, tasks and ideas. 1991. viii, 252 pp.

14 **SCHWARTZ, Ursula V.:** Young Children's Dyadic Pretend Play. A communication analysis of plot structure and plot generative strategies. 1991. vi, 151 pp.

13 **NUYTS, Jan, A. Machtelt BOLKESTEIN and Co VET (eds.):** Layers and Levels of Representation in Language Theory. A functional view. 1990. xii, 348 pp.

12 **ABRAHAM, Werner (ed.):** Discourse Particles. Descriptive and theoretical investigations on the logical, syntactic and pragmatic properties of discourse particles in German. 1991. viii, 338 pp.

11 **LUONG, Hy V.:** Discursive Practices and Linguistic Meanings. The Vietnamese system of person reference. 1990. x, 213 pp.

10 **MURRAY, Denise E.:** Conversation for Action. The computer terminal as medium of communication. 1991. xii, 176 pp.

9 **LUKE, K. K.:** Utterance Particles in Cantonese Conversation. 1990. xvi, 329 pp.

8 **YOUNG, Lynne:** Language as Behaviour, Language as Code. A study of academic English. 1991. ix, 304 pp.

7 **LINDENFELD, Jacqueline:** Speech and Sociability at French Urban Marketplaces. 1990. viii, 173 pp.

6:3 **BLOMMAERT, Jan and Jef VERSCHUEREN (eds.):** The Pragmatics of International and Intercultural Communication. Selected papers from the International Pragmatics Conference, Antwerp, August 1987. Volume 3: The Pragmatics of International and Intercultural Communication. 1991. viii, 249 pp.

6:2 **VERSCHUEREN, Jef (ed.):** Levels of Linguistic Adaptation. Selected papers from the International Pragmatics Conference, Antwerp, August 1987. Volume 2: Levels of Linguistic Adaptation. 1991. viii, 339 pp.

6:1 **VERSCHUEREN, Jef (ed.):** Pragmatics at Issue. Selected papers of the International Pragmatics Conference, Antwerp, August 17–22, 1987. Volume 1: Pragmatics at Issue. 1991. viii, 314 pp.

5 **THELIN, Nils B. (ed.):** Verbal Aspect in Discourse. 1990. xvi, 490 pp.

4 **RAFFLER-ENGEL, Walburga von (ed.):** Doctor–Patient Interaction. 1989. xxxviii, 294 pp.

3 **OLEKSY, Wieslaw (ed.):** Contrastive Pragmatics. 1988. xiv, 282 pp.

2 **BARTON, Ellen:** Nonsentential Constituents. A theory of grammatical structure and pragmatic interpretation. 1990. xviii, 247 pp.

1 **WALTER, Bettyruth:** The Jury Summation as Speech Genre. An ethnographic study of what it means to those who use it. 1988. xvii, 264 pp.